D1220328

Transnational Communism across the Americas

Transnational Communism across the Americas

EDITED BY MARC BECKER,
MARGARET M. POWER,
TONY WOOD, AND
JACOB A. ZUMOFF

**UNIVERSITY OF
ILLINOIS PRESS**
Urbana, Chicago, and Springfield

© 2023 by the Board of Trustees
of the University of Illinois
All rights reserved
1 2 3 4 5 C P 5 4 3 2 1
∞ This book is printed on acid-free paper.

Cataloging data available from the Library of Congress

ISBN 9780252045226 (hardcover)
ISBN 9780252087363 (paperback)
ISBN 9780252054747 (ebook)

Contents

Transnational Communism
across the Americas

Introduction

From the National to the Transnational

MARC BECKER, MARGARET M. POWER,
TONY WOOD, AND JACOB A. ZUMOFF

In March 1935, the radical U.S. writer Josephine Herbst traveled to eastern Cuba to visit Realengo 18, a peasant community fighting against eviction from its lands in what is now Guantánamo Province. Reporting on her trip for the U.S. communist magazine *New Masses*, Herbst noted the privations these peasants had to endure, as well as their determination to resist. She also noted their marked internationalism: "the names of [Augusto César] Sandino and Pancho Villa come into the discussion often," she wrote, adding that one gathering ended with the singing of the "Marseillaise" and the "Internationale." Herbst described how one of the peasants began drawing a map on the earthen floor of his hut with a stick. He started with the island of Cuba, then she watched "its smallness . . . being related to the world," as the outlines of the United States and then Europe took shape. Then "a sudden great bulge of the stick moved by an inspired curve makes the Soviet Union. Everyone in the room smiles."[1]

Herbst had visited the Soviet Union in 1930 as part of a delegation to a writer's conference. When the Cuban peasants learned that she had a stamp from the self-proclaimed workers' state in her passport, they decided that she should also have a visa from Realengo 18, which they held to be a "soviet" in its own right. A document was solemnly drawn up using the community's single typewriter and duly signed by its leader, Lino Alvarez, a veteran of the Cuban independence struggle. In Herbst's telling, the making of this visa—an act that linked this embattled community to the USSR half a world away—was enough to elevate the spirits among those gathered. She commented, "We have been looking at the map and feeling the powers that are against this small island in its battle for freedom. The visa is a kind of magic that restores everyone."[2]

The incident captures in miniature the broad reach of the Soviet Union's example—its hold on the imaginations of people in many parts of the globe—in the years following the October 1917 Revolution. The kinship that these Cuban *campesinos* (peasants and rural workers) clearly felt with the Soviet Union is one of the many kinds of transnational connections between the Latin American left and the wider world in the early twentieth century. The essays in this volume depict and analyze the relationships communists in Latin America forged with each other and with their counterparts throughout the world, as well as with other social and political movements. These links took many forms. Beyond direct contacts between individual Latin American communist parties and the Communist International (Comintern), the world communist organization founded in 1919 and headquartered in Moscow, there were also interpersonal relationships and dynamics that crossed borders and continents, as well as ideological alignments and solidarities with distant and not-so-distant comrades.[3]

Transnational Communism across the Americas draws attention to transnational linkages and how they influenced and drove local actions. In doing so, it breaks with two broader tendencies in historical studies of communism: on the one hand, a focus on the global level and, on the other, an emphasis on the nation-state. Recent contributions have rightly addressed communism as a global phenomenon, but they largely fail to shed sufficient light on the dynamic interactions among different parts of that global movement.[4] The majority of scholars, instead, have concentrated on the history of a particular country's communist movement or, at best, the connections between one national Communist Party and the Comintern or the Soviet Union. Many of these studies have added to our understanding of their subjects, but by limiting their approach to individual countries, they, too, overlook the influence and relationships that existed between communists and communist movements across national boundaries.

It is understandable why historians have approached their subjects in this way. Most universities, of course, emphasize *national* history. And during the Cold War, anticommunist writers emphasized the "foreign" nature of communism, a charge that many scholars more sympathetic to communism tried to defend against by emphasizing the national elements of each Communist Party. The result, however, has been to treat most communist movements in the Americas in isolation from one another and from the broader communist movement in the Americas and internationally.

This emphasis on the nation-state is ironic given that the communist movement stressed internationalism, taking up Karl Marx and Friedrich Engels's slogan "Workers of the world unite," and that between 1919 and 1943, the movement's highest organization was called the Communist *International*. The Comintern's origins effectively lie in World War I: V. I. Lenin and other Bolsheviks were disgusted that many leaders of the Socialist (or Second) International in Germany, France, and other belligerent countries supported their own countries' war efforts, betraying international socialism by jettisoning their duty, as the Bolsheviks saw it, to struggle against the imperialism of their own bourgeoisies. This motivation (proletarian internationalism in Lenin's words) guided the Bolsheviks after their own revolution in October 1917 in tsarist Russia. The Bolsheviks stressed the need for workers to take power throughout the world, especially in developed capitalist countries, to safeguard the revolution in Russia and lay the basis for constructing an international socialist society. In March 1919 they organized a Third *Communist* International to win over left-wing socialists and forge communist parties throughout the world.[5]

The Russian Revolution deepened and consolidated long-standing divisions between revolutionaries and reformists within the European social-democratic and labor movements. Soon left-wing militants—including socialists who opposed their parties' support for the war as well as anarchists and syndicalists opposed to the traditional social-democratic emphasis on parliamentarism and electoralism—rallied to the Bolsheviks. In much of Europe, communist parties developed out of sizable left-wing tendencies within the established socialist parties. In Latin America, by contrast, the early communist movement was much weaker and, from the Comintern's perspective, not a strategic priority. Nevertheless, militant workers, radical intellectuals, and anarchist and socialist activists across Latin America looked to the triumphant Bolshevik Revolution, which had occurred in a backward, peasant country, as an inspiration for their own liberation.

The first communist party in the Americas was organized in Argentina in January 1918 as a split from the Socialist Party, and over the next decade, other parties formed across the region. No one from Latin America, however, attended the First Comintern Congress in Moscow in March 1919, and few participated in the next several congresses. While many Bolshevik leaders knew German and French, and some had even learned English while in exile in Great Britain or the United States, few knew Spanish or Portuguese, and there were few direct links between the fledgling communist movement and Latin America or the Caribbean. Nor did the Comintern leadership seem to expend much thought on the problems facing Latin America. Nonetheless, by 1925, eight communist parties

(Argentina, Brazil, Chile, Cuba, El Salvador, Guatemala, Mexico, and Uruguay) had been organized in Latin America and the Caribbean, and by 1930 eight more had formed (Colombia, Costa Rica, Ecuador, Haiti, Honduras, Panama, Paraguay, and Peru). Communist parties later emerged in Bolivia, the Dominican Republic, Nicaragua, Puerto Rico, and Venezuela in the 1930s and 1940s.[6]

Latin American communists worked with each other and the Comintern to establish several transnational initiatives in the region in the 1920s and 1930s. One of the first was the Anti-Imperialist League of the Americas, founded in Mexico City in 1925.[7] By 1928 there were chapters in eleven Latin American countries.[8] In Mexico the league set up branches in several states and organized regular anti-imperialist events in the major cities. These featured a diverse array of speakers and drew in a cross-class range of participants, from peasant farmers to urban middle classes. The league was also particularly successful in advancing the Comintern's goals of "promoting and developing communist movements" in the circum-Caribbean region. According to Sandra Pujals, the league became the "command center for a regional movement directed by several of the most committed Caribbean communists," including Cubans Julio Antonio Mella and Jorge Vivó and Venezuelans Gustavo Machado and Salvador de la Plaza.[9] The league published *El Libertador* in Mexico City and sponsored the Hands Off Nicaragua campaign, a hemispheric effort to generate solidarity with the anti-imperialist forces of Augusto César Sandino in Nicaragua. (See the chapter by Lazar Jeifets and Víctor Jeifets in this volume.)

Although few Latin American delegates journeyed to Moscow for the first five congresses of the Comintern, the region contributed a total of twenty-five votes at the Sixth Congress in 1928. Numerous activists had traveled to Moscow for the tenth anniversary celebrations of the Bolshevik Revolution in 1927 and remained there for other meetings, including the Comintern congress the following year. Delegates from the Sixth Congress returned to Latin America dedicated to implementing the program that they had drafted in Moscow. Two pivotal meetings took place in 1929. The first, the Constituent Congress of the Confederation of Latin American Labor Unions, was held in Montevideo, Uruguay, from May 18 to 26, 1929. The idea for the Montevideo conference first emerged in December 1927 at a meeting of delegates from Latin America who were in Moscow for the tenth anniversary commemoration of the October Revolution. Labor groups from fifteen countries sent delegates to the Montevideo labor conference. Out of this meeting emerged the Confederación Sindical Latino Americana (CSLA, Latin American Trade Union Confederation).[10] After the conclusion of the Montevideo conference, many of these same delegates crossed the Río de la Plata to participate in the First Latin American Communist

Conference from June 1 to 12, 1929, in Buenos Aires. In total, thirty-eight delegates from fifteen countries gathered for this historic meeting.[11]

In 1931 the Comintern established the Caribbean Bureau in New York City. Political exiles from Venezuela and Cuba administered the Bureau, along with representatives from the Communist Party of the United States (CPUSA). The Bureau sought to promote left activity in New York among Caribbean immigrants and throughout the larger Caribbean region.[12] Indeed, Bureau leaders understood that part of their mission was to train Caribbean radicals living in New York City so they could return to their country of origin and foment revolutionary consciousness, communist organization, and close ties with the Bureau and the Comintern. Puerto Rican Alberto Sánchez, who appears in Margaret M. Power's chapter in this volume, exemplifies this practice. Sánchez became a member of the CPUSA after moving to New York City in 1926. The Caribbean Bureau sent him to Moscow to participate in the International Red Aid Congress in 1932, and in 1934 he went to Puerto Rico where, working with four others, he launched the Puerto Rican Communist Party.[13] In 1931 the Bureau also sent two Comintern cadres to Venezuela to "coordinate the efforts of the dispersed communist groups" that operated there.[14]

Ties to the Comintern brought Latin American communists into contact not only with each other and the new Soviet state but also with communists from across the globe, linking Latin America to broader struggles. At the same time, starting in the mid-1920s, the Soviet Union and the Comintern underwent important political changes. First came the struggle for the leadership of the Soviet Union and the international communist movement after Lenin's death in 1924. Thereafter, the rise of Joseph Stalin led to an emphasis on "socialism in one country," which increasingly prioritized the interests of the post-Lenin Soviet government over those of international revolution. In 1928 the Comintern entered what its leadership called the Third Period, adopting a more combative stance that reflected Moscow's conviction that the demise of capitalism was imminent. Yet with the onset of the Great Depression, it was right-wing forces in the capitalist world that profited most dramatically, as exemplified with the rise of Adolf Hitler. In 1935 the threat of fascism prompted the Comintern's shift to the Popular Front strategy, which called for alliances among communists, social democrats, bourgeois liberals, and moderate nationalists. In 1943, in the midst of World War II, Stalin sought to reassure his capitalist allies by dissolving the Comintern altogether.

The Cold War that developed after 1945 was marked by increasing hostility between the advanced capitalist countries (especially the United States) and the Soviet Union and its allies in Eastern Europe and, later, China. It intensified conflict between communist and anti-imperialist forces on one side and pro-capitalist elements and the United States on the other across the globe. These tensions played out in Latin America and the Caribbean, where a variety of popular movements sought to challenge entrenched, U.S.-backed elites. Across much of the region, authoritarian and liberal-democratic regimes alike seized hold of Cold War anticommunism to legitimate their harsh repression of these challenges, regardless of whether they had any actual connection to the region's communist parties. Although much weakened by state violence, Latin American communists were, nonetheless, a significant presence within the political landscape up until the end of the Cold War.

The National and the International in Latin American Communism

As noted above, a key political question that communists faced—and which is echoed in the scholarly literature—was to what extent communism was an international movement and to what extent it reflected the individual historical developments of each country. A transnational approach to communism in the Americas simultaneously allows us to address this question and provides an opportunity to approach it from a different perspective by observing how broader trends in the communist movement—such as the rise of Stalin, an emphasis on fighting racial and women's oppression, the move to form alliances with non–working-class or left forces during the Popular Front and World War II—played out in different national contexts. The opening of the Comintern archives in Moscow after the collapse of the Soviet Union in 1991, the subsequent release of Cold War–era documents from other sources, and a reappraisal of familiar archives across the region have all facilitated this transnational approach.[15]

Communist parties in Latin America and the Caribbean commonly grappled with several different issues. A party frequently had particularly strong roots in a sector of the working class (such as copper miners in Chile or banana plantation workers in Costa Rica), which often related to the role of a particular country in the world capitalist economy; in other countries (such as Mexico), the party's support was fragmented among urban workers, artisans, and peasants. The diverse ethnic and racial composition of Latin America was something else communists had to grapple with, some more concertedly and successfully than others. Cuban communists took up an antiracist agenda in the 1930s, for example, while around the same time communists in Mexico, Chile, Ecuador, and elsewhere began to pay more attention to Indigenous questions. As if the social, ethnic, and geographical diversity of their countries were not enough of a challenge, Latin American communist parties were also for the most part illegal in their early years, which forced them to operate clandestinely within a turbulent and repressive political climate. As several of the chapters in this volume demonstrate, each party also had complex, often highly conflictive relations with other forces on the left, giving rise to long-running tensions that severely constrained attempts to forge broader alliances. Finally, each party had its own relationship with the Comintern and Soviet Union, in some cases mediated through contacts with larger "sibling" parties, such as the CPUSA. The links between Latin American parties and their U.S. counterparts—often constructive and cooperative, though also laced with tensions—is another recurrent theme in these chapters.

By placing communist movements in the Americas in a transnational frame, the essays in this volume shed fresh light on the complex and dynamic interaction among these factors. The diversity of programs, policies, and analyses the different parties developed emerged out of a confluence of the global and local. A transnational approach that concentrates not on the Communist Party in one country or the Comintern itself but that, instead, examines the interactions and relationships among communist forces in different countries, creates a unique opportunity to capture the variety of scales on which Latin American communist politics unfolded.

The essay by Jeifets and Jeifets, for example, explores how political changes in the Comintern affected the relationship between the Mexican Communist Party and Sandino's struggle against the U.S. occupation in 1920s Nicaragua. Tony Wood's chapter on Latin American communist cadres in the Soviet Union helps us understand the development of the Comintern's conception of Latin America and the role communists from Latin America played in this process. They were involved closely enough to feel the influence of shifts in Soviet politics, yet they were unable to wield decisive influence on Comintern strategy.

Frances Peace Sullivan's chapter on the "Negro Question" in Cuba highlights the relation between the Cuban Communist Party's stance on race in the 1930s and the shifting attitudes of the Comintern and the CPUSA, while Jacob A. Zumoff's chapter examines this relationship as it played out in U.S., Panamanian, and Costa Rican communism. Jacob Blanc draws attention to how the transnational experiences of the Communist Party of Brazil's longtime leader Luís Carlos Prestes during his time in exile shaped his politics. Power's chapter scrutinizes how changes in the international communist movement—such as the move from the Third Period to the Popular Front—affected the relationship between the communist parties in the United States and Puerto Rico and how it influenced their connection with Puerto Rican Nationalists.

The formal dissolution of the Comintern in 1943 changed the dynamics of how communists in the Americas related to each other and the broader communist movement. Marc Becker uses Central Intelligence Agency (CIA) documents to explore the links that communist youth in Latin America forged with their comrades in Europe and China during the early Cold War period. By highlighting the role Argentine writer María Rosa Oliver played in promoting peace and cultural exchanges, Adriana Petra reveals the often-unacknowledged importance of women in developing and maintaining communist networks in the 1950s.[16] Patricia Harms makes two important and intertwined arguments. First, women played a critical, if largely overlooked, role in the communist movement in Guatemala before the 1954 coup. Second, their ties to transnational women's organizations facilitated their ability to do so. Kevin A. Young's examination of the Frente Farabundo Martí para la Liberación Nacional (FMLN, Farabundo Martí National Liberation Front) shows that transnational ties remained integral to revolutionary communism in the post-Comintern period. He argues that the FMLN studied the thinking and practice of communists in China and Vietnam and applied the lessons learned to the guerrilla war its members carried out in El Salvador in the 1980s. Finally, Tanya Harmer's afterword draws together the themes of the volume and highlights the contributions that the chapters collectively make to ongoing scholarly debates.

These chapters come from a variety of historiographical and political perspectives. The transnational approach employed in this collection helps historians better understand the activities of individual communist parties and the relationships between and among them throughout the Americas. More importantly, it provides a way to reevaluate the importance of communist movements in Latin America and around the world.

The essays in this volume do not exhaust the possibilities. One could envision, for example, fruitful investigations of attitudes toward the Spanish Civil War, the role of European immigrants, critiques of CPUSA leader Earl Browder's accommodationist position, differing conceptions of the Indigenous question, and the emancipation of women among Latin American communists. As well as these specific areas for future research, important broader questions remain open for debate, such as the role communists played in the building of political and social democracy in Latin America and the shifting relationships between internationalist and regional, "Latin Americanist" perspectives over time.[17] Our hope is that these chapters spur researchers to explore the history of Latin American communism in a transnational way.

Notes

1. Herbst, "Passport from Realengo."

2. Herbst, "Passport from Realengo."

3. We have not attempted to define "communism" in a uniform way throughout this collection; some authors use it to refer only to the Communist Party, while others include a constellation of political groups and trends under this rubric.

4. For examples of important global contributions, see Pons, *Cambridge History of Communism*, and Pons and Cameron, *Global Revolution*.

5. Studies of the Comintern in English include C. L. R. James, *World Revolution*; E. H. Carr, *Foundations of the Planned Economy* and *Twilight of the Comintern*; Claudín, *Communist Movement*. For a broader recent history of the communist movement, see Priestland, *Red Flag*.

6. Caballero, Latin America and the Comintern, 43–53.

7. B. Carr, "Pioneering Transnational Solidarity," 148. According to Carr, the league began "under the auspices of the Comintern and the U.S. Workers Party [CPUSA]."

8. Melgar Bao, "Anti-Imperialist League." The definitive work on the league is Kersffeld, *Contra el imperio*.

9. Pujals, "Embarcados!" 108.

10. Confederación Sindical Latino Americana (CSLA), *Bajo la bandera.*

11. Secretariado Sudamericano de la Internacional Comunista, *El movimiento revolucionario latino americano*.

12. Pujals, "Soviet Caribbean," 259–60.

13. Pujals, "De un pájaro," 270; Díaz, "El gobierno," 16–17.

14. Jeifets and Jeifets, "La inserción internacional," 3.

15. Examples of recent transnational approaches to communism include Drachewych and McKay, *Left Transnationalism*; Studer, *Transnational World of the Cominternians*; McGuire, *Red at Heart*; and Stevens, *Red International and Black Caribbean*.

16. For a larger discussion of women communists in Latin America, see Valobra and Yusta Rodrigo, *Queridas camaradas*.

17. For a version of this argument as applied to Guatemala, see Grandin, *Last Colonial Massacre*; for Cuba in the 1930s, see Rojas, "Comunistas en democracia."

PART I

Bolshevism and the Americas (1917–1943)

The Comintern, the Communist Party of Mexico, and the "Sandino Case"

The History of a Failed Alliance, 1927–1930

LAZAR JEIFETS AND VÍCTOR JEIFETS

The most important challenge facing Bolshevism after its triumph in Russia in October 1917 was the spread of the world revolution. In that respect, the militants of the Third International (Comintern) were worthy followers of the French Revolution of 1789, as they sought to internationalize their revolutionary process. Until the Sixth Congress of the Comintern (1928), the priorities of the Third International were centered on Germany, England, France, and China, while Latin America remained marginal to its plans.[1] Yet, events in Nicaragua forced the Comintern headquarters in Moscow to pay attention to the armed struggle of the Ejército Defensor de la Soberanía de Nicaragua (EDSN, Army for the Defense of Nicaraguan Sovereignty). In this way, the guerrillas led by Augusto César Sandino became involved in the Comintern's international anti-imperialist campaign. Moreover, a complicated triangle of relations developed between the EDSN, the communists, and the Mexican government.

The Liga Antiimperialista de las Américas (LADLA, Anti-Imperialist League of the Americas), founded in 1925 under the auspices of the Partido Comunista de México (PCM, Communist Party of Mexico), was the main tool of the Comintern's "united front" policy.[2] Its history is by no means a historiographical lacuna.[3] Most research, however, has focused on anti-imperialist activities in Mexico, Argentina, and Cuba, the three countries where the LADLA was most important. The league rapidly achieved renown among popular movements in various parts of the American continent, enabling the development of a tenacious opposition to the Yankee empire. The anti-imperialist movement that Sandino led is one example of this. To this day, however, Sandino's place within the orbit of international communism remains little studied, despite some attempts to fill this gap.[4]

How did the links between Sandino and the Comintern emerge? What role did people involved in solidarity campaigns play? And, ultimately, what was the balance of contacts between the Comintern and the Sandinistas? The following text addresses these questions in four sections. The first concentrates on the origins of the campaign for solidarity with the Sandinistas that began in the United States. The second section explores the activities of the Manos Fuera de Nicaragua (MAFUENIC, Hands Off of Nicaragua) committee founded in Mexico in 1928. The third section is devoted to early relations between Sandino and the Mexican government. Finally, we analyze the triangle formed by Sandino, the Mexican government, and the PCM while also investigating the reasons for the breakdown in relations between the EDSN and the Comintern.

We use newspaper sources and printed documents, but documents from Russian and Mexican Archives form the base of our analysis. By comparing this material with what has been written on the subject, we can reach an adequate and detailed understanding of the misunderstandings among the Comintern, the Mexican left, and Sandino.

The Beginnings of the Pro-Sandinista Campaign

LADLA's initial propaganda campaigns met with little enthusiasm among most of the region's population. The issues on which they focused—support for Puerto Rican independence and the closure of the U.S. Navy base at Guantánamo, as well as calls for the withdrawal of U.S. troops from Haiti and Santo Domingo, among others—were widely seen as rather-distant concerns. But in the campaign to support the struggle of the EDSN, LADLA leaders saw a promising possibility for winning the sympathies of a broad cross-section of Latin Americans. The nature of events in Nicaragua, a country that had become a fiefdom of foreign monopolies, changed drastically after Sandino's irruption into political life. In 1927 the civil war between Nicaraguan liberals and conservatives ended after the Tipitapa Pact,[5] which both sides signed thanks to U.S. mediation. The presence of U.S. troops, however, caused unease among large sectors of the population. Sandino, one of the former liberal generals, rejected the pact and the disarmament of the liberal detachments. On July 16, 1927, the Sandinistas began fighting against the pro-U.S. government of José María Moncada and the U.S. Marines. The EDSN gradually came to consider its struggle as part of the broader world anti-imperialist movement.

In Latin America it was common to reject the statements of U.S. President Herbert Hoover, who later called Sandino a "bandit" operating "outside the civilized pale."[6] On the contrary, anti-imperialists praised the "crazy little army" that was challenging Washington's might. For example, the French writer Henri Barbusse called Sandino "the general of free men." The EDSN carried out its own publicity campaign. Prominent Honduran writer Froylán Turcios was Sandino's representative in Central America and later throughout the continent. Establishing links with the communists and the LADLA opened up possibilities for Sandino to add the efforts of the Anti-Imperialist League to his struggle.[7] According to historian Daniel Kersffeld, even allowing for the significant ideological differences between them, the EDSN's alliance with the communists gave both parties many benefits: while the EDSN gained international projection, the PCM became one of the key intermediaries between Sandino and the world.[8] In January 1927 the Comintern Executive Committee (ECCI) published its appeal "Against the Rapacious Imperialism of the United States" in which it declared: "From the Rio Grande to Tierra del Fuego the popular masses of Latin America have to organize the broad movement of protest against the exploitation and robbery carried out by the United States. [. . .] The workers and peasants of the whole world have to show their solidarity with the people of little Nicaragua."[9]

According to the ECCI, U.S. intervention in Nicaragua could be the beginning of armed aggression against Mexico. The ECCI, therefore, ordered the Communist Workers' Party of America to organize resistance under the slogan "Hands off Mexico and Nicaragua!" thus turning the U.S. branch of the Anti-Imperialist League into a mass organization.[10]

The workers' party had a special anti-imperialist department headed by Charles Phillips, a.k.a. "Manuel Gómez," who at the same time was the leader of the U.S. section of the LADLA. LADLA lacked influence in the organized labor movement, but the campaign in favor of Sandino changed the situation, and numerous anti-imperialist rallies stirred things up in several cities of the Empire of the North.

The pro-Sandinista campaign in the United States quickly stalled, however, because of communist factional infighting. The majority of workers' party members, led by the party's secretary general Jay Lovestone, seized hold of any errors made by the league to criticize their opponents, foremost among them Manuel Gómez. The party leader mocked the slogan "Stop the flow of Nicaraguan blood," calling it "Gomez's Kotex [sanitary pad] campaign."[11] It seemed that many U.S. communists, suffering from a hidden "communist nationalism," were unwilling to carry out a sincere struggle for the national emancipation of Latin Americans, believing that they themselves should be the main center for any communist work in the continent simply because they lived in the most developed country in the hemisphere. Anti-imperialists in Latin America, obviously, did not welcome this attitude. The LADLA in Mexico publicly declared that if the Latin Americans themselves did not help the EDSN and Sandino, no one would be capable of doing so. A declaration by the Congress against Imperialism and Colonial Oppression in Brussels (February 1927), proposed by eleven Latin American and U.S. delegates, demanded the immediate withdrawal of U.S. troops. It also called for the organization of a broad movement in favor of these demands.

The Formation of the MAFUENIC and Its First Tasks

On January 19, 1928, the Hands Off Nicaragua Committee was founded in Mexico City, the fruit of the efforts of Fritz Bach, the representative of Socorro Rojo Internacional (SRI, International Red Aid, also commonly known by its Russian acronym MOPR) in Mexico.[12] The MAFUENIC (constituted as a united front) was formed by the League against Imperialism (LAI), the SRI, the LADLA, the Central American and Antilles Union, the International Anti-Fascist League, the Teaching Workers International, and the Mexican Anti-Clerical League.[13]

Among the members of the committee were the Peruvian Jacobo Hurwitz (secretary general), PCM members Luis G. Monzón and Rafael Ramos Pedrueza, and the Venezuelan Carlos León, president of the Partido Revolucionario Venezolano (PRV, Venezuelan Revolutionary Party). Fritz Bach, the de facto leader of the MAFUENIC, thought it urgent to bring several "well-known people with good connections" onto the committee to ensure its efficacy. For example, Ramos Pedrueza was appointed as treasurer because of his prestige, not because he knew anything about accounting. Contacts with the government were to be maintained through Belén de Zarraga, head of the Anti-Clerical League, who was a friend of Mexican President Plutarco E. Calles. Although the communists wanted to have a majority, they needed the MAFUENIC to look like an independent structure.[14] It was no coincidence that the committee's first appeal was published in national newspapers with a large circulation, *Día* and *El Universal* (Mexico City); the communist biweekly *El Machete* (Mexico City) came into play only later.[15]

The MAFUENIC was not going to limit itself to collecting money and medicines; it would be considered the basis of the future broad front. For this reason, LADLA's organ, *El Libertador*, was put at the committee's disposal. The organizers of the pro-Sandinista campaign hoped to bring together several Latin American progressive forces. Their first activity was to send a telegram to the Pan American Congress in Havana, demanding a discussion of the Nicaraguan issue and the withdrawal of the interventionist troops.[16]

In Bach's view, support for the Nicaraguan resistance was more conducive to the deployment of the anti-imperialist movement in the United States than activities in favor of the remote and poorly understood Chinese Revolution. The Mexican MAFUENIC established contact with the Nicaraguan rebel leader through Carleton Beals, a reporter for the *Nation*. In May 1928 the MAFUENIC delegate, Venezuelan Gustavo Machado, visited Sandino's general staff to propose a plan of cooperation. His main idea was to unite the anti-imperialist forces so that they would form a single army with a single program and similar tactics.[17]

Sandino wanted to make good use of the possibilities MAFUENIC offered to forge international links for his movement and decided to appoint Machado as the EDSN's representative in Mexico. Perhaps, the Venezuelan's declarations about wanting to obtain arms for the Sandinistas from the authorities were the basic reason for Sandino's decision. However, the general was disappointed by the slow results of Machado's activities. The reasons for this were obvious: upon his return from Nicaragua to Venezuela, Machado concentrated entirely on national priorities, primarily preparing an armed expedition against the dictator Juan Vicente Gómez. At that time, he did not consider it a liability to neglect his role as Sandinista emissary because, in the event of the virtual triumph of the Venezuelan revolution, the continental anti-imperialist struggle would in any case receive a strong boost.

Nevertheless, Sandino continued to have confidence in the MAFUENIC, and on January 18, 1929, he commissioned the committee to be his general representative in Latin America. The committee received, indeed, a gift of fate, since it had the chance to become a link between Sandino and the world. The MAFUENIC, however, gave no official response and after four months demanded that Sandino explain his plans for the provisional government in Nicaragua. Sandino was more than surprised and considered such behavior to be a mistake.[18]

Although at first glance there seems to have been a lack of consistency in the MAFUENIC's reactions, its line was more than consistent. The Third International demanded that its partners not only participate in a common struggle but that they also accept communist control and, ultimately, accept Marxist ideology or communist aims. From the beginning, united-front strategies were accompanied by acute sectarianism, which caused disagreements in the

1920s and early 1930s. Among them was the rupture with the Alianza Popular Revolucionaria Americana (APRA, American Popular Revolutionary Alliance) in Peru and with the Liga Nacional Campesina (National Peasant League) in Mexico.

In the case of Sandino, the Comintern affiliates hoped that the "general of free men" would begin to identify fully with the Third International, and they did not understand at all how unrealistic such bets could be. At the same time, the MAFUENIC tried to form a Latin American legion, composed of volunteers united by blood, language, and race. Mexican Andrés García Salgado, Peruvian Esteban Pavletich, Salvadoran Agustín Farabundo Martí, Venezuelan Carlos Aponte, and other volunteers joined the ranks of the EDSN.[19] The legion never became very large. More important was the confidence that the Sandinistas gained in MAFUENIC due to the daily participation of the latter's representatives in the fighting in the Nicaraguan mountains. The EDSN general staff even discussed some military operations with the MAFUENIC.[20]

The Comintern, however, was stung by the defeats suffered by revolutionary movements in Europe and China—in particular, the 1927 massacre of Chinese communists by their former allies in the Kuomintang—and was never interested in plans to assist Sandino militarily. The Soviets also considered the risk of a strong U.S. response to the direct involvement of the Third International in these matters. These motives were probably reasonable, but they buried the possibilities of making use of Sandino.

The propaganda that the MAFUENIC put out proved to be quite successful. During the first months, thousands of people attended meetings that the committee organized in Mexico, and the circulation of *El Libertador* reached five thousand copies. This work gave a boost to the whole international communist campaign in favor of the Sandinista cause and was one of the reasons for the Comintern's growing interest in Latin America.

At that time, the PCM did not receive substantial aid from Moscow and carried the entire weight of the work on its own shoulders. Demanding support and directives from the Comintern and the SRI day after day, the Mexican communists and the LADLA did not hesitate to say that, owing to the lack of resources, the communists were on the verge of losing their leading role in the anti-imperialist movement.[21]

The SRI's representative in Mexico, Vittorio Vidali, had the necessary money, but he preferred to carry out his own pro-Sandinista campaign without collaborating directly with the MAFUENIC.[22] In these conditions, the organizers of the MAFUENIC no longer expected the Comintern to be their only source of financial support. Thus, they proposed to their Latin American branches to use 20 percent of the money collected for propaganda and give the rest to the MAFUENIC. *El Libertador* was considered as having the capacity to finance the whole campaign, so the MAFUENIC started propaganda activities to increase regular subscriptions all over Latin America. The first revenues inspired many hopes but at the same time led to a serious mistake: the decision made in 1928 to change the magazine's format from its original combined emphasis on workers' and peasants' issues to one that aimed to be a workers' press organ. But *El Libertador* had already gained prestige among intellectuals as an anti-imperialist publication, while it was not very well received among the workers, who were in many cases illiterate and did not have the money to subscribe.

Declaring that Sandino's struggle was a symbol for all peoples oppressed by imperialism, the MAFUENIC argued that the League against Imperialism had some serious decisions to make.[23] The Comintern, for its part, amid a growing confrontation with the Mexican government, wanted to take advantage of the pro-Sandinista campaign in its struggle against President Emilio Portes Gil, whom the communists accused of betraying the ideals of the Mexican revolution and serving the "Yankee empire." The organization assumed that the Nicaraguan insurgent general should make a statement in opposition to Portes Gil, since he was considered a tool of U.S. imperialism.

The Comintern demanded that the PCM and LADLA avoid any "harmful" commitments and that they separate Sandino from liberal elements, while Moscow set itself the task of establishing contact with other anti-imperialist forces in Nicaragua fighting against the United States (the ECCI referred to the Nicaraguan Communist Party, not realizing that such a party did not exist) in order to protect itself in the case of a break with Sandino.[24] These tasks were in line with the approach of the Sixth Congress of the Comintern in what it called the "Third Period": the new stance adopted in 1928 that envisaged the general weakening of the capitalist system, a deepening political crisis, and the growth of U.S. imperialism. According to the Communist International, Latin America was rapidly entering the enormous sphere of U.S. influence.[25]

The Mexican Government Speaks Out

In late spring 1929 the Nicaraguan guerrillas lacked weapons, while the U.S. Marines already controlled most of the country's territory. Seeking to stave off a catastrophe, Sandino turned to the Mexican president to help him "leave Nicaragua honorably" through the efforts of an EDSN officer, Mexican José de Paredes.[26] Sandino only hoped to obtain temporary asylum, thinking he would receive the ammunition necessary to restart the struggle: "The man who conceives transcendental projects to guarantee the future of a race, does not base his hopes on obtaining a monthly pension to live in exile."[27]

For Mexico this situation was not new. Already in May 1926 the government had sent money, arms, and ammunition to the Nicaraguan liberals, without regard for the tensions this would create with Washington.[28] But the Mexican political panorama had visibly changed by 1929. The establishment of the Maximato—from 1928 to 1934, Plutarco Elías Calles remained the "maximum leader," pulling the strings behind three successive presidents—and the formation of the hegemonic Partido Nacional Revolucionario (PNR, National Revolutionary Party) came to define many governmental decisions. This limited the prospects of the national left and led to growing tension between the PCM and the government.

Portes Gil, Mexican president from 1928 to 1930, had to resolve an important dilemma. Despite his personal sympathies for the Sandinistas, he could not give them the weapons they requested because Mexico was only now reestablishing friendly relations with the United States.[29] In granting asylum to Sandino, the only condition Portes Gil made was that Sandino not attack the United States verbally while he was on Mexican soil. In April 1929 Portes Gil proposed that the Nicaraguan president Moncada go to Washington and request the withdrawal of U.S. Marines from the territory. Likewise, Portes Gil also conveyed to the U.S. ambassador in Mexico, Dwight Morrow, the need to put an end to the armed conflict, promising to make the EDSN submit to the Nicaraguan government. According to Portes Gil, Sandino agreed with these proposals. Moncada, however, rejected the plan, explaining that he would not be able to stay in power without the U.S. Marines.[30] In the end Portes Gil confirmed his government's willingness to give Sandino asylum without providing him with weapons, offering the Nicaraguan and members of his general staff transportation from Costa Rica to Mérida, Mexico, in the Yucatán Peninsula.

According to the testimony of EDSN representative Pedro José Zepeda, Captain José de Paredes was the unintentional culprit of the misunderstanding between Sandino and Portes Gil. The young and excited Mexican volunteer failed to explain the Mexican president's point of view accurately, making Sandino believe that the Mexican authorities were willing to guarantee all the conditions for continuing the struggle for the liberation of Nicaragua. Speaking with Portes Gil, Captain Paredes only listened to what he wanted to hear and then convinced Zepeda about the complete success of the mission, advising the general to leave the guerrilla camp as soon as possible. Zepeda was cautious and would not give concrete recommendations. Nevertheless, he confirmed Portes Gil's sympathies for the Sandinista cause.[31] There are few testimonies about Portes Gil's precise attitude toward the asylum granted to Sandino, but they suggest that the chain of events that occurred between the summer of 1929 and the spring of 1930 had a subjective cause. The primary source of the strained relations in the Sandino–Portes Gil–PCM triangle was Paredes's misunderstanding of the Mexican president's words.

Finally, in June 1929 Sandino arrived in Mexico, complicating the situation in a country where repression of the communist left had already begun. The EDSN leader explained that he had traveled to Mexico to have his army recognized as a legitimate party to the conflict in Nicaragua. He also planned to visit several Latin American nations in order to call for an inter-American conference against the U.S. Monroe Doctrine, and he also wanted to discuss the issue of a Nicaraguan canal as a project capable of bringing Latin American countries together. Sandino expressed himself clearly: "Our struggle is the struggle for independence and we think that all Latin America understands this and does not consider it as the struggle of a single social class. [...] The Communist Party supports us more than any other party, but it is not because we presumably are communists."[32]

Upon entering Mexico, Sandino and his people were, in effect, interned as prisoners. While the Nicaraguan rebel considered himself a political and military leader, the Mexican government treated him as a political refugee and nothing more.[33] The EDSN militants were transferred to Yucatán, where they found themselves penniless; for a month, they only received meager aid from local unions. Upon learning of Sandino's desire to return to his country, the government notified him that it would give him a farm. The Nicaraguan general considered this an insulting proposal and proof of the Mexican government's inability to resolve the matter because of the elections due in November of the same year. Nevertheless, the EDSN leader was forced to accept the proposal and told journalists that he had no doubt that before November 1929, he would return to Las Segovias, Nicaragua, to restart the armed struggle "against the Yankee bandits."[34]

Sandino insisted on having a personal conversation with the Mexican leader to remind him of the original reasons for his arrival. He promised Portes Gil that he would return to the Nicaraguan jungle, waiting for better times, with his hopes placed in the Mexican people (whom he adored), regardless of Mexico's attitude toward the conflict in Nicaragua. The EDSN leader was not asking for free financing but for the possibility of a $10,000 loan.[35] But Portes Gil avoided all personal contact, which left Sandino feeling desperate. The EDSN commander was isolated from events in his country and even suspected that his own representative, Dr. Zepeda, was a confidential agent of the Mexican government.[36]

Only toward the end of November did it become known that Paredes had misinterpreted the instructions that Sandino had given. The captain hoped that this would help the Nicaraguan receive asylum in Mexico, so he did not warn the general. Given the situation, Sandino explained to Portes Gil that he wished to leave Mexico and expressed his apologies for the inconveniences that Paredes's activities caused in these "difficult moments for Mexican politics." Sandino suggested, however, that the president clearly define Mexico's stance with regard to the conflict in Nicaragua. He further noted the reasons he had left Las Segovias for Mexico and the failure of those plans and tried to emphasize Mexico's moral duty "not to allow the colonization of Central America by Yankee bandits."[37] It was all in vain. Portes Gil did not reply.

The Crisis and Rupture of Relations between the PCM and Sandino

The PCM and the MAFUENIC found themselves in an ambiguous position after the Nicaraguan's arrival in Mexico. Both groups were concerned by the nature of relations between Sandino and the Mexican government, which at the time was repressing the left and the autonomous unions. These organizations began to lose confidence in each other because of a media campaign. In January 1930 Sandino complained to the secretary general of the PCM, Hernán Laborde that *El Universal* and the *New York Times* had published reports on the alleged delivery of $60,000 to Sandino by the Mexican government to stop his war activities in Nicaragua, citing an anonymous PCM representative as their source.[38]

Sandino branded the articles as malicious slander and gently but firmly asked the PCM to find out the source of the information.[39] He also demanded that the PCM explain why the EDSN never received the money that the MAFUENIC promised. He referred to the acknowledgment of receipt for $1,000 that Sandino had signed and given to Machado. The Venezuelan had not made clear to the EDSN that this was not money that had been collected but the sum that they were just about to collect.[40]

Those in the PCM suffered a real shock when they read these statements. According to Laborde, his party and the LADLA had had nothing to do with the publication of the aforementioned news.[41] Apparently, the PCM was not aware of the money that had been collected and the mechanism of their delivery to Sandino by the MAFUENIC.

While the central committee of the PCM demanded a financial report from the Venezuelan, people close to the MAFUENIC (Bach, León, and Ramos Pedrueza) showed little interest in participating in the inquiries.[42] The investigation was part of the conflict between the PCM and a Venezuelan communist group accused of being an imperialist agent for cooperating with the Mexican government. Formally, those words referred to the anonymous leaders of the Venezuelan Revolutionary Party, but the communists de la Plaza and Machado, founders of the PRV, were sure that the PCM was referring to them. De la Plaza was quick to accuse Laborde of sacrificing Machado to reach an understanding with Sandino.[43]

Laborde rejected the allegations, saying that the activities of the PCM were only intended to clarify things and that de la Plaza had no right to decide on the capacity of the PCM leaders. In any case, the investigation was quickly forgotten when the Comintern lost interest in the Sandinista struggle.

The PCM hoped to organize a direct conversation with Sandino to discuss the possibilities of reestablishing the activities of the MAFUENIC, which had been halted when the PCM was made illegal. It took the communists a long time to reach an agreement with Sandino, and it was their fault. The party did not have the resources to send its representatives to see Sandino in Mérida.[44] The situation changed, however, after Sandino's personal secretary, Salvadoran Farabundo Martí, received word about Sandino's willingness to accept the aid that the LADLA and the PCM had offered. Faced with the impossibility of reaching an agreement with the Mexican government, Sandino was forced to look for money to return to Nicaragua.

The Nicaraguan leader flatly rejected the Machiavellian twists and turns of the foreign policy of the new Mexican president, Pascual Ortiz Rubio, suspecting that the authorities were inclined to recognize Moncada as the leader of Nicaragua. This would be an offense to the EDSN.[45] At that time the PCM concluded that it could take advantage of Sandino's disillusionment to continue using his name in anti-imperialist propaganda.[46]

In January 1930 the central committee of the PCM made clear to Sandino the rigid conditions of their aid: immediate departure for Nicaragua or for an anti-imperialist tour under the aegis of the League against Imperialism; a declaration condemning the Mexican government as a tool of Washington; and the publication of all correspondence between Sandino and Portes Gil.[47] Obviously, the PCM wanted to force Sandino either to accept the Comintern's stance, which would mean the radicalization of the Nicaraguan's position, or to reject it altogether. In the latter case, the communists were ready to initiate an anti-Sandinista campaign.

The meeting between Sandino and the communists took place on February 3, 1930. Laborde, Enea Sormenti (a.k.a. "Vidali"), and Gastón Lafarga represented the PCM, while the EDSN sent five people: Sandino himself, José Constantino González, Enrique Rivera Bertrand, Esteban Pavletich, and Farabundo Martí.

Also present were the Cuban Juan Ramón Brea as delegate of the LADLA; León, Bach, and Ramos Pedrueza, for the MAFUENIC; and the Costa Rican Vicente Sáenz, on behalf of Central American intellectuals. At the meeting Sandino insisted that the MAFUENIC should resume its work. In addition, it was confirmed that this organization had given Sandino a fraudulent check for $1,000. In general, all parties agreed that the anti-imperialist struggle would achieve its objectives through confrontation with foreign imperialism and its national allies. This struggle should be combined with the political movement of the oppressed masses of Latin American workers and peasants.[48]

The parties ignored the contradictions in the document. While Sandino referred to the right of all anti-imperialists to participate in the struggle, the communists insisted on the class character of the movement. In addition, the PCM succeeded in getting the general to condemn the Mexican government (albeit indirectly). Bach and Ramos Pedrueza did not sign the document, apparently, because they did not agree with the right of the PCM to control the activities of the MAFUENIC. Sáenz also declined to sign, but his reasons are unknown.

In any case the MAFUENIC was no longer able to provide any help. The Venezuelans Machado and de la Plaza left Mexico, the government deported Italian Tina Modotti as a pernicious foreigner, and Sormenti left Mexico illegally. A few months earlier, agents of the Cuban government had assassinated Mella, and the PCM expelled Bach, Ramos Pedrueza, and Diego Rivera.[49] There was no formal record of the closure of the MAFUENIC, but it effectively disintegrated. The PCM had just changed most of its leaders, was disoriented, and did not have much idea what attitude to take in its relations with the EDSN general.

On February 6, 1930, Sandino declared his willingness to carry out the world propaganda tour under the aegis of the League against Imperialism, and to "go directly to Moscow to [. . .] request the resolute support of the Comintern, giving the struggle a mass character, with a concrete program in accordance with the program of the Comintern for the colonial and semicolonial countries."[50] He communicated the same to Barbusse and Willi Münzenberg, emphasizing that he was ready to act against any Latin American government as far as the anti-imperialist struggle was concerned.[51]

Sandino rejected his old ideas of forming a Latin American nation through the anti-imperialist struggle and with the participation of Latin American governments. Now he joined a classist anti-imperialist struggle against foreign imperialism and its national agents: the governments, sellout union leaders, and "the phony left nationalists." He declared his willingness to confront "yellow" unionism and imperialist pan-Americanism by organizing the workers under the banner of the Confederación Sindical Latino Americana (CSLA, Latin American Trade Union Confederation), this being one of the pillars of revolutionary anti-imperialism.[52]

Nevertheless, the PCM was unable to get Sandino to Europe to confirm the agreements they had reached. The party then had to turn to communists in the United States for help with subsidies.[53] In these weeks it appointed Martí as its representative to the EDSN. The EDSN leader was quick to point out that he considered the Salvadoran to be his representative to his general staff and not within the EDSN.[54] Sandino was not going to tolerate political commissars coming into immediate contact with his people, especially on the eve of his planned departure for Europe, and he did not want to turn cooperation with the PCM into PCM control over the movement he was leading.

Meanwhile, the Mexican government was very uncomfortable with the contacts between Sandino and the now illegal PCM, so it ordered the arrest of the guerrilla commander's secretaries.[55] The new cabinet did not want to help Sandino. Moreover, President Ortiz Rubio preferred to keep the Nicaraguan out of the country and out of the PCM's sphere of influence. Finally, the secretary of the interior, former president Portes Gil, cut the Gordian knot by offering Sandino arms and money on the condition that he leave quickly for Nicaragua and that the EDSN transport everything itself.

Caught between the Mexican government and the Comintern, Sandino preferred to take the bird in his hand without waiting for the hundred others that were flying around Moscow. He left Mexico but tried to save his relations with the PCM by promising that his return to Las Segovias was temporary, until the money for the European tour arrived. Angry and disappointed, Sandino only needed a pretext for the break with the PCM, and he quickly found it. During the journey to Nicaragua, Martí got drunk and declared that "he cared little for Sandino, the army, and Nicaragua, and only the party's decision motivated his stay as a spy to expose Sandino."[56] Martí's work in the EDSN lasted barely two weeks. Sandino's representative in Mexico, Zepeda, explained that what justified Martí's intervention was his membership in the PCM and his espionage work.[57] It must be assumed that the insurgent general was aware of Martí's communist militancy but that he considered his statements as a lack of personal loyalty. The rupture was clear and definitive.

The PCM canceled its agreement with Sandino and recognized that the government had triumphed in the competition to win over the Nicaraguan insurgent. With a certain mischievous glee, Laborde predicted the further course of events: "On receiving the promise of help [that would never arrive] in a few months, [Sandino] will find himself in the same situation as when he had to leave Nicaragua. He will finally meet with failure [he will be assassinated or flee] or with the need to make an agreement with the Yankees."[58]

The central committee of the PCM publicly accused Sandino of betraying the working class by accepting the support of the Mexican government and renouncing the role of "the main fighter against continental imperialism linked to the workers and peasants movement; now he has become a caudillo seeking power in Nicaragua."[59] With some minor modifications, this version was published in the pages of *El Machete* in June 1930.[60] Sandino and the PCM did not return to the subject of their relations, although occasionally *El Machete* published brief information on Nicaraguan events, calling for anti-imperialist unity under the banners of the communist party of Nicaragua.

Martí became a symbol of the failure of relations between the communists and the EDSN. While Sandino believed that all militants in his movement had to obey the directives of the EDSN, Martí was sure that the discipline of the Comintern should be above the discipline of the EDSN. Martí, therefore, did not think he was betraying Sandino because Martí communicated information to communist allies with the aim of strengthening a solidarity campaign in favor of the Nicaraguan cause. At the time of the rupture, he branded his former boss as a "petty-bourgeois liberal caudillo who wished to rule by semi-colonial and semi-feudal methods."[61] Years later, however, he recognized Sandino's sincerity and spiritual integrity.[62] The Salvadoran Army executed Martí in 1932 during an uprising that the Communist Party and peasant groups had organized. Sandino was kidnapped and killed by National Guard officers in February 1934, after a peace agreement between the EDSN and government of Nicaragua had already been signed.

Final Considerations

The triumph of the Bolshevik Revolution over a backward regime had repercussions across the world. Even so, the global goal of the Comintern, a world revolution, could not be achieved. It was difficult for Russia to become the base for the advancement of communism. The bureaucratic mechanism of the Third International failed to function in tune with sociopolitical processes in many parts of the world. The case of Sandino is an example of the deficiencies of the Comintern structures. While the organization saw early on the possibilities that Sandino's struggle opened up for the whole of Latin America and succeeded in initiating a solidarity campaign, it did not provide genuine support for the EDSN. The communist attempt to control Sandino's army by making use of the contradictions between the Nicaraguan and the Mexican government failed because the Comintern tried to start building the house from the roof: it insisted on communist hegemony in the future revolution without establishing the need for a joint struggle at the beginning. In the end all the allies of the EDSN lost: the Comintern, the PCM, the LADLA, and, obviously, Sandino himself. The winners were the U.S. government and its Nicaraguan satellites. The Mexican government, involved in this process, managed to keep a positive image without many political consequences. Nevertheless, the two key characters of this historical drama, Sandino and Martí, paid for their own and other people's mistakes with their lives.

Notes

1. This chapter was originally published as "La Comintern, el PCM y el 'caso Sandino': historia de una alianza fracasada, 1927–1930," in *Anuario Colombiano de Historia Social y de la Cultura* 44, no. 2 (2017): 63–86. It appears here by kind permission of the *Anuario*'s editors. It is licensed under the Creative Commons Attribution 4.0 International License (CC BY). Read the license at https://creativecommons.org/licenses /by/4.0/legalcode. Caballero, *La Internacional Comunista*, 114–16.

2. Adopted by the Comintern in 1922, the "united front" policy involved building a broad working-class alliance across party-political lines; in Latin America and elsewhere, it sought to harness anti-imperial and anticolonial sentiment.

3. Piazza, *Die Liga gegen Imperialismus*; Melgar Bao, "Anti-Imperialist League"; Kersffeld, *Contra el imperio*.

4. Kersffeld, "El Comité Manos"; Carr, "Pioneering Transnational Solidarity."

5. The Tipitapa Pact is also known as the Espino Negro Pact, signed in May 1927.

6. Presidential News Conference of April 21, 1931, in Hoover, *Public Papers*, 191. See also Kalmykov, *Historia de America Latina*, 63; Selser, *Cronología*, vol. 3, and McPherson, *Invaded*, 45–55.

7. Formally called the League against Imperialism and Colonial Oppression, this Comintern-sponsored organization was founded in 1926. Headed by Willi Münzenberg and Virendranath Chattopadhyaya, it brought together anticolonial activists from Africa, Europe, South and East Asia, Latin America, and the Caribbean; it was dissolved in 1937.

8. Kersffeld, *Contra el imperio*, 140.

9. Ivanovich, *¿Por qué los EE.UU.*, 31–32.

10. El telegrama sobre la situación en Nicaragua, January 12, 1927, F. 515, op. 1, exp. 929, folio 7, Russian State Archive of Social and Political History (hereafter referred to as RGASPI), Moscow.

11. Shipman, *It Had to Be Revolution*, 161–62, 167. Unfortunately, Kersffeld in his work ignores the contradictory attitude of the American Anti-Imperialist League and only highlights its achievements in the struggle in favor of Sandino. Kersffeld, *Contra el imperio*, 146–49.

12. On the Swiss-born communist Fritz Sulzbachner, aka Federico Bach (1897–1978), see Jeifets and Jeifets, *América Latina*, 66.

13. Bach to Willi [Münzenberg], Mexico, January 10, 1928, f. 542, op. 1, d. 28, ff. 1–2 reverse, RGASPI; "El Comité Manos Fuera de Nicaragua," *El Universal* (Mexico City), January 20, 1928.

14. Bach to Willi [Münzenberg], Mexico, January 16, 1928, f. 542, op. 1, d. 28, f. 3, RGASPI.

15. Bach to Willi [Münzenberg], Mexico, January 20, 1928, f. 495, op. 1, d. 28, f. 17, RGASPI.

16. ¡Comité Manos Fuera de Nicaragua! Boletín diario (Mexico City), January 19, 1928.

17. Ramírez, *El pensamiento vivo de Sandino*, 2:26. Contrary to Kersffeld's assertions, Machado or other emissaries were not sent to the EDSN by the Comintern but by MAFUENIC. Kersffeld, *Contra el imperio*, 150–52.

18. Ramírez, *El pensamiento vivo de Sandino*, 2:34–35.

19. Jeifets, Jeifets, and Huber, *La Internacional Comunista*.

20. Ramírez, *El pensamiento vivo de Sandino*, 1:287, 285.

21. "Depto. de agitación y propaganda del PCM al Depto. de agitación y propaganda del CEIC," March 15, 1928, f. 495, op. 108, d. 84, ff. 31–32, RGASPI.

22. Bach to the CC of the SRI, December 6, 1928, f. 495, op. 108, d. 92, f. 13, RGASPI.

23. *El Libertador* (Mexico City) 21, 1928, 35, and 14, 1928.

24. [The Comintern] to the CC [Central Committee] of the PCM,F. 495, op. 108, d. 105, f. 39, RGASPI.

25. MacKenzie, *La Comintern y revolución mundial*, 146–47.

26. "José de Paredes al Presidente Interino de los Estados Unidos Mexicanos," Mexico, February 16, 1929, Fondo Particular de Emilio Portes Gil, box 28, exp. 3, n.d., Archivo General de la Nación, Mexico City (hereafter referred to as AGN); Ramírez, *El pensamiento vivo de Sandino*, 1:304.

27. Sandino to Portes Gil, Mérida, January 1, 1929, Fondo Particular de Emilio Portes Gil, box 28, exp. 3, n.d., AGN.

28. Buchenau, "Calles y el Movimiento," 3.

29. Portes Gil, *Quince años*, 351. The typewritten sheet of the memoirs is missing a phrase from the printed book: "una ayuda, con que Sandino no lograría triunfar" (an aid, with which Sandino would not succeed). "Memoirs of Emilio Portes Gil," Fondo Particular de Emilio Portes Gil, box 28, exp. 3, n.d., AGN.

30. Francisco Navarro, "Informe de la misión confidencial desempeñada por el suscrito ante el gobierno del Presidente Moncada, de Nicaragua, en 1929," Oslo, October 31, 1939, Fondo Particular de Emilio Portes Gil, box 28, exp. 3, n.d., AGN.

31. Zepeda to Licenciado Emilio Portes Gil, Mexico, 1934, Mexico City, Fondo Particular de Emilio Portes Gil, box 28, exp. 3, n.d., AGN.

32. X. Campos Ponce, *Los yanquis y Sandino*, 27.

33. "Sandino al Presidente de la República Mexicana Emilio Portes Gil," Veracruz, June 30, 1929, Mexico City, Fondo Particular de Emilio Portes Gil, box 28, exp. 3, n.d., AGN.

34. Sandino to Zepeda, Mérida, January 25, 1930, Fondo Particular de Emilio Portes Gil, box 28, exp. 3, n.d., AGN.

35. "Sandino al Presidente de los Estados Unidos Mexicanos Emilio Portes Gil," May 31, 1929, El Chipotón, Fondo Particular de Emilio Portes Gil, box 28, exp. 3, n.d., AGN.

36. Sandino to Zepeda.

37. Ramírez, *El pensamiento vivo de Sandino*, 1:404–5.

38. Sandino to Laborde, Mérida, January 8, 1930, F. 495, op. 108, d. 134, f. 1, RGASPI.

39. Sandino to Laborde.

40. Ramírez, *El pensamiento vivo de Sandino*, 2:28–29, 36–37.

41. Laborde to Moreau, New York, February 1930, F. 495, op. 108, d. 133, f. 5, RGASPI.

42. Laborde to Machado, Mexico, April 16, 1930, F. 495, op. 108, d. 134, ff. 7–8, RGASPI.

43. Laborde to de la Plaza, Mexico, June 6, 1930, F. 495, op. 108, d. 134, f. 29, RGASPI.

44. Sandino to Laborde.

45. Sandino to Zepeda, general representative of the EDSN, Fondo Particular de Emilio Portes Gil, box 28, exp. 3, n.d., AGN.

46. Laborde to Moreau, New York, February 1930, F. 495, op. 108, d. 133, f. 6, RGASPI.

47. Laborde to Moreau, Mexico, January 1930, F. 495, op. 108, d. 133, f. 3, RGASPI.

48. Copy of the Minutes of the Meeting between the representatives of LADLA, MAFUENIC, Central American intellectuals and the EDSN delegation, Mexico, February 3, 1930, F. 495, op. 108, d. 134, f. 30, RGASPI.

49. Martínez Verdugo, *Historia del comunismo*.

50. Laborde to Moreau, Mexico, February 7, 1930, F. 495, op. 108, d. 133, f. 14, RGASPI.

51. Ramírez, *El pensamiento vivo de Sandino*, 2:62–66.

52. Ramírez, *El pensamiento vivo de Sandino*, 2:69, 70–72.

53. Laborde to Moreau, Mexico, February 7, 1930, f. 14.

54. Ramírez, *El pensamiento vivo de Sandino*, 2:109.

55. *Daily Worker* (Chicago), February 26, 1930.

56. The PCM to the Comintern, June 8, 1930, F. 495, op. 108, d. 131, ff. 69–70, RGASPI.

57. Laborde to the CC of the CP of the US, Mexico, April 30, 1930, F. 495, op. 108, d. 131, ff. 60, RGASPI.

58. PCM to the Comintern, ff. 73–74.

59. Circular letter from Laborde, Mexico, April 30, 1930, f. 495, op. 108, d. 128, ff. 30–31, RGASPI.

60. "La traición de Augusto C. Sandino," *El Machete* (Mexico City), June 1930.

61. Arias Gómez, *Farabundo Martí*, 53.

62. Petrukhin and Churilov, *Farabundo Martí*, 48.

Black Caribbean Migrants and the Labor Movement and Communists in the Greater Caribbean in the 1920s and 1930s

JACOB A. ZUMOFF

In the 1920s and 1930s, Black workers in the United States, Panama, and Costa Rica became increasingly important to the labor movement in each country, even as they faced multisided racial oppression. All three countries were home to a significant population of Afro-Caribbean migrants (often from the Anglophone Caribbean) and their descendants. These "West Indians" were among the most transnational populations in the Americas and played important roles in North and Central American societies.[1] Although the communist movement in all three countries began with a similar "colorless" approach to Black oppression, within a decade, the Communist Party in the United States (CPUSA) became well-known for opposing Black oppression, while the Costa Rican and Panamanian communist parties remained indifferent.

This chapter examines the approach taken by the Comintern to the Afro-Caribbean population in the United States, Panama, and Costa Rica and Afro-Caribbean migrants' role in the international Communist movement. This requires a comparative and a transnational perspective: to analyze the Comintern's broader approach to Black oppression, it is useful to compare the efforts the communist movement in each country took (or did not take) to recruit Afro-Caribbean migrants. While the Comintern leadership recognized the importance of the struggle for Black liberation, among these three parties, only the CPUSA translated this understanding into increased work among the Black population. In Costa Rica and Panama, founding communist leaders did not see Black liberation as central to forging communist parties, and the Comintern was not in a position to force these early communists to focus on the "Negro Question." As a result, communists in Panama and Costa Rica failed to recruit many Caribbean migrants.[2]

West Indians were transnational in origin, destination, and outlook; their cosmopolitanism and radicalism had been forged by slavery and abolition, European colonialism, and U.S. imperialism. In the late nineteenth and early twentieth centuries, tens of thousands of Afro-Caribbean people migrated throughout the region—and beyond. Migration from different European colonies to various host societies, often in succession, helped forge a transnational identity shaped by what Michelle Stephens has referred to as "two acts of displacement," slavery and migration. These Afro-Caribbean migrants "attempted to imagine a transnational form of Black nationality that could both transcend nationalism and reimagine the state itself."[3] This international identity contributed to support for communism among some West Indian migrants—but only when communists attempted to recruit them.

In the interwar period, Black people in the Greater Caribbean underwent great political ferment, most strongly demonstrated by a wave of militant strikes in the British Caribbean from 1919 to the mid-1930s, which further made them open to radical politics. The first Black cadres recruited by the CPUSA were from the Caribbean, and when the party recruited cadres from the African Blood Brotherhood (ABB) in the early 1920s, they tapped into this current. These Afro-Caribbean communists mediated between the struggle for Black rights in the United States and the international fight against imperialism and colonialism. Neither communists in Panama nor Costa Rica did this, for reasons discussed below.[4]

The Comintern recognized the importance of Black oppression but struggled to develop a Marxist analysis that connected the fight for Black liberation to the struggle for workers' revolution. This difficulty was understandable. The Bolsheviks' conception of special oppression developed in the tsarist empire, but much of the early Comintern focus on Black oppression centered on the United States, home to a relatively large communist movement. But none of the more than one hundred oppressed peoples in the tsarist empire experienced the same type of oppression as Black people in the United States, which differed as well from colonial oppression in Africa or Asia or even Black oppression elsewhere in the Americas. Black people in the United States did not form a nation, having been integrated into the capitalist system, while being forcibly segregated at the bottom of society. They had no distinct language, religion, territory, or economy. They were an oppressed caste, set apart by their color and the North

American concept of race (the so-called one-drop rule). Furthermore, similar to pan-African Black intellectuals and activists, such as W. E. B. Du Bois or Marcus Garvey, the Comintern tended to generalize the Black experience and create an international Negro Question, comprising the different forms of oppression of Black people in South Africa, West Africa, the Caribbean, and in Latin America.

Much of the early work of the Comintern toward the Negro Question was aimed at Afro-Caribbean migrants from the Caribbean. New York City, Panama City, and Colón and Limón (Costa Rica) were major hubs for the West Indian diaspora. Between 1881 and 1921, roughly forty-five thousand Jamaicans migrated to Panama; thirty-three thousand migrated to Costa Rica and other Central American countries; and forty-six thousand migrated to the United States. Large numbers of Afro-Caribbean people migrated from other British colonies.[5] The CPUSA recruited the leaders of the African Blood Brotherhood, a New York–based group of Afro-Caribbean radicals, but as will be seen, communist parties in Panama and Costa Rica did not recruit significant numbers of Afro-Caribbean migrants nor pay much attention to the connections between the struggle against Black oppression and the fight for socialism.

Communists and the Negro Question in the United States

After the leading sections of Second (Socialist) International supported their "own" capitalist governments' war efforts in World War I, the Bolsheviks sought to forge a new international of revolutionary Marxists to replace what they termed as the rotting corpse of social democracy, which they saw as irreparably compromised by its support for imperialism. The Comintern envisioned the struggle for Black liberation as central to fighting against imperialism and to breaking the workers' movement from social-democratic "social chauvinism." The Comintern forced the (white) CPUSA leadership to address Black oppression, and, in turn, Black Communists struggled to make the party's leadership assimilate Comintern directives. As a result of these efforts, communists in the United States began to fight to make the Negro Question central to the struggle for socialism there. Communists transformed the struggle for Black liberation from a local issue into a concern for the international proletariat.[6]

Since his *What Is to Be Done?* (1902), V. I. Lenin argued that revolutionaries must take up the fight against ethnic, racial, national, and other types of non-class oppression. This stemmed from the Bolshevik experience in the Russian empire, where tsarist oppression rested on numerous forms of special oppression. Because of this, oppressed national, religious, and ethnic minorities comprised a large part of the Bolshevik leadership. Lenin believed the fight for Black liberation was central to the fight for international revolution and was not just a local issue to be dealt with by communists in the United States. At the Comintern's Second Congress (1920), Lenin insisted the CPUSA make a presentation on Black oppression. (Since there were no Black delegates, this fell to John Reed, a white delegate who only agreed to do so after Lenin stressed it was "absolutely necessary.")[7] The Third Congress a year later again discussed Black oppression. Two Afro-Caribbean delegates from the United States attended the Fourth Congress (1922), allowing for a fuller discussion. The Fifth (1924) and Sixth Congresses (1928), the first two post-Lenin conferences, dealt with the question in more depth.[8]

The first significant breakthrough by the Comintern in recruiting Black radicals was in the United States, even though the early CPUSA inherited the "colorless" approach of its forebears in the left wing of the Socialist Party, who opposed racism but did not see Black oppression as central to maintaining capitalism in the United States. The Socialist Party (including antiracist left-wing leaders, such as Eugene V. Debs) did not offer a revolutionary answer to Black oppression nor try to mobilize the working class to defend Black workers during the "Red Summer" of 1919, when several cities erupted in pogroms against Black people.[9] The CPUSA was founded during the post-Reconstruction period of Jim Crow segregation, Black disenfranchisement, the rebirth of the Ku Klux Klan, and tremendous anti-Black violence. During the Great Migration, tens of thousands of Black people left the rural south and moved to the urban north—where they encountered segregated housing, poor jobs, and racist violence. To Marxists, especially those outside the United States, the central role of Black oppression to capitalism in the United States was clear. Furthermore, Black people were becoming an important component of the industrial proletariat. The fight against Black oppression had the potential to be a motor force for broader social struggle. Despite this, the Socialist Party did not see the need to mobilize the working class to fight racist attacks or make Black liberations central to socialist politics. The early Communist Party did not differ much from their socialist forebears; they denounced racist violence but did not focus on Black oppression.

Without Comintern intervention, communists would not have made Black liberation central to their work. The only Black communist at the foundation of the CPUSA was Otto Huiswoud, originally from Dutch Surinam, who joined the CPUSA through his association with the Dutch left-wing social-democratic movement, underlining the transnational dimension of the communist fight for Black liberation.[10] For the Comintern leadership, the CPUSA's lack of attention to the fight for Black liberation was a profound social-democratic weakness inherited from the party's socialist origins.

The African Blood Brotherhood

Cyril V. Briggs, a Harlem journalist from St. Nevis, organized the African Blood Brotherhood in late 1919. Several leaders of the ABB belonged to the Socialist Party in Harlem, including W. A. Domingo, Grace Campbell, and Richard B. Moore (all born in the Caribbean except Campbell, whose father was Jamaican). They drew upon the heritage of Caribbean radicalism and viewed the struggle against Black oppression as part of a global fight against colonialism and imperialism.[11] The ABB's magazine *Crusader* (published in New York) was read throughout the West Indian diaspora, including Panama. Briggs and most of the ABB leadership joined the CPUSA in the autumn of 1921, attracted by the Comintern's anticolonialism and anti-imperialism, not by the work of CPUSA itself.[12]

Claude McKay, a poet from Jamaica, was around the ABB and the CPUSA in the early 1920s. After moving to the United States in 1912, McKay lived in London from 1919 to 1921, where he contributed to the left-wing socialist journal *Workers' Dreadnought*.[13] That the first Black CPUSA cadres were Caribbean immigrants reflects the centrality of transnationalism to the appeal of communism. West Indian immigrants—a significant minority of the Black population in New York City—tended to be well educated and to come from societies where, although forged through slavery, day-to-day life was not determined by the color line. In the United States they confronted the one-drop rule and a rigid color line, forced segregation, and racist violence. This daily experience with Black oppression, combined with the anticolonial attitude of many migrants, further radicalized many West Indians in the United States; as historian Winston James demonstrated, many Black militants and radicals in the United States came from a Caribbean background.

This West Indian immigrant dynamic helps explain the rise of the Universal Negro Improvement Association (UNIA), led by Marcus Garvey, a Jamaican living in New York. Arguing that Black "redemption" could only be accomplished in Africa, the UNIA mixed accommodationism and militancy, insisting on race pride while accepting that the United States was a white country. To the Garvey movement, Black freedom would be gained outside of the United States. The UNIA's newspaper, the *Negro World* was transnational and multilingual and stressed the plight of Black people in the Caribbean and the world. As scholar Catherine Bergin put it, "Garvey's Pan-Africanism enabled a global vision of a Black politics—one that was structured outside of the boundaries of the nation state." The Comintern and the UNIA offered competing transnational perspectives for West Indians concerned with the fight against Black oppression. Despite Garvey's procapitalist views, the UNIA, as the largest Black organization in the world, attracted radicals. Domingo, the first editor of the *Negro World* before joining the ABB, underlines that both perspectives often appealed to similar constituencies.[14]

Except for Domingo, most of the ABB cadres joined the CPUSA. As communists, they provided leadership for recruiting more Black communists, including workers and intellectuals born in the United States. These Afro-Caribbean recruits served as a tribune for Black concerns within the communist movement and stressed the need to fight Black oppression and took the (still mainly white) leadership to task for neglecting the Negro Question in defiance of the Comintern leadership. They appealed to the Comintern to continue to pressure the (white) party leadership to emphasize Black liberation and pressured the leadership to carry out Comintern directives. The former ABB cadres helped forge transnational communist networks. As Bergin has argued, "in their responses to the Russian Revolution, African Americans, and Afro-Caribbean migrants living in the US, created a new transnational politics of liberation."[15] Much of the ABB's activity after joining the CPUSA was directed toward supporters of Garvey's UNIA. The ABB's communism and the UNIA's Pan-Africanism offered competing visions of transnational Black politics: Black liberation tied to the struggle for working-class power internationally versus Black empowerment under capitalism. Communists sought to polarize Black politics (including UNIA) along class lines and convince militant Black intellectuals and activists that socialism offered the way forward for Black liberation. In the 1920s the CPUSA recruited few Black people but met with more success in the 1930s.[16]

In 1922 McKay and Huiswoud attended the Fourth Comintern Congress. In his report to the Congress, Huiswoud complained communists in the United States had neglected the Negro Question, because "little attention has been paid to this matter and that it has not received the attention it deserves as a component of the world-revolution." The Fourth Congress established a Negro Commission and passed a resolution on the Negro Question. This resolution tended to collapse the situation of Black people throughout the world: "The history of Blacks in the United States has prepared them to play an important role in the liberation struggle of the entire African race." There was a tendency to conflate the tasks of communists in the United States and South Africa, ignoring the particularities of Black oppression in each country.[17]

In his remarks, McKay criticized the CPUSA: "They do not want to take up the Black question" and noted that "prejudice was noticeable" among white communists. McKay met with leading Bolsheviks, and Leon Trotsky commissioned him to write a study of Blacks in the United States. The resulting *Negroes in America*—published only in Russian translation and not appearing in English until the 1970s—denounced the CPUSA's leadership for neglecting the Negro Question and for not fighting for social equality between Black and white people in the United States. (McKay left the communist movement later in the decade, in part due to these frustrations.)[18]

Over the next years, the CPUSA addressed Black oppression in response to pressure from the Comintern and Black communists, largely former ABB members. Progress was not linear and was marked by fits and starts. In 1925 Texas-born Lovett Fort-Whiteman and other communists organized the American Negro Labor Congress (ANLC) to recruit Black workers to the communist movement. These efforts did not bear much immediate fruit, and the CPUSA remained a largely white organization, with its few Black members likely to be Afro-Caribbean.[19]

Through the ANLC the CPUSA recruited James W. Ford (born in Alabama) and George Padmore (born in Trinidad). Both would play central roles in the international communist movement's approach to the Negro Question, through the International Trade Union Committee of Negro Workers (ITUCNW), under the purview of the Red International of Labor Unions (Profintern). The ITUCNW, headquartered in Hamburg until the Nazis' rise to power in 1933, published the newspaper *Negro Worker*, aimed at Black workers throughout the world.[20]

The "Theses on the Revolutionary Movement in the Colonies and the Semi-Colonies," adopted by the Sixth Comintern Congress in July and August 1928, contained a lengthy section on the Negro Question but only examined Black oppression in the United States, Africa, and "Negro states, which are in fact imperialist colonies or semicolonies (Liberia, Haiti, Santo Domingo)." Although there was a section on Latin America, the theses did not address Black oppression in the region.[21]

However, the first issue of the *Negro Worker*, published in July 1928, stated its goal as laying "a basis for the Unity and Solidarity of the Negro workers against imperialist and capitalist oppression" and to struggle for the "*World Unity* of black, brown, yellow and white workers and imperialist oppression in the colonies and the imperialist countries upon the workers."[22] As Padmore put it in 1930, "The Negro toilers goaded to desperation are answering the imperialist offensive by increasing mass struggles" in Africa, the United States, the Caribbean, and Latin America, which "all show that the Negro masses have awakened and are adding new and powerful forces to the struggle against capitalist imperialism."[23] The roles of Huiswoud, McKay, and Padmore demonstrate the centrality of Afro-Caribbean communists to the Comintern's struggle for Black liberation and to the Comintern's transnational approach. The editorial board of the *Negro Worker* in late 1931, for example, included Padmore (as editor), Briggs, and Huiswoud, with other representatives from the United States, Africa, and the West Indies.[24]

Padmore's *Life and Struggles of Negro Toilers,* published by the ITUCNW in 1931, contains sections on Africa, the United States, the Caribbean, and Latin America. He concluded, "The general situation in Latin America demands the closest attention, especially the Negro question, which is becoming more and more complicated," because of "the importation of foreign Blacks to compete against the native labourers."[25] Most communist parties in Latin America, including Panama and Costa Rica, however, did not display the attention to the Negro Question that Padmore called for.

In contrast, in the 1930s communists in the United States made headway among the Black population, especially in northern cities, such as Chicago and New York, and among Black militants in the south. Communists helped forge interracial industrial unions, unlike existing, white-dominated craft unions. Communists, including the ITUCNW, championed the Scottsboro youth who had been framed and sentenced to death on bogus charges of raping two white women in Jim Crow Alabama. Highlighting the power of internationalism, communists built a transnational campaign to free the youth, making their case an international symbol of "lynch rope justice" and Black oppression in the United States. As Frances Peace Sullivan indicates in her chapter in this volume, the Scottsboro campaign resonated among Black people in Cuba.[26]

In 1931 the Comintern established a Caribbean Bureau, located in New York City, which was responsible for coordinating activity in the Caribbean islands, Central America, Mexico, and part of South America. The leadership of the Caribbean Bureau came from the CPUSA, with the assistance of exiled Cuban and Venezuelan communists.[27] The Caribbean Bureau drew attention to Black oppression in the Greater Caribbean as part of the struggle for unity between the region's working class and peasants, across linguistic, national, cultural, racial, ethnic, and gender divisions. Sandra Pujals argues, "Bringing the racial issue to the political frontline was most likely one of the most significant contributions of the Comintern's Caribbean agenda to the future development of a sense of unity and identity in the region" and "perhaps also the most enduring yet controversial, since racial discrimination was not even contemplated as an item within Caribbean radical politics at the time."[28] Nonetheless, the work of communist parties in the Greater Caribbean was uneven.

The political program and nature of the CPUSA in the 1930s were different than at its founding in 1919, reflecting changes in the international communist movement from Lenin's time to Joseph Stalin's time. The CPUSA had embraced Stalin's program of "socialism in one country," which rejected the necessity of international revolution. The rise of Stalinism overlapped with the Comintern's increased emphasis on Black oppression, which was one reason why several leading Black militants supported Stalin. The Comintern's formal position on the Negro Question reflected the rise of Stalinism, including an emphasis on a "two-stage" revolution that insisted that backward countries would first need to go through a democratic, anti-imperialist stage before becoming ready for socialist revolution. In the late 1920s and early 1930s the CPUSA, in accord with the Comintern, adopted the "Black belt" line that largely Black areas in the southern part of the United States comprised an oppressed nation with the right to self-determination, that is, the right of independence from the United States if the Black-belt nation desired.[29]

This theory shoehorned the Black experience in the United States into a European national-colonial question. The concept of an independent Black republic seems better fitted to the Caribbean—where racism, colonialism, and imperialism overlapped—than mainland North America, where the Black population had been an integral part of society for hundreds of years despite slavery and oppression. This approach attempted to divide the struggle for Black liberation into "stages" as Stalin prescribed in the struggle for colonial liberation. Many Black communists (including Afro-Caribbean immigrants) opposed the Black-belt position as a concession to segregation, and in its day-to-day work the CPUSA emphasized the fight for racial equality and downplayed "self-determination."

Communists and Antillanos in Panama and Costa Rica

In the 1930s the influence of the Bolshevik Revolution and the CPUSA's opposition to racial inequality attracted Black workers and intellectuals to communism. Black Caribbean immigrants, although a small portion of the Black population in the United States, served as a bridge to the broader Black population, facilitating future communist recruitment among the Black population more broadly. It might be expected that Black West Indians would have played a similar role in the communist movements in Panama and Costa Rica as they did in the United States. That they did not reflects differences between Panama and Costa Rica and the United States, including the role of Black Caribbean migrants in the labor and workers' movement, the relationship of these communist parties to the Comintern, and the weight of the Garvey movement. Communists in Panama and Costa Rica did not make the fight for Black liberation central to their work. Neither party recruited many West Indians, and militant West Indians looked elsewhere, especially to the Garvey movement.

The Republic of Panama was nominally an independent country, although in practice it was a protectorate created and dominated by the United States and saddled (like Cuba) with a constitutional provision granting the United States military the power to intervene at will. Cutting across the republic was the Canal Zone of more than 1,400 square kilometers, controlled by the United States and essentially a company town run by the U.S. military.[30] Many Panamanians saw their society as marked by fluid racial categories and the lack of overt racist violence common in the United States. This situation hid the oppression of Black people and stressed *cultural* unity instead of *racial* divisions, emphasizing a shared *hispanidad* among Black, mixed-race, and white Hispanic Panamanians, centered on Spanish-derived culture and Catholicism.[31]

Afro-Caribbean migrants ("Antillanos") played a central role in the working class in the isthmus, especially during the construction of the Panama Canal from 1904 to 1914. As historian Luis Navas has indicated, the working class in Panama developed earlier than the Panamanian bourgeoisie. Canal workers— foreigners laboring in a foreign-owned enterprise—were the most important section of the proletariat. Capitalists in Panama consisted mainly of landlords and merchants, at once dependent on and threatened by the canal's dominance in the economy.[32]

Antillanos faced racism as well as cultural, linguistic, and religious hostility in the Republic of Panama, and Jim Crow–style segregation in the English-speaking Canal Zone. Black workers from throughout the West Indies (called silver workers because they were originally paid in silver) did most of the physical labor in the Canal Zone, facing low pay, mistreatment, police abuse, and segregated housing and recreational facilities. White workers (called gold workers because they were originally paid in gold), largely from the United States, did most of the skilled work, received higher wages, and enjoyed a North American suburban existence in the middle of the tropics.[33]

West Indians in the Canal Zone formed a powerful section of the working class in the isthmus and repeatedly went on strike in the late nineteenth and early twentieth centuries.[34] Given the importance of the canal to the development of U.S. imperialist economic and military power, the U.S. military oversaw the canal's construction and operation and brooked no labor militancy. Gold workers' privileges reflected the Jim Crow–style racism of the U.S. government and lowered labor costs. Hispanic Panamanians, excluded from canal jobs, looked at West Indian workers as privileged while West Indians feared being replaced by Hispanic Panamanians. These divisions prevented unified labor struggle in the isthmus and blunted the development of an inclusive proletariat in Panama.[35]

Thousands of West Indian workers were laid off as the canal neared completion. In October 1916 almost a quarter of the West Indian workers in Panama struck after the authorities announced gold workers would be granted rent-free housing, but silver workers would not. The strike brought the zone to a standstill and won support by Hispanic workers in the Republic of Panama, posing the possibility of a unified labor movement of West Indian and Hispanic workers. Even though U.S. and Panamanian government repression broke the strike after five days, the strike underlined the power of West Indian workers and their ability to organize—and their strategic position in the working class of the isthmus.[36]

In late February 1920 almost all silver workers went on strike in the Canal Zone. The governor of the Canal Zone evicted strikers from their housing in the Canal Zone and mobilized some two thousand Panamanian and Colombian scabs (and some gold workers). Leaders detained in the Canal Zone were deported to the West Indies. In the wake of the strike, significant numbers of West Indians left Panama, many going to Cuba or the United States.[37]

After the 1920 strike the organized labor movement in Panama was at best indifferent to Antillano workers, while most West Indian workers had little to do with the labor movement. The Federación Obrera de la República de Panamá (Workers Federation of the Republic of Panama) was organized shortly after the strike but included few if any West Indians in its ranks, and several of its constituent unions supported expelling Antillanos from Panama. Understandably, the left and the labor movement focused on ridding Panama of U.S. domination, but the movement's Hispanic leadership tended to see West Indians as complicit in that domination, not as possible allies. This, in turn, fed Anglo chauvinism among some West Indian workers, who spoke English, were Protestant, and took pride in their attachments to Britain.

These divisions within the working class undercut the proletariat's historical continuity and hindered the working class's ability to assimilate the lessons of past struggles. Even Hispanic radicals in the labor movement viewed the transnational vision of Antillano workers as a threat, not a possible strength to the revolutionary workers' movement. In the face of indifference on the part of the Panamanian left and the labor movement, the greatest beneficiary of the silver workers' militancy was the Garvey movement. The UNIA had forty-six branches in the Republic of Panama and two in the Canal Zone. As scholar Kofi Barina stressed, through the efforts of the UNIA, "under the banner of race first, a cadre of radicals hailing from Barbados, Jamaica and Panama were able to unify around a Pan-African ideology." Although the Garvey movement initially supported union organizing, after the defeated 1920 strike, the movement turned away from working-class militancy, became anti-union, and opposed Hispanic-Antillano working-class unity.[38]

In Panama the Grupo Comunista was founded in 1921 under the guidance of a Spanish anarchist and Peruvian exiles.[39] The group's first major action was the September–October 1925 tenants' strike, led by the Liga de Inquilinos y Subsistencia (Tenants' Subsistence League) against high rents and poor housing conditions. On October 10 police attacked protesting tenants, killing several and bloodying dozens more.[40] The rent strike is seen as the beginning of a tradition of social struggle in Panama and the start of the modern labor movement. However impressive, militant, and important the rent strike was, few West Indians seem to have been involved even if West Indians suffered from the same poor housing and high rents as other residents of Colón and Panama City. Antillanos were vulnerable to expulsion, and the Panamanian government warned foreigners to keep out of the strike and expelled foreign leaders in the tenants' strike.[41]

Anti–West Indian racism and xenophobia were common in Panama. Right-wing Hispanic nationalists founded Acción Comunal (AC) in 1923. In 1924 Olmedo Alfaro, a contributor to AC's newspaper, published a racist pamphlet titled *El Peligro Antillano en la América Central: La Defensa de la Raza* (The West Indian danger in Central America: Defense of the race) that asserted Afro-Caribbean immigrants and their descendants threatened the Hispanic culture and sovereignty of Panama.[42] At the time of the strike, AC blamed West Indians for the conditions that caused the strike and tried to co-opt anger among Hispanic Panamanians over high rents and U.S. domination. In contrast, the Tenants' Subsistence League appealed to West Indians to join the strike, but there is no indication that the league addressed the special oppression of West Indians, for example, through demanding citizenship rights or an end to racial segregation in the Canal Zone or racial discrimination in the republic.

By 1925 the left-wing labor movement (which gave birth to the Communist Party in 1930) and the West Indian movement developed on different tracks. In 1928 the National Assembly made it harder for Antillanos born in Panama to obtain citizenship at the same time Britain and the United States sought to wash their hands of this population. AC capitalized on opposition to foreign-domination of Panama and in 1931 seized power through a coup. According to historian Michael Conniff, anti-Antillano attitudes "permeated all layers of society."[43]

The failure of the organizers of the tenants' strike to deal with the role of West Indians in Panamanian society meant the organizers could not combat the anti-Antillano sentiment common among Hispanic Panamanians nor confront Anglo chauvinism among West Indians. By the time Panama's Communist Party was founded, the Panamanian labor movement and the Antillano population had already diverged. An article from 1931 in *El Comunista*, published by the Comintern's Caribbean Bureau in New York, about how the communists organized May Day protests in Panama City, Colón, and elsewhere, does not mention West Indians at all. This would suggest that both the broader communist movement (the Caribbean Bureau) and communists in Panama did not see a revolutionary potential in the Antillano population and did not see recruitment from the transnational population as crucial.[44]

In the summer of 1932, communists and socialists participated in a two-month tenant strike that won a modest reduction in rents.[45] An article in the New York–based communist newspaper *El Mundo Obrero* highlighted Black oppression:

> The greatest effort must be expended to secure unity of Black and white tenants. This must be done through defending Black tenants, especially Jamaicans, against discrimination, segregation, abuse, etc. We must remember that the exploiters try to divide the workers' ranks, making Black workers the object of special attacks. In 1925, the police carried out the massacre in the Plaza de Santa Ana under the cry, *"Kill the Negroes."* Black tenants must be included in all [strike] committees and in the struggle's leadership.[46]

An article in December repeated in similar terms the need for Black-white unity and to defend West Indians.[47] However, the role of Antillanos in the 1932 strike is not clear. None of the arrested leaders was West Indian, and local newspaper accounts did not mention Antillano involvement, but the Tenants' Subsistence League printed leaflets in English.[48] The June *Mundo Obrero* had an article on communist work among young tenants in Panama that did not mention Black youth.[49] During the strike, the Comintern's *International Press Correspondence* published an article with the headline "Party Cadres in the CPs of South America and Caribbean America" and asserted the necessity of "the formation of reliable political Party cadres from among the Indians and Negroes, who know the language and the conditions of life of the oppressed nationalities." Without mentioning Panama, the article stated, "Most of the sections of the C.I. in South America have done nothing."[50]

After the 1932 tenants' strike and amid the devastation of the Great Depression, anti-Antillano sentiment descended into what Conniff called "the worst agitation against West Indians yet experienced" in Panama.[51] Amid this, communists in Panama did not stress fighting for Antillano rights as part of the struggle for national liberation and workers' power. The lack of communist attention to Antillanos left the field open to its competitors in the Socialist Party. The Socialist Party, not the communists, emphasized the issue and, according to historian Marixa Lasso, "openly defended the West Indian."[52]

Antillanos in Costa Rica

Unlike most of Latin America, the concept of national identity in Costa Rica was constructed around the idea of the nation's being "white." In the late 1800s more than ten thousand West Indians migrated to Costa Rica, first to work on a railroad from the Caribbean coast to the capital, San José, and then as workers for the U.S.-owned United Fruit Company (UFC) on the Caribbean coast.[53] This growing Antillano population was Black, English-speaking, and Protestant in a predominantly white, Hispanic, and Catholic country.[54]

West Indian banana workers organized as West Indians, not as workers. They demanded respect for West Indian culture and history and the end to racial discrimination along with higher wages and better working conditions. Between 1879 and 1911, West Indian workers struck more than a dozen times, but they often lost in the face of violent repression and the use of Hispanic strikebreakers.[55] Ethnic divisions separated the Antillanos' labor struggle in Limón from the national labor movement and broader national politics. The UFC favored Anglophone workers over Hispanic workers, playing one section of the working class against the other, causing each to blame the other, and deflecting criticism from the UFC.[56]

The Partido Comunista de Costa Rica (PCCR, Communist Party of Costa Rica) was founded in 1931. The PCCR was a distant star in the Comintern universe: there were no regular Comintern emissaries nor direct correspondence with the Comintern. Instead, the Comintern's Caribbean Bureau in New York City communicated with the party. The PCCR did not become a full member of the Comintern until the Seventh Congress of the Comintern in 1935. As a result, unlike with the CPUSA, the Comintern did not force the PCCR to address Black oppression.[57]

Given the stability of Costa Rica compared to its Central American neighbors, the party was able to remain legal (until the Civil War of 1948), publish a regular newspaper, and stand (and win) elections.[58] The focus on elections further blinded the PCCR to the concerns of Antillanos, most of whom were not citizens. An article in *El Comunista* from January 1932 elaborated "immediate demands" for its electoral platform, including a fight against wage cuts and unemployment, social welfare and social security programs at the expense of the rich and the government, confiscation of large estates to be redistributed to the peasantry, and a workers' and peasants' government. There was no demand aimed at Antillanos. An overview of the early PCCR by historian Vladimir de la Cruz does not mention efforts directed toward Black workers.[59]

The 1934 Banana Workers' Strike and West Indians

In 1934 Communist organizers led a strike of banana workers in Costa Rica for almost three weeks in August. This strike established the PCCR as an important force in the nation and the banana workers as the vanguard of the Costa Rican proletariat.[60] Most Antillanos in Limón did not participate in this strike. Many West Indians had become small planters instead of agricultural workers and depended on the UFC's good graces.[61] The Costa Rican government's expulsion of pro-strike foreigners (mainly, Nicaraguan workers), further militated against Antillano support for the strike.[62]

The PCCR did not entirely ignore West Indian workers. This might reflect the importance of the Negro Question in the broader Comintern, although the PCCR efforts were minimal. In August, *Trabajo*, the party's paper published in San José, hailed the "Colored Workers of the Atlantic Zone" for their "valiant attitude" and for "giving an outstanding example of bravery, fighting shoulder to shoulder with your companions in slavery in that great battle against the United Fruit Company."[63] The CPUSA's *Daily Worker* claimed, "More than half of the strikers are Negro workers, many brought into the country under semi-slave contracts from Haiti, Nicaragua and other countries."[64] These claims for Antillano participation are undercut by correspondence of communist leaders. In a letter to a Limón cadre, communist leader Manuel Mora observed that the UFC "has been fomenting division between Blacks and whites because when the workers are divided they are not able to struggle against the company." He instructed his comrades to "try to move forward and win over with care each day more Blacks to our ranks; struggle against the ignorance and lack of comprehension of many of them." He claimed that the UFC was "skillfully manipulating the situation with the Blacks to make the whites think that Blacks are the enemy."[65] This attitude is similar to Debs's position, stressing the need for class unity but lacking an appreciation of the special oppression of Black people. Unlike with the CPUSA, Comintern insistence did not propel the PCCR to transcend this narrow color blindness.

Communists in Costa Rica offered nothing special to Black workers. Instead of formulating demands dealing with the special oppression experienced by West Indians—such as demanding full citizenship rights and opposing racial discrimination—the communists blamed West Indians for not joining the strike.[66] Even when seeking to recruit Antillanos, the PCCR's lack of engagement with West Indians and lack of a special analysis or demands addressed to West Indians hindered these efforts.

The Comintern, CPUSA, and Caribbean Bureau

During the mid-1920s, with the rise of Stalinism and its "two-stage" theory of revolution, the Comintern stressed opposition to imperialism over class struggle within colonial and semi-colonial countries, seeking allies with liberals and other capitalist politicians.[67] One result was to downplay issues such as racial oppression that might challenge national unity in oppressed countries. In Latin America as a whole, the Comintern tended to emphasize the struggle against U.S. imperialism, which dominated national politics. In Panama and Costa Rica, this took the form of fighting against the Panama Canal authorities and the United Fruit Company, and West Indian workers tended to be associated with the bad influence of these companies in the popular imagination. Unlike in Central America, West Indians in the United States were often found in the front ranks of opposition to imperialism, given their experience as colonial subjects.

A key difference between communism in the United States, on one hand, and in Panama and Costa Rica on the other, is the role of the Comintern. The Comintern repeatedly intervened into the CPUSA to force the party to pay attention to the fight against Black oppression; Black communists in the United States, including cadres from the ABB, helped formulate the Comintern's approach to Black liberation. This sustained effort did not happen in Panama or Costa Rica, which were on the periphery of the Comintern and did not receive much Comintern attention.[68]

As noted above, the Comintern's *International Press Correspondence* observed in 1932 that "the rise of the revolutionary movement among oppressed minorities—Indians and Negroes—which has been noticeable recently raises before all the CPs of South [i.e., Latin] America the urgent task of the leadership of this movement." The article criticized "the unsatisfactory national composition of the Party cadres" in Latin America and urged that communists carry out sustained work to correct this.[69] However, the article did not mention Central America, and at least in Panama and Costa Rica, such literary attention was not matched by concrete efforts. The Liga Antiimperialista de las Américas (LADLA), the Latin American affiliate to the Comintern-aligned League against Imperialism (LAI), was founded in 1925 in Mexico City. As historian Anne Garland Mahler observed, "in its early years, it was generally silent on problems facing Black communities."[70] The 1927 Congress of the LAI in Brussels passed a resolution on the Negro question that asserted: "In Latin America, except in Cuba, Negros do not suffer the yoke of whatever special oppression. (In Panama, the Yanqui intervention has transplanted the barbaric customs against the Negros from the United States, which is the same origin of social inequalities in Cuba.)"[71] Through the Comintern's Caribbean Bureau, communists in the United States—and not the Comintern leadership in Moscow—paid the most attention to the Central American parties. While some individual CPUSA cadres did try to prompt communists in Central America to address Black oppression, as described below, these efforts lacked either the force or persistence of the Comintern's emphasis.

This understanding of the importance of race, especially connecting the fight for Black rights to the fight against imperialism, was uneven. The connection between national liberation and Black liberation was obvious for overwhelmingly Black Caribbean societies that were European colonies (such as Jamaica) or under U.S. occupation (such as Haiti) but less so in the United States, with an oppressed Black minority population.[72] Further, the Black-belt theory transformed Black oppression in the United States into a question of national liberation but said nothing about oppressed Black minorities in Costa Rica and Panama, which were themselves oppressed by U.S. imperialism. As Sullivan demonstrates in the current volume, the Cuban Communist Party emphasized the struggle against Black oppression (and adapted a version of the Black-belt theory). This reflects the importance of the Comintern (mediated through the Caribbean Bureau and the CPUSA) and of Black Cuban communists in the early 1930s, who stressed the Negro Question.[73]

An article in the CPUSA's *Daily Worker* in 1925 opposing U.S. intervention in Panama did not mention West Indian workers in Central America, even when it denounced the deportation of labor militants, some of whom had English-sounding names and might have been West Indian.[74] More awareness was shown in February 1929 by a Chinese-born member of the CPUSA who set sail from San Francisco and passed through the Panama Canal en route to Cuba.

Although most of the report dealt with work among Chinese people in Cuba, he reported:

> I do not know whether there are comrades working among the Negroes in the Canal Zone. In view of the fact that imperialist war is impending, that the Panama Canal is a powerful instrument of American imperialism, that the population in the canal zone is largely Negro, and that they are doing all the rough and essential work there, it is important that our comrades in the Republic of Panama and Central American countries should pay special attention to the Negro work in that region and the American Party, in its fight against imperialism, must not overlook the Panama Canal.[75]

There is no evidence that this led to work in the Canal Zone.

El Mundo Obrero and the Negro Question

Starting in 1930, the CPUSA helped publish *El Mundo Obrero* (Workers World) in New York, a monthly Spanish-language journal "dedicated to the revolutionary proletariat movement and national liberation, especially in the countries of the Caribbean." Its editorial team comprised representatives from the communist movement in Central America, Colombia, Cuba, Venezuela, and Cuba, along with CPUSA members Michael Gold, John Dos Passos, and managing editor Walter Carmon.[76] As its name indicates, *El Mundo Obrero* took a transnational perspective, but this did not include much emphasis on the Afro-Caribbean population.

El Mundo Obrero underlined the partial nature of Communist attention to the Negro Question in the Greater Caribbean. The journal regularly featured the struggle to save the Scottsboro youth but had little to say about Black oppression in the Caribbean. As shown by its language and editorial board, the Caribbean that *El Mundo Obrero* envisioned was the Hispanic Greater Caribbean; occasional articles on non-Hispanic Caribbean countries were outnumbered by articles on Mexican immigrants in the United States or on the Spanish Civil War—that is, non-Caribbean themes of interest to a Spanish-speaking population. The *Negro Worker* carried more frequent articles about Blacks in the Caribbean, showing that the Negro Question was seen as separate from normal communist work in the region.

In 1931 *El Mundo Obrero* published articles on the communist movement in Panama, stressing the struggles of workers and the peasants and the fight for national liberation. But none discussed winning Antillano workers to these struggles or connecting them to the fight for Black liberation.[77] During the 1932 tenants' struggle, as noted above, articles on Panama in *El Mundo Obrero* empha-sized the fight against anti-Black racism, but it is unclear if this reflected a broader change. More research is necessary to uncover what discussion, if any, there was about Black oppression in the Caribbean among *El Mundo Obrero*'s editors.

The CPUSA's lack of coverage of Black oppression in its propaganda about Central America reflected the party's larger lack of attention to Central America and its division of "Negro work" from "anti-imperialist" work. The CPUSA organized the Anti-Imperialist League of the Americas (AIL) in the 1920s, but this group remained small. In 1932 its organizer complained its work was "being done without adequate guidance from the CC [central committee] or from the DC's [district committees]." Work among Spanish speakers in the United States was the purview of the party's Spanish bureau, while the anti-imperialist frac-tion was responsible for organizing against U.S. imperialism in the Philippines, the Caribbean, Latin America, China, and Korea. The same document proposed that the CPUSA leadership assign Briggs to the AIL's executive committee and requested that "the Negro Department" meet with the AIL leadership to "work out plans for establishing the AIL as an organization among the Negroes." There is no indication in the archives that these proposals were implemented.[78]

El Mundo Obrero featured articles on Costa Rica, usually about the PCCR's election campaigns. One article from September 1931, titled "The Next Elec-tions in Costa Rica," argued, "The Communist Party is the party of the working class and thus the leader of the oppressed masses, of the peasants, of the poor in the cities, and of all those oppressed by imperialism." Antillanos were not listed among the oppressed. An article in July 1932 predicted, "As a measure of the worsening hunger and misery of workers and peasants, there exists a great possibility of spontaneous movements in Costa Rica, especially in the United Fruit Company plantations and the large estates in the coffee region." But while the article mentioned workers, peasants, and students, it did not mention Black people. This points to the separation between the CPUSA's "Negro work" and its "anti-imperialist" work.[79]

In 1933 a CPUSA youth leader, Dora Zucker, attended a Central American student congress in San José before being expelled from Costa Rica. She noted the prominence of Black oppression in Costa Rica and advocated work among Black workers and building support for the Scottsboro youth.[80] After Zucker's departure, neither the CPUSA nor the PCCR continued this work. When the International Labor Defense, affiliated with the CPUSA, organized a protest at the New York City headquarters of the UFC in October 1934, the *Daily Worker* did not mention Black workers."[81]

In neither Costa Rica nor Panama did the communist movement recruit significant numbers of West Indians, even though West Indians were an important component of the working class. There was only one leading communist in Costa Rica of West Indian descent, Harold Nichols, a tailor educated in San José, who joined the party in the 1930s.[82] This lack of communist attention helps explain the continued strength of the Garvey movement in Panama and Costa Rica among West Indians.[83]

In the early twentieth century, Afro-Caribbean migrants were one of the most transnational populations in the Americas; they played a prominent role in the United States, Panama, and Costa Rica. In the aftermath of World War I and the Bolshevik Revolution, the Communist International attempted to forge a transnational movement to destroy capitalism. Only in the United States did key West Indian leaders become communists, while few West Indians joined the communist movement in either Panama or Costa Rica. The Comintern regularly and forcefully intervened into the CPUSA to emphasize Black liberation, which helped the CPUSA recruit Afro-Caribbean migrants, who, in turn, helped develop the party's approach to the Negro Question. Neither the Comintern nor the CPUSA played such a role in the communist parties of Panama or Costa Rica, which meant the communist movement in these countries did not transcend "colorlessness" nor recruit many Afro-Caribbean migrants.

Notes

1. The traditional English term for this population, "West Indian," is problematic, not least because it accepts a European colonial term. However, there is no entirely suitable replacement; the current chapter uses "Afro-Caribbean," although this includes not only migrants from the British and French Caribbean but also Hispanic Caribbean. In Spanish the same population was usually referred to as Antillano, although this does not make sense in the U.S. context. Thus, rather clumsily, this chapter uses Afro-Caribbean, West Indian, and Antillano to refer to the same population. *Hispanic* refers to the native Spanish-speaking populations of Latin America.

2. The present work draws on previous publications by the author, which contain extensive historiographic discussion and references: Zumoff, "Black Caribbean Labor Radicalism in Panama, 1914–1921"; *Communist International and U.S. Communism*; "1925 Tenants' Strike in Panama"; and "Ojos Que No Ven."

3. Stephens, *Black Empire*, 2, 5.

4. Cardoso da Silva, "Do antirracismo local," 152.

5. Putnam, *Radical Moves*, 29 (table 2). There was a significant West Indian population in Cuba, which is examined in Frances Peace Sullivan's chapter in the current volume.

6. I have developed this relationship in more detail in Zumoff, *Communist International and U.S. Communism,* chapter 14.

7. Reed to Lenin, with Lenin's handwritten reply, fms Am 1091:533, John S. Reed Papers, Harvard University.

8. Pateman, "V. I. Lenin"; Riga, "Ethnic Roots."

9. See Debs, "Negro in the Class Struggle." The term "colorless" is taken from Debs's statement in this article that "the class struggle is colorless." Scholars have also referred to this as "color-blind" socialism. See Kelly, "Du Bois's Prolific 'Error,'" and Zumoff, *Communist International,* 289.

10. On Huiswoud, see Enkevort, "Life and Works," and Cardoso da Silva, "Do antirracismo local," 174.

11. On the ABB, see Bergin, "Unrest among the Negroes"; Gatto, "Harlem Radical African Blood Brotherhood"; James, *Holding Aloft.*

12. James, *Holding Aloft,* 155–60. Garland Press has published a facsimile edition of the *Crusader,* with an introduction by Robert A. Hill.

13. James, "In the Nest."

14. Bergin, "Russian Revolution," 70; Hanglberger, "Marcus Garvey." There is a voluminous research on Garvey; for an introduction, see Stein, *World of Marcus Garvey,* and Grant, *Negro with a Hat.*

15. Bergin, "Russian Revolution," 66.

16. Drachewych, "Communist Transnational," 3.

17. See Huiswoud's and McKay's reports in Riddell, *Toward the United Front,* 800–811. The resolution is on 947–51.

18. McKay, *Negroes in America.*

19. Zumoff, *Communist International,* 319–28.

20. For an extensive history of the ITUCNW, see Weiss, *Framing a Radical African Atlantic.* Padmore later became hostile to the communist movement. On Padmore, see James, *George Padmore*; Oliveira de Mattos, "Silent Hero."

21. Communist International, *VI Congreso,* 1:236.

22. *Negro Worker,* July 15, 1928.

23. *Negro Worker,* October 15, 1930.

24. *Negro Worker,* October–November 1931.

25. Padmore, *Life and Struggles,* part 2.

26. On CPUSA work among Black people in the United States in the 1930s, see Kelley, *Hammer and Hoe,* and Naison, *Communists in Harlem.* On the ITUCNW and Scottsboro, see Drachewych, *Communist International,* 51–52, and Swagler, "Russian Revolution," 624.

27. Pujals, "Soviet Caribbean" and "Con Saludos Comunistas."

28. Pujals, "Soviet Caribbean," 265–66. See also Mahler, "South-South Organizing."

29. The clearest expression of this idea is in Haywood, *Road to Negro Liberation.* Section 39 of the "Theses on the Revolutionary Movement in the Colonies and

Semicolonies," adopted at the Sixth Comintern Congress (1928), states that Black people in the southern United States have the right to self-determination. See Communist International, *VI Congreso*, 1:237.

30. Beluche, "El problema nacional," 30.

31. Porras, "Configuraciones de identidad nacional"; Guerrón-Montero, "Racial Democracy and Nationalism."

32. Conniff, *Black Labor*, 4; Navas, *El movimiento obrero*, 62–64; Gandásegui, Saavedra, Achong, and Quintero, *Las luchas obreras en Panamá*, 13; Greene, *Canal Builders*, 396–99.

33. In addition to the material cited in the previous note, see Donoghue, *Borderland on the Isthmus*; O'Reggio, *Between Alienation and Citizenship*; Senior, *Dying to Better Themselves*.

34. Zumoff, "Black Caribbean Labor Radicalism," 433.

35. Navas, *El movimiento obrero*, 142–50; Zumoff, "Black Caribbean Labor Radicalism," 434–45.

36. Zumoff, "Black Caribbean Labor Radicalism," 436–37.

37. Zumoff, "Black Caribbean Labor Radicalism," 436–40.

38. Barima, "Caribbean Migrants," 54; Ewing, "Caribbean Labour Politics," 31–35.

39. The only synthetic study of early communism in Panama is Del Vasto, *Historia del Partido Comunista*.

40. The best source on the strike is Alexander Cuevas, whose study has been reprinted in several forms, most recently as Cuevas, *El movimiento inquilinario de 1925*. See also Zenger, "West Indians in Panama," chapter 3.

41. Soler, *Panamá*, 59; Zumoff, "1925 Tenants' Strike," 530–33; *Workman*, October 24, 1925; Arango Durling, *La inmigración prohibida*, 27.

42. Beluche, "El problema nacional," 28; Alfaro, *El peligro antillano*; Lasso de Paulis, "Race and Ethnicity," 72; Milazzo, "White Supremacy."

43. *Workman*, October 24, 1925; Conniff, *Black Labor*, 66, 80; Arango Durling, *La inmigración prohibida*, chapter 5; Corinealdi, "Envisioning Multiple Citizenships," 92.

44. *El Comunista* (New York), June 1931.

45. On the strike, see Diógenes de la Rosa's chapter "Informe del Representante de los Inquilinos" (1934), *Diógenes de la Rosa*, 1:93–116; Pizzurno Gelós and Araúz, *Estudios sobre el Panamá Republicano*, 201–2; Zenger, "West Indians in Panama," 112.

46. *Mundo Obrero* (New York), September 1932.

47. *Mundo Obrero* (New York), December 1932.

48. Conniff, *Black Labor*, 83; Zenger, "West Indians in Panama," 104–16.

49. *Mundo Obrero*, June 1933.

50. Gómez, "Party Cadres," 743–44. The journal used "South America" to mean all Latin America.

51. Conniff, *Black Labor*, 83.

52. Lasso de Paulis, "Race and Ethnicity," 72–73; see also Conniff, *Black Labor*, 84.

53. Soto-Quirós, "Reflexiones sobre."

54. *La Tribuna* (San José), August 13, 1930, cited in Harpelle, "Bananas and Business," 62.

55. Bourgois, *Ethnicity at Work*, chaps. 6 and 7; Soto-Quirós, "Un otro significante," 8; Anderson, "Imperial Ideology," esp. chap. 1; Botey, *Costa Rica entre guerras*, 76; Chomsky, "Afro-Jamaican Traditions," 837; Echeverri-Gent, "Forgotten Workers," 289–93; Harpelle, *West Indians of Costa Rica*, 46–50.

56. Olien, "Negro in Costa Rica," 101–6; Chomsky, *West Indian Workers*, 235–37.

57. Chacón Araya, "Recordando la Fundación," 125–28; Ching, "El Partido Comunista"; Alexander, *Rómulo Betancourt*.

58. Herrera Zúniga, "Nueve preguntas."

59. *El Comunista* (New York), January 1932; de la Cruz, "El Primer Congreso."

60. Botey and Cisneros, *La crisis de 1929*, 114; Rosas Sandoval, "La cultura de las clases trabajadoras urbanas"; Acuña Ortega, *La huelga bananera de 1934*.

61. See Zumoff, "Ojos Que No Ven," 222.

62. Acuña Ortega, *La huelga bananera de 1934*, 29, 35, 37; Bourgois, *Ethnicity at Work*, 108.

63. *Trabajo*, August 11, 1934, qtd. in Bourgeois, *Ethnicity at Work*, 107.

64. *Daily Worker* (New York), August 28, 1934.

65. Qtd. in Bourgois, *Ethnicity at Work*, 59.

66. See Bourgois, *Ethnicity at Work*, 109.

67. This culminated in the disastrous alliance with Chiang Kai-shek and his Nationalist Party (Goumindang) in 1927, in which thousands of workers and communists were massacred.

68. Cerdas-Cruz, *Communist International in Central America*, 149.

69. Gómez, "Party Cadres," 744.

70. Mahler, "Global Solidarity," 49. See also Melgar Bao, "Anti-Imperialist League."

71. *El Libertador* (Mexico City), June 1927, qtd. in Mahler, "Global Solidarity," 57. I have slightly modified Mahler's English translation.

72. Stevens, "Hands Off Haiti!"

73. Wood, "Semi-Colonials and Soviets," in the current volume; Mahler, "Red and the Black in Latin America."

74. *Daily Worker* (Chicago), October 21, 1925.

75. Tontien [Shi Huang] to Dear Comrades, January 16, 1929, in f. 515, op. 1, d. 1662, Russian State Archive of Social and Political History (hereafter referred to as RGASPI).

76. On *El Mundo Obrero*, see Campos Domínguez, "La Revista *Mundo Obrero*."

77. *El Mundo Obrero* (New York), August 1931 and October 1931.

78. Proposals made to the Secretariat, CC, by the fraction of the Buro of the Anti-Imperialist League, October 15, 1932, in f. 515, op. 1, d. 3028, RGASPI.

79. *El Mundo Obrero* (New York), September 1931 and July 1932. None of the articles mentioned women, which may be a result of an electoral bias.

80. Caribbean Bureau to PCCR Central Committee, April 19, 1933, in Ching, "El Partido Comunista," 37–39; *Daily Worker* (New York), June 3, 1933, and June 20, 1933; *El Mundo Obrero* (New York), August–September 1933.

81. *Daily Worker* (New York), October 8, 1934.

82. Molina Jiménez, "Afrocostarricense y Comunista."

83. On Costa Rica, see Leeds, "Toward the 'Higher Type of Womanhood,'" 2; On Panama, see Barima, "Caribbean Migrants," and Ewing, "Caribbean Labour Politics."

The "Negro Question" in Cuba, 1928–1936

FRANCES PEACE SULLIVAN

In the early 1930s communists across the globe were calling for international working-class solidarity *and* Black liberation, and the Partido Comunista de Cuba (PCC, Communist Party of Cuba) was no exception. The PCC and its sister organizations fought against U.S. lynch justice, advocated for Black self-determination, and put international proletarian solidarity into practice by defending Black immigrants, a rare position among communist parties (or any political party) in the Americas. They even criticized their own previous inaction on the issue of race; at its IV Congreso Nacional Obrero de Unidad Sindical (Fourth National Labor Union Unity Congress) in 1934, the communist-affiliated Confederación Nacional Obrera de Cuba (CNOC, National Workers Confederation of Cuba) conceded, "One of our fundamental failures had been to neglect . . . the Negro Question in general."[1] In short, during the first half of the 1930s, Cuban communists firmly believed that the fight for Black liberation was essential to revolutionary struggle on the island.

Cuban historiography of the communist approach to race tends to place the party firmly on the side of Black liberation in the 1930s without close attention to the nuances of how the PCC articulated that support or how policies around race fit into an international agenda.[2] At the same time, a robust and more transnationally oriented literature on Black communism largely focuses on the Anglophone world, overlooking places like Cuba.[3] More recently, historians addressing Black communism in the Spanish-speaking world have illuminated how Black organizers often "pushed Communists and their vision of world revolution to the left."[4] This chapter builds on these works to examine specifically the Cuban party apparatus and how it tackled issues particular to Black people—a matter referred to as the "Negro Question"—and the evolution of that approach in dialogue with the global communist movement. As historian Barry Carr has demonstrated, the PCC evolved from a "Caribbean backwater" in communist circles to having "the most substantial Comintern presence seen in Latin America" between the years 1932 and 1934.[5] In light of this early 1930s conjuncture of Comintern-PCC cooperation *and* a concerted effort to tackle racism, the Negro Question in Cuba offers a unique window into transnational communist thinking on race and the local applicability of international directives.

The PCC, like most communist parties in the Americas, initially neglected the particular concerns of Black workers, instead prioritizing social class over race and concentrating on penetrating the established labor movement. In the early 1930s, however, a changing international communist landscape and voices from within the party itself pushed the PCC to act, and the party moved Black liberation to the forefront of its agenda. Documents from the Workers Movement collection at the Instituto de Historia de Cuba in Havana reveal that the PCC took on the Negro Question with three main campaigns: defense of the Scottsboro Nine in Alabama, the right to self-determination in the Black-majority regions of the island, and a campaign against anti-Black racism and terror.

In particular, the PCC came to see Cuba's multinational sugar workforce as an essential constituency. In the first third of the twentieth century, as many as six hundred thousand Haitians and British West Indians migrated to labor in Cuba's sugar fields and factories.[6] Cuba's foremost industry, dominated by foreign capital, relied on these Antillano workers, and they continued to arrive in a special concession to sugar companies until the late 1920s. Much of Cuban society largely resented this migratory stream, with some openly opposing Black immigration on racist grounds, while others complained that foreigners imported by imperialist companies lowered wages and hampered labor organizing.[7] So in 1933, when the Partido Comunista de Cuba came to the defense of Antillano workers, it stood alone in advocating for their rights. Indeed, defense of Antillanos was a rare position among communist parties in the Americas. During the Popular Front, however, this vision of proletarian internationalism in practice would come to clash with Cuban nationalism and lead the PCC to reverse course on foreign workers while reframing the Negro Question in national terms. The PCC's shifting approach to the Negro Question reflects larger attempts to balance international directives with local realities and to Cubanize a transnational communist agenda.

The Negro Question in Cuba

Founded in 1925, the PCC was not an immediate ally to Afro-Cubans, let alone Black immigrants. Rather, the party only slowly moved to a position of racial solidarity, thanks in large part to internal and external pressures. The PCC spent its early years small in numbers, dominated by Spanish and Eastern European immigrants, and focused on wresting union leadership away from anarcho-syndicalists.[8] By the late 1920s, however, having faced severe repression from the regime of President Gerardo Machado and the deportation of many leaders, the PCC regrouped and entered a stronger phase due to several factors. At home, the Great Depression and rising opposition to the Machadato made the party and its fierce anti-imperialism popular. Internationally, at its 1928 Sixth Congress, the Communist International (Comintern) had made the "discovery of Latin America," and American communist parties began receiving newfound attention and limited funds.[9] Thus, began a period of transnational collaboration through a vibrant press, party and labor congresses, and institutions like the Caribbean Bureau.[10]

While the Comintern's Sixth Congress is most famous for launching the "Third Period," a time characterized by rejecting collaboration with the noncommunist left in favor of "class against class" struggle, the congress also marked a watershed moment for the communist approach to Black liberation, though the change was long in the making.[11] As early as 1913 V. I. Lenin expressed support for African Americans in the United States, a stance formalized in the Comintern's 1920 "Theses on the National and Colonial Question," which argued that communist parties must support "revolutionary movements among the dependent nations and those without equal rights (e.g., in Ireland, and among the American negroes), and in the colonies."[12] Encouraged by Lenin's position and by the Bolshevik victory, several "New Negro" intellectuals—voices in the postwar surge of Black political mobilization—joined communist parties and pushed for an aggressive approach to Black liberation. In 1922 Dutch Surinam–born Otto Huiswoud and Jamaican Claude McKay, leaders of a New York organization of Black communists called the African Blood Brotherhood (ABB), addressed the Communist International's Fourth Congress.[13] The congress issued "Thesis on the Negro Question," which acknowledged the "awakened race consciousness" and "spirit of rebellion" of African-descended peoples worldwide and proclaimed that "the Negro problem has become a vital question of the world revolution."[14] Later, Lovett Fort-Whiteman, an ABB leader, addressed the 1924 Fifth Congress, and "Black Bolshevik" Harry Haywood studied at Bolshevik schools in Moscow before attending the Sixth Congress. African American James W. Ford (who would later attend the 1934 fourth CNOC conference in Havana) represented the Communist Party of the United States of America (CPUSA) at the Red International of Labor Unions and was heavily involved in debates at the 1928 Sixth Congress.

In short, Moscow's evolving thinking on the national and colonial questions, engagement with diasporic figures urging a concerted approach to race, and awareness of a rise in Black activism all pushed the Comintern to move forcefully on the Negro Question. The 1928 Sixth Congress declared,

> The Negro race everywhere is an oppressed race. Whether it is a minority (U.S.A., etc.), majority (South Africa) or inhabits a so-called independent state (Liberia, etc.), the Negroes are oppressed by imperialism. Thus, a common tie of interest is established for the revolutionary struggle of the race and national liberation from imperialist domination of the Negroes in various parts of the world.[15]

The Comintern directed local parties to "struggle for the complete equality of rights for the Negroes" and urged organizing Black workers, largely through the International Trade Union Committee of Negro Workers (ITUCNW) and its paper, the *Negro Worker*.[16]

Not all communist parties embraced the call for action on the Negro Question. Party leaders often believed that Latin America experienced less racism than the United States or that racism was mainly entrenched among elites, not the working classes. In a different but related vein, Peruvian José Carlos Mariátegui argued that ethnic-based organizing would further marginalize Indigenous peoples.[17] The PCC, too, was slow to move on the Negro Question.[18] Yet, by the early 1930s, it had begun a concerted effort to reach out to Afro-Cubans. There are several reasons for this shift, including encouragement from Moscow, exchanges with other communist parties, and the efforts of prominent Afro-Cuban communists, including Sandalio Junco.

Junco, who led a bakers' union, was a prominent member of the PCC in the late 1920s and represented Cuba in the ITUCNW.[19] In May 1929 he attended the founding meeting of the Confederación Sindical Latino Americana (CSLA, Latin American Trade Union Confederation) in Montevideo, Uruguay, as the CNOC's international secretary. His speech, "El problema de la raza negra y el movimiento proletario" (The problem of the Black race and the proletarian movement), detailed the unique situation of disadvantage and oppression facing Black people across the Americas, critiqued the idea that racism was absent in Latin America, and called on communist parties to organize Black workers. Significantly, he also addressed the exploitation of Haitian, Jamaican, and other Antillano laborers working for U.S. commodity-export companies in the Caribbean and Central America, condemning "the modern slave trade carried out by imperialist companies."[20] Junco called on all labor unions to open their doors to foreign Black workers and suggested the formation of unions of Antillean workers in places where export industries were reliant on immigrant labor, like Cuba.[21] His proposal made it into the final resolution, which included a statement of the need to organize Afro-Caribbean workers.[22] A few weeks later in Buenos Aires, Junco attended the first (and only) conference of Latin American communist parties. Junco again argued that anti-Black racism, in fact, did exist in Latin America and pointed to its particular forms in Cuba. Similarly, in a 1930 article for the newspaper *El Trabajador*, Junco insisted on the importance of reaching out explicitly to Black workers.[23] In short, Junco (who would later be expelled from the PCC for Trotskyism) pushed to organize Black workers as uniquely subjugated. He was not alone in encouraging the PCC's firm stance on the Negro Question.

The early 1930s were a period of heightened transnational communist collaboration both in ideology and in practice. Individuals traveled the region, often as representatives of the Comintern, emphasizing the importance of expanding the party reach. These included CPUSA leaders Huiswoud and Ford, both of whom visited in Cuba in 1930.[24] To be clear, local parties and their affiliates often complained of lack of support, especially material resources, yet the Comintern's influence was clearly felt during this period through outfits like the International Red Aid (IRA) and regional bodies like the Caribbean Bureau, all of whom took up the Negro Question.[25]

In particular, the New York–based Caribbean Bureau of the Comintern, founded in 1931, served as a nexus for Marxist intellectuals, party members, and union organizers from across the Caribbean, facilitating communication between the Comintern and American communist parties. As Sandra Pujals writes, the bureau "added a more inclusive, local idiosyncrasy to an altogether Eurocentric and ideologically orthodox entity." The Caribbean Bureau connected Cuban communists—including the intellectual voice of the PCC, Rubén Martínez Villena, who coedited the bureau's New York newspaper, *Mundo Obrero*— with a community of New York, West Indian, Venezuelan, Dominican, and Puerto Rican intellectuals. Together, they grappled with pressing questions shared by societies with histories of slavery. Caribbean Bureau voices centered "special forms of national oppression and discrimination" and called upon local parties to address racial oppression.[26] In 1931 the bureau took the PCC to task for having "very few Negro workers, though a third of [Cuba's] population is Negro." A letter claimed that "because the Party does little among the Negro workers, there are practically no Negros in the party" and called for a more aggressive Black-recruitment campaign.[27] The *Mundo Obrero* explicitly suggested Caribbean communists organize workers on foreign-owned plantations.[28]

The Caribbean Bureau was not alone. In the early 1930s the Comintern and the CPUSA also urged the Cuban party to expand its membership base. In Cuba, where at least a third of the population was Black or of mixed race, this necessarily meant reaching out to workers of color.[29] The CPUSA, in a 1930 open letter, charged the Cuban party to "energetically penetrate the masses with its own slogans and demands, expressing the immediate needs of these masses."[30] By 1932 Moscow was directly pressuring the PCC to become a "true organization of the masses." At its 1932 conference, the Comintern's International Red Aid urged affiliate organizations to convert themselves into popular organizations with expansive memberships. Its Cuban arm, Defensa Obrera Internacional (DOI, International Workers' Defense), was to work with labor unions, the unemployed, and local peasantries in an effort to "grow extraordinarily."[31] These messages were consistent with Third Period priorities, which included, above all, a call for communist parties to assume leadership of the proletariat. In Cuba the PCC could not become an "organization of the masses" without action on the Negro Question, and one of the most important components of this work was the campaign in defense of the Scottsboro Nine.

Defense of the Scottsboro Nine

In April 1931 white juries convicted nine young African Americans on false rape charges in Scottsboro, Alabama, and sentenced all but one to die. The CPUSA took up the case and demanded their release.[32] Almost immediately, the campaign reached global proportions, as demonstrations erupted in Latin America, the Caribbean, Japan, South Africa, Australia, India, and New Zealand and across Europe.[33] Several factors internationalized the Scottsboro case, not the least of which was a CPUSA-organized European tour in 1932 by Ada Wright, mother of two defendants.[34] The International Red Aid, its U.S. arm called International Labor Defense (ILD), the Red International of Labor Unions (RILU or Profintern), and its ITUCNW all spread word about the trial and mobilized workers in defense of the "Scottsboro boys." As historian Hakim Adi explains, Scottsboro's "global significance was largely a consequence of the campaign organized by the Comintern and its organizations."[35] Communist newspapers, like the *Negro Worker*, the *Daily Worker*, and the *Mundo Obrero*, kept readers abreast of the trials, called for protests, and covered agitation around the case. As "a central episode in the global racial politics of the 1930s," Scottsboro linked the struggle against racial discrimination with anti-imperialism *and* workers' rights.[36] After all, the Scottsboro Nine were victims of lynch justice, certainly, but they were also poor youths and men riding the rails in search of work like so many others during the Great Depression.

Taking a cue from its parent body, Defensa Obrera Internacional spearheaded the Cuban campaign and launched a series of protests and letter-writing assemblies. Scottsboro defense had widespread traction on the island.[37] Labor unions sent messages of protest to the U.S. embassy as early as July 1931. The CNOC issued a statement calling for the defendants' release sponsored by an "endless" list of organizations, including unions of drivers, typographers, commercial employees, carpenters, and metallurgical workers.[38] Informal groups of laborers paused work to send cables to the governor of Alabama.[39] Across the island, demonstrations erupted near spaces of U.S. power, including consulates and company offices.[40]

Sympathy for the Scottsboro Nine resonated beyond communist circles, as even the conservative Havana newspaper *Diario de la Marina* declared the "entire world is interested in [their] acquittal from death sentences."[41] Members of the elite Afro-Cuban society, Club Atenas, called the case an example of "racial prejudice and capitalist cruelty," indicating that PCC language around the case as a failure of "capitalism" had taken wider hold.[42] In Santiago, an Afro-Cuban man entered a relief kitchen serving mainly Spaniards and agitated for a march mentioning Scottsboro.[43] The police murdered at least one Scottsboro protestor in Cuba, white Communist Youth League member Domingo Ferrer.[44]

The PCC harnessed this popular outrage toward its Third Period goals of growing its member base, moving forcefully on the Negro Question, and advancing international proletarian solidarity. Party affiliates issued instructions about how to tailor Scottsboro messages to particular constituencies, including peasants, workers, young people, and intellectuals.[45] The DOI directed local divisions to "take advantage of all events related to the nine youths in Scottsboro to recruit new Black members to our ranks."[46] Scottsboro, however, was about more than recruitment. It became a tool to "advance the international education of the Cuban masses" and a prism through which to condemn the intertwined problems of imperialism, racism, labor exploitation, and political repression, all of which united workers across the Americas.[47]

With Scottsboro at the forefront of its messaging and "For the Liberty of the Scottsboro Nine!" appearing in a majority of party circulars and manifestos, the PCC successfully recruited Afro-Cubans during the early 1930s.[48] Both leadership and rank and file increased their proportions of Black members. In 1933 the DOI claimed that of its 500 members, 175 were Black.[49] According to some estimates, over a third of PCC rank and file were Black, and by mid-decade, Cubans of color led the longshoremen's union, builders' guild, the sugar workers' union, and the CNOC. Several Black and mixed-race activists, including sugar organizer Jesús Menéndez and PCC general secretary Blas Roca, rose to prominence during this period.[50]

The vigorous campaign in defense of the Scottsboro Nine exemplified the PCC's commitment to Black liberation. That the first major episode in the party's antiracism struggle was an overseas event is not a coincidence. The late nineteenth-century independence struggle had established the ideal of multiracial brotherhood as an essential component of nationalist rhetoric.[51] Political organizing on the basis of race had been illegal since 1910, and Black organizations were often accused of stirring up race hatred.[52] The PCC's Scottsboro campaign thus walked a careful line between circumspection about openly tackling racism at home and the global turn toward the Negro Question. While condemning imperialist racism proved popular, however, two other approaches had mixed results.

The "Faja Negra"

The idea of Black self-determination first appeared on the PCC agenda in 1932.[53] The position stipulated that because Black residents in the *oriental* region stretching between Santiago de Cuba and Baracoa formed a majority of the population, they constituted an "oppressed nation" and had the "right to self-determination, even to the formation of a separate state."[54] Moscow had long debated the nationalities question and, at the Sixth Congress in 1928, addressed its applicability to Black-majority states (South Africa), states with significant Black populations (Cuba, the United States), and states with Indigenous populations (Australia, Ecuador).[55] At issue was whether the Negro Question was one of race or of nationality, and the Sixth Congress resolved that the CPUSA "must come out openly and unreservedly for the right of Negroes to national self-determination" in the U.S. south.[56] After a year of inaction, the U.S. party took up the position and maintained that African Americans had the right to self-determination in Black-majority regions.[57] The Cuban party adopted a position by the same name, "Black belt" or "*faja negra*," in late 1932 and announced it in *El Trabajador* in 1933.[58] The party reiterated that the region's Black residents had the right to form a separate state and would be supported by the party if they so chose.[59]

Practical problems and criticism plagued the Black-belt policy from the start. What, many Cuban intellectuals asked, was to become of more than three-fourths of Afro-Cubans residing outside of the faja negra.[60] Moreover, with its claim that the Black belt constituted a distinct nation, the PCC failed to consider that much of the Black population in Oriente was composed of Haitians and British West Indians working in the sugar industry.[61] To what extent did they share a nationality? Moreover, Black self-determination seemed a poor fit with Cuban ideologies of racial brotherhood. Essayist Alberto Arredondo argued that Black Cubans could not be distinguished from white Cubans in terms of territory, religion, language, and culture. In the wars of independence, he claimed "*El Negro* did not struggle for [Cuba's] division, but for its integration. NATION and NEGRO cannot be separated in Cuban society."[62] Similarly, party spokesman Agustín Alarcón later wrote an *Adelante* article titled "Black Nation?! No!" condemning the policy and arguing, "The Cuban nation is singular and indivisible."[63] As Tony Wood demonstrates, the idea of self-determination was not entirely clear even within party circles, and it opened the PCC to critique from anticommunists, who spread rumors of impending Black rule and obligatory miscegenation.[64] In other words, while self-determination marked an effort to assert Black rights (and, in fact, entailed calls for Black land ownership, access to the professions, and desegregation), it was sometimes confusing to militants and easily caricatured by outsiders.

Criticism of the faja negra idea continued from its inception through Cuban historiography immediately after the 1959 revolution and beyond.[65] In 1986 scholar Pedro Serviat argued that the Black-belt position had been a "theoretical and practical error" and that the Cuban national process had been one of racial integration since 1868.[66] Wood summarizes this historiography: "The self-determination policy thus appears as at best a passing folly, of little consequence within the larger trajectory of Cuban Communism."[67] Recently, some scholars have challenged the idea that self-determination was a mistake or diversion from the struggle for Black equality. Historian Margaret Stevens writes that "advocating for workers' right to self-determination in the 'Black Belt' of the U.S. and Cuba formed a critical component of Communist praxis against American imperial power and Cuban native elites."[68] Wood concludes that "black equality and self-determination in Oriente were not contrasting or alternative paths, but complementary strategies to be pursued in different parts of Cuba." He argues that these "geographic complements" were parts of a coherent struggle for Black equality and a sincere PCC effort to tackle discrimination internally and externally.[69]

Indeed, while the PCC and its sister organizations proclaimed the *right* to self-determination in the Black belt, they never demanded the formation of a separatist state. In late 1933, as the DOI prepared for its first national congress, it proclaimed itself in favor of "political, social, and economic equality for Black people" in the same breath as declaring support for "self-determination in the '*faja negra*' of Oriente."[70] Another DOI circular defended the organization against accusations of "fomenting race war," called for full racial integration, and instructed DOI members to personally desegregate social spaces. "White and black *compañeros* [comrades]" were to hold meetings together in "those places in which *negros* have not been permitted."[71] The DOI, in other words, saw no incongruence between the *right* to self-determination and integration. At its second congress in April 1934, the PCC explained, "It is necessary to put the struggle for self-determination in its proper place, which, these days, is not the central, daily issue[, that is,] the daily and systematic struggle against racial discrimination and anti-Black oppression. [We must] develop struggles for the right of Blacks to work in any factory, office, and in commerce [and] to be admitted to all hotels, theaters, cinemas, parks, etc., linking this in all cases to the slogan of Black self-determination."[72] The everyday struggle, then, was not for a separatist state but for social and economic equality, equal representation in the workplace, and integration of public and private spaces.

In short, the faja negra was often unclear and occasionally put the party on the defensive. While condemning the obvious case of U.S. lynch justice of the Scottsboro trials was a straightforward endeavor, convincing the Cuban people to apply the Soviet take on nationalities to racial matters was a harder sell for the Communist Party in Cuba, where nationalist ideology had been integrationist, at least rhetorically, since the nineteenth century. In light of this lack of traction, the PCC no longer mentioned self-determination in written materials by the end of 1934, and in a speech in October 1935, Roca announced a turn away from the position.[73] This change coincided with the Popular Front era of international communism, which emphasized cross-class collaboration over proletarianism and national unity over internationalism, as detailed below. Ultimately, the faja-negra story sheds light on the careful line the PCC walked when trying to balance international directives with local realities. While the Black-belt policy exposed the limitations of the Third Period position on subjugated nations, party support for Afro-Caribbean immigrants would expose the limits of an internationalist praxis at home during the rise of Great Depression–era nativism.

Defense of Antillano Workers

In the early 1930s Afro-Caribbean immigrants had been laboring in Cuba's fields, factories, and cities for well over a decade.[74] Despite Junco's early calls for the mobilization of Afro-Antillean immigrants, the PCC made little effort to reach out to Caribbean workers, even after launching its Black-recruitment campaign. The party believed Antillanos were too linguistically, socially, and geographically isolated and too easily exploited for organizing.[75] This changed after the PCC spent a year working with sugar laborers.

By 1931 a consensus had emerged among communists on and off the island that organizing Cuba's sugar workforce was an essential step toward anti-imperialist revolution. Newspaper articles and party leaders proclaimed the importance of the sugar proletariat, with the *Mundo Obrero* writing that the success of all other campaigns "depends on organizing sugar workers."[76] In February 1932 the PCC set up a commission to build a national sugar-worker union through the CNOC.[77] Even then, however, the call to organize sugar workers made no mention of immigrants, despite the fact that they were often the majority of field hands.[78]

The PCC surveyed working conditions and organized sugar laborers over the course of 1932, a process that raised their awareness of the plight and potential of Antillanos.[79] By the time the founding congress of the Sindicato Nacional de Obreros de la Industria Azucarera (SNOIA, National Union of Sugar Industry Workers) gathered in Santa Clara in December 1932, declarations explicitly included Haitians and British West Indians. The SNOIA's founding manifesto condemned abuses committed against Antillanos during the previous harvest, including several cases of forced labor and deportation, as well as at least one murder at the hands of the armed force charged with protecting property in the countryside, the Rural Guard. The manifesto called for a general strike and, like the CNOC's February plans, provided a strike how-to guide. Unlike earlier, however, this included a clear role for Antillanos: strike committees should be "elected and formed by all workers, by whites and blacks, by native and foreign, by Haitians, Jamaicans, and Chinese [workers], by adults and young people, by men and women, . . . by agricultural and mill workers." The SNOIA specifically addressed British West Indians and Haitians in its demands, calling for "equal pay for equal work and the right to all work positions for *negros*, Jamaicans, and Haitians."[80] In short, over the course of 1932, organizers shifted from overlooking immigrants to advocating for their full inclusion in party actions.

If Cuba's communists were just coming to grips with the plight of foreign workers by the end of 1932, Afro-Caribbean participation in events known as the Revolution of 1933 convinced the PCC of Caribbean immigrants' revolutionary potential. That year, rising political opposition to President Machado came to a head with a general strike in August. Machado fled the island on August 12, and by early September, Ramón Grau San Martín led a left-leaning government.[81] Nevertheless, strikes continued in Cuba's sugar towns through the fall, with heterogeneous groups of workers, including British West Indians, Haitians, and Cubans, taking over dozens of mills and establishing workers councils, which they sometimes called soviets.[82] Carr has demonstrated that Antillanos joined strike committees and workers councils, blocked roads, and carried out labor stoppages.[83] PCC organizers later admitted their previous doubts about immigrant workers and surprise at their militancy: "[I]n past years when we discussed sugar work we believed that this was difficult and that the main obstacles were the Haitian and Jamaican workers whom we could not reach because they spoke English or patois. But our assumption was built on complete ignorance. . . . Haitian and Jamaican workers demonstrated a high degree of combativeness in the recent labor struggle. They fought more like members of a slave rebellion who had nothing to lose. In many mills they were in the front line of the struggle."[84] By the end of 1933, the PCC had completely reversed course, from denying the revolutionary potential of Afro-Caribbean immigrants to calling for their organization and celebrating their role in the sugar insurgency. The party had come to see the largely Black multinational workforce laboring at the heart of the imperialist-dominated sugar industry as essential to revolution in Cuba.

While Cuban and foreign sugar workers were striking and seizing factories, the wider Cuban public continued to resent Black immigrants for, as many claimed, bringing down wages and taking jobs. Amidst the Revolution of 1933, several organizations dedicated to promoting anti-immigrant legislation sprang up, including the Association of National Reconquest and the Pro-80% Committee promoting Cuban majorities in workplaces.[85] The Grau administration, which was largely prolabor and had established the eight-hour workday and the Ministry of Labor, moved to exclude foreigners from workplaces. An October decree ordered the repatriation of all unemployed foreigners without resources. The next month, the Nationalization of Labor Law, dubbed the 50% Law, stipulated that one-half of all employees in most industries must be Cuban, though fieldworkers were exempted in a major concession to sugar companies. Finally, December regulations mandated the deportation of all foreign workers who failed to comply with previous laws.[86] "Forceful repatriation" was to be carried out by local municipal authorities, under supervision from the Ministry of the Interior, and with army support.[87]

Haitians in eastern Cuba were most affected by anti-immigrant policies. Thousands were forcibly deported, many of whom were, in fact, employed. They were not given the opportunity to collect belongings, settle affairs, or say good-bye to family, and repatriation conditions were brutal.[88] The communist newspaper *Bandera Roja* (Havana, Cuba) reported that the steamer *Julián Alonso*, where deportees awaited embarkation, had a maximum capacity of seventy but held five hundred individuals without adequate food.[89] Deportations continued after U.S.-supported military strongman Fulgencio Batista replaced Grau in January 1934. In all, 4,943 Haitians were deported between November 1933 and July 1934.[90]

Throughout this period of nationalist legislation and violent deportations, the Communist Party and its sister organizations, CNOC, SNOIA, and DOI, ardently defended immigrant workers in a manner consistent with Third Period calls for cross-national solidarity. Protesting deportations was a means to put internationalism into practice. The PCC labeled the new legislation maneuvers "intended to divide the working classes" and to "increase racial tensions."[91] The CNOC and the SNOIA argued that laborers should be careful not to listen to "words of 'Cuban chauvinism' and other hollow messages about 'our patria' because we are all workers, native and foreign. We do not see differences of race, nationality, or gender."[92] The party urged workers, "ABOVE ALL IN ORIENTE" to organize "meetings, demonstrations, strikes, [and] protest resolutions" against the new laws and emphasized organizing Black *compañeros* in opposition.[93]

Amid the sugar strikes, CNOC and SNOIA proclamations and manifestos called for working people to stand together regardless of race or nationality. Organizers exchanged letters with striking sugar workers, encouraging them to remain firm in their resistance and warning of the divisive threat represented by nativism. To workers at the Mabay mill, the CNOC wrote that the government was attempting "a campaign to place against each other whites and blacks, Cubans and foreigners (especially Jamaicans and Haitians)" and reminded strikers that they should remain clear on their positions: "against the 80% [movement], against the expulsions of Haitians and Jamaicans, and against all forms of nationalist propaganda-patriotism intended to divide the working class."[94] One of the SNOIA's key tasks for its January 1934 conference was "drawing up specific demands for Antillean workers (Jamaicans, Haitians, etc.)."[95] The SNOIA condemned the 50 percent law as a "criminal maneuver" attempting to "deceive the masses of workers and to break the unified front."[96]

In late 1933 the DOI launched an aggressive "campaign against anti-Black terror." According to *Defensa*, "Black masses are terrorized so that they may be better exploited," a practice that is particularly "savage" toward Antillanos. After condemning Grau for "throwing Haitian workers from the land in the east," the group called on members to "fight against every incidence of violence and against the deportations of Haitians and the stripping of their lands," referring to the practice of denying deportees a chance to tend to affairs and subsistence plots. DOI told *oriental* workers: "In the Oriente there should be a massive mobilization using all the troops to stop the dispossession and deportation of Haitians. We should have meetings, demonstrations, etc. in every place where they have taken a Haitian. . . . We should have protest resolutions sent to the consul of Haiti, the Secretary of State and the President of the Republic." *Defensa* added a suggestion: "also [send protests] to the yankee consuls and to President [Franklin D.] Roosevelt demanding the freedom of the Scottsboro *negros*," fusing the PCC's two great Black-defense campaigns of the early 1930s.[97]

In short, the PCC used solidarity with Antillanos to put Third Period ideals of international proletarian solidarity and Black liberation into practice. As praxis, however, the campaign was less than successful. Labor nationalization laws were popular across the Americas, as states erected border controls and often targeted Black immigrants working for foreign companies.[98] In Cuba, national-ist fervor around the Revolution of 1933 meant that communist opposition to labor nationalization pitted the PCC against its working-class base, especially Afro-Cubans, just as it was in the middle of a campaign of Black solidarity. In Cuban cities, the 50 percent law principally affected Spanish-owned commer-cial establishments, where Spaniards privileged their own countrymen, and was especially popular among unemployed Afro-Cubans.[99] Arredondo explained that Afro-Cubans, often the last to be hired and the first to be fired, were the principal beneficiaries of nationalization. He called the measure "an indisput-able step advancing towards the elimination of prejudice and discrimination and toward jobs for thousands of unemployed individuals."[100] Communist oppo-sition to the anti-immigrant legislation, then, put the party in the same camp as powerful employers who also opposed the laws.

In December 1933, the PCC attempted to organize a general strike against labor nationalization, but the strike failed as most rank-and-file members favored the laws. In fact, that same month, over twenty thousand people marched to the presidential palace in a show of support.[101] In Havana, crowds headed by Afro-Cubans confronted shopkeepers and business owners who had refused to comply. Supporters of the law clashed with communist protestors and threatened to seize businesses that did not nationalize. The party, which had expanded considerably from a few hundred people in 1929 to over three thousand in 1932, was again struggling to survive by mid-1934, burdened by severe repression from the Batista government and diminished popularity.[102] In the face of rising nativism, the PCC's support for foreign workers hindered its efforts to widen its rank-and-file appeal. Internationally, the heyday of pro-letarian internationalism was over, and communists were shifting gears. As it had with the Black belt, the PCC reversed its position on labor nationalization, this time as part of its turn to the Popular Front.

Dawn of the Popular Front

The mid-1930s marked a turning point for the PCC's approach to the Negro Question. While not abandoning Afro-Cubans, the party reframed its antiracism work in terms of Cuban nationalism, as not only the PCC but also the global communist movement emphasized cross-class alliances. In March 1935, the Communist Party organized a general strike, which Batista violently suppressed.[103] After the strike, which Stevens has called "the final hurrah of the working-class–oriented Third Period," the PCC found itself isolated and many of its unions illegal. That July and August, at the Seventh World Congress of the Communist International, Moscow launched the Popular Front. Jettisoning the Third Period emphasis on class struggle, the Comintern encouraged class-collaboration and coalition as a strategy to fight fascism. Local communist parties followed suit.

Roca's speech at the Seventh Congress emphasized the need for collaboration with "national reformist and national revolutionary parties" and criticized the PCC for having underestimated potential allies on the left. Thanking the Comintern for its "mighty assistance" and its "brother Party," the CPUSA, for assisting the Cuban struggle, Roca suggested a new "national stage" of his party's work, one of collaboration with opposition groups they had previously eschewed. These included the Auténticos, led by left-leaning Grau San Martín, whom the PCC had vehemently opposed during his brief presidency in 1933, and Joven Cuba, a militant anti-Batista and anti-imperialist group. (Roca bragged that the PCC had responded to a rebuff from the leader of the Auténticos "without calling him a fascist!") The PCC Cubanized the Comintern line. Whereas Moscow emphasized unity against fascism, the PCC agreed but also urged communist parties to remember the threat that imperialism posed, claiming the two were deeply linked; the united front had to be an "anti-imperialist front."[104]

This new national message meant jettisoning the Black belt. Roca explained, "Such slogans as the self determination of the Negro nation and the confiscating of the lands of the large estates have been withdrawn as conditions of the united front, bearing in mind that our most important task now is the organization of the *national front* for the unified struggle of the people of Cuba *against imperialism and the national traitors*." This did not mean, however, abandoning solidarity with Black workers and "the importance of the Negroes."[105] Roca highlighted the need to develop demands with the Black population in mind and advised against any policies that might alienate Black people.

As Roca's speech makes evident, the matters of labor nationalization and solidarity with foreign workers were still tricky ones for the PCC in 1935, and the

50 percent law was an issue "which must be solved in the next months." Roca acknowledged that the PCC's opposition to popular nationalization measures could be held against the party and break the potential for unity. He still hoped to "struggle against" labor nationalization but suggested "as a last resort" that the party could settle for the "maintenance of the Grau law 'status quo,'" which had "great popularity."[106] In other words, as late as mid-1935, the PCC wished to avoid supporting the 50 percent law but openly feared the political risks. The facts that anti-immigrant legislation had succeeded in pushing immigrants out of the country or to the margins or to integrate themselves into Cuban society likely helped the party allow solidarity with Antillanos to fade quietly from the platform.

By 1936 the party formally reversed course on labor nationalization and went from being the 50 percent law's most vigorous opponent to an ardent defender. The position change sheds light on how Negro Question policies fared the transition from the Third Period to the Popular Front. The PCC did not abandon its Black-solidarity work, but the struggle for Black rights was no longer a matter of proletarian internationalism. Rather, it was essential to national liberation, of ridding the country of the vestiges of colonialism and neo-imperialism. For Afro-Antillean immigrants, this meant the loss of an ally.

The CNOC announced its revision on labor nationalization in a May 1936 open letter, which acknowledged the "erroneous" nature of its previous position and that the party had not understood how popular the legislation was with its "deep national content." CNOC now demanded "comprehensive compliance" and called for an end to exemptions. The letter encouraged members to monitor compliance personally, suggesting that unions watch "constantly and daily in every industry, every workshop, in every department . . . so that we avoid transgressions of the law." It concluded with a moderate call for foreigners with Cuban wives or children and nationalized Cubans to be considered citizens but also, in a complete change of heart, demanded prohibition of all future immigration.[107] Whereas the party's previous opposition to labor nationalization had been expressed in terms of proletarian solidarity with exploited Antillano workers, the new position in favor of nationalization was articulated as a means of ridding the country of Spanish privilege. This rhetorical shift allowed the PCC to reverse position while never formally disavowing proletarian internationalism.

Two versions of this open letter are filed together at the Instituto de Historia de Cuba in Havana, a draft and the final pamphlet.[108] Comparing them sheds light on the CNOC's move out of the Third Period and into the Popular Front. Whereas the draft included several expressions of support for proletarian internationalism, the unemployed, and Black workers of all nationalities, the final document replaced each of these with emphases on alliances beyond the traditional proletariat and on Cuban patriotism. Several references to "proletarian emancipation" were replaced or dropped entirely. The draft advocated "Cuban preponderance [in workplaces] so that the proletariat, the class most interested in the struggle against national and racial oppression, achieves an international unified front of the oppressed and exploited." In contrast, the final document advocated "Cuban preponderance" for the sake of "our country's national liberation," and stressed the importance of placing Cubans in "professional and better paid technical positions," and dropped mention of the "international united front."[109] The draft ended with, "Long Live the Proletarian United Front of All Nations and Races!" but the printed version ended with a quotation from the independence leader and icon of Cuban patriotism José Martí: "¡¡UNITY—as Martí said—IS THE RALLYING CRY!" This was a significant shift for the party that had, not too long before, decried as "hollow" expressions of patriotism.

Both versions claimed that the CNOC had "not broken with proletarian internationalism," but caveats reaffirming the party's friendliness toward foreign labor were removed entirely from the final version. The earlier draft argued that Yankee and Spanish privilege had historically been maintained on the backs of exploited "Cuban and foreign" workers, while the final document omits "and foreign." Mentions of Antillanos as the "most exploited foreign workers" were removed from the final version, and the printed pamphlet added a description of Haitian and Jamaican immigrants as constituting "a cheap and poorly paid workforce."[110] This is a major concession to popular claims that immigrant labor undermined Cuban working conditions and indicates the party's move away from solidarity with Antillanos.

The comparison also highlights a move away from class-against-class struggle toward cross-class collaboration among workers, peasants, and professionals. Both versions of the letter end with strong calls for unity, but unity of whom varies. Whereas the preliminary draft calls for unity of the "exploited natives and foreigners," the published version called for unity of Cuban "workers, employees, and professionals . . . from one end of the island to the other." The draft called for continued "struggle against national and racial chauvinism," a message dropped completely from the final document's penultimate paragraphs, which addressed technical and professional trades. Finally, as printed the open letter minimized the draft's language about Afro-Cubans. Although both documents argue that Afro-Cubans suffered the greatest discrimination when *peninsular* privilege prevailed, the pamphlet shaved five of eight paragraphs from the section "Support for the Unemployed and Defense of the *Negro*."

Specific mentions of Black women domestic servants and unemployed Black workers were dropped entirely from the final version.

The multiple drafts of the open letter reveal that, as the party heeded Comintern calls for Popular Front nationalism, it no longer saw Antillanos, and sugar workers more generally, as essential to its struggle in Cuba. Instead, it refocused on the urban centers of Cuban political life and entering the political mainstream. The party did not abandon the Negro Question, however. Immediately after the Seventh Comintern Congress, the PCC launched a campaign denouncing the Italian invasion of Ethiopia. As historian Ariel Mae Lambe explains, the party framed this Hands-Off Ethiopia as part and parcel of its anti-imperialist work—Cuba and Ethiopia shared a struggle against imperialist aggressors—and sought to direct outrage over the invasion toward building a Cuban Popular Front.[111] Moreover, as Wood's forthcoming book details, the PCC remained an advocate for Afro-Cubans through the late 1930s.

Conclusion

During the Third Period, when the PCC was under pressure from the Comintern and the CPUSA to penetrate the working classes and to struggle against racism, the Negro Question was a matter of proletarian internationalism. From 1928 to 1934, the PCC moved from overlooking Black laborers to advocating forcefully for Black rights abroad and at home. Most dramatically, the party launched a campaign in defense of Afro-Antillanos, a position which, as Jacob A. Zumoff and Carr illustrate, was unique among Latin American communist parties.[112] That Cuban communists put the call for international proletarian solidarity into local practice makes sense in light of Cuba's particular circumstances. After all, the island's foremost industry was operated by a largely Black, multinational workforce, whose 1933 insurgency epitomized Third Period international proletarian solidarity against imperialism.

In transitioning from the Third Period to the Popular Front, however, the Negro Question underwent a significant reframing in Cuba. Like elsewhere, Cuban Communists contended with rising nationalism at home and a new set of transnational imperatives from Moscow, not the least of which was to pay greater attention to local realities. In 1935, as communists in Moscow, Cuba, and much of the globe shifted gears, internationalism in Cuba clashed with nativism, and Black liberation was nationalized. Cuban Communists never abandoned the antiracist cause, but their shift away from solidarity with foreign sugar workers reveals the inherent challenges and limitations of lasting internationalist struggle.

Notes

1. For CNOC's conference, see CNOC, "Resolución sobre el trabajo."

2. Serviat, *El problema negro*, 118; Fernández Robaina, *El negro en cuba*, 134–36.

3. Makalani, *In the Cause of Freedom*; Boyce Davies, *Left of Karl Marx*; Solomon, *Cry Was Unity*; McDuffie, *Sojourning for Freedom*.

4. Stevens, *Red International and Black Caribbean*, 2; Mahler, "Red and the Black."

5. Carr, "From Caribbean Backwater," 248.

6. McLeod, "Undesirable Aliens," 599.

7. Chomsky, "Barbados or Canada?"; de la Fuente, "Two Dangers, One Solution." Regarding Afro-Cuban responses to immigration from the British West Indies and Haiti, Chomsky explains that some Black Cuban intellectuals embraced the idea that *cubanidad*—not race—was central to their position in society. In this vein they recognized the racism implicit in hostility toward Antillano immigration yet still rejected immigration. Rather than identify Afro-Caribbean workers as the main threat to Cubans on the job market, these intellectuals rejected *all* forms of immigration, especially the much-larger influx of Spaniards.

8. Rojas Blaquier, *El primer*; Carr, "From Caribbean Backwater."

9. Caballero, *Latin America and the Comintern*, 65.

10. Caballero, *Latin America and the Comintern*, 65; Carr, "From Caribbean Backwater"; Pujals, "Soviet Caribbean."

11. Adi, *Pan-Africanism and Communism*; Kelley, *Freedom Dreams*, chap. 2; Stevens, *Red International and Black Caribbean*; Zumoff, *Communist International*, chaps. 14–17.

12. "Thesis on the National and Colonial Question Adopted by the Second Comintern Congress," July 28, 1920, reproduced in Degras, *Communist International*, 1:142.

13. Jacob A. Zumoff addresses the ABB in his contribution to the current volume.

14. "Thesis of the Fourth Comintern Congress on the Negro Question," November 30, 1922, reproduced in Degras, *Communist International*, 1:399–401.

15. Political Secretariat, Communist International, "Resolution on the Negro Question in the United States," October 26, 1928, reproduced in Degras, *Communist International*, 2:555.

16. "Extracts from the Theses on the Revolutionary Movement in Colonial and Semicolonial Countries Adopted by the Sixth Comintern Congress," reproduced in Degras, *Communist International*, 2:546.

17. Becker, "Mariátegui."

18. Adi, *Pan-Africanism and Communism*, 295.

19. Adi, *Pan-Africanism and Communism*, 296; Mahler, "Red and the Black," 3–4.

20. Junco, "El problema," 65.

21. Junco, "El problema," 64. Junco explicitly cited Marcus Garvey's Universal Negro Improvement Association as a reason local communist parties needed to be more aggressive in recruiting Black workers. Junco, "El problema," 172–73.

22. Melgar Bao, "Rearmando la memoria," 156–58.

23. Mahler, "Red and the Black," 13–14.

24. Stevens, *Red International and Black Caribbean*, 126, 122; Carr, "Identity, Class, and Nation," 98.

25. Carr, "From Caribbean Backwater"; Rojas Blaquier, *El primer*; Caballero, *Latin America and the Comintern*.

26. Pujals, "Soviet Caribbean," 260, 266.

27. Rodriguez, "Our Present Tasks in Cuba," *Communist* (Chicago), June 1931, 524.

28. "El Mundo Obrero," *Mundo Obrero* (New York), [July] 1931, 1. For example, see "Organicemos los obreros azucareros en Cuba," December 1, 1931, 16–17, 22, and "La dictadura de United Fruit Company," April 1, 1932, 5, 22, both in *Mundo Obrero*.

29. De la Fuente, "Race and Inequality in Cuba," 135.

30. "Letter of the Central Committee of the CPUSA to the Central Committee of the CP of Cuba," *Communist* (Chicago), October 1930, 66.

31. Alberto Sánchez, "El Congreso Mundial del S.R.I. y las Secciones de los Países del Caribe," *Mundo Obrero*, February 1, 1933, 7, 18.

32. For summaries, see Carter, *Scottsboro*; Kelley, *Hammer and Hoe*, chap. 4; Solomon, *Cry Was Unity*, part 2.

33. Solomon, *Cry Was Unity*; Adi, *Pan-Africanism and Communism*, 264–67; Stevens, *Red International and Black Caribbean*, 127.

34. Miller, Pennybacker, and Rosenhaft, "Mother Ada Wright."

35. Adi, *Pan-Africanism and Communism*, 127.

36. Miller, Pennybacker, and Rosenhaft, "Mother Ada Wright," 389.

37. I have written elsewhere about Cuba's Scottsboro campaign. See Sullivan, "For the Liberty of the Nine Boys."

38. "Protesta por la condena de 8 Negros," *Diario de la Marina* (Havana, Cuba), July 8, 1931.

39. "Entrevista efectuada a Compañeros que participaron en el Soviet del Central Nazabal: La compañera María Tomasa González," fondo 5, sig. 5/19:104/207/Lit, Instituto de Historia de Cuba (hereafter referred to as IHC), Havana.

40. "Luchemos por la libertad de los Negros de Scottsboro," *Mundo Obrero* (New York), June 1, 1932; Bertot, American consular agent at Manzanillo to Edwin Schoenrich, American Consul at Santiago de Cuba, May 23, 1932, telegram, vol. 23, no. 800, Record Group 84, National Archives and Records Administration, College Park, Maryland; Edwin Schoenrich to Edward L. Reed, American Chargé d'Affaires, Havana, April 11, 1933, vol. 377, no 600, Record Group 84, National Archives and Records Administration, College Park, Maryland; Grant Watson to John Simon, South and Central America, Confidential Report, December, 13, 1933, Record Number 371/16576, National Archives, London, England.

41. "Lo de Scottsboro," *Diario de la Marina* (Havana, Cuba), October 14, 1932, 3. See also "El caso sobre los 7 negros se falla hoy," *Diario de la Marina* (Havana, Cuba), November 7, 1932, 1.

42. Guridy, *Forging Diaspora*, 135.

43. Edwin Schoenrich to Harry F. Guggenheim, July 13, 1931, vol. 338, no. 800, Record Group 84, National Archives and Records Administration, College Park, Maryland.

44. Stevens, *Red International and Black Caribbean*, 119.

45. "Luchemos por la libertad."

46. "El Organizador: Boletín del Departamento de Organizacion del Comité Ejecutivo Nacional de DOI," November 1934, fondo 1, sig. 1/8:223/11.1/1-7, IHC.

47. "Circular sobre la reunión y preparación del Primer Congreso Nacional de 'Defensa Obrera Internacional,'" ca. late 1933/early 1934, fondo 1, sig. 1/8:223/2.1/1-42, IHC.

48. An informal survey of documents in IHC, fondo 1: Primer Partido, and fondo 8: Museo Obrero, reveals that a majority of PCC manifestos and circulars between 1931 and 1934 ended with some form of the slogan.

49. DOI, "Composición de DOI," 1933, fondo 1, sig. 1/8:223/5.1/1-109, IHC.

50. De la Fuente, *Nation for All*, 190–93; Pappademos, *Black Political Activism*, 217; Carr, "Identity, Class, and Nation."

51. De la Fuente, *Nation for All*; Ferrer, *Insurgent Cuba*.

52. The clearest example of this was the Partido Independiente de Color (PIC, Independent Party of Color), an organization of Black independence veterans who demanded pensions and in 1912 were violently suppressed. The ensuing massacre extended well beyond the PIC and remained a potent reminder of the risks associated with race-based organizing. See Castro Fernández, *La masacre*; Helg, *Our Rightful Share*.

53. Serviat, *El problema negro*, 116; Fernández Robaina, *El negro en Cuba*, 136; Arredondo, *El negro en Cuba*, 87–88. By far the most thorough analysis of the PCC's self-determination position is Wood, "Problem of the Nation." I'm grateful Tony Wood shared chapter 5 with me.

54. Serviat, *El problema negro*, 117–18.

55. Zumoff, *Communist International*, 355.

56. "Extracts from the ECCI Resolution on the Negro Question," October 26, 1928, repr. in Degras, *Communist International*, 2:554; Adi, *Pan-Africanism and Communism*, chap. 2.

57. Tomek, "Communist International"; Campbell, "Black Bolsheviks"; Zumoff, *Communist International*, chap. 16; Adi, *Pan-Africanism and Communism*; Solomon, *Cry Was Unity*.

58. "Las masas negras y el partido comunista," *El Trabajador* (Havana, Cuba), September 9, 1933, 3; Carr, "Identity, Class, and Nation," 98–99.

59. "Testimonio: preguntas y respuestas sobre los años 30: Fabio Grobart en la escuela de historia," *Revista de la Universidad de la Habana* 200 (1973): 135, repr. in Grobart, "Preguntas y respuestas"; Wood, "Problem of the Nation," chap. 5; Serviat, *El problema negro*, 117–18; "Las masas negras y el partido comunista," *El Trabajador*, September 9, 1933, 3; Instituto de Historia de Cuba, *Historia del movimiento obrero*, 1:560–61.

60. Fernández Robaina, *El negro en Cuba*, 136–37.

61. Arredondo, *El negro en Cuba*, 88.

62. Arredondo, "El negro y la nacionalidad," 6.

63. Alarcón "¿Nación Negra?" 12.

64. Wood, "Problem of the Nation," chap. 5. See also Carr, "Identity, Class, and Nation," 102.

65. For early Revolution-era criticism, see Grobart, "Preguntas y respuestas," 94–98. For later historiography, see Instituto de Historia de Cuba, *El movimiento obrero cubano*, 2:560–61; Fernández Robaina, *El negro en Cuba*, 135; Serviat, *El problema negro*, 118–19.

66. Serviat, *El problema negro*, 118.

67. Wood, "Problem of the Nation," 3.

68. Stevens, *Red International and Black Caribbean*, 109.

69. Wood, "Problem of the Nation," 11, 51.

70. "Circular sobre la reunion."

71. DOI, Sección Cubana del Socorro Rojo Internacional–Comité Ejecutivo Nacional, "Circular—Asunto: 3 de Enero, culminación de la campaña contra el terror a los negros y embarque de Haitianos," December 21, 1933, fondo 1, sig. 1/8:223/5.1/1-109, 41–42, IHC.

72. II Congreso Nacional del Partido Comunista de Cuba, "Resolución sobre la situación actual, perspectivas y tareas," April 1934, repr. in Instituto de Historia de Cuba, *El movimiento obrero cubano*, 2:718–53.

73. Wood, "Problem of the Nation," 55.

74. Casey, *Empire's Guestworkers*; Giovannetti, *Black British Migrants*.

75. For Carr's superb discussion of party attitudes toward azucareros antillanos, see Carr, "Identity, Class, and Nation," 100.

76. William Simons, "Organicemos los Obreros Azucareros en Cuba," *Mundo Obrero*, December 1, 1931, 16–17, 32.

77. Carr, "Mill Occupations and Soviets," 135–37.

78. CNOC, "Llamamiento de la comisión pro organización del sindicato de obreros de la industria azucarera," February 8, 1932, reproduced in Instituto de Historia de Cuba, *El movimiento obrero cubano*, 2:265–73.

79. The survey is discussed in SNOIA, "Adherido a CNOC y la Confederación Sindical Latino Americana—Comité Ejecutivo Nacional—Buró Nacional "Documento No. 2, Carta Circular," December 13, 1933, fondo 1, sig. 1/8:87/6.1/5-6, IHC.

80. "Manifestó de la Primera Confederación de Obreros de la Industria Azucarera, celebrado bajo de las auspicios de la CNOC y de la Confederación Sindical Latino-Americana," December 1932, fondo 1, sig. 1/8:87/2.1/1-8, IHC.

81. Soto, *La revolución del 33*; Whitney, *State and Revolution in Cuba*.

82. Carr, "Mill Occupations and Soviets"; García and Mironchuk, *Los soviets obreros*; García Domínguez and Rovira González, "Los 'Soviets'"; Portuondo Moret, *El "Soviet" de Tacajó*.

83. Carr, "Identity, Class, and Nation," 109–14; McLeod, "Undesirable Aliens," 604; Carr, "Mill Occupations and Soviets."

84. "Juan" to "estimados compañeros," December 2, 1933, Cuban Party, f. 495, op. 105, d. 68, Russian State Archive of Social and Political History (RGASPI), Moscow, cited in Carr, "Identity, Class, and Nation," 110.

85. De la Fuente, *Nation for All*, 195–96.

86. Pérez de la Riva, "Cuba y la migración antillana," 70–71; Commission on Cuban Affairs and Buell, *Problems of the New Cuba*, 211–17. For the sugar exemption, see Carr, "Identity, Class, and Nation," 108.

87. "Repatriación forzosa de extranjeros sin trabajo ni recursos; Decreto no. 2232 de 18 de octubre de 1933," in Pichardo Viñals, *Documentos*, 4:80–82.

88. Carr, "Identity, Class, and Nation," 106–7; McLeod, "Undesirable Aliens," 605; Casey, *Empire's Guestworkers*, 139–42.

89. "En Oriente cazan haitianos," *Bandera Roja (Havana, Cuba)*, January 5, 1934, 1–5, repr. in Instituto de Historia de Cuba, *El movimiento obrero cubano*, 2:653–54.

90. McLeod, "Undesirable Aliens," 604–5.

91. CNOC, César Vilar, Secretario General del Pleno del Comité Ejecutivo Confederal a Central Mabay, November 2, 1933, fondo 1, sig. 1/8:7/4.1/1-3, 1, IHC; DOI, Comité Ejecutivo Nacional, "Circular—Asunto: 3 de Enero, culminación de la campaña contra el terror a los negros y embarque de Haitianos," December 21, 1933, fondo 1, sig. 1/8:223:5.1/1-109, IHC.

92. CNOC, SNOIA, "A las masas," September 27, 1933, fondo 1, sig. 1/8:87/22.1/1, IHC.

93. "En Oriente cazan haitianos," *Bandera Roja* (Havana, Cuba), January 5, 1934, 1–5, repr. in Instituto de Historia de Cuba, *El movimiento obrero cubano*, 2:653–74, emphasis in original.

94. CNOC, César Vilar, Secretario General.

95. CNOC, SNOIA Adherido a la Confederación Sindical Latino Americana, "La zafra actual y las tareas de los obreros azucareros," January 1934, fondo 1, sign. 1/8:87/1.1/2-11, IHC.

96. CNOC, SNOIA Adherido a la Confederación Sindical Latino Americana, "La zafra actual."

97. DOI, Comité Ejecutivo Nacional, "Circular."

98. Putnam, *Radical Moves*, chap. 3.

99. De la Fuente, *Nation for All*, 195; Whitney, *State and Revolution in Cuba*, 116; Carr, "Identity, Class, and Nation," 109.

100. Arredondo, *El negro*, 146–47.

101. Whitney, *State and Revolution in Cuba*, 117.

102. De la Fuente, *Nation for All*, 195–98; Carr, "Identity, Class, and Nation," 103, 109.

103. Stevens, *Red International and Black Caribbean*, 220.

104. Blas Roca, "Forward to the Cuban Anti-Imperialist People's Front," *Communist*, October 1935, 955–67, emphases in original.

105. Blas Roca, "Forward."

106. Blas Roca, "Forward."

107. CNOC, Mesa Ejecutiva, "La Nacionalización del Trabajo: Una Reinvindicación Imperiosa del Pueblo Cubano—Carta Abierta, mayo 1936," May 1936, fondo 1, sig, 1/8:7/11.1/1–8, IHC.

108. The first draft is filed as given in CNOC, Mesa Ejecutiva, "La Nacionalización del Trabajo. The printed pamphlet is located in the same folder with "p. 50" added to the *signatura* (catalog number).

109. Paragraphs 13 and 14 in each version.

110. Paragraphs 8 and 9.

111. Lamb, *No Barrier Can Contain It*, 55–58.

112. Zumoff, current volume; Carr, "Identity, Class, and Nation," 114–16.

Semicolonials and Soviets

Latin American Communists in the USSR, 1927–1936

TONY WOOD

At the opening of the Comintern's Sixth Congress in Moscow on July 17, 1928, the organization's chairman, Nikolai Bukharin, observed that "South America is for the first time widely entering the orbit of influence of the Communist International."[1] More Latin American countries were represented at the gathering than ever before, and delegates from Mexico, Brazil, Argentina, Ecuador, Colombia, Uruguay, and Paraguay all played an active role in the deliberations. But a few days later, when a Brazilian delegate took to the podium, he politely objected to Bukharin's remark. "Comrades, this is not quite true," said Fernando Lacerda. It was "not [that] the Communist movement has manifested itself for the first time in Latin America" but, rather, that "the Communist International has for the first time taken an interest in the Communist Movement of Latin America."[2] Across the region, communist parties had begun to spring up in the wake of the 1917 Bolshevik Revolution, in many cases building on existing socialist, anarchist, and trade-union organizations, and they had expanded over the course of the 1920s. Yet it was only now, Lacerda noted with more than a hint of resentment, "that the Communist International is beginning to take up questions relating to Latin America."[3]

This exchange condenses many of the tensions between the Comintern and its Latin American affiliates toward the end of the 1920s. While Latin America was represented at Comintern congresses in the first half of the decade, the delegates themselves were often not from the region: those speaking on behalf of the Mexican Communist Party, for example, included Indian revolutionary M. N. Roy and U.S. communists Bertram Wolfe and Charles Phillips.[4] In the second half of the 1920s, however, the flow of Latin Americans to Moscow increased as the Soviets began to pay more sustained and systematic attention to the region—in large part because of their growing awareness of the geopolitical and economic weight of the United States, which the Comintern saw as the main rival to the British Empire.[5] This made Latin America a key front in the worldwide battle against capitalism and imperialism, and the Comintern established a new Latin American secretariat within its Moscow apparatus to reflect the region's rising importance.

Yet this increased attention was double-edged, since it coincided with the Comintern's adoption of a new strategy of "class against class" at its 1928 congress. Based on the premise that capitalism was about to enter its terminal crisis, it called for a sharp radicalization of communist parties and labor movements across the globe. Comintern officials weighed in energetically about the policies communists should adopt, in many cases seeking to override the views of the local parties and impose a more confrontational line. Latin American communists, then, found themselves welcoming their newfound prominence in the Comintern's thinking even as they fought to defend their view of their own region's specificities and their convictions about the best strategies to pursue.

This chapter looks at the experience of Latin American communists in the Soviet Union in the late 1920s and early 1930s as a prism for understanding the shifting relations between Latin American communist parties and the global movement to which they belonged. Many previous studies have explored this subject from the standpoint of individual national parties or with regard to the fate of the Comintern as a whole.[6] Yet while such works have contributed a great deal, they tend to overlook the influence of transnational dynamics.[7] Drawing on the Comintern archives in Moscow, sources from Mexico and Cuba, and the published testimonies of communists themselves, I argue that the experiences of Latin Americans in the Soviet Union in the 1920s and 1930s provide a privileged window onto a key phase in the development of the region's communist movement. Their encounters with Bolsheviks and revolutionaries from elsewhere not only took place at key moments in the elaboration of the Communist movement's global strategy; they also posed with unusual clarity many of the core dilemmas that beset the Latin American radical left.

How did Latin Americans in the Union of Soviet Socialist Republics (USSR) attempt to shape the Comintern's understanding of Latin America, and to what extent did they succeed? How did their Soviet sojourns shape their personal and political trajectories thereafter? This chapter explores these questions by focusing on two main areas: the role of Latin American delegates in Comintern debates, and the experiences of the more than one hundred Latin Americans who went to study in Comintern schools. Questions of translation—literally and figuratively—were central throughout. Especially prominent was the issue of whether concepts and strategies developed for other parts of the world were relevant to Latin America. As we will see, in some cases these discussions led to important misunderstandings or *desencuentros*. First, however, it may be helpful to get an overall picture of the different varieties of Latin American radicals who spent time in the USSR in the 1920s and 1930s.

Visitors to the Future

In the 1920s and 1930s, scores of Latin Americans went to Moscow to attend Comintern congresses, to work for longer spells in the Comintern's apparatus, or to study in its cadre schools.[8] They were part of a much larger flow of international travelers, which included members of communist parties from across the world as well as trade unionists, peasant delegates, students, writers, and artists. But while Latin American leftist publications frequently carried reports and testimony on the nascent workers' state, in the first half of the 1920s direct personal links between Latin America and the USSR remained relatively infrequent.[9] Manuel Díaz Ramírez, one of the founders of the Partido Comunista de México (PCM, Communist Party of Mexico), attended the 1921 Comintern congress and took part in the establishment of Comintern's trade union organization, the Profintern.[10] Representatives of Mexico's most radical peasant league, the Liga de Comunidades Agrarias del Estado de Veracruz (LCAEV, League of Agrarian Communities of the State of Veracruz), were among a handful of Latin Americans to travel to the USSR for gatherings of the Comintern and of its affiliated organization for rural workers and peasants, the Peasant International (Krestintern); in 1923, for instance, LCAEV leader Úrsulo Galván shared a stage with Ho Chi Minh.[11] The Peruvian student leader Víctor Raúl Haya de la Torre also spent four months in the Soviet Union in 1924, attempting to drum up support for a pan-Latin American anti-imperialist movement that eventually took shape in 1926 as the Alianza Popular Revolucionaria Americana (APRA, American Popular Revolutionary Alliance).[12] Such contacts laid important groundwork, creating channels of communication between Moscow and the various national Communist parties in Latin America. But they remained sparse until 1927, when a qualitative and quantitative leap occurred.

That year, the Bolshevik regime invited an extensive cast of visitors to the USSR to celebrate the tenth anniversary of the October 1917 Revolution. This included cultural luminaries, such as U.S. writers Theodore Dreiser and Scott Nearing, German artist Käthe Kollwitz, and Mexican muralist Diego Rivera.[13] Several other Latin Americans attended the festivities, including Ramón de Negri, the Mexican government's envoy to Berlin; Venezuelan communist Salvador de la Plaza; and four members of the Mexican Liga Nacional Campesina (National Peasant League). These peasant delegates were included in a forty-person group that met with Mikhail Kalinin, president of the Supreme Soviet.[14]

Late 1927 also brought the arrival of the first batch of Latin American students to attend the International Lenin School (ILS). Established in 1926, the ILS was one of a series of educational institutions attached to the Comintern, designed to provide political and theoretical education to the cadres of communist parties from around the world. The first Latin American ILS cohort consisted of eight militants from Argentina, Brazil, Chile, Colombia, Ecuador, Peru, Uruguay, and Venezuela.[15] This marked the start of an important stream of Latin American contacts with the USSR. According to calculations made by Víctor Jeifets and Lazar Jeifets, over the next decade a total of 120 Latin American students went to the ILS, most of them arriving after 1930.[16] Not only did they account for a substantial portion of the overall total of Latin American communists in the USSR, they were also an especially significant segment, since students were often chosen because they were being groomed for leadership roles. As we will see, many of these students also took part in Comintern and Profintern deliberations.

The largest category of Latin Americans communists to spend time in Moscow consisted of official party delegates. Again, their numbers notably increased after 1927. At the Profintern Congress the following April, the organization's head, Solomon Lozovsky, referred to having made a "second discovery" of the Americas—thanks in large part to the presence of more delegates from the region than ever before, which enabled much more substantive discussion of the region.[17] Dozens of Latin Americans attended the two Comintern congresses held in 1928 and 1935. They included prominent figures such as Blas Roca, longtime leader of the Partido Comunista de Cuba (PCC, Communist Party of Cuba), and Mexican Marxist writer José Revueltas. A number of Latin Americans also worked in the structures of the Comintern and Profintern in the early 1930s. For example, Cuban trade unionist Sandalio Junco was employed by the Profintern in 1930 to 1932, serving on the international committee of the International Trade Union Committee of Negro Workers (ITUCNW), while his fellow Cuban communist, poet Rubén Martínez Villena, spent several months attached to the Comintern's Latin American Secretariat in 1930 to 1932.[18] Brazilian revolutionary Luís Carlos Prestes was also in Moscow between 1931 and

1934, taking part in Comintern Executive Committee (ECCI) discussions; his sister Heloiza worked as a translator for the ECCI from 1932 to 1943, staying in Moscow until 1945.[19]

A final category of Latin Americans in Moscow worth mentioning comprised nonparty members and sympathizers, who in many cases wrote enthusiastically about their experiences. Peruvian poet César Vallejo, for example, visited the USSR three times between 1928 and 1931, producing a stream of positive portrayals of Soviet life, describing Moscow as "the city of the future."[20] Mexican labor leader Vicente Lombardo Toledano, who was in Moscow in 1935 for the Seventh Comintern Congress, gave a series of lectures on his return to Mexico in which, echoing Vallejo, he labeled the USSR "the world of the future."[21]

The idea that the Soviet system provided a glimpse of a better world to come was an important part of its appeal to radical visitors. Another recurrent trope was that of homecoming—that is, of arriving in the homeland of the international working class. On his first day in Leningrad in August 1930, Martínez Villena wrote to his wife in Havana describing the cityscape in stirring terms: "The red sun was rising, magnificent. On one side of the river, a string of factories, with their tall and uneven chimneys, all throwing their pavilions of black smoke into the air. . . . There, we thought, the proletariat is in power." According to Martínez Villena, an elderly American worker standing next to him pointed to the scene and said, "as if [giving] the title of a painting: 'Sunrise in the *patria*.'"[22]

This positive image did not always last. In Martínez Villena's case, his time in the USSR was marred by worsening physical health: afflicted by tuberculosis he had contracted in Cuba, he spent several months ailing in sanatoria by the Black Sea.[23] In other cases, prolonged contact with Soviet realities led to disillusion and even rupture with the communist movement. The Mexican radical feminist Concha Michel, for example, spent several months in the USSR in 1932 and 1933 and concluded that the Bolshevik Revolution had not liberated women at all and that the worldwide movement was not only failing to advance the struggle for women's rights but actively blocking it. She was expelled from the PCM for publicly expressing these views in 1934.[24]

The encounter with the Soviet Union generated disparate responses in individual communists, from deepening loyalty to stark estrangement. The variety and vehemence of these responses in themselves reflect the formidable tensions of the time: neutrality was not an option. The 1930s were, after all, marked by a global crisis of capitalism, with the Wall Street Crash of 1929 and other financial meltdowns leading to a prolonged depression. The rise of fascism, meanwhile, raised the political stakes worldwide: leftists felt they were engaged in a struggle over the fate of humanity itself. In this context, strategic differences took on an urgency that often had polarizing effects.

Moreover, in these same years the land of the Soviets was itself going through convulsive and often lethal changes—most notably the rapid industrialization program under the First Five-Year Plan and the forced collectivization of agriculture after 1929. The mass arrests of the Great Terror did not truly begin until 1937, but the shadow of Stalinist repression also began to loom as early as 1934. As noted at the beginning of the chapter, all of this coincided with the Comintern's Third Period and its adoption of a "class against class" line. Latin American delegates, students, and travelers all had to navigate these treacherous crosscurrents, seeking a balance between their adherence to the global communist movement and their need to carve out strategies adequate to their countries.

Classifying Latin America

The relative paucity of Latin American delegates at Comintern congresses prior to 1928 meant that the region was given little specific attention at these gatherings. In this respect, it shared the fate of much of the non-European world: at the Third Congress in 1921, for example, Roy upbraided the organization for only allocating him five minutes to speak on the situation in the entire Indian subcontinent, while at the Fourth Congress in 1924, Ho Chi Minh similarly criticized the lack of attention paid to the colonized world.[25] The Comintern's strategic perspective and analyses remained for the moment centered on workers' movements in Europe—and on the foreign policy needs of the USSR itself.[26] As far as Latin America was concerned, this meant that the entire region was subsumed into the larger category of "colonial and semicolonial" countries, which included both formal colonies and territories that were under the sway of foreign powers, such as China.

Yet Latin American communists themselves were divided as to the relevance of this category to their region. At the Sixth Comintern Congress in Moscow in 1928, Latin American delegates voiced objections to their region being classed as semicolonial. On August 9, during a discussion of the Comintern's overall program, Ecuadorian delegate Ricardo Paredes observed that "one cannot establish a strict classification between so-called semicolonial countries because there is a considerable number of intermediary forms."[27] He proposed the adoption of "a new category" that would "consist of the 'dependencies' which have been penetrated economically by imperialism but which retain a certain political independence."[28] Paredes was effectively proposing a finer-grained schema in which Latin America's specific features would emerge more clearly; the implication here was also that an appreciation of these specificities would then prompt the development of a differentiated strategy.

For the Comintern, however, these details made little difference to the overall strategy to be followed, which was the same for Latin America as for other semi-colonial regions: revolutionary movements should lead the masses to power and carry out an immediate leap to socialism, skipping the bourgeois revolutionary stage required in industrialized countries. On August 16, when Swiss communist and Comintern Executive Committee member Jules Humbert-Droz presented his report on Latin America, he laid out a broad strategy for the region as a whole, which he saw as falling increasingly under the sway of the United States.[29] Noting that some comrades from the region became "indignant" when their countries were described as semicolonial—implicitly chastising them for nationalist pride—Humbert-Droz argued that while they had indeed gained political independence from Spain and Portugal, they then "became gradually the prey of British and subsequently also of Yankee imperialism."[30] The growing penetration of U.S. power into the region took a variety of forms, ranging from Wall Street investments to direct military interventions and protectorates in Nicaragua, Haiti, and Panama. Humbert-Droz also cited the Platt Amendment in Cuba as an example of Washington's political reach and the economic missions to Colombia, Ecuador, and Chile led by U.S. "money doctor" Edwin Kemmerer in the 1920s as instances of indirect financial control.[31] On this reading, Latin America was well on the way to becoming an effective colony of the United States.

What were the strategic consequences of this? For Humbert-Droz, imperialism's growing penetration of Latin America meant that "there is no base for the development of an independent national capitalism" and that "the capitalist regime is only developing as a colonial regime."[32] Communists, therefore, needed to adopt a radical program: expropriation and nationalization of land, confiscation of foreign-owned enterprises, destruction of the power of the land-owning classes and the Church, and the organization of "workers,' peasants' and soldiers' soviets."[33]

While many Latin American communists concurred with Humbert-Droz about the absence of a national bourgeoisie, they disagreed with his strategic recommendations. In Moscow, however, the Latin American delegates were in no position to challenge the organization's overall strategic shift—and there is little sign they wanted to do so. Rather, their interventions took the form of attempts to complicate or nuance the picture. Thus, for example, Paredes's introduction of the category of "dependent" countries was designed to make clear the region's differences from colonial and semicolonial areas, while Lacerda's comments, with which this chapter began, highlighted the degree to which Latin America's communist movement had already been developing for some time independent of Comintern directives.

Such interventions did not lead to major shifts in the Comintern's line, but they added to the organization's knowledge about and awareness of Latin America's specificities. Reports and comments by Humbert-Droz and others clearly make use of information supplied by Latin American delegates. However, the latter's attempts to distinguish their region from other parts of the world were not always well motivated. For example, when the Comintern discussed the "Negro Question" in August 1928, the Colombian delegate's contribution was to deny that the problem of racial discrimination existed in Latin America. The debate centered primarily on the discrimination endured by people of African descent in the United States, a sign of the leading role played by the U.S. Communist Party—and in particular by African American members, such as Harry Haywood—in Comintern discussions of race.[34] The Colombian delegate sought to differentiate Latin America from the United States and categorically asserted, "There is no race hatred in Latin America towards the Negroes and the laws provide the same rights for blacks and whites."[35] These arguments were repeated at subsequent communist gatherings in Buenos Aires and Montevideo in 1929, and it was often Comintern representatives from outside the region who backed the few delegates of color present in condemning this blindness to the realities of racism.[36]

One area where the Comintern began to show an increased awareness thanks to Latin American delegates was the Indigenous question. In April 1928 Mexican muralist David Alfaro Siqueiros had raised the Indigenous question during a meeting of the Profintern Congress. (He had arrived in the city at the end of 1927, as part a delegation of Mexican workers and peasants.)[37] In the midst of a presentation on how the communist movement should organize the predominantly peasant populations of Latin America, Siqueiros called for "absolute recognition of the right of the Indians to be organized in [their] communities" and then added a series of concrete policy measures, including reduced taxes, water rights, and the right to bear arms for self-defense.[38] At the same April 10 meeting, Paredes twice signaled the need to give more attention to Indigenous peoples in Latin America and, in particular, to their revolutionary potential and to the specific racial oppressions they endured.[39] It was, in fact, thanks to Paredes that the gatherings in Buenos Aires and Montevideo the following year included "the problem of race" on their agendas at all.[40]

A few months later, during the Comintern Congress sessions devoted to the "colonial question," delegates from Latin America repeatedly returned to the Indigenous theme, in a bid to press the Comintern to address it more substantively. On August 14, 1928, Humbert-Droz had noted in passing the importance of "the Indian tribes" in the social structure of several countries and observed that they had "taken an active part" in revolutionary movements among the peasants in recent years.[41] Several delegates found this insufficient. On August 18, Vittorio Vidali, representing the PCM, observed, "The colonial and semicolonial thesis paid very little or hardly any attention to the native [Indigenous] problem."[42] Yet there were twenty-five million Indigenous people in Latin America, he said, "a mass of exploited and enslaved people who are not even entitled to a plot of land."[43] Vidali then went on to argue that the Comintern's program should specify that "under a regime of workers' and peasants' democratic dictatorship they will have the right of self-administration and of developing their own culture, etc." He added that this was not only a question for the future: "also under the present regime we must struggle for the recognition of these rights."[44] Wolfe, the U.S. communist who had represented the PCM at the 1924 Comintern Congress, echoed Vidali's recommendation, saying that Indigenous uprisings were "the greatest reserve of revolutionary energy that exists in Latin America" and that the region's communist parties "must work out a whole series of special measures" to address the problems of the Indigenous population, including self-determination.[45]

These interventions lent further impetus to the Comintern's idea that the right of self-determination should be extended to the Indigenous and peoples of African descent in the Americas. This Third Period initiative, best known in the form of the Black Belt Thesis adopted by the Communist Party of the United States for the U.S. South, was also taken up by communist parties in Cuba, Chile, and Mexico. Though it has largely been dismissed in the literature, the concept of self-determination had a significant impact on the Cuban Communist Party's stance on race and left its imprint on Mexican Marxist ideas about Indigenous autonomy.[46] In Chile, meanwhile, the Communist Party's endorsement of Mapuche sovereignty was central to an Indigenous uprising in Lonquimay in 1934.[47] Without the transnational encounters that took place in Moscow, it is doubtful whether this distinctive approach to race and indigeneity would have taken the form it did.

Dilemmas of the Third Period

The Comintern's 1928 adoption of a "class against class" strategy came in the wake of a steady centralization of policy making in Moscow. Strategy worldwide was increasingly subordinated to decisions made by the executive committee. This meant, in turn, that Latin American parties, even as they figured more prominently in the Comintern's thinking, found themselves more constrained by that thinking after 1928. Across the region, Communist parties took a more antagonistic attitude than before, not only toward their political opponents but also toward erstwhile allies, such as the APRA movement and other anti-imperialist forces. In many cases, Latin American parties began to advocate for the immediate establishment of Soviet power, while in Mexico, the sectarian turn led to a rupture in 1929 between the PCM and the peasant leagues that had been one of the PCM's most substantial bases of support, drastically weakening the party even as it was forced to operate clandestinely.[48] But the greatest disaster of Third Period adventurism in Latin America was the 1932 insurrection in El Salvador, in which the Communist Party played a leading role and which was crushed by the dictatorship of Maximiliano Hernández Martínez at the cost of tens of thousands of lives.[49]

At the same time, it would be a mistake to see the Third Period strategy as entirely an external imposition. Many Latin American communists eagerly endorsed the new turn, in part because their countries were already in the grip of deepening polarization and confrontation. In mid-1929, Siqueiros referred to the likelihood that the Mexican government, then in the midst of a battle with the Catholic Cristero rebels, would turn its guns on the communists and called for insurrection. "The party's hour has sounded, "he insisted. "Our task will be to create a Sandino in every state, to wage a guerrilla war."[50] More important, the radicalization of the Comintern's strategy posed more sharply than before the central question with which revolutionaries were concerned: When and how did communists envisage being able to seize power, and how would they wield it to bring about the promised transformation? In Latin America, a further question was what kind of revolution should be pursued: A broad struggle for liberation from U.S. and European imperialism, which would then develop in a socialist direction, or on the contrary a struggle in which anti-imperialist and socialist agendas were intertwined, heralding a direct leap into the socialist future?

At the turn of the 1930s, debate over the sequencing and character of the coming revolution was so intense that even the most minimal differences in phrasing could give rise to fundamental strategic disagreements. An exchange of letters between two Cuban communists in the USSR in 1930 and 1931 gives a sense of this heightened pressure, representing in linguistic microcosm the starkly divergent options then being weighed. Here, questions of translation became intertwined with arguments over strategic priorities, revealing the extent to which the adequacy of Comintern policies to Latin American realities was not simply an abstract conceptual issue but a matter of concrete political choices.

In the autumn of 1930, Martínez Villena was sent to Sukhumi on the Black Sea coast to receive treatment for his tuberculosis. That November, a conference of Latin American parties was to be held in Moscow, and Martínez Villena was anxious to convey his views of the Comintern's current program, dictating his remarks to Junco before departing.[51] But to Martínez Villena's consternation, he discovered that there were significant differences between his arguments and the text Junco presented, centering above all on whether the proletarian revolution was to occur *simultaneously and parallel with* the bourgeois-democratic one or whether it would take place *after* the latter.[52]

Martínez Villena was furious, expressing his anger in distinctly Cuban fashion. "In baseball terms," he wrote to Junco in January 1931, "I tell you that you have never messed it up [*pifiado*] in such a sustained and inexplicable way."[53] He especially upbraided Junco for a translation error that revolved around just two words. In presenting Martínez Villena's remarks, Junco had cited a Comintern document stating that the dictatorship of the proletariat "cannot be established all at once [no puede establecerse de golpe]." According to Martínez Villena, however, the correct translation should read, "does not have to be established all at once [puede no establecerse de golpe]."[54]

This apparently minor disparity could have major strategic consequences. Junco's phrasing implied a sequential view, ruling out an immediate seizure of power; this would then prompt a search for broader alliances, as well as suggesting an openness to taking part in elections. Martínez Villena, on the other hand, wanted to hold onto the possibility of a direct revolutionary leap into socialism, implying a confrontational position that was in line with the Comintern's Third Period strategy. The placement of two words thus opened up a massive strategic gulf, in which the communist movement's entire approach to the question of revolution was at issue.

This exchange between Martínez Villena and Junco was only one small example of the contention that would roil Latin American communist parties over these alternatives, both in the 1930s and in subsequent decades. But it captures very effectively the heightened stakes of the Third Period, as well as demonstrating that the Comintern's line was not simply imposed on the Latin American parties at a distance: there were supporters of the different positions within those parties themselves, and often close friends and comrades ended up on opposing sides. Latin Americans in the USSR, such as Martínez Villena and Junco, found themselves at the sharp end of these debates, representing their own parties' views to the Comintern even as they mediated between the two forces and at the same time grappled with their own convictions. These tensions are also very visible in the experiences of

Latin American students at the International Lenin School, to which I now turn.

A "Forge for Cadres"?

The International Lenin School (ILS) was only one of several Comintern cadre schools: there were also the Sun Yat-sen University, the Communist University for National Minorities in the West (KUNMZ in the Russian acronym), and the Communist University for Toilers of the East (KUTV). Alumni of the latter include key figures in twentieth-century communism and anticolonialism, such as Deng Xiaoping, Ho Chi Minh, Jomo Kenyatta, Nazim Hikmet, Josip Broz Tito, and many more besides. But while a handful of Latin Americans did study at KUTV in the late 1920s—a reflection of the region's inclusion at the time within a global, colonized "East"—the majority of Latin American students in Moscow attended the more globally oriented ILS.[55]

Between its founding in 1926 and its closure in 1938, as many as thirty-five hundred students passed through the doors of the ILS.[56] The overwhelming majority of them came from European countries and the United States, with a much smaller representation from the colonized world. Latin American countries accounted for another relatively minor portion of the overall total, sending over a hundred students. The numbers drawn from each country reflected the size and relative strength of each national party. The Cuban party grew rapidly in the 1930s, going from only a few thousand members to become one of Latin America's largest, with twenty-three thousand members by 1939; among Latin American parties, it contributed the most ILS students, with twenty-four.[57] The Mexican Party shrank drastically in the early 1930s due to government repression, but it recovered after 1935 to reach a similar size to the Cuban CP by the end of the decade; it sent twenty-one students.[58] Argentina sent eighteen students, Colombia thirteen; most Latin American countries sent a handful of students, and only two countries—Nicaragua and Bolivia—didn't send any.[59] Although they made up only a small proportion of the ILS student body, up until the mid-1930s Latin Americans accounted for the majority of the school's Spanish-language sector students.[60] (It was only with the arrival of Spanish communists in the run-up to the Civil War that Latin Americans began to be outnumbered.)

The purpose of the ILS was to improve the quality of party cadres, and in several cases, its Latin American alumni went on to become (or already were) leaders of their respective parties: Eudocio Ravines in Peru (secretary general, 1930–42), Héitor Ferreira Lima in Brazil (1931), Ignacio Torres Giraldo in Colombia (1934–38), Ricardo Paredes in Ecuador (1933–52), and Hernán Laborde in Mexico (1929–39). But often, Latin American parties—generally small and embattled—did not feel they could afford to lose key people for one or two years at a stretch. As a result, it was for the most part younger, up-and-coming members who were sent, with uneven results, as we will see.

There were other problems with recruitment that pointed to conflicting priorities between Moscow and the Latin American parties. The Comintern repeatedly criticized those parties for failing to send enough industrial workers and for sending artisans or intellectuals instead. But one major reason for this was that initially instruction was not available in Spanish; students had to be literate in English, French, German, or Russian. This in itself skewed the selection of students away from the working class. However, recruitment patterns also reflected these parties' social bases and the economic structure of the countries in question. Industrial proletariats across the region were generally small, and few Latin American communist parties at this time could boast of a strong peasant base; their members tended, rather, to be drawn precisely from among artisans and intellectuals. Other discrepancies, meanwhile, shed an unflattering light on Latin American parties' composition and internal cultures: they also failed to meet the Comintern's quota of 25 percent female students or to send enough Black or Indigenous students for the Comintern's liking.[61]

In 1930 the Comintern finally formed a Spanish-language section within the school (sector "L"). Soviet functionaries who either had some experience of Latin America or who had acquired surprisingly in-depth knowledge of the region at a distance provided the teaching. To give only a few examples, Stanislav Pestkovsky, who had served as the first Soviet ambassador to Mexico from 1924 to 1926, taught at the ILS in the 1930s.[62] Olga Meshkovskaia, who had served in the Red Army cavalry in the Russian Civil War, lived in Argentina for two years before working for the ILS and for the Comintern's Latin American secretariat from 1931 to 1935.[63] By contrast Genrikh Yakobson seems never to have been to Latin America. Another Red Army veteran, he taught at KUTV as a specialist on "the Orient" before working on Latin American issues at the Profintern and the ILS. Yakobson also intervened numerous times in Comintern meetings on Latin America—in fluent Spanish, which he somehow acquired in the space of a few years in Moscow.[64] Georgi Skalov, a.k.a. "Sinani," was a member of the Petrograd Soviet in 1917 and was centrally involved in the establishment of Bolshevik power in Central Asia, before being attached to the Comintern's Latin American Secretariat at the end of the 1920s and teaching at the ILS.[65]

On arrival, students were required to assume a revolutionary pseudonym and to sign an oath of secrecy as part of their training for clandestine work.

Their personal files in the Comintern archive contain ILS questionnaires in which they briefly lay out their social background and political formation. In many cases, they also produced lengthy, handwritten autobiographical statements. The course of study at the ILS included heavy doses of political economy and dialectical materialism, as well as immersion in the history of the Russian Communist Party—at that point the foremost example of a successful revolutionary organization. Some students, in fact, joined the Bolshevik Party while in the Soviet Union: Torres Giraldo and the Mexican muralist painter Xavier Guerrero both did so in 1929.[66] But for the most part they remained members of their national parties. Many also worked within the structures of the Comintern or one of its affiliated bodies, such as the Profintern.[67] During the summers, students were able to travel to other parts of the USSR or in many cases were assigned to temporary positions in Soviet industry.

Judging by the archival evidence and by the testimonies left by students, life at the ILS was intense and austere to the point of being monastic.[68] Ferreira Lima, a former tailor originally from Matto Grosso, spent three years at the school from 1927 to 1930 and was there at the same time as Guerrero and Venezuelan Carmen Fortoul, among other Latin American students.[69] He recalled long days of study, from 9 a.m. to 8 p.m., with political discussions continuing into the night in students' rooms. They lived together in close quarters in the ILS building at 25 Vorovsky Street, an elegant nineteenth-century manor house in central Moscow. Food was a recurrent problem for the many nationalities gathered there (though some of the hardships were relative: in 1930 a group of French students complained about not having enough wine).[70] Ferreira Lima also recalls trips to the cinema and theater, but aside from this there was seemingly little contact with the world outside the school or the corridors of the Comintern.

ILS students underwent a strange combination of isolation and tremendous pressure, in an atmosphere of dramatically raised ideological stakes. During his time as an ILS student in Moscow, for example, Junco clearly experienced a great deal of strain: his personal file records several absences due to ill health and a spell in a sanatorium in 1931 for what a doctor described as "psycho-neurosis with epileptoid features."[71] By contrast, Ferreira Lima's experience seems to have been positive: in his memoirs he describes his time in the USSR as "extremely valuable," enabling him "to considerably improve my general culture" and giving him "a global overview, economic, political, and social, of all countries," thanks to daily contact with comrades from across the world.[72] But he also noted that even then, it was clear that the Comintern was falling prey to the sectarianism and bureaucratism that had begun to overtake the Bolshevik Party under Stalin.[73] He referred in particular to the intraparty struggles that unfolded in the second half of the 1920s, through which Stalin exerted an increasingly tight grip on the Bolshevik apparatus and neutralized his opponents, expelling them from the party and, in the case of Trotsky, from the country. ILS students could not help but be affected by the precedents this set. While some came out of the school steeled for the battles ahead, many others would emerge from it deeply disillusioned. This is why, as Jeifets and Jeifets put it, the ILS turned out to be "not only a forge for cadres but also a factory for dissidents."[74]

The Hair's-Breadth Universe

As noted above, a number of Latin American ILS students went on to play prominent roles in their national parties, fulfilling the school's purpose in doing so. But in many other cases, they parted ways with the movement after their return. Thanks to his training at the ILS, Ferreira Lima briefly served as secretary general of the Brazilian Communist Party in 1931 and was put in charge of its cadre training school in 1935. But he was accused of Trotskyist leanings and expelled from the party in 1937.[75] Junco, meanwhile, returned to Cuba in 1932 seemingly a changed man: he became one of the leaders of an internal opposition current within the Communist Party. For this he was ultimately expelled from the PCC in September 1932, after two fractious meetings full of angry exchanges and sectarian sniping.[76] Here, his having spent time in Moscow proved double-edged: originally a sign of trust, it was now turned against him, as his detractors accused him of trying to hoodwink them with his greater knowledge after living at the expense of the Russian proletariat for two years.[77] Within a year of his expulsion, Junco had cofounded the Trotskyist Partido Bolchevique Leninista (Bolshevik Leninist Party).[78] For the rest of the 1930s, he would be vilified by the PCC as a traitor. In May 1942—two years after Trotsky was assassinated in Mexico—Junco was gunned down in Sancti Spíritus in central Cuba, with the PCC widely suspected to have ordered the killing.[79]

The early 1930s were, as noted, a period of heightened ideological tension within the communist movement. Later that decade this would reach murderous extremes in the USSR with the unleashing of the Great Terror, many of whose victims were from the Communist Party's own ranks. Tens of thousands of dedicated militants were accused of treason, imprisoned, and summarily executed. As historian William Chase and others have shown, dozens of foreign Comintern personnel were also imprisoned and executed.[80] This included several of the ILS's teachers and staff. Skalov, Meshkovskaia, and Pestkovsky were arrested between 1935 and 1937; accused of Trotskyism, Meshkovskaia was executed in 1938, while Skalov and Pestkovsky died in prison, apparently in 1936 and 1943, respectively.[81]

The wave of repression also swept up students at the ILS—including one Latin American, Mexican lawyer Evelio Vadillo. Originally from Campeche, Vadillo was born in 1903 and spent time in Cuba in the mid-1920s, becoming active in radical politics there.[82] After returning to Mexico in 1927, he joined the PCM and often spoke at student events and party rallies. In the first half of the 1930s he was repeatedly imprisoned, enduring two spells in the Mexican penal colony in the Islas Marías. It was after his release in 1935 that the PCM sent him to Moscow to study at the ILS, where he enrolled under the pseudonym "Pedro Arapos." That August he attended the Seventh Comintern Congress as a PCM delegate. Revueltas, who was also in Moscow for the Congress, later recalled spending time with Vadillo that summer, drinking beer on Pushkinskii Boulevard and dining together with Pestkovsky.[83]

But Vadillo was soon to fall foul of the climate of increasing suspicion that had settled over the USSR, especially since the assassination of the Leningrad Bolshevik Party chief Sergei Kirov in December 1934, which sent the Soviet state's repressive apparatus into overdrive. In early 1936 the People's Commissariat of Internal Affairs (NKVD) arrested Vadillo. The apparent trigger was trivial: in January 1936 some graffiti reading "Viva Trotsky" was discovered in the toilets at the ILS. Suspicion initially fell on students from Spain, but the finger of blame quickly moved to Vadillo.[84] Very likely under torture, he admitted to being part of a "terrorist group" along with Meshkovskaia. Perhaps because he was a foreigner, Vadillo was imprisoned but not executed. The reprieve was a bitter one: he spent the next two decades in prison or in distant internal exile in the USSR, shuffled back and forth from Moscow to the Kazakh steppe to Siberia. Despite efforts by the Mexican authorities to secure his release during World War II, it was not until after Stalin's death that Vadillo was finally able to return home, arriving in Mexico in November 1955.[85] Not surprisingly, his experience turned him against the ideals that had taken him to the USSR in the first place: at a press conference held on his return, he stated, "I placed the most precious years of my youth at the service of sterile activities that earned me persecution, imprisonment, deportation, etc., for ideals that it is impossible to square with or adapt to our specific realities."[86] His health broken, he lived for only another three years, dying in 1958.[87]

Vadillo's case is a particularly tragic illustration of the dilemmas and dangers facing Latin American communists in the interwar period—an exception, perhaps, but also a fearsome limit case for what could befall them in these years. It prompted anguished reflection in some of his comrades. In 1964, in the wake of his own break from the PCM, Revueltas dramatized these concerns in his novel *Los errores*. Set in the 1940s, the novel's characters include Jacobo, a communist intellectual who repeatedly wonders about the fate of "Ezequiel Padilla," a comrade who had disappeared in the USSR. Jacobo asks himself what it means to be a communist if it entails a willingness to stay silent about the disappearance of a comrade. Didn't this self-silencing imperil or even invalidate the movement's larger goals and principles? Jacobo doesn't arrive at any real answer—except to say that since errors are intrinsic to the human condition, "reducing the error to the width of a hair is the highest victory that can be obtained."[88] And yet, he observes, in reality that hair's breadth itself contains "a measureless abyss, deeper and wider . . . than the galaxy" we inhabit; in effect, it could constitute a whole other universe. Vadillo suffered the most drastic consequences, but Latin American communists in the USSR in the 1920s and 1930s were all trying to edge their way along that razor-thin, and razor-sharp, boundary.

Conclusion

For many years, the conventional picture of relations between the Comintern and its Latin American affiliates involved a Stalinized, top-down dynamic in which Moscow imposed its will regardless of local realities. With the opening of the Comintern archives in the 1990s, this Cold War–era picture was substantially modified by scholarship that captured a more complicated reality, in which national parties sought to forge their own paths within, and often in spite of, the broad strategic guidelines laid down by the Comintern. Yet such studies often remain beholden to a dual framework that treats Moscow and the national parties as separate, distant components.

Through the experiences of Latin American communists in the USSR, this chapter has sought to capture the distinctive transnational dynamics that marked the evolution of the Latin American radical left in the 1920s and 1930s. Many of the key ideological struggles and strategic rifts that would strongly affect the region's communist parties were initially played out in Moscow. These debates did not affect Latin America at one remove after taking place within the Comintern; rather, Latin Americans were directly involved in them as observers and participants. While their attempts to alter Comintern strategy during its Third Period (1928–35) fell short, they were able to use their knowledge to expand the Comintern's understanding of the region's political, socioeconomic, and ethnic realities. The experiences of Latin Americans who studied in the Comintern's schools, meanwhile, shed light on how the foot soldiers of communism's world revolution saw life under Bolshevik rule. For many, their sojourn in the USSR strengthened and validated their commitment to the cause, while for others it brought disillusionment and rupture. Either way, the time they spent in the Soviet Union was politically formative. In journeying from their homelands to the USSR and back, Latin American communists embodied the border-spanning radical collectivity their movement aspired to create; their experiences, in all their transnational splendor and misery, are as integral a part of Latin American communism's history as the varying fortunes of individual national parties.

Notes

1. "Comrade Bukharin's Opening Speech" [July 17, 1928], 706.
2. "Discussion on the Report of Comrade Bukharin" [July 25, 1928], 819.
3. "Discussion on the Report of Comrade Bukharin" [July 25, 1928], 819.
4. On the roles played by Roy, Wolfe, and Phillips in the early history of the Mexican Communist Party, see Carr, *Marxism and Communism*, 18–27.
5. See, for example, "Comrade Bukharin's Speech in Reply" [July 30, 1928], 871.
6. Among many others, see Broué, *Histoire de l'Internationale communiste*; Claudín, *Communist Movement*; Rees and Thorpe, *International Communism*; and Cerdas Cruz, *La hoz y el machete*.
7. A number of recent studies have begun to address this imbalance, however; see Drachewych, "Communist Transnational."
8. On Latin American students, see Jeifets and Jeifets, "La Comintern y la formación." See also Jeifets and Jeifets, *América Latina*, 28–30. This is an indispensable resource for anyone studying communism in Latin America, and I join many others in being greatly indebted to it.
9. For the case of Chile, see Aránguiz Pinto, "El 'viaje revolucionario.'"
10. Jeifets and Jeifets, *América Latina*, 179–80.
11. For a list of delegates, see Protocols of the First Krestintern Congress, October 10, 1923, f. 535, op. 1, d. 1:4–6, Russian State Archive of Social and Political History (hereafter referred to as RGASPI), Moscow.
12. See, for example, Haya to Stirner (the Swiss Comintern functionary and former PCM member Edgar Woog), January 1, 1925, f. 495, op. 118, d. 2:26–32, RGASPI. On Haya's relations with the Comintern and his time in Moscow, see Jeifets and Jeifets, "Haya de la Torre."
13. "Statisticheskaia svodka o poseshchaemosti VOKS inostrantsami za 1925–1929 gg," f. R5283, op. 8, d. 60, 67, State Archive of the Russian Federation, Moscow. On

foreign visitors to the USSR during this period more generally, see David-Fox, *Showcasing the Great Experiment*.

14. Record of delegates' conversations with Kalinin, November 10, 1927, f. 535, op. 1, d. 142:90–123, RGASPI.

15. Respectively, Solomón Elguer, Héitor Ferreira Lima, Rufino Rosas Sánchez, Guillermo Hernández Rodríguez, Ricardo Paredes, Eudocio Ravines, Carlos Imaz, and Carmen Fortoul. Jeifets and Jeifets, *América Latina*, 28–29.

16. Calculations by Jeifets and Jeifets, "La Comintern y la formación," 151.

17. "Conférence Latino-Américaine, 3ème séance (matin)," April 8, 1928, f. 495, op. 79, d. 45:62, RGASPI.

18. Jeifets and Jeifets, *América Latina*, 317–18, 398–99.

19. Jeifets and Jeifets, *América Latina*, 503–5. On Prestes's trajectory, see Jacob Blanc's essay in the current volume.

20. Vallejo, *Camino hacia*, 113–28.

21. Lombardo Toledano and Villaseñor, *Un viaje al mundo*.

22. Martínez Villena to Asela Jiménez, August 30, 1930, Moscow, in Martínez Villena, *El útil anhelo*, 2:55.

23. See Núñez Machín, *Rubén Martínez Villena*, 221–45.

24. See Michel's personal file, f. 495, op. 241, d. 28, RGASPI, and the pamphlet she wrote after returning, *Marxistas y "marxistas,"* fondo PCM Folletos, serie 2, 59, Centro de Estudios del Movimiento Obrero y Socialista, Mexico City. See also Olcott, "Plague of Salaried Marxists."

25. M. N. Roy, "Speech in Discussion of Eastern Question," July 12, 1921, in Riddell, *To the Masses*, 855–56; Ho Chi Minh, "Report on the National and Colonial Questions at the Fifth Congress of the Communist International" [July 8, 1924], in Ho Chi Minh, *Selected Works*, vol. 1.

26. Claudín, *Communist Movement*, 86–88.

27. "Discussion on the Report of Comrade Bukharin on the Draft Programme of the Comintern" [August 9, 1928], 1177.

28. "Discussion on the Report of Comrade Bukharin on the Draft Programme of the Comintern" [August 9, 1928], 1177.

29. "Questions of the Latin-American Countries: Co-Report of Comrade Humbert-Droz" [August 16, 1928].

30. "Questions of the Latin-American Countries: Co-Report of Comrade Humbert-Droz" [August 16, 1928], 1300.

31. "Questions of the Latin-American Countries: Co-Report of Comrade Humbert-Droz" [August 16, 1928], 1301. On the Kemmerer missions, see Drake, *Money Doctor in the Andes*.

32. "Questions of the Latin-American Countries: Co-Report of Comrade Humbert-Droz" [August 16, 1928], 1304.

33. "Questions of the Latin-American Countries: Co-Report of Comrade Humbert-Droz" [August 16, 1928], 1304–5.

34. On these discussions, see, among many others, Adi, *Pan-Africanism and Communism*, chaps. 1 and 2; Haywood, *Black Bolshevik*, chap. 8.

35. "To the Commission on Work among Negroes" [August 9, 1928]," f. 495, op. 155, d. 56:108–9, RGASPI. The Colombian delegate was Jorge Cárdenas of the Partido Socialista Revolucionario (PSR, Revolutionary Socialist Party). See Jeifets and Jeifets, *América Latina*, 130.

36. As the Black Cuban trade unionist Sandalio Junco put it in Buenos Aires in 1929, "on many occasions when we have discussed this question, some comrades representing parties have denied the existence of this problem in many Latin American countries. However, the problem exists and compels us ever more urgently to address it." Secretariado Sudamericano de la Internacional Comunista, *El movimiento*, 291. On the Buenos Aires debates, see Becker, "Mariátegui," and Mahler, "Red and the Black in Latin America."

37. For Siqueiros's own account of his time in Moscow, which centers largely on his ideological disputes with Diego Rivera, see Siqueiros, *Me llamaban el Coronelazo*, 229–38.

38. "6ème séance de la Conf. Latin. Américaine, 10 avril 1928 (soir)," f. 495, op. 79, d. 46:10, RGASPI.

39. "6ème séance de la Conf. Latin. Américaine, 10 avril 1928 (soir)," f. 495, op. 79, d. 46:10, RGASPI, 17–20, 73.

40. "6ème séance de la Conf. Latin. Américaine, 10 avril 1928 (soir)," f. 495, op. 79, d. 46:10, RGASPI, 73. Calling for a "point on the Indigenous," Paredes also noted the absence of any discussion of women. This was not taken up, however.

41. "Questions of the Latin-American Countries," 1302–3.

42. "Continuation of the Discussion on the Questions of the Revolutionary Movement in the Colonies" [August 17 and 18, 1928], 1394. The term "native" is what appears in the English translation published in *International Press Correspondence*. I was unable to consult the original record of Vidali's remarks; however, given that the French translation of the proceedings has Vidali referring here to "*le problème indigene*," it seems plausible that he used the Spanish phrase "*el problema indígena*." See "VIe Congrès Mondial de l'International communiste," 1419.

43. "Continuation of the Discussion," [August 18, 1928], 1394.

44. "Continuation of the Discussion," [August 18, 1928], 1394.

45. "Continuation of the Discussion," [August 18, 1928], 1407.

46. I develop these arguments at greater length in my dissertation, "Problem of the Nation."

47. Ulianova, "Levantamiento campesino."

48. Carr, Marxism and Communism, 44–45.

49. Gould and Lauria-Santiago, *To Rise in Darkness*.

50. "Acta de plática con los delegados mexicanos durante la primera conferencia comunista latinoamericana," Buenos Aires, May 28, 1929, f. 495, op. 108, d. 99:15, RGASPI.

51. Martínez Villena to Asela Jiménez, October 4, 1930, in Martínez Villena, *El útil anhelo*, 2:93.

52. Martínez Villena to Sandalio Junco, November 11–12, 1930, in Martínez Villena, *El útil anhelo*, 2:141–53.

53. Martínez Villena to Sandalio Junco, January 27, 1931, in Martínez Villena, *El útil anhelo*, 2:216.

54. Martínez Villena to Sandalio Junco, January 27, 1931, in Martínez Villena, *El útil anhelo*, 2:230.

55. On the KUTV and the significance and scope of the concept of "the East," see Kirasirova, "'East' as a Category."

56. On the International Lenin School, see Kirschenbaum, *International Communism*, chap. 1; on the schools overall, see Studer, *Transnational World*, 90–107.

57. Rojas Blaquier, *El primer*, 2:43–44; Jeifets and Jeifets, "La Comintern y la formación," 151.

58. Carr, *Marxism and Communism*, 10; Jeifets and Jeifets, "La Comintern y la formación," 151.

59. Jeifets and Jeifets, "La Comintern y la formación," 151.

60. Calculations based on "Svedeniia ob ispol'zovanii studentov 1931–32 uch. g.," f. 531, op. 1, d 39:10, and "Svedeniia o nalichnom sostave studentov MLSh po sostoianiiu na 10/XI-35-g. vkliuchit.," f. 531, op. 1, d. 84:12–13, RGASPI.

61. Latin American Ländersekretariat to South American Bureau, June 1931, f. 495, op. 79, d. 153:54, RGASPI; Latin American Ländersekretariat to South American and Caribbean Bureau, April 28, 1933, f. 495, op. 79, d. 188:51–53, RGASPI.

62. Jeifets and Jeifets, "La Comintern y la formación," 143–44. On Pestkovsky's time in Mexico, see Spenser, *Impossible Triangle*, 98–110.

63. Jeifets and Jeifets, *América Latina*, 417–18.

64. Yakobson personal file, f. 495, op. 65a, d. 8811:1–2, 6, 28, 32–33, RGASPI. For examples of Yakobson's contributions to Comintern and Profintern discussions, see "Stenogramma Latinoamerikanskogo LS IKKI: meksikanskii vopros," April–May 1930, f. 495, op. 79, d. 105, RGASPI; "Materialy latinoamerikanskoi sektsii Ispolbiuro Profinterna," January 1, 1929, f. 534, op. 3, d. 463:4, 5–7, RGASPI.

65. Jeifets and Jeifets, *América Latina*, 582–84.

66. Jeifets and Jeifets, *América Latina*, 285; Torres Giraldo, *Cincuenta meses en Moscú*, 42.

67. See, for example, Torres Giraldo, *Cincuenta meses en Moscú*, 30–35, 53–58.

68. See, for example, the account by Ferreira Lima, *Caminhos percorridos*, 80–88.

69. Ferreira Lima, *Caminhos percorridos*, 81.

70. "Protokol utrennego zasedaniia po chistke kollektiva VKPb pri MLSh ot 6.1.1930," f. 495, op. 137, d. 91:4–5, RGASPI.

71. Sandalio Junco's personal file, f. 495, op. 241, d. 27:18–19, RGASPI.

72. Ferreira Lima, *Caminhos percorridos*, 130–31.

73. Ferreira Lima, *Caminhos percorridos*, 134–35.

74. Jeifets and Jeifets, "La Comintern y la formación," 154.

75. Heitor Ferreira Lima's personal file, f. 495, op. 197, d. 91:13–19, RGASPI.

76. "Reunión del Comité Central, Septiembre 20 and "Sesión ampliada del Comité Central del Partido Comunista de Cuba (S. de la I.C.) celebrada el 24 de septiembre de 1932," f. 495, op. 105, d. 50:1–9, 10–21, RGASPI.

77. "Sesión ampliada," 10–11, 20.

78. For the PBL's founding manifesto, dated September 25, 1933, see "A todos los Obreros y Campesinos. Al Pueblo de Cuba," fondo especial leg 1, exp 136, Archivo Nacional de Cuba, Havana.

79. "Tres muertos y varios heridos en un acto que tenía lugar en memoria de Antonio Guiteras, en Sancti Spíritus," *Diario de la Marina* (Havana, Cuba), May 9, 1942.

80. Chase, *Enemies within the Gates*.

81. On Meshkovskaia, see her entry in Memorial's database "Zhertvy politicheskogo terrora v SSSR," http://lists.memo.ru/index13.htm; on Pestkovsky and Skalov, see Jeifets and Jeifets, *América Latina*, 485–87, 582–84.

82. Biographical details are taken from the autobiographical statement in Vadillo's personal file, f. 495, op. 241, d. 42:9–10, RGASPI; Jeifets and Jeifets, *América Latina*, 618–19.

83. "[Evelio Vadillo]," October 4, 1963, in José Revueltas, *Las evocaciones requeridas*, 2:147–50.

84. See the handwritten notes on the case dated January 12, January 23, and August 28, 1936, f. 531, op. 1, d. 185:6, 10–11, 12, RGASPI.

85. See the diplomatic documents relating to Vadillo's case, leg. 4, exp. 3:1–16, 21–23, Fondo Archivo de la Embajada de México en la URSS, Archivo Histórico Genaro Estrada, Mexico City.

86. "Testimonio de Evelio Vadillo Martínez," November 15, 1955, Mexico City, document 72110, leg. 997, Fondo Histórico Vicente Lombardo Toledano, Universidad Obrera de México, Mexico City.

87. For a series of articles reconstructing Vadillo's fate, see Héctor Aguilar Camín, "El camarada Vadillo," *Nexos*, 147, March 1990, and "En busca de Vadillo," *Nexos*, 149, May 1990; and Rodrigo García Treviño, "El regreso de Evelio Vadillo," *Nexos*, 156, December 1990.

88. Revueltas, *Los errores*, 67.

A Relationship Forged in Exile

Luís Carlos Prestes and the Brazilian Communist Party, 1927–1935

JACOB BLANC

Luís Carlos Prestes served as the secretary-general of the Partido Comunista Brasileira (PCB, Brazilian Communist Party) from 1942 to 1980, making him one of the longest-tenured leaders of a Communist Party anywhere in the world. His initial engagement with the party, however, was disjointed and often contentious. In the late 1920s the PCB initially sought to recruit Prestes, even inviting him to run as its candidate in Brazil's 1930 presidential election. Soon afterward, though, the PCB denounced him as a petty-bourgeois obstacle to proletarian revolution. But by 1935 the PCB had swung back again, and Prestes was henceforth held aloft as one of its most important leaders.

What explains this political whiplash, and how could one person be seen in such diverging ways within a relatively short period of time? Drawing on Brazilian and Soviet archives, this chapter traces the back-and-forth history of Prestes and the PCB through the transnational linkages that shaped both the man and the party. Prestes became radicalized in the late 1920s and early 1930s while living in exile in Bolivia, Argentina, Uruguay, and the Soviet Union. Prior to his exile, he rose to fame for having led a two-year rebellion across Brazil's vast interior regions—the eponymously named Prestes Column. Yet, it was only when he left the country in 1927 that he began to discard his liberal, reformist views in favor of a Marxist critique. This radicalization culminated in 1935, when he helped lead a failed communist insurrection in Rio de Janeiro.

Like Prestes, the Brazilian Communist Party also evolved in relation to communist militants outside of Brazil, most notably the shifting policies from the Comintern in Moscow—often mediated through the South American Bureau located in Buenos Aires. The PCB had to navigate Comintern directives between two major summits held in Moscow, the Sixth World Congress in 1928—which ushered in the so-called Third Period and its program of class warfare—and the Seventh World Congress in 1935, which called for a broader Popular Front approach. The PCB's vacillating stance on Prestes was thus driven by its own attempts to recalibrate its platform according to the changing wishes of Moscow.

Scholarship on Prestes and the PCB is robust, including recent biographies from Daniel Aãrao Reis (one of Brazil's most prominent historians) and Anita Prestes (Luís Carlos's eldest daughter).[1] Whereas most studies tend to treat the early history of Prestes and the PCB as an almost predetermined prologue to his eventual leadership position, this chapter uses a transnational perspective to chart a more nuanced view of Prestes's trajectory. Transnational politics not only influenced the disjointed relationship between the man and the party—they made the relationship possible in the first place.

The period from 1927 to 1935 highlights the complicated collaborations sparked by the flow of militants and debates between Brazil, Latin America, and the Soviet Union. During this time, Prestes was a key player in the exchanges between the PCB and the Comintern. In the late 1920s, when the PCB was originally in favor of Prestes, the Comintern was against him. Then in 1930, when the PCB began denouncing Prestes—partly as a way to show that it could follow the Third Period directives of Moscow—the Comintern, at the urging of a Latvian Bolshevik leader stationed in South America, reversed course and saw him as redeemable, going so far as to invite him to live in the Soviet Union. It was only in the lead-up to 1935, when Prestes returned from Moscow to help plan an armed revolt, that the two organizations held a common view toward Prestes. From that point forward, Prestes became the guiding figure of the PCB for most of the twentieth century.

New Paths in the 1920s

The Brazilian Communist Party was founded in 1922 with barely seventy members. Most of its early leaders came from anarcho-syndicalist backgrounds in the industrial strikes of 1917 to 1920.[2] As Reis writes, "the creation of the PCB went completely unnoticed by public opinion," and for several years the party was "insignificant to the point of being almost ridiculous."[3] The growing pains of building a new organization were exacerbated by events at the national level.

In the 1920s a series of rebellions took place in Brazil, led not by communists or other Marxists but, rather, by liberal sectors of the military, including Luís Carlos Prestes. This movement of reform-minded military leaders came to be known as *tenentismo*, from the Portuguese word for lieutenant, *tenente*. The tenente campaign began in 1922, with a barracks revolt that ended in a famous shootout along the Copacabana beach in Rio de Janeiro. It then resurfaced in 1924, when an uprising in São Paulo gave way to the Prestes Column's fifteen-thousand-mile march across the country. The tenente campaign failed to overthrow President Artur Bernardes, but it became the largest opposition movement of the decade.

The rise of tenentismo had adverse effects on Brazil's recently formed Communist Party. In response to the tenente revolts, the federal government enacted heavy censorship and repression. Between the first tenente revolt in 1922 and the end of the Prestes Column rebellion in 1927, Brazil was placed under martial law for all but seven months. The repressive climate of the 1920s forced the PCB to operate in a semi-clandestine manner and hindered its ability to build its membership base. By 1928, over five years after its founding, the party remained small, with just over six hundred members.[4]

In contrast to the PCB's slow start, Prestes rose to national fame for his role in the tenente rebellion. Prestes had not participated in the initial revolt of 1922, but over the course of the 1924 uprising, he became the movement's unquestioned leader. By the time the column crossed into exile in early 1927, Prestes was a living legend. As evidenced in an article from the Rio de Janeiro newspaper *A Gazeta de Noticias,* written three days after the rebels took up exile in Bolivia: "for those who bind themselves body and soul to the cause and the work of the revolution, he is a demigod."[5] Tenentismo represented a loosely defined form of "revolution" based on liberal reformist demands that included a new president, the secret ballot, a balance of power among the three branches of government, and universal primary-school education. Prestes's fame emerged from the heroic narrative of the rebel journey across Brazil. Although Prestes and his troops had done very little to help local communities directly, popular depictions presented him as a liberating figure. A 1929 article in another Rio de Janeiro newspaper, *A Manhã,* for example, proclaimed that "the platform of Luis Carlos Prestes, traced in blood, across the geographic map of Brazil, is the only one the people can trust, after so much dishonesty and ridicule. So any politicians who right now want to win over the hearts of the people, will have to speak to them about Prestes and in the name of Prestes."[6] As a wildly popular leader connected to a broad-based liberal movement, Prestes became an appealing symbol to a wide range of audiences.

During the column's long march through the interior, Prestes came to see the demands of tenentismo as insufficient. The most-telling example of his changing views came in late 1926, as the column inched along its final push toward exile. Across four pages of handwritten text, Prestes wrote an essay on agrarian reform: "Having walked amongst the Brazilian people, especially the poor, we have seen the most ferocious despotism being practiced. . . . [And] considering that public lands should be shared by the poor who need the means of subsistence. . . . [And] considering that instead of giving unused lands to small farmers, state governments have put the nation in danger by giving it freely to those who own vast latifundio [estates]. . . . We resolve to create land deeds for whichever man requests it."[7] Although Prestes's experience in the interior had begun to shift his worldview, it took several years for his emerging social critique to find a larger framework.

Prestes did not engage with Marxism until he and the tenente rebels took up exile in Bolivia, where they worked for an English logging company in the town of La Gaiba—Prestes had trained as an army engineer, and he oversaw several construction projects in exile. His first encounter came via Rafael Corrêa de Oliveira, a journalist from Rio de Janeiro's *O Jornal*, who had traveled to Bolivia to interview him. Corrêa de Oliveira left Prestes with a handful of books, including some on political theory, and their subsequent correspondence helped nudge along Prestes's radicalization. In a letter a few months after their time together in Bolivia, Prestes even quoted V. I. Lenin as saying that "theory can become a material force when it grips the masses."[8] Yet, in a reflection of how rudimentary his politics were at this early stage, Prestes attributed the quotation to the wrong radical: the phrase was written by Marx, not by Lenin as Prestes had confidently stated in his letter.

In December 1927, almost a year after arriving in Bolivia, Prestes was visited by Astrojildo Pereira, the secretary-general of the Brazilian Communist Party. At this point, the PCB was oriented to a strategy of building a Worker and Peasant Bloc—the Bloco Operário e Camponês. As described in a 1927 statement from the PCB's central committee, the bloco sought to build "an independent class politics [to run candidates] who would maintain permanent contact with the working class through representational sectors—unions and politicians—and public rallies."[9] Although the bloco was envisioned to cover peasants as well as urban workers, in practice the PCB had not done much in the countryside; as Pereira himself admitted, "the 'peasant' element was little more than a word inserted into the bloco, it was a wish."[10] As the PCB sought to increase its profile and make inroads with rural sectors, Pereira traveled to Bolivia to meet with Prestes. Pereira wanted to recruit Prestes to the PCB, with the explicit goal of establishing an "alliance between the communists and the soldiers of the Prestes Column, or, in other words, between the revolutionary proletariat under the influence of the Party and the . . . peasant masses under the influence of [Prestes]."[11]

Prestes, it should be emphasized, had done almost nothing to help communities in Brazil's interior. Aside from a few instances of destroying tax records or making alliances with local leaders during the march, the rebellion did very little that could be considered a direct act of solidarity or justice. More often than not, the encounters were defined either by indifference (engaging just enough to receive supplies and keep the column marching forward) or violent conflict; although Prestes attempted to maintain a code of discipline and accountability throughout the long march, rebel soldiers committed numerous acts of looting, rape, and murder. As part of its campaign to overthrow the government—and in desperate need of reinforcements—the column called on rural communities to rise up and join the rebellion. Almost none did. Despite the reality of what took place during the column, a mythology grew that depicted Prestes as a guiding symbol of Brazil's impoverished rural masses. While living in exile, a nickname coalesced around Prestes that stuck with him throughout his life, o Cavaleiro de Esperança—the Knight of Hope. For urban leaders seeking to appeal to the Brazilian countryside, Prestes was a captivating folk hero. As such, the PCB sent its secretary-general all the way to Bolivia to recruit the mythic Knight of Hope. After two days of discussion, Prestes declined the PCB's offer, though he was intrigued and kept the Marxist literature that Pereira had brought him, including texts from Karl Marx, Friedrich Engels, and Lenin, as well as a dozen issues of *L'Humanité*, the Parisian newspaper of the French Communist Party.[12]

Two months after his meeting with Pereira, Prestes left Bolivia and moved to Buenos Aires, where he would live for the next two and a half years.[13] Unlike in Brazil, the Argentine Communist Party was legal, and Prestes frequented the party's headquarters and began spending time with local leaders, including Victorio Codovilla and Rodolfo Ghioldi. Argentine communists suggested Marxist books for him to read. Several decades afterward, Prestes recalled that two texts in particular shifted his political orientation: *State and Revolution* by Lenin, and volume one of Marx's *Capital*. Prestes considered *State and Revolution* the single most influential text on his changing worldview: "it made me realize just how false and misguided my conception of the State was, which had been engrained in me during my university studies and that made me think that the State was an institution above social classes." And in volume 1 of *Capital*, Prestes claimed to have discovered "the secrets of capitalist exploitation, [it] changed me into a socialist by scientific conviction."[14]

While Prestes began to embrace a Marxist worldview, the Comintern moved in a direction that precluded an alliance with someone like him. In July 1928 Moscow hosted the Sixth World Congress of the Communist International, a watershed gathering that initiated the so-called Third Period, a reference to the third phase of postwar capitalist development. The congress overturned the previous united-front approach of collaborating with non-communist revolutionary groups—such as the Prestes Column—replacing it with a more confrontational program of class warfare. For the PCB and militants elsewhere in the region, the 1928 congress also represented what scholar Manuel Caballero calls the "Red Columbus," the point at which the Comintern finally "discovered" Latin America.[15] With a new interest in this part of the world, the Comintern directed the delegates from Latin America to reorient their campaigns toward a platform of "agrarian and anti-imperialist" revolution. Leôncio Basbaum, one of the three Brazilian delegates, felt heartened that the congress was taking an interest in Latin America, though also discouraged that the Europeans seemed to know very little about the region: "They felt that everything was semicolonial, and they projected the problems of Asia onto Latin America as if everything were the same." At one point, Basbaum recalled, he was asked what language people speak in Brazil.[16]

At the end of the year, from December 29, 1928, to January 4, 1929, the PCB held its Third Party Congress in Niterói, an industrial port city across the bay from Rio de Janeiro. With the directives from the recent Moscow summit in mind—particularly, the Comintern's emphasis on agrarian revolution for Latin America—the PCB reaffirmed its commitment to the bloco program. As mentioned above, the party knew that it had thus far failed to engage the peasant element of the bloco. Seeking to implement the policies of the Third Period, the PCB discussed at length how to best expand its presence in the countryside. The congress's final report observed, "For the first time in the history of the Party . . . peasants and the agrarian problem were taken seriously. . . . The Third Congress did not resolve [the problem], nor did it give a definitive solution, nor could it have; but crucially, the question was put on the table, in its full magnitude."[17] At a time when Prestes was, rightfully or not, seen as someone who could unite rural Brazilians, the PCB considered the Knight of Hope a potential catalyst to fulfill its program. The appeal of Prestes also drew from the Party's attachment to its so-called Third Revolt thesis. Articulated by Octávio Brandão, the Third Revolt thesis postulated that Brazil's revolution had recently progressed through its first two stages: the two tenente revolts of 1922 and 1924. From these initial phases led by the petty bourgeoisie, a third stage would soon take place: "The third revolutionary eruption will be characterized . . . as a continuation of the revolution of 1924 and the Prestes Column, which was never defeated. It was only ever interrupted." The PCB thus envisioned itself as the inheritor of the Prestes Column rebellion.

The Comintern's Third Period left the PCB in a delicate position. The emphasis on an agrarian and anti-imperialist revolution called for a vigorous campaign in the countryside. Pereira, the former head of the PCB now living in Moscow, declared to the Comintern Executive Committee (ECCI): "Comrades, it was said on the occasion of the Sixth World Congress that the Communist International has discovered Latin America. I believe that Latin America is now sufficiently discovered, and that it is no longer enough to feel satisfied with this happy statement, or with good resolutions on paper. The resolutions must be energetically carried out."[18] Yet, the policy of class warfare now complicated an alliance with the person that the PCB saw as its key to such an approach. Although Prestes had begun to embrace Marxism, he had not yet joined the Communist Party. Moreover, he remained a potent symbol of the liberal tenente rebellion, precisely the sort of non-communist group from which the Comintern sought to distance itself at the Sixth World Congress.

At this juncture, the PCB decided that Prestes's potential as a leader of the peasantry—however romanticized the notion may have been—outweighed the risks of collaborating with the former head of a petty-bourgeois movement. In June 1929 the PCB invited Prestes to run as the party's candidate for the 1930 presidential elections. While in Buenos Aires for the First Conference of Latin American Communist Parties, two PCB leaders, Paulo Lacerda and Basbaum, met with Prestes and pitched the idea of a presidential run. As Basbaum recalled, "our hope was to recruit Prestes and use his national and popular prestige to win over the masses."[19] While claiming to agree with much of the PCB platform, Prestes rejected the offer: "I cannot accept [the candidacy] because I am still loyal to the tenentes. Only after speaking with them can I take a position."[20]

The visit to Prestes reflected the complicated process through which communist parties in Latin America implemented the changing policies of the Comintern. Lacerda and Basbaum had been two of the Brazilian delegates to the Sixth World Congress in Moscow, and they were fully aware of the Comintern's new directives. The archival record does not clarify whether the PCB's decision to approach Prestes was taken consciously against the Comintern, though it, nonetheless, showed that the party still saw the legendary Knight of Hope as its best avenue for organizing the countryside—and also for building a larger national profile. By the end of 1929, the party counted only twelve hundred members, and its leaders surely imagined that Prestes would expand its base.[21] The PCB's proposed collaboration with Prestes hinted at how the party's relationship with Moscow would soon grow tense. In the ensuing debates about how to build a revolutionary movement in Brazil, Prestes remained a central point of contention.

The Comintern's top leadership rarely sent instructions directly to the PCB. Instead, it generally operated through two bodies: the Latin American secretariat in Moscow and the South American Bureau in Buenos Aires. In Moscow, the secretariat held several deliberations on Brazil and Prestes. A secretariat meeting in October 1929, for example, observed, "The question is not simply: either a bloc with Prestes, or a critique of Prestes. Prestes organizes and leads the peasants . . . while [the PCB] is not yet linked to these peasant masses. Without a doubt, [the party] must begin to denounce and fight against the program of Prestes which is confused, petty bourgeois, semi-liberal, and already halfway to treason."[22] And in Buenos Aires, the South American Bureau included Latin American communists as well as party members who had come from Europe to help enact Moscow's policies. The bureau was established in 1926, and toward the second half of Prestes's exile in Buenos Aires, it was run by the Latvian Abram Heifetz, who went by the name Guralsky—though most Latin Americans referred to him as El Rústico—literally translated as The Rustic (meaning old) but playing as well with the Spanish word for The Russian, El Ruso. During this period, the bureau derided the PCB for its misplaced interpretation of—and desire to collaborate with—Prestes. At one meeting in November 1929, Codovilla stated, "I have the impression that the [Brazilian] comrades talk a lot about their thesis for revolution, but that they do very little to actually prepare it, or that they're just waiting for the Prestes Column to bring it about."[23] And in late January 1930, the bureau called for the PCB to conduct a thorough self-critique and acknowledge its failure: "The party must make great strides toward its independence from the petty bourgeoisie and, at all costs, make a serious criticism of the democratic [forces] that control the peasantry, like the Prestes Column. The party must understand that it has committed a series of very serious mistakes and has transformed the bloco into a political arm of the petty bourgeoisie."[24]

While the Comintern was urging the PCB to distance itself from Prestes, another group was busy courting him. In the years after the Prestes Column, tenente leaders helped form the Liberal Alliance, a coalition of military officers, industrialists, and urban liberals led by Getúlio Vargas, the governor of the southern state of Rio Grande do Sul, who was running for president in the 1930 elections. At Vargas's invitation, Prestes had returned clandestinely to Brazil to meet in Porto Alegre, first in September 1929—three months after Prestes had met with the PCB leaders—and again in January 1930. Vargas wanted the Knight of Hope to endorse him for president.[25] At both meetings, Prestes declined to back Vargas. Their discussions kept a potential partnership on the table, and Vargas gave Prestes a fake passport and pledged to send money to Buenos Aires to help organize an armed rebellion in the event that he lost the election. Vargas's inclination proved prescient, and on March 1, 1930, he lost the presidency by nearly 20 percentage points to the president of the state of São Paulo, Júlio Prestes—no relation to Luís Carlos. After losing what he claimed was a rigged election, Vargas began preparing an armed uprising and again sought out Prestes, this time offering him the role of military chief of the revolution. As he had before, Prestes rejected Vargas. With Prestes moving increasingly toward communism, he saw Vargas as an insufficient vehicle for change, and, moreover, he felt that Vargas only wanted to "lean on the prestige of the [Prestes] Column in order to increase his power."[26]

In the aftermath of the 1930 elections and having turned down the entreaties of both the PCB and the Liberal Alliance, it was uncertain which position Prestes would take. In this climate of political instability, Prestes was an attractive force. An article in the Rio de Janeiro–based *Correio da Manhã* the week after Vargas's presidential defeat commented, "Luís Carlos Prestes is a symbol. In light of the legend that has formed around him . . . he is the embodiment, perhaps, of the only hope capable of leading Brazil to better days."[27] Despite the influence of Prestes's symbolism, during his two years in exile, he had made few direct contributions to Brazilian politics, and there was a risk that his influence could diminish if he stayed on the sidelines too long.

The May Manifesto

Still refusing to join either the PCB or Vargas, Prestes opted for his own path by releasing what became known as the May Manifesto. On the May 29 front cover of the *Diário da Noite*—a liberal Rio de Janeiro newspaper—Prestes's manifesto was printed in full under the title of "Captain Luís Carlos Prestes defines his current views."[28] Short of fully embracing a communist orientation, which came the following year, the May Manifesto was a direct rebuke of Vargas's Liberal Alliance. And although Prestes lifted a few phrases from official Comintern policy—most notably an emphasis on the "agrarian and anti-imperialist revolution"—the manifesto did not mention the Communist Party. Its opening lines were addressed "to the suffering proletariat of our cities, to the workers oppressed by plantations and ranches, [and] to the wretched masses of our backlands." Calling on workers and peasants to rise up, Prestes outlined his vision for an "agrarian and anti-imperialist revolution . . . [fighting] for the complete liberation of our agricultural workers, of all forms of exploitation, feudal and colonial; for the seizure, nationalization and redistribution of lands, for handing the land back to those who work it." Prestes also denounced Vargas, offering a tacit acknowledgment of his own complicity in the tenente movement that had paved the way for the Liberal Alliance: "The Brazilian revolution cannot be achieved with the Liberal Alliance's anodyne program. The simple swap of politicians, the secret vote, promises of electoral freedom, administrative honesty, respect for the Constitution. . . . these solve nothing, nor can they in any way appeal to the vast majority of our population."

The May Manifesto was widely disparaged. This antagonism came swiftly from the tenentes in the Liberal Alliance, who felt betrayed by their former leader. Juárez Távora and Isidoro Dias—two of Prestes's most important former tenente comrades—issued public denunciations, and previously allied newspapers now spoke out against him.[29] A front-page editorial in the *Diario Carioca* explained that while the newspaper had supported Prestes—"the flag-bearer of the movement . . . the young soldier who crossed Brazil from one extreme to the other"—it must now withdraw its backing in light of his "strange" new manifesto.[30]

For Brazil's communists, on the other hand, Prestes's May Manifesto did not go far enough. The central issue was that Prestes did not see the working class as leading the revolution. Less than two weeks after the manifesto's release, Brandão issued a statement declaring that "the document and its author are not communists."[31] National media seemed fascinated, if not a little confused, with the PCB's reaction to the manifesto; in its article on Brandão's statement, *O Jornal* commented, "Even the Communist Party repels all contact with the ideas of that ex-revolutionary." In an interview with the *Diário de Notícias* (Rio de Janeiro), Brandão said, "Prestes approached it all wrong. . . . The working classes will never be freed by Knights of Hope."[32] And in *A Classe Operária* (Rio de Janeiro), the party's official newspaper, the PCB warned, "Luís Carlos Prestes, with his revolutionary words, seeks to build his movement for the petty bourgeoisie. . . . [Our party] must denounce him to the working masses [for] deceiving the proletariat, [and] masking his true nature with revolutionary phrases."[33]

The PCB's seesaw approach to Prestes must be seen as part of the party's delayed responses to the policies of the Comintern. Although a year earlier the PCB had asked Prestes to run as its candidate for president, the mounting pressure from the bureau in Buenos Aires appears to have finally broken through. Brandão in particular, whose Third Revolt thesis had come under heavy criticism from the bureau, seemed eager to denounce Prestes and thus gain standing with the Comintern. The pressure to implement the class warfare policies of the Third Period had come not only from the bureau in Buenos Aires but also from the Latin American secretariat in Moscow, which called for the PCB to be hostile to democratic and reformist elements.[34] Prestes could not have fully known about the tensions between Moscow and Brazil, and he had likely thought that the PCB would celebrate his manifesto—if the party had sought to recruit him beforehand, surely they would embrace him even more now that he had publicly broken from the tenentes. To Prestes's surprise, the PCB did not.

In the fallout from the May Manifesto, Prestes sought to appease his communist critics by publishing a second manifesto. In July he announced the creation of a Liga de Ação Revolucionária (LAR, Revolutionary Action League). Prestes envisioned the LAR as an independent force that could build an alliance with the Communist Party. In response, the PCB doubled-down on its criticism of Prestes, declaring, "the League would be a confused party. [Prestes only] provides evasive formulas for revolutionary struggle. . . . He is the most dangerous enemy of the Communist Party."[35] Aside from trying to buy weapons in France for a potential insurrection in Brazil, the LAR never got off the ground, and Prestes abandoned it within a few months. Living in exile in Argentina and disowned by both the tenentes and the communists, Prestes could only watch from a distance what soon unfolded in Brazil.

In the five months following Prestes's May Manifesto, a series of political and military conflicts culminated in Vargas's seizure of power on October 24. The Revolution of 1930, as it became known, signaled the end of the First Republic political system that had ruled Brazil since 1889. For communists in Brazil and beyond, the success of Vargas's liberal revolution accelerated debates on how to build a proletarian movement. Prestes, who until very recently had been an icon of the liberal militarism that now ruled Brazil, began to move decisively toward communism. This process accelerated when he was forced to move to a different country. Prestes had been arrested in Buenos Aires on October 2, 1930, for denouncing Argentina's recently installed military government—a month earlier, General José Félix Uriburu had staged a coup against the democratic government of Hipólito Yrigoyen.[36] After three days in prison, Prestes was freed on the condition that he leave the country. He then moved to Montevideo, Uruguay, where he found work as a foreman for a plumbing construction company.[37] In Montevideo, Prestes began spending time with the Uruguayan Communist Party, and he also reconnected with "El Rústico" Guralsky—after the military coup in Argentina, Guralsky and the South American Bureau had relocated to Montevideo.[38]

Born in Riga, Latvia, Guralsky joined the Bund, the Jewish socialist organization, in the early 1900s and spent much of the next two decades in and out of tsarist prisons.[39] After the Russian Revolution in 1917, Guralsky went to Ukraine as part of the Bund's central leadership, where he began collaborating with Bolsheviks in Odessa and Kiev. He joined the Bolsheviks while organizing in Kiev, and in the coming years he rose up through various leadership positions, including in the attempted 1923 revolt in Germany. He was eventually assigned to the Latin American secretariat in Moscow, and at the Sixth World Congress in 1928, he helped author the reports on Latin America, which led to him being dispatched in early 1930 to Buenos Aires, where he headed the South American Bureau. As the Comintern's leading representative in South America, Guralsky oversaw the party's engagement with the PCB and Luís Carlos Prestes. Despite the Comintern's distrust of Prestes, Guralsky saw potential in his May Manifesto and began a two-pronged strategy to shape and recruit him. As journalist William Waack has written, "Guralsky decided to work two parallel angles. At the same time that he cultivated a close relationship with Prestes, he gave orders for the Communist Party to adopt a firm line against him."[40]

Guralsky's conversations with Prestes had their intended effect and helped push the Knight of Hope to an explicitly communist program. Prestes credited Guralsky as one of the single most influential people in his trajectory, saying, "he helped me choose the correct path . . . that freed me from strange beliefs and converted me to a soldier of the only true revolutionary movement."[41] In particular, Guralsky emphasized the mistake of Prestes's earlier platforms, comparing them to the petty bourgeois phases of the Russian Revolution: "Rústico talked to me about Lenin's fight against the populists, the economists, and the Mensheviks. Those were real lessons about the history of the Bolshevik movement, which made me understand the path of revolution." While privately mentoring Prestes, Guralsky also led the bureau's critique of him. In late 1930 and early 1931, the bureau issued declarations against Prestes, calling him "the greatest obstacle to building a Communist Party in Brazil" and exclaiming, "If Prestes wants to move forward [with the party], he must recognize the confusion that his platform [has created], which will lead him to a treasonous end."[42] The bureau's public criticism greatly affected Prestes. In February 1931, the German militant Arthur Ewert—a member of the bureau—wrote to Moscow reporting that Prestes had been thrown into "a situation of great isolation, and because we are simultaneously attacking him, it has left him quite depressed."[43]

Influenced by his conversations with Guralsky and eager to gain the approval of the bureau, the Comintern, and also the PCB, Prestes wrote a third manifesto. In March 1931 he issued a declaration that emphasized his newly hardened commitment to the PCB. The text provided a full-throated denunciation of his previous politics, including his original role as a tenente and also his two prior manifestos.[44] In contrast to his first manifesto—which the Comintern had denounced as a petty-bourgeois evasion of the proletariat—Prestes declared, in the document's closing lines, that the revolution can only come about "under the unquestioned hegemony of the party of the proletariat, the Brazilian Communist Party."

In a sign that the Comintern and the PCB were still not aligned, the two groups had different reactions to Prestes's new position. For the South American Bureau in Montevideo, the manifesto showed that Prestes had finally embraced the program of the Communist International. As Ewert reported to Moscow a few weeks after the manifesto's release, "Prestes is now speaking our same language. He is in favor of the 'party of the proletariat' . . . and I have the impression that he is doing everything he can to avoid the path taken by his old [tenente] friends."[45] The PCB, on the other hand, maintained its recently adopted criticism of Prestes. This was the start of a new phase for the PCB, when it sought to purge reformist elements from the Party, including through expelling top leaders from the 1920s, such as Pereira, the former secretary-general, who had spearheaded the proposed alliance with Prestes. In May, the party circulated a statement, "Against Luís Carlos Prestes," among its branches across Brazil, calling him the representative of "the most impoverished faction of the petty bourgeoisie." The following month, the PCB continued its attacks by grouping Prestes with various other groups that it saw as obstacles to a proletarian revolution in Brazil, including Vargas's Liberal Alliance, as well as Trotskyists and anarchists.[46]

The PCB's reluctance to be swayed by Prestes's new manifesto was surely conditioned by the ongoing criticism that it had received from the bureau. In November 1930, for example, the bureau issued a fairly scathing critique of the PCB: "The activity of our party in Brazil during these past few months clearly shows the full merit of the [Comintern's] criticism of the [PCB's] errors and shortcomings. Its organizational defects, its missteps, its political weaknesses, have become even more evident in the present situation. . . . The party has not been able to develop, in either the city or the countryside, a truly energetic and effective campaign. . . . It has not yet broken with its petty bourgeois illusions."[47] Prestes thus became a point of misalignment between the Comintern and the PCB. While the Comintern began to soften its view of Prestes after his third manifesto, the PCB did not, and the party in Brazil resisted Prestes for several more years. As the PCB embraced a more hardened position of class warfare, Prestes represented the alliance-based program of the late 1920s that a new leadership in Brazil now sought to overturn. In contrast, Guralsky's influence— through both his personal interactions with Prestes and also his role as the head of the South American Bureau—helped make Prestes acceptable to communists outside of Brazil. We see then how the policies of the Third Period were contingent on various factors as they disseminated outward from Moscow, through regional offices, and down to the national level. Whether from the personal intervention of Comintern leaders like Guralsky or the efforts of a new central committee in Brazil seeking to differentiate itself from former national leaders now deemed to be reformist, transnational policies could foster dissonance in the very spaces they were meant to unite.

In the middle of 1931, the Comintern accelerated its approval of Prestes. At the suggestion of the Uruguayan Communist Party and with the approval of Moscow, Prestes was invited to live in the Soviet Union. This was the period when the Soviet government, as part of Stalin's first Five-Year Plan, hired foreign engineers, an especially appealing offer for Prestes given the precarious nature of his construction work in Montevideo. In August, a month before Prestes would travel to Moscow, the bureau wrote to the PCB explaining the Comintern's new stance toward Prestes: "Luís Carlos Prestes has finally put himself on the side of the Communist Party of Brazil. He is going to the Soviet Union. . . . Our goal must now be to take advantage of [his] political progression, given his importance, to reinforce the ideological and organizational strength of the PCB."[48] At the bureau's insistence, the PCB then issued a statement to its members explaining the party's about-face: "The declaration from Prestes is, without a doubt, a great success for our party. It clearly proves that for a petty bourgeois revolutionary who genuinely wants to fight against imperialism and feudalism, the only path . . . is to march with the proletarian movement, led by the only revolutionary party, the Communist International."[49]

The Knight of Hope in Moscow

With the official endorsement of the Comintern—and the nominal acquiescence of the PCB—Prestes left South America for the first time. In late September 1931 he sailed from Montevideo to Le Havre, France, and having arranged for his mother and three sisters to join him, the family reunited in Berlin and continued to the Soviet Union, where they arrived in November.[50] In Moscow, Prestes was welcomed by Dimitri Manuilsky, the secretary of the ECCI. Like Guralsky in Buenos Aires and Montevideo, Manuilsky had a profound influence on Prestes, particularly concerning the policies of the Sixth World Congress. He also helped arrange a job for Prestes in the People's Commissariat of Heavy Industry, a newly created ministry that oversaw large industrial projects.

Prestes eventually transferred jobs and became a communications officer in the Comintern's International Agrarian Institute, where he wrote articles on topics such as land reform, and he even hosted an event on the Prestes Column's march across Brazil. Prestes also spent time with other visiting militants from across Latin America, and he went on delegation trips to cities across the Soviet Union, including to Kiev, Kharkov, Rostov, and Leningrad.

Although Manuilsky had told Prestes that he could officially join the Communist Party after a year of work, Stalin's purges in the early 1930s led the Comintern to pause new memberships in 1933. Unable to join the Communist Party in Moscow, Prestes renewed his efforts to join the PCB. At Manuilsky's urging, in March 1934, the ECCI approved a resolution asking the PCB to extend membership to Prestes. The PCB did not reply to this request, and when the ECCI sent two additional follow-ups in the coming months, the PCB ignored those as well. It was only in June that the PCB finally replied, confirming that they would allow Prestes to join.[51] Even then, the PCB remained skeptical and did not admit Prestes to the Central Committee leadership until the night before its revolt in 1935.

In July 1934 Moscow hosted the Third Conference of Latin American Communist Parties. At the summit, the ECCI under Manuilsky, with input from the Brazilian delegation led by the new Secretary-General Antônio Maciel Bonfim, decided that Prestes should return to Brazil to help organize an armed insurrection against Vargas. According to Reis, the 1934 conference in Moscow served as a culminating moment in the alignment of the PCB and the Comintern.[52] In the early 1930s, as Prestes settled into his life in Moscow, the Comintern had continued to criticize the PCB; in June 1933, for example, the ECCI wrote directly to the PCB declaring, "Owing to the lack of ideological form and the organizational looseness of the party in Brazil, owing to the fact that the party is littered with class hostile elements, [and] owing to the weakness of its leading cadres . . . the party has failed to capitalize on the favorable moment for revolutionary action."[53] But under the leadership of Bonfim, the PCB accelerated its orientation to Moscow by expelling certain leaders, reorganizing its structure to prioritize workers over "intellectuals," and undertaking a self-critique of its previous failures.[54] The party had also grown, now counting some five-thousand members.[55] At the 1934 Moscow conference, Bonfim made a compelling presentation on the revolutionary potential of Brazil. Guralsky, who attended the conference, remarked that "the Brazilian comrades did not exaggerate the ripeness of the country's revolutionary potential," which could then set in motion other revolts across Latin America.[56]

To safeguard Prestes's journey back to Brazil, the Comintern prepared an alias by assigning him a bodyguard: a German militant of Jewish descent named Olga Benário. Twenty-six years old when she met Prestes—ten years her senior—Benário had been a leader in the Communist Youth International, with experience organizing cadres in Germany, Great Britain, France, and the Soviet Union. Benário and Prestes were introduced only a few days before departing for Brazil, traveling incognito as Portuguese newlyweds on their honeymoon; famously, while pretending to be a couple, Prestes and Benário fell in love. The two left Moscow on December 29, 1934, and with fake documents in hand they made a four-month journey across Europe, to the United States, and down to South America. They eventually arrived clandestinely in Rio de Janeiro on April 17, 1935.[57] After eight years in exile, the Knight of Hope had returned.

The Seventh World Congress, the ANL, and the 1935 Revolt

While Prestes lived underground in Brazil, laying the groundwork of an armed revolt, delegations from across the world traveled to Moscow for the Seventh World Congress. For nearly a month beginning in late July 1935, the congress debated and ultimately approved a sweeping set of policies that marked a sharp departure from the previous platform established in 1928. Motivated by the rising specter of fascism across Europe, the Seventh Congress discarded the previous program of class warfare in favor of a new "Popular Front" through which communist parties could build coalitions to advance their revolutionary goals. As a sign of Prestes's rising profile, he was elected, in absentia, to the Comintern Executive Committee.

A few months prior to the Seventh World Congress, Brazil had offered a test case for the type of actions that the Popular Front program would soon facilitate. In March, a month before Prestes and Benário secretly returned to Brazil, a wide swath of the Brazilian left formed the Aliança Nacional Libertadora (ANL, the National Liberating Alliance). The ANL, as the historian John French notes, was an "exhilarating if short lived revolutionary adventure . . . [that] promised the imminent replacement of the established order with a 'popular government' that would oppose fascism, imperialism, and the large landowners."[58] Between March (when the ANL was launched) and July (when it was banned by the government), the ANL grew to over fifteen hundred chapters and a hundred thousand members, with fifty thousand in Rio de Janeiro alone.[59] The ANL brought together the anti-Vargas wing of the tenentes along with several groups of socialists, Trotskyists, and anarchists. At the Comintern's directive, the PCB did not initially join the ANL, despite the fact that Prestes—the party's most popular member—had been chosen as the ANL's honorary president. Though as evidenced in a letter from the ECCI in late May, Moscow soon saw the ANL as a way to "develop the legal status of the PCB at the same time as it consolidates the illegal apparatus" currently planning an armed revolt.[60] With input from the Comintern agents who had traveled to Brazil to help plan the uprising, Prestes wrote a manifesto that was read aloud at an ANL rally on July 5. The ANL had not adopted an official platform—let alone a discourse—of armed insurrection, but Prestes now declared, "This is a situation of war and everyone must take their post . . . Brazilians: All of you who are united by misery, by suffering and by humiliation across the country. . . . You have nothing to lose and the immense riches of Brazil to win."[61]

On the heels of four months of unprecedented mobilization, Prestes's manifesto had an immediate, and unintended, consequence. Rather than catapulting the ANL into a new—more PCB-leaning—phase, it gave Vargas the perfect excuse to shut down the movement. Less than a week after the manifesto's release, Vargas declared the ANL an illegal organization, and police raided its headquarters and arrested several leaders. By October the ANL had dissipated completely. This left the PCB in a difficult situation. Although the Seventh World Congress now sanctioned precisely the sort of coalition building witnessed in the ANL, government repression had left the PCB as the only organization in Brazil still willing, and able, to take up arms. After Vargas shut down the ANL, the South American Bureau in Montevideo recommended to Moscow that the PCB "accelerate preparations for the insurrection. . . . It is impossible at the moment to set a date, but it is advisable to prepare for it quickly."[62]

Despite the PCB's confident projections that Brazil was ready for a proletarian revolution, conditions on the ground proved otherwise. When an uprising broke out on November 23, 1935, its strongest showing came not from the PCB but from disenchanted officers in the military—echoes of the tenente movement of the previous decade. The revolt, moreover, took place in the northeastern garrisons of Natal and Recife, far from the party's stronghold in Rio de Janeiro. Although the PCB had begun preparing a potential uprising, it did not envision such a move being ready until December or January. But when the northern barracks revolt erupted in November, the PCB decided that it had to act quickly in order to build on the current momentum.[63] On November 27 Prestes and the PCB led an uprising in Rio de Janeiro.[64] By that point, Vargas's forces had had plenty of time to prepare, and the government correctly anticipated that the revolt in Rio de Janeiro would be launched by rebels in the Third Infantry

Regime stationed at Praia Vermelha. The insurrection, which never spread to the working classes, was quelled by the early afternoon.

Conclusion: Imprisoned but on the Rise

After the PCB's failed revolt, the government arrested thousands of people, including most of the PCB leadership. Prestes and Benário eluded capture and stayed on the lam for almost half a year; the police eventually discovered their location and arrested them in March 1936. Determined to make an example of Prestes, Vargas ordered the deportation of Benário. In September 1936, when Benário was seven months' pregnant with Prestes's child, the Vargas regime sent her back to Nazi Germany. Given that Benário was Jewish, her deportation has become one of the most infamous events in Vargas's history. Upon arrival in Germany, Benário was detained in a women's prison in Berlin and was later shipped to a series of Nazi concentration camps. She was killed in the gas chambers of Bernburg in 1942.

Prestes, for his part, was found guilty of sedition and thrown in jail. During his imprisonment from 1937 to 1945, Prestes became the face of a global solidarity campaign that sought to denounce not only the repression under Vargas's regime in Brazil but also the persecution of communists across the region. To help win Prestes's freedom, some of Latin America's most famous communists made statements in support of Prestes, including Chilean poet Pablo Neruda, Argentine writer Alfredo Varela, and Brazilian novelist Jorge Amado, himself living in exile in Buenos Aires. The spotlight cast on Prestes, in turn, helped expand the profile of the Brazilian Communist Party. And in 1942 the PCB elected Prestes, still in jail, as its secretary-general, completing his rise to the top of a party that less than a decade earlier had refused him membership.

Prestes's trajectory occurred amidst a changing series of political debates in Brazil, across Latin America, and across the globe. A close reading of the web of relationships that formed between Prestes, the PCB, and the Comintern helps elucidate how communist parties in Latin America navigated the evolving policies dictated by Moscow. As seen in the case of Prestes, this process was not seamless. The back-and-forth positions on display in this chapter were influenced by the opinions of particular communist leaders in Latin America and Moscow, as well as the changing contexts in Brazil and across the world. Although this transnational flow of people and ideas often made Luís Carlos Prestes an obstacle of the Communist Party, so, too, did it eventually pave the way for his ascent as the leader of the PCB.

Notes

1. Reis Filho, *Luís Carlos Prestes*; A. L. Prestes, *Luiz Carlos Prestes*.

2. For more, see Dulles, *Anarchists and Communists*, 41–98.

3. Reis, *Luís Carlos Prestes*, 114–15.

4. "Relatório á I.C. apresentado pela delegação brasileira por occassião do IV Congresso da I.S.V.," 1928, no. 1, 358–63 series Internacional Comunista, Arquivo Edgard Leuenroth, Campinas, Brazil (hereafter referred to as AEL).

5. "Entra Prestes!" *Gazeta de Noticias* (Rio de Janeiro), February 6, 1927, 2.

6. "Imperativos do momento politico," *A Manhã* (Rio de Janeiro), April 26, 1929, 3.

7. Luís Carlos Prestes, "Liberdade ou morte—titulo de domínio," likely written between October 1926 and January 1927, series JT 1924.05.10, IV:–118, Fundacão Getúlio Vargas, Centro de Pesquisa e Documentação de História Contemporânea do Brasil, Rio de Janeiro.

8. The letter, originally written on May 25, 1927, was reproduced in "Uma Carta escripta em 1927 for Luiz Carlos Prestes," *Correio da Manha* (Rio de Janeiro), February 5, 1929, 1.

9. PCB leadership, open letter, January 5, 1927, as reproduced in Pereira, *Formação do PCB*, 116–20.

10. Pereira, *Formação do PCB*, 125.

11. Pereira, *Formação do PCB*, 132.

12. Pereira, *Formação do PCB*, 131.

13. Prestes, *Luiz Carlos Prestes*, 105–6.

14. L. C. Prestes, "Como cheguei ao comunismo," 7.

15. Caballero, *Latin America and the Comintern*, 70.

16. Basbaum, *Uma vida*, 62.

17. PCB Third Party Congress program, February 12, 1929, series Internacional Comunista, no. 3, 537–74, AEL.

18. Dulles, *Anarchists and Communists*, 392.

19. Basbaum, *Uma vida*, 69.

20. Moraes and Viana, *Prestes*, 44.

21. South American Bureau, meeting, October 24, 1929, no. 1, 116, series Internacional Comunista, AEL.

22. Latin American Secretariat, meeting, October 31, 1929, no. 1, 137, series Internacional Comunista, AEL.

23. South American Bureau, meeting, November 6, 1929, f. 503, op. 1, d. 27, 57–68, Russian State Archive of Social and Political History (hereafter referred to as RGASPI), Moscow.

24. Latin American Secretariat, January 28, 1930, no. 2, 573–79, series Internacional Comunista, AEL.

25. Moraes and Viana, *Prestes*, 47–49.

26. L. C. Prestes, "Como cheguei ao comunismo," 7

27. "Os dois Prestes," *Correio da Manhã* (Rio de Janeiro), March 9, 1930, 4.

28. "O capitão Luiz Carlos Prestes define a sua atitude actual," *Diário da Noite* (Rio de Janeiro), May 29, 1930, 1.

29. "As novas ideas de Luiz Carlos Prestes e o problema brasileiro," *Diário Carioca* (Rio de Janeiro), June 19, 1930, 1; "O marechal Isidoro Dias Lopes discorda do commandante Luis Carlos Prestes," *Diário Carioca* (Rio de Janeiro), June 4, 1930, 12.

30. "A nova directriz do Commandante Prestes," *Diário Carioca* (Rio de Janeiro), May 29, 1930, 1.

31. "Ainda o manifesto do commandante Luiz Carlos Prestes," *O Jornal*, June 11, 1930, 3.

32. "A replica dos comunistas ao sr. Luiz Carlos Prestes," *Diário de Noticias* (Rio de Janeiro), September 2, 1930, 1.

33. *A Classe Operária*, January 17, 1931, no. 3, 6–10, series Internacional Comunista, AEL.

34. For example, Americo Ledo (pseudonym of Astrojildo Pereira) in Moscow to the PCB, September 5, 1929, no. 4, 21, series Internacional Comunista, AEL.

35. *A Classe Operária*, no date attributed, likely late July 1930, in Moraes and Viana, *Prestes*, 52.

36. L. C. Prestes, "Como cheguei ao comunismo," 10.

37. A. L. Prestes, *Luiz Carlos Prestes*, 135.

38. A. L. Prestes, *Luiz Carlos Prestes*, 13–39.

39. Jeifets and Jeifets, *América Latina*, 287–88.

40. Waack, *Camaradas*, 39.

41. L. C. Prestes, "Como cheguei ao comunismo," 10.

42. South American Bureau, "Statement on Brazil," January 1931, f. 503, op. 1, d. 46, RGASPI; Latin American Secretariat, bulletin 12, November 1, 1930, f. 495, op. 79, d. 119, 99–130, RGASPI.

43. Arthur Ewert report, February 1931, f. 495, op. 79, d. 151, RGASPI, in Waack, *Camaradas*, 41. Ewert's code name in Latin America was Harry Berger.

44. "Carta Aberta," open letter reproduced in Bastos, *Prestes e a revolução social*, 220–31, citing full text published in *Diário da Noite* (Rio de Janeiro), March 12, 1931.

45. Berger to unknown recipient, March 20, 1931, in Waack, *Camaradas*, 42.

46. Reis, *Luís Carlos Prestes*, 144.

47. Latin American Secretariat, bulletin 12, November 1, 1930, f. 495, op. 79, d. 119, 99–130, RGASPI.

48. South American Bureau to PCB, August 29, 1931, f. 503, op. 1, d. 44, 19–21, RGASPI.

49. PCB, statement, November 1, 1931, no. 5, 270–72, series Internacional Comunista, AEL.

50. Unless otherwise noted, details on Prestes's time in the Soviet Union from A. L. Prestes, *Luiz Carlos Prestes*, 140–62.

51. Details on the exchanges from Waack, *Camaradas*, 58, and Moraes and Viana, *Prestes*, 58.

52. Reis, *Luís Carlos Prestes*, 167.

53. ECCI, "Resolution on the Brazilian Communist Party," June 10, 1933, no. 1, 235–38, series Internacional Comunista, AEL.

54. Reis, *Luís Carlos Prestes*, 162–63.

55. Dulles, *Anarchists and Communists*, 517.

56. Qtd. in A. L. Prestes, *Luiz Carlos Prestes*, 154.

57. Reis, *Luís Carlos Prestes*, 172–73.

58. French, *Brazilian Workers' ABC*, 62–63.

59. Reis, *Luís Carlos Prestes*, 175–76.

60. Cited in Waack, *Camaradas*, 138.

61. "O manifesto do sr. Luiz Carlos Prestes," *O Jornal*, July 6, 1935, 11.

62. Qtd. in A. L. Prestes, *Luiz Carlos Prestes*, 127.

63. Moraes and Viana, *Prestes*, 76.

64. For a more detailed account of the uprisings, particularly the actions of Prestes, see A. L. Prestes, *Luiz Carlos Prestes*, 173–84; Reis, *Luís Carlos Prestes*, 181–88.

A Political and Transnational Ménage à Trois

The Communist Party USA, the Puerto Rican Communist Party, and the Puerto Rican Nationalist Party, 1934–1945

MARGARET M. POWER

In April 1944 Juan Antonio Corretjer, former secretary general of the Partido Nacionalista de Puerto Rico (PNPR, Puerto Rican Nationalist Party), addressed the constituent convention of the Communist Political Association (CPA) in New York City. The CPA replaced the Communist Party USA (CPUSA), after the party's secretary general, Earl Browder, dissolved it the previous year. Corretjer lauded the formation of the CPA, drawing on the language and politics of the Popular Front: "[T]he Communist Political Association . . . will facilitate the unity of the democratic forces of [the United States] in the struggle to defeat fascism and obtain victory in the war." That was not, however, the only reason he backed the development of the CPA. He also believed it would contribute to ending U.S. colonial rule of Puerto Rico: "The organization of this association will assist the democratic forces of this nation to find greater and more efficient means with which to help my people obtain the recognition of their national independence." He then announced that he refused to renounce support for Puerto Rican independence, despite CPUSA backing the U.S. President Franklin D. Roosevelt administration, which colonized Puerto Rico. "For despite well-meaning counsels that Puerto Rico postpone the demand for her independence until after the war, the Puerto Rican people insist that independence be recognized immediately. Yes, independence for Puerto Rico now."[1] Corretjer admired the CPUSA, but he valued the fight for Puerto Rican independence even more.

Like other Nationalists, he refused to put the struggle for Puerto Rican independence on hold until the United States won the war.

This chapter explores the complex and dynamic transnational relationships between and among the PNPR and the CPUSA and the Partido Comunista de Puerto Rico (PCP, Communist Party of Puerto Rico) from the mid-1930s through the mid-1940s. The PCP and the CPUSA had close, mutually supportive ties with each other and a more uneven connection with the PNPR. Political directives emanating from the Communist International (Comintern), which shifted in accordance with changing global politics and Moscow's agenda, influenced both communist parties' positions on the PNPR. All three parties supported a free Puerto Rico, but only the Nationalists consistently prioritized ending U.S. colonialism. While the Nationalists opposed fascism, they persisted in their efforts to achieve independence before, during, and after World War II. Both the CPUSA and the PCP upheld the demand for Puerto Rican independence, even though they backed the Roosevelt administration in the United States and the Partido Demócrata Popular (PPD, Popular Democratic Party) in Puerto Rico, in accordance with Popular Front politics.[2] After Germany invaded the Union of Soviet Socialist Republics (U.S.S.R.) in 1941, the PCP and the CPUSA subordinated the demand for independence and called for full-out support for the Allied war effort. One other disagreement divided the Communists and the Nationalists. Both of these parties linked independence to socialism and the working class. The Nationalists, however, called on all Puerto Ricans, regardless of class, to unite against colonialism and deferred discussion of other issues until Puerto Rico was a sovereign republic.

. . .

Left-wing militants from the socialist, trade-union, and anarchist movements in the United States joined together to establish the CPUSA in 1919. This rather fractious grouping experienced political differences, even the creation of two different organizations both calling themselves communists, until the Comintern directed them to form one unified party in 1921.[3] Although the party suffered numerous internal divisions, much of its core and leadership faithfully followed the Comintern's political directives, adjusting the party's policies to keep in line with the international organization's political zigzags. In the late 1920s, in accordance with the Comintern, the party adopted the class versus class political line and rejected alliances with any social democratic forces.[4] Faced with the growing threat of fascism, the Comintern's Seventh World Congress adopted Popular Front politics in 1935, which mandated communists seek alliances with all those that opposed fascism, even capitalists.[5]

The CPUSA adopted Popular Front politics and pivoted from attacking the Roosevelt administration to backing it in the mid-1930s. As George Charney, a New York–based member of the CPUSA, recalled, "Overnight we adjusted our evaluation of Roosevelt and the New Deal. . . . We were reassured that patriotism was not necessarily reactionary[,] . . . that there was a difference between bourgeois democracy and fascism . . . and, above all, . . . a basis existed for common action between the Soviet Union and the bourgeois democratic tradition of the West."[6]

Browder, CPUSA secretary general, declared, "Fascism is un-American," exalted the nation's "Revolutionary Heritage," ceased to refer to the United States as an "oppressor nation," and defined the main issue of the 1936 U.S. presidential election as "Fascism vs. Democracy."[7] Under Browder's direction, the CPUSA called on its members to "Americanize" themselves, get involved in their communities, and work to improve people's lives that the Great Depression had ripped apart and devastated.[8] At the same time, the CPUSA held up the Soviet Union as the model to aspire to and the leader in the global fight against fascism. "The camp of progress and peace finds its stronghold in the Soviet Union, the country of socialist prosperity. To its banner are rallying all the growing armies of those who would resist fascism and war."[9]

Then, in response to the Molotov-Ribbentrop nonaggression pact between the Soviet Union and Nazi Germany (1939–41), the CPUSA abruptly abandoned the anti-fascist fight and, adopting the Soviet line, hailed the pact as providing "a firm step to peace."[10] It opposed U.S. involvement in the war, supported draft resisters, and blamed U.S. oligarchs, such as the Morgans, Du Ponts, and Rockefellers, for pushing the United States to get involved "in the imperialist struggle for the redivision of the world," which is how U.S. Communists characterized prowar sentiment.[11]

The CPUSA pivoted back to antifascism following Germany's 1941 invasion of the Soviet Union and rallied its forces to rejoin the antifascist struggle, defend the U.S.S.R., and support the war. In a move to allay Allies' fears of the so-called Red Peril, the Comintern dissolved itself in 1943.[12] Browder was so convinced that the U.S.S.R. and the United States were no longer enemies that he disbanded the CPUSA in 1943 (after the Comintern had dissolved itself).[13] The above-mentioned Communist Political Association (CPA) formed in 1944 as its replacement. Far from promoting class struggle or denouncing U.S. capitalism or imperialism, the CPA would "carry . . . forward and consolidat[e] nearly a century's efforts to establish a firmly-rooted American working-class organization of Marxists, inspired by our nation's democratic traditions and dedicated to the national interest and democratic aspirations of the American people."[14]

After the allies defeated Nazi Germany and fascist Italy in 1945 and Cold War rivalry replaced antifascist collaboration, Browder's predictions proved false and his position untenable. In July 1945 the CPUSA was reconstituted, and the national committee of the CPUSA expelled Browder and up to several thousand other members for "political deterioration."[15] The committee accused Browder of being a "renegade" and a "class enemy" who created "certain illusions among the workers and masses of people regarding the future relations between the capitalist and socialist systems."[16] William Z. Foster, who had challenged "the whole structure and essence of Browder's revisionist 'theories,'" became the new secretary general of the CPUSA, a position he held until his retirement in 1957.[17]

The history of the Puerto Rican Nationalist Party (PNPR) followed a very different trajectory than that of the CPUSA, although the political twists and turns described above brought the two parties together from the late 1930s through the early 1940s. The PRNP formed in 1922, more than two decades after the United States invaded and colonized Puerto Rico in 1898. For the next eight years, it focused on protecting Puerto Rican culture in the face of U.S. inroads into the archipelago's educational, political, and economic institutions and maintained cordial relations with the United States. That changed in 1930 when Pedro Albizu Campos was elected party president. Under his direction, confrontation, not conciliation, defined PNPR policies toward Washington. The party unambiguously demanded the end of U.S. colonialism and worked to expand its base to include poorer strata of Puerto Rican society. It formed armed militias to train men and some women to militarily challenge individuals and institutions that represented and perpetuated U.S. rule.[18]

Puerto Rican dissatisfaction with U.S. rule, manifested in strikes and protests, increased during the turbulent 1930s. In response, the U.S. government appointed Colonel Francis E. Riggs to head the Puerto Rican police force and General Blanton Winship as governor. Their mission: eliminate the Nationalists. Winship's and Riggs's repressive policies initiated an upward cycle of armed confrontations between proindependence and colonial forces. In 1936 Puerto Rican police killed four Nationalists as the latter drove in front of the flagship university in Río Piedras. In response, two Nationalists assassinated Riggs later that year; the police swiftly arrested and murdered them. The U.S. government further escalated tensions by arresting and charging the leadership of the Nationalist Party with sedition and other offenses. In response, several hundred peaceful Nationalists gathered in Ponce, a city on the southern coast of Puerto Rico, on March 21, 1937 (Palm Sunday), to demand their leaders' release. In what has come to be known as the Ponce Massacre, the police opened fire on the crowd, murdering nineteen marchers and wounding somewhere between 150 and 200 men, women, and children from among the Nationalists, onlookers, and even their fellow officers.[19]

A carefully selected jury found seven of the Nationalist leaders guilty in the second trial in 1937 and sent them to the Atlanta Federal Penitentiary (AFP) in Georgia to serve sentences of between six to ten years.[20] The exile of the PNPR leadership and the wave of anti-Nationalist repression that followed debilitated the party. Legal expenses, monetary support for the exiled prisoners and their families, a drop in membership, and declining contributions depleted the party treasury, which was never that abundant.[21] The party ended the decade in a considerably weaker position than it had begun it.

In contrast to the PRNP's history, that of the PCP was closely tied to the CPUSA. In 1934 the Comintern sent Alberto Sánchez, a Puerto Rican member of the CPUSA, to Puerto Rico to establish a Communist Party.[22] He arrived at the height of the Great Depression, a time when Puerto Ricans were experiencing increased immiseration, anger at and disenchantment with the capitalist system and U.S. colonialism, and a concomitant upsurge in protests and strikes. Sánchez embodied both the transnational nature of the communist movement in the early decades of the twentieth century and the fluid relationship that existed between Communists and Nationalists in the United States and Puerto Rico. First a Nationalist, Sánchez became a Communist after he emigrated to the United States in 1926, found work in different factories, and joined the CPUSA. In 1932 he was a CPUSA delegate to the International Red Aid Congress in Moscow.[23] After Sánchez arrived in Puerto Rico, he joined with five other men to form the PCP in 1934.[24] The fledging party affiliated with the Comintern in 1935.[25]

To symbolize the dual nature of its struggle, the PCP, which considered itself the "authentic party of the working class," was founded on September 23, 1934, the anniversary of the 1848 Grito de Lares (the Cry of Lares), when anticolonial rebels unsuccessfully rose up to end Spanish rule and establish the independent republic of Puerto Rico.[26] Unlike the PNPR, the PCP defined the working class, which at the time included agricultural, primarily sugar cane, workers; dockworkers; the transportation sector; and women who labored in the textile industry as the sole class capable of achieving real independence. César Andreu Iglesias, alternatively PCP president or secretary general from 1946 to 1953, stated, "The working class has the greatest interest in transforming society so as to obtain justice. The first stage of this transformation is to convert the ideals of the founding fathers of Lares into reality: conquer political sovereignty for the people."[27]

The PCP enjoyed a close relationship with the CPUSA. PCP members and leaders took CPUSA-directed courses in the United States. For example, Sánchez and Andreu Iglesias attended a six-week course at the National Communist School, known as Camp Unity, in upstate New York. Their subjects covered the history of Puerto Rico, propaganda, "how to proceed if the Party is declared illegal," use of the mimeograph and press, and organization.[28] Membership in the two parties was fluid. Two of the leaders of the PCP had first been members of the CPUSA. PCP leader Andreu Iglesias met his wife, U.S. Communist Jane Speed, when he was studying communism in the United States. She returned to Puerto Rico, joined the PCP, and became one of two women in the party's leadership.[29] The *Daily Worker*, the CPUSA newspaper, routinely carried news about the PCP and Puerto Rico; often the articles were translated versions of PCP articles.

The PCP was never large, and membership figures are hard to come by, although scholars agree that membership numbered six hundred at most in 1943.[30] The PCP dissolved itself in 1944, following the lead of the CPUSA, and reconstituted itself in 1946, once again mirroring the example set by the CPUSA, but apparently it never regained many members. Despite its small numbers, the party exercised substantial influence in the labor movement and held leadership positions in the left-wing Confederación General de Trabajadores (CGT, General Confederation of Workers). Nonetheless, it had no success in the electoral arena, as party candidates consistently failed to win races. Sánchez, one of the PCP founders and later its secretary general, did win election to the Puerto Rican House of Representatives but only after he quit the party and joined the Popular Democratic Party (PPD).[31]

From Conflict to Collaboration: Nationalists and Communists

The primary point of contact between the CPUSA and the PNPR was New York City, which simultaneously boasted the largest population of Puerto Ricans outside Puerto Rico and served as headquarters for the CPUSA.[32] Interactions between the two organizations were rocky in the early to mid-1930s, primarily due to political differences and each party's drive to win the allegiance of the Puerto Rican community for itself. The parties' relationships hit rock bottom in 1932, when tensions between the two groups ran particularly high. At issue was the Nationalists' position that Puerto Ricans' political priority was to end U.S. colonial rule over the archipelago. The proindependence party believed Puerto Ricans outside the archipelago were "exiles," whose primary duty was to redeem "our native soil," rather than focus on improving their conditions in New York. The CPUSA, on the other hand, supported independence and the fight against "exploitation being suffered by Puerto Ricans in New York." Differences between the two groups escalated and members of the two parties challenged each other at public rallies, which occasionally led to street fights, and once culminated in a communist killing—or at least being accused of killing—a Nationalist, Angel Feliú.[33]

Connections between the parties improved as the decade progressed, for four reasons. First, the CPUSA and PCP's adoption of Popular Front politics encouraged the CPUSA to seek common ground with the Nationalists. Second, all three parties opposed colonialism and imperialism and backed independence for Puerto Rico, which provided a basis for joint work. Third, both the PNPR and CPUSA received concrete benefits from enhanced links with each other, as discussed below. Fourth, Browder, secretary general of the CPUSA, developed friendships with the Nationalist leaders when they were imprisoned together in the Atlanta Federal Penitentiary. These personal relationships enriched the political ties between them, which enhanced their ability to work together.

PCP overtures to the PNPR in Puerto Rico demonstrate the former's attempts to implement Popular Front politics by drawing on the two parties' shared goals of independence and improving Puerto Rican' lives. They also reveal persistent tensions between the two parties. The PNPR planned to hold its annual national assembly in December 1935. In November 1935, PCP leader Sánchez wrote to Albizu Campos. After extending his good wishes for the assembly's success, Sánchez stated that the PCP "wanted to contribute all its forces and ideology to avoid disunity among those who sincerely and honorably struggle for the total economic and political independence of Puerto Rico." He listed four points with which the PCP "was in total agreement with the Nationalist Party": the absolute independence of Puerto Rico; opposition to Yankee imperialism and imperialist war; opposition to the barbaric and selfish exploitation of the Puerto Rican productive class (*brazo productor*); and for an education system democratically led by Puerto Rican teachers and students. (Proindependence forces demanded Puerto Ricans control the archipelago's educational system and that classes be taught in Spanish.) Sánchez then asked the PNPR to name a commission to work with a similarly appointed commission from the PCP to "create a popular, united, and anti-imperialist front" that would forge "a unified struggle and a free Puerto Rico for Puerto Ricans."[34]

Although the PNPR welcomed the PCP's support, it insisted on maintaining its independence and, consequently, invited the Communists to join the Nationalist Party. A series of letters between Sánchez and Albizu Campos after Puerto Rican police shot and killed the aforementioned Nationalist Party members in front of the University of Puerto Rico in Río Piedras in October 1935 illustrates where each party stood on the issue of unity. The day after the police murders, Sánchez wrote a letter to Albizu Campos, which three members of the PCP personally delivered to the Nationalist Party during the memorial service it held for its four assassinated comrades. Sánchez expressed the PCP's wish that "the blood shed by the self-sacrificing fighters for our nation's and our people's liberation will not be in vain." He closed the letter calling for "our people's free-dom from the foreign yoke."[35]

Juan Juarbe, Albizu Campos's secretary, responded to Sánchez two weeks later. Juarbe first thanked Sánchez for the "act of solidarity, which reflects the standards established by the great teachers of communism, Marx, Lenin, Engels, and Trotsky, who have stated that Nationalism constitutes the united front of occupied nations."[36] He then called on PCP members to "join the Nationalist ranks . . . since any division in this time of foreign intervention only favors imperialism, which tries to destroy us." Juarbe clarified the differences between the two parties: "Our mission ends with the foundation of an independent, free, and sovereign republic. Only then can we freely determine the social consti-tution that will suit our nation's needs."[37] In other words, the PNPR refused to advocate socialism or any economic policy prior to independence. Despite the rebuff, the PCP persisted in its efforts to work more closely with the PNPR, as we see below. However, in a reflection of the influence the CPUSA had over the PCP, ties between the PCP and the PNPR advanced in tandem with improved relations between the CPUSA and the PNPR in the United States.

A combination of Popular Front policies, shared support for independence, mutual advantages, and individual friendships paved the way to better relations between the Nationalists and the Communists. As noted above, the imprison-ment of Nationalist Party leaders in the Atlanta Federal Penitentiary and gov-ernment repression of party members and supporters contributed to a decline in the party's membership, base of support and, consequently, finances. The scarcity of funds severely limited the prisoners' ability to pay their legal fees or purchase necessities in the commissary, let alone cover their families' expenses, given the imprisoned men had been their family's breadwinner. Vito Marcan-tonio, one of Albizu Campos's lawyers and congressional representative from East Harlem, the New York City neighborhood in which many Puerto Ricans lived, worked to ameliorate the prisoners' conditions.[38]

Marcantonio fought tirelessly for the independence of Puerto Rico and the freedom of the Nationalist prisoners.[39] Although not a member of the CPUSA (he was a member of the American Labor Party), he played a critical role in advancing its politics and interests. He not only advocated the party's political agenda in Congress but he also served as a national spokesman for progressive causes the CPUSA supported. For example, he called for the release of Tom Mooney, a political prisoner and labor and left-wing activist; backed the Spanish Republic; and fought for the end of the U.S. poll tax that discriminated against poor people, especially Blacks.[40] He also headed the International Labor Defense (ILD), a CPUSA-sponsored organization that supported political prisoners in the United States and was the U.S. branch of the Comintern's International Red Aid.[41] In addition to his legal work on behalf of the Nationalist prisoners, Marcantonio made sure that the ILD sent them a check of between $3 to $5 every month to cover their commissary purchases.[42] When Albizu Campos arrived in New York City after his release from the AFP, Marcantonio, along with Browder, was there to meet him.[43]

The alliance among Marcantonio, the CPUSA, and the PRNP, while based on shared values, also brought distinct advantages to each party. Because Marcantonio was such a valuable figure in the CPUSA's political constellation, the party devoted time, energy, and resources to ensuring his election. The party understood that Nationalist support of Marcantonio greatly enhanced his chances of winning. CPUSA leader Charney noted, "The nationalist movement in Puerto Rico, headed by Pedro Albizu Campos, dominated the politics of 'El Barrio.'"[44] Support for the Nationalist Party and its prisoners and opposition to U.S. repression and rule ran high in East Harlem. For example, ten thousand Puerto Ricans marched through East Harlem in 1936 "to protest the attitude and actions of 'Imperialistic America' in making 'slaves' of the natives of the island." As they marched, they shouted, "Free Puerto Rico!" and "Down with Yankee Imperialism!"[45] The CPUSA and Marcantonio provided the Nationalists with legal counsel and financial resources, and the PNPR, in turn, helped get out the vote that returned Marcantonio, the voice of the CPUSA in Washington, to Congress.[46]

Friendships between Browder and the imprisoned Nationalist Party leaders served to cement the tripartite relationships. Convicted of passport fraud, Browder arrived at the AFP in January 1940. Imprisoned in harsh conditions and isolated from the family he loved and his political comrades, Browder turned to the Nationalist prisoners for conversation and companionship. Their joint imprisonment, lengthy discussions, and political compatibility increased Browder's, and by extension the CPUSA's, and the Nationalists' willingness and ability to work together.[47] The relationships they forged in prison persisted after they were released from the AFP and subsequently reunited in New York City in 1943.[48] When he was still in prison, Browder had promised Albizu Campos the CPUSA would throw its political weight and organizational resources into building a solidarity movement in the United States in favor of Puerto Rican independence, an offer the Nationalists welcomed and the CPUSA pursued.[49]

One of the most important projects that resulted from this relationship was *Pueblos Hispanos*.

Pueblos Hispanos

Pueblos Hispanos, a Spanish-language newspaper published in New York City in 1943 and 1944, was a joint project of the PNPR and the CPUSA.[50] James W. Ford, a CPUSA leader who had represented the party on issues relating to Latin America, helped to develop the publication.[51] In his April 1943 report to party leaders, he clarified that "the paper is not to be a Communist Party paper," but it "supports its broad win-the-war and anti-fascist program." Indeed, the paper aimed to "unit[e] Spanish-speaking peoples to win the war, concentrating on the Puerto Rican people, their problems here in the United States as well as for [the] independence of Puerto Rico within the framework of the United Nations coalition to defeat the Axis powers."[52]

Pueblos Hispanos encompassed and projected U.S., transnational, and international forces and politics. Consuelo Lee Tapia, a Puerto Rican member of the CPUSA, administered the paper, and Corretjer, secretary general of the PNPR, directed it. Its editorial committee included Lee Tapia, Corretjer, Ford, Ernestina González (who represented Spanish Republicans), and Armando Román, a leader of the Lower Harlem section of the Communist Party.[53] The newspaper featured Popular Front politics, Puerto Rican nationalism, and transhemispheric and global coverage and perspective.[54] Although it was primarily distributed in New York City, it was disseminated elsewhere in the Americas. The CPUSA, which provided the financial backing, and Spanish-language organizations, such as the Lower Harlem section of the Communist Party, delivered the paper to sixty newsstands across New York City. The paper was also sent to Latin American embassies in Washington and to some Latin American countries, including Cuba.[55]

Each issue reflected the distinct and combined goals of both parties. *Pueblos Hispanos* simultaneously centered Puerto Rico and positioned it in the context of Latin America, while antifascist politics shaped the newspaper's coverage. The paper consistently featured activities and campaigns jointly sponsored by the two parties. For example, the first issue included a column on the Spanish Civil War by Leonard Lamb, Lee Tapia's husband and a captain in the International Brigades; congratulatory messages from Mexican labor leader and Marxist Vicente Lombardo Toledano and poet and Chilean Communist Party member Pablo Neruda; Corretjer's report on Albizu Campos, who was still a prisoner in the AFP; and an analysis of fascism in Europe.[56] The first page of the second issue featured an article by Charles Collins, "Puerto Rico Is the Key to the Liberation of All the Peoples of the Caribbean," and one by Valentina Martín, a "Spanish Mother," titled "I Accuse: They Have Killed Six of My Children" (figure 1).[57]

A trio of news items exemplifies how the editors closely intertwined their shared perspectives on fascism and antifascism, Puerto Rico, and progressive

Figure 1. This cover of *Pueblos Hispanos*, a PNPR-CPUSA–produced newspaper, brings together support for Puerto Rican independence and the Spanish Republic, February 27, 1943. Source: The New York Public Library, microfilm, American Historical Newspapers.

politics in the United States through their national and international coverage. The first article critiqued bilingualism in Puerto Rico, the second condemned the arrest of Argentinian Communist and Comintern envoy Victorio Codovilla, and the third backed Marcantonio's opposition to the poll tax for U.S. Blacks.[58] The article on Puerto Rico, "Negación oficial del bilinguismo" (Official denial of bilingualism), criticized U.S. government policy that forced Puerto Rican teachers to teach in English and condemned José Gallardo, the U.S.-appointed Puerto Rican commissioner of public education, who imposed the practice.[59] Both the PCP and the nationalists advocated classes be taught in Spanish. *Pueblos Hispanos* editors characterized Gallardo as lacking "even an ounce of patriotic consciousness" because he favored English, the language of the invader, over Spanish, Puerto Rico's language. Gallardo's preference for English aligned with his belief that Puerto Rico was part of the United States, not an occupied nation. Indeed, Gallardo wanted to make sure that "the next generation of Puerto Rican citizens acquires absolute facility in the English language," which, according to him, "is the language of our nation!"[60]

The article, "Victorio Codovilla encarcelado" (Victorio Codovilla imprisoned), highlights how Argentine Communists' participation with noncommunist forces (the Radical Party) in antifascist activities led to government repression directed against the former. It recounts that Codovilla, the "notable Argentine Communist leader [who is] admired throughout Latin America" was engaged in "preparations for . . . the historic anti-fascist demonstration in Buenos Aires." As he was speaking about the activity with a leader of the Argentine Radical Party, "Special Police" force arrested him and sent him to "a concentration camp in the Southern desert of Argentina."[61]

The third article, "Marcantonio defiende legislación contra impuesto sobre el voto" (Marcantonio defends legislation opposing a poll tax), consisted of reprinted excerpts from Marcantonio's speech that was first published in the *Daily Worker*, the CPUSA newspaper. Reflecting the Browder line that communists are patriotic Americans, Marcantonio first referenced Thomas Jefferson, who declared, "All men have been created equal," and, therefore, are similarly entitled to vote. He then pointed out how important such a measure was in times of war. It would not only "raise the morale of our thirteen million loyal Negro citizens," it would also offer "clear evidence . . . to our allies . . . and to the colonized peoples of India, Africa, Latin America and the Caribbean . . . of our absolute determination to win this war for a free and democratic world."[62]

Pueblos Hispanos ceased publication somewhat abruptly in October 1944. Corretjer wrote to Browder to inform him that "after 20 intense months of struggle in the antifascist front and for the independence of Puerto Rico," *Pueblos Hispanos* had "suspended publication." The reason Corretjer gave was that he wanted to "help the development of *La Voz de la CGT*, the official organ of the General Confederation of Puerto Rican Workers, which recently began publication in San Juan, Puerto Rico."[63] Of course, the real reasons are more complicated. Corretjer, who had been moving closer to the CPUSA, fell in love with Lee Tapia, as she did with him. She, in turn, sought membership in the Nationalist Party. Albizu Campos rejected her petition for membership because he considered her more of a Communist than a Nationalist and because he feared that her affair with Corretjer, which led to her divorce from CPUSA hero Lamb, would damage the PNPR's relationship with the CPUSA. Albizu Campos similarly expelled Corretjer from the party because of his growing affiliation with communism and the threat his relationship with Lee Tapia potentially posed for CPUSA-PNPR relations.[64]

The CPUSA and PNPR's collaboration on *Pueblos Hispanos* encouraged improved relations between the PNPR and PCP in Puerto Rico. Unlike in 1935, when the PNPR rebuffed the PCP's suggestion to "create a popular, united, and anti-imperialist front," the PNPR invited the PCP to address its 1943 annual assembly in Puerto Rico, a turn of events that received positive coverage in *Pueblos Hispanos*. Yet, despite the notably better relations of the three parties, marked differences remained, as two *Pueblos Hispanos* articles on the Nationalist assembly illustrate.

The first article, which Corretjer probably wrote, reflected the PNPR's assessment of the meeting. It reported on the election of Albizu Campos as party president, Corretjer for general secretary, and a dozen or so other officers to the PNPR Junta Nacional (the National Board, which served as the party's governing body). The article then focused on one of the party's key resolutions, which affirmed the party's commitment to incorporate "the principles of a true democracy, which include all the democratic and social conquests that animate the spirit of our times." After confirming the party's alignment with democracy and democratic nations and condemnation of fascism, the newspaper asserted Puerto Rico's right to independence: "The only way the United States can consolidate and establish friendship and trust with the free peoples of the Americas and strengthen inter-American solidarity, which is essential for the preservation and survival of the democratic institutions and security of the hemisphere, is if it immediately welcomes a Puerto Rican [delegation] to negotiate the U.S. military's exit from the Island and recognizes the Republic of Puerto Rico."[65] It further called on Roosevelt and British prime minister Winston Churchill to fulfill the promise they made in the Atlantic Charter to "establish a purely democratic order in the world, inspired by respect for the legitimate right of peoples to live their life according to the principle of self-determination."[66] In other words, the PNPR pledged its support for democracy and to democratic forces and, at the same time, maintained its right to struggle for a free Puerto Rico even as the global war against fascism raged.[67]

The second article focused on PCP president Juan Santos Rivera's speech at the Nationalist assembly. Santos Rivera framed the struggle for independence as part of the antifascist battle and, unlike the Nationalists, explicitly referenced the working class and peasants, the "vast majority of whom resolutely support independence." The article continued, "The war we are waging against Nazi fascism is a revolutionary war of national defense of all the peoples of the world." Instead of denouncing U.S. forces that occupied the island, as the Nationalists did, Santos Rivera condemned prostatehood elements in Puerto Rico who support colonial rule because it allows them to perpetuate the "exploitation, hunger, and misery" of the working class and peasants. Santos Rivera made no mention of the U.S. government. The PCP president concluded that the party was fighting for a "free and democratic republic" and that by "defending the immediate interests of all the people, it would not only improve the economic [well-being] of the masses it would also . . . reinforce unity among the democratic nations against Hitlerism."[68]

In short, the PNPR prioritized the struggle for an independent nation. It upheld democracy and aligned itself with democratic forces but pointedly called on both the United States and, secondarily, the United Kingdom to follow through on their promises to end colonialism and grant independence to their colonies. The PNPR spoke from the perspective of colonized Nationalists who knew that the defeat of fascism would not deliver Puerto Rican independence because the nation that ruled them would emerge victorious from the war. And, unlike the PCP, it viewed Puerto Ricans as one people and largely ignored class.

The PCP, however, positioned Puerto Rico's independence as dependent upon the global defeat of fascism and Puerto Rican prostatehooders, the Puerto Rican version of the nonnational bourgeoisie. In line with Popular Front politics, the PCP refrained from mentioning, let alone criticizing, the United States or demanding independence. It, like the CPUSA, championed the Roosevelt administration and defined an Allied victory in World War II, which represented the triumph of the Soviet Union, as the central task of communists globally. It portrayed victory against Nazism as both indispensable and the prelude to achieving better lives for Puerto Rican workers and peasants. Fascism abroad and prostatehood forces domestically, not Washington, were the adversary. These two distinct perspectives on who the enemy is and what the goal is encapsulate the key differences between the Nationalists and the Communists in this period, as did the question of whether or not Puerto Ricans should serve in the U.S. armed forces.

The PNPR argued that patriotic Puerto Ricans should not be part of the military that occupied their homeland.[69] As a result, one hundred Nationalist men refused military service during World War II and received sentences ranging from one to five years.[70] The U.S. government also convicted four successive committees of Nationalist Party leaders for "conspiring to obstruct the draft" and exiled them to prisons in the United States.[71] The PCP, on the other hand, encouraged members to join the U.S. military both to defeat fascism and to strengthen Puerto Rico's demand for independence. PCP members, including Andreu Iglesias, enlisted in the U.S. military in a show of patriotic and political duty.[72] Santos Rivera related, "Our soldiers march to the battle fields of Europe and the Pacific along with the U.S. armed forces." They did so, he argued, "because Puerto Ricans understand we need to join with [those fighting] the war[s] of national liberation because that is the only way to obtain and guarantee freedom for all peoples, including our own."[73]

Political Differences Persist

The CPUSA's backing of the Roosevelt administration in the joint fight against fascism contradicted its support for Puerto Rican independence. U.S. military strategists considered Puerto Rico essential to Washington's ability to control the Caribbean area against Nazi incursions.[74] Roosevelt Roads Naval Base, comprising land on Puerto Rico's east coast and the island of Vieques, was one of the largest U.S. Navy bases in the world, big enough to shelter the entire British Navy, should such refuge be required.[75] Ernest Gruening, one of Roosevelt's key advisers on Latin America and the director of the federal Division of Territories and Island Possessions, regarded U.S. control of Puerto Rico as vital to the promotion of U.S. policies across Latin America.[76] Naturally, U.S. officials rejected independence.

By the early 1940s, Luis Muñoz Marín, the leader of the Popular Democratic Party (PPD), was the Roosevelt administration's man in San Juan. The PPD advocated greater autonomy for Puerto Rico in the framework of an ongoing colonial relationship with the United States. (In 1952 the party presided over the establishment of the Free Associated State.) Even though the CPUSA promoted independence, it backed Muñoz Marín and other PPD candidates and embraced New Deal appointees and plans for the archipelago. Corretjer's comments that open this chapter reflected his awareness of this contradiction and his refusal to conform to policies that would backpedal independence.

The CPUSA's and the PCP's endorsements of Washington's New Deal poli-cies in Puerto Rico were clear in the July 1939 Congress of Youth held in New York City.[77] Julia Rivera, likely a PCP member, represented Puerto Rico at the meeting. Instead of unequivocally demanding independence, she said, "We feel it is time the present status of Puerto Rico be terminated," a statement vague enough to be open to multiple interpretations. In an apparent nod to the New Deal, she added the archipelago needed "concrete aid . . . through public works programs and better educational facilities."[78] The general resolutions of the Congress did not ask the U.S. government to end colonial rule but to "Give a New Deal to Puerto Rico," offering one more indication that Communists were willing to back the Roosevelt administration's plans and shelve the demand for independence.[79]

The PCP fell in line behind the CPUSA.[80] Despite its commitment to inde-pendence, it, too, backed the PPD.[81] The PCP defended its support for the PPD by claiming the party was better than other Puerto Rican parties, which sup-ported statehood and were "enemies of the working class and independence."[82] Instead, the PPD was "anti-corporations and backed by the masses of workers and peasants."[83] Further, the PPD represented "the interests of the Puerto Rican nationalist bourgeoisie," which, "in this historical moment, coincide with the immediate interests of the working and peasant class."[84]

• • •

Over the next few years, some of the individuals described above changed positions, both politically and geographically. The reconstituted CPUSA ousted Browder in 1946 and replaced him with Foster. Foster and the CPUSA continued to call for Puerto Rican independence, but the new secretary general failed to develop the close relationship with Albizu Campos or the Nationalist Party that Browder did.[85] Foster did, however, travel to Puerto Rico and wrote articles and a pamphlet and spoke in public about the miserable conditions Puerto Ricans living in the U.S. colony endured.[86]

Albizu Campos remained in New York City until 1947, when his parole ended, and he could return to Puerto Rico. Rapturous crowds met him at the dock to celebrate his arrival.[87] Corretjer and Lee Tapia married, returned to Puerto Rico via Cuba, and joined the PCP. PCP leader Andreu Iglesias called for Corretjer's expulsion in March 1948 due to his "ingrained insurrectional tendencies," which are "the logical result of his bourgeois-nationalist sectarianism."[88]

Examining the CPUSA, PCP, and PRNP's tri-partite relationship through a transnational lens and in connection with each other illuminates each party's political positions more clearly. It illuminates how closely the PCP's position on the Nationalist Party mirrored that of the CPUSA, which suggests, ironically, that the ties between the two communist parties reflected, to some extent, Washington's colonial connection to Puerto Rico. Although the CPUSA and PCP opposed colonialism, their commitment to Puerto Rican independence was often shaped by the global communist movement's political priorities, as was their relationship to the Puerto Rican Nationalist Party. During the class-versus-class period in the early 1930s, the CPUSA considered the PRNP bourgeois nationalists and targeted them as a rival if not a threat. While the CPUSA called for independence, it focused on organizing Puerto Ricans in New York City to join the class struggle, which it led, against U.S. capitalism.

Popular Front politics led to a radical reorientation of both communist parties' politics and practices. They then considered the Nationalist Party a significant ally against fascism and worked to shore up their relations with it. It is not clear how the Molotov-Ribbentrop Pact affected relations, if, in fact, it did. But after Germany invaded the Soviet Union in 1941, the CPUSA and PCP both reverted to the Popular Front politics of the late 1930s and intensified their backing of the Allied war effort to defeat fascism. In the process the PCP threw its support behind the PPD, which was allied with the Roosevelt administration and, therefore, an ally in the fight against fascism. The PCP even backed the PPD's candidates in the 1940 elections, a decision that weakened its standing among the labor movement. However, the PCP's 1943 dissolution, which one historian has characterized as "a colonial mandate from the CPUSA," dealt the party a blow from which it never recovered.[89] As historian Luis Díaz points out, when the party reconstituted itself in 1946, only "a nucleus of its founding members and [some] young activists remained."[90]

The Nationalist Party, for its part, never wavered in its determination to secure a free homeland. It was quite willing to work with the Communists, when their politics aligned and when it suited its interests, but it refused to tailor its struggle for independence to the fight against fascism or the Comintern's agenda. It opposed Puerto Rican men serving in the armed forces of the nation that colonized Puerto Rico because the Nationalist Party believed, correctly, that the defeat of fascism would not lead to the end of U.S colonialism. However, it was quite willing to carry through on the plans Albizu Campos, Browder, and Corretjer had made when they were imprisoned together in the AFP to produce *Pueblos Hispanos*, which promoted antifascism and independence for Puerto Rico.

Notes

1. Communist Political Association, *Path to Peace*, 97.
2. Under the leadership of Luis Muñoz Marín, the PPD sought and obtained backing and resources from the Roosevelt administration. The PPD, in turn, opened the archipelago to U.S. military installations, supported the drafting of Puerto Rican men,

and declared "immediate social reforms," not Puerto Rico's status, was its key electoral issue in 1940. Ayala and Bernabe, *Puerto Rico*, 137.

3. For a discussion of the party's founding, early days, the different organizations that comprised it, and the numerous divisions that occurred within it during the 1920s, see Zumoff, *Communist International and U.S. Communism*, esp. chap. 1.

4. Eley, *Forging Democracy*, chaps. 17 and 18.

5. Dimitrov, "Fascist Offensive," in Dimitrov, *Selected Works*.

6. Charney, *Long Journey*, 59.

7. Browder, *Democracy or Fascism*, 9.

8. Gosse, "'To Organize in Every Neighborhood,'" 112–13. Browder sought to make U.S. communists, the majority of whom were foreign born, less different and more like regular "Americans." Draper, *American Communism and Soviet Russia*, 189.

9. Browder, *Democracy or Fascism*, 6.

10. "A Smashing Blow at Munich Treachery and Aggression," *Daily Worker* (New York), August 25, 1939.

11. "Opponents of Draft Get a Year and a Day," *Daily Worker* (New York), November 15, 1940; "The Peace Issue and the Voters," *Daily Worker* (New York), November 15, 1940. George Charney remembered the policy shift as "revolting," yet "in spite of these shattering experiences, our faith held. The Soviet Union could not be wrong. It was still the socialist fatherland." Charney, *Long Journey*, 60.

12. As Dimitrov put it, "fascism, desirous of winning these masses to its own side, tries to set the mass of the working people in town and countryside against the revolutionary proletariat, frightening the petty bourgeoisie with the bogey of the 'Red Peril.'" See Dimitrov, "Anti-Fascist People's Front," in Dimitrov, *Selected Works*.

13. The only other party that followed suit was the PCP, which was both dependent on and under the sway of the CPUSA.

14. Communist Political Association, *Path to Peace*, 93.

15. Isserman, *Which Side Were You On*, 240.

16. Thompson, *Path of a Renegade*, 4. Further, Thompson declared Browder ignored "the inherently reactionary class character of monopoly capital and its role and objectives in relation to imperialist expansion, imperialist super-profits, and exploitation of the working class and people."

17. Thompson, *Path of a Renegade*, 7; Isserman, *Which Side Were You On*, 240–41.

18. For a succinct history of the PNPR, see Power, "Rise of the Puerto Rican Nationalist Party."

19. For an authoritative analysis of the event, see Hays, *Report of the Commission of Inquiry*.

20. Rosado, *Pedro Albizu Campos*, 255; Paralitici, *Sentencia Impuesta*, 413.

21. It is not clear that the PNPR kept membership records, or if they did, I have not located them. According to Federal Bureau of Investigation records, PNPR membership peaked in 1936 at 3,000 and declined to 565 in 1950. Although these numbers are likely too low and fail to consider supporters, they do offer a picture of the decrease in membership that occurred in this period. Federal Bureau of Investigation, *Nationalist*

Party of Puerto Rico (NPPR), San Juan, Puerto Rico, July 31, 1952, SJ 100-3, 23:6, https://archive.org/.

22. In the early 1920s, the Comintern sent U.S. communist James Sager to create a communist party in Puerto Rico. His efforts failed. For background on Sager's attempt and the history of the PCP, see Pujals, "La presencia," and Díaz, "El gobierno." Comintern agent Charles Phillips, a cofounder of the Mexican Communist Party and later a member of the CPUSA, coordinated Sager's mission. Shipman, *It Had to Be Revolution*.

23. Jeifets and Jeifets, *América Latina*, 559; Díaz, "El gobierno," chap. 3, 15; Pujals, "Una perla," 137.

24. Díaz, "El gobierno," chap. 3, 16–17.

25. Díaz, "El gobierno," chaps. 4 and 5.

26. Andreu Iglesias, *Independencia y Socialismo*, 43; Jiménez de Wagenheim, *Puerto Rico's Revolt*. In the 1930s the Nationalist Party resurrected the largely ignored anticolonial battle and traced the origins of the Puerto Rican nation to it. Power, "Nationalism in a Colonized Nation," 124.

27. Andreu Iglesias, *Independencia y Socialismo*, 43. For a biography of Andreu Iglesias, see Fromm, *Cesar Andreu Iglesias*. Andreu Iglesias joined the PCP in 1936, rose to prominence in its trade union secretariat, and was elected to the executive committee of the Confederación General de Trabajadores (CGT, General Confederation of Workers). Andreu Iglesias, *Independencia y Socialismo*, 145–46.

28. Committee on the Judiciary, "Communist Threat to the United States," 1311.

29. "Jane Speed de Abreu: Former Communist," file 48, box 9, Robert J. Alexander Papers, Special Collections, Rutgers University, Rutgers, New Jersey. The other woman was Consuelo Burgos, sister of Julia de Burgos, famous Puerto Rican poet and Nationalist.

30. Ayala and Bernabe, *Puerto Rico*, 138.

31. Ayala and Bernabe, *Puerto Rico*, 138–40; Pujals, "Soviet Caribbean," 263–64.

32. In 1910 roughly 2,000 Puerto Ricans lived in the United States; by 1940 that number had shot up to 69,967, primarily in New York City, where they were concentrated in the Upper East Side. Acosta-Belén, *Puerto Ricans*, 13; Gosse, *Where the Boys Are*, 20.

33. Vega and Andreu Iglesias, *Memoirs of Bernardo Vega*, 171–72. These brawls occurred during the Third Period (1928–34), when the Comintern promoted "class against class" politics and called on communist parties around the world to oppose alliances with forces, such as the Nationalists, that rejected class struggle.

34. "Un mensaje comunista," *El Mundo* (San Juan, Puerto Rico), November 7, 1935. Sánchez wrote in the name of "the Political Bureau of the Communist Party (Puerto Rican Section and the Communist International)."

35. "Correspondencia de hombres," *La Palabra* (San Juan, Puerto Rico), November 18, 1935.

36. Although Leon Trotsky had been expelled from the Bolshevik Party by then and was soon to be exiled from the Soviet Union altogether, the Nationalists included him in

the list. Trotsky supported both the Nationalist Party and Puerto Rican independence. When he was in exile in Mexico, he lauded the Nationalists because they denounced imperialism in general, not just in "its fascist form." Ayala and Bernabe, *Puerto Rico*, 110.

37. Ayala and Bernabe, *Puerto Rico*, 110.

38. Marcantonio's papers, which are housed in the New York Public Library, bulge with letters from Puerto Ricans in New York City and in Puerto Rico and his responses to them.

39. For the speeches he delivered and the bill he presented in Congress in favor of Puerto Ricans, independence, and the release of the nationalist prisoners, see Rubinstein, *I Vote My Conscience*, 375–439.

40. Rubinstein, *I Vote My Conscience*, iii, 172–76; Schaffer, *Vito Marcantonio*, 89–91.

41. Meyer, "Pedro Albizu Campos," 97.

42. FBI, *Nationalist Party*, 185–86. Ironically, this alerted the FBI to the budding relationship between the PNPR and the CPUSA. In one of the agency's first memos on the issue, a Puerto Rico–based FBI agent informed director J. Edgar Hoover in 1939 that the "International Labor Defense in New York sent an air mail to the [Atlanta] prison enclosing $5.00 to each one of the seven Nationalists saying to use this money for cigarettes and to keep their spirits up." FBI, *Nationalist Party*, "Memo from Special Agent to J. Edgar Hoover," December 5, 1939, https://archive.org/; Vito Marcantonio to Juan Antonio Corretjer, July 21, 1939, box 46, "Correspondence of Juan Antonio Corretjer," Marcantonio Papers, New York Public Library.

43. "Pedro Albizu Campos," May 11, 1954, memo, FBI file 105-11898, 2, https://archive.org.

44. Charney, *Long Journey*, 107.

45. "10,000 Parade Here," *New York Times*, August 30, 1936.

46. PNPR leaders observed, "In 1936, [the Nationalists] played an active part in the elections . . . by backing the candidacy of Vito Marcantonio. . . . Again in 1938 the organization threw its forces behind the candidacy of Marcantonio, *and its support was one of the deciding factors of his overwhelming victory*." Testa, "Puerto Rican Nationalist Movement," 2 (emphasis added). I thank Lorrin Thomas for sharing copies of the *Spanish Book* with me.

47. When Browder applied for a passport in 1934, he failed to report he had traveled to the Soviet Union, Germany, Italy, and China in the 1920s under an assumed name, which was a crime. Flynn, Earl Browder, 13, 20, 22; "Browder Is Loser in Supreme Court," *New York Times*, February 18, 1941.

48. For an exploration of their friendship and its political consequences, see Power, "Friends and Comrades."

49. Rodríguez-Fraticelli, "Pedro Albizu Campos," 29.

50. As Cristina Pérez Jiménez notes, PH "sought to strengthen ties between supporters of the Puerto Rican Nationalist Party and CPUSA members and sympathizers." "Puerto Rican Colonialism," 51.

51. Jeifets and Jeifets, *América Latina*, 220. Ford was also the party's vice-presidential candidate in 1932, 1946, and 1940. In 1932 the presidential candidate was William Z.

Foster; in 1936 and 1940 it was Earl Browder. The CPUSA candidates received 102,785, 80,259, and 46,251 votes, respectively, in those years. Gregory, "Mapping American Social Movements."

52. James W. Ford, "Concerning the Spanish Language Paper P.H.," April 1, 1943, "Pueblos Hispanos, 1944," box 30, Earl Browder Papers, Special Collections Research Center, Syracuse University Libraries, Syracuse, New York.

53. Lee Tapia had first joined the PCP in 1937 but joined the CPUSA after she moved to New York City. Pérez Rosario, *Becoming Julia de Burgos*, 2.

54. For the CPUSA's perspective on PH and its relevance to the antifascist fight, see "Everybody in Spanish-Speaking Harlem Is at War against Axis," *Daily Worker* (New York), February 3, 1943, 3.

55. Ford, "Concerning the Spanish Language Paper P.H.," 1; Rosado, *Pedro Albizu Campos*, 289; Meyer, "Pedro Albizu Campos," 102.

56. *Pueblos Hispanos* (New York), no. 1, February 20, 1943.

57. *Pueblos Hispanos* (New York), no. 2, February 27, 1943.

58. *Pueblos Hispanos* (New York), no, 3, March 6, 1943.

59. For a discussion of U.S. education policies in Puerto Rico and how Puerto Rican teachers negotiated them, see Del Moral, *Negotiating Empire*.

60. *Pueblos Hispanos* (New York), no. 3, March 6, 1943, 5.

61. *Pueblos Hispanos* (New York), 5, 11. According to the *Daily Worker* (New York), Codovilla was meeting with a commission from the Radical Party to "promote a National Union organization." The Argentine Minister of the Interior issued a statement declaring, "The government doesn't desire the unity of Radicalism with the Communists." "Fight Castillo Gestapo, Argentine Communists Call," *Daily Worker* (New York), February 26, 1942, 2.

62. *Pueblos Hispanos* (New York), no. 3, March 6, 1943, 5.

63. Juan Antonio Corretjer, "Letter to Earl Browder," October 30, 1944, box 30, "Pueblos Hispanos, 1944," Earl Browder Papers, Special Collections Research Center, Syracuse University Libraries, Syracuse, New York.

64. Corretjer had been the PNPR representative to the CPUSA, and Lee Tapia had been the CPUSA representative to the PNPR, which heightened Albizu Campos' concerns regarding how their romance could affect relations between the two parties. For a fuller discussion of the situation, see Power, "Friends and Comrades."

65. "Puerto Rico: Republicanos, Comunistas en Convención Nacionalista en Caguas," *Pueblo Hispanos* (New York), March 13, 1943, 10.

66. "Puerto Rico: Republicanos, Comunistas en Convención Nacionalista en Caguas," *Pueblo Hispanos* (New York), March 13, 1943, 5, 10.

67. The article echoes Corretjer's speech at the founding of the Communist Political Association, which opens this chapter.

68. "El Partido Comunista Puertorriqueño Pide la Independencia de la Isla," *Pueblos Hispanos* (New York), April 3, 1943.

69. Paralitici, *La repression*, 74.

70. Paralitici, *Sentencia Impuesta*, 80.

71. Medina Ramírez, *El movimiento libertador*, 209–10; Paralitici, *Sentencia Impuesta*, 85, 418.

72. Díaz, "El gobierno," 26.

73. Santos Rivera, *Puerto Rico ayer*, 14–15.

74. Rodríguez Beruff, "Rediscovering Puerto Rico"; Qayum, "German Blockade."

75. García Muñiz, "U.S. Military Installations," 55.

76. Johnson, "Anti-Imperialism," 96.

77. Marino, "Pan-American Feminism," 6; Reiman, *New Deal*, 42. The American Youth Congress was the U.S. branch of the World Congress of Youth, which was "organized by the popular-front International Committee of Youth."

78. "Proceeding of Congress of Youth," July 1–5, 1939, New York City, box 2, Communist Party Pamphlets 1934–1939, Special Collections, University of Illinois at Chicago.

79. "Proceeding of Congress of Youth," July 1–5, 1939, New York City, box 2, Communist Party Pamphlets 1934–1939, Special Collections, University of Illinois at Chicago.

80. "Puerto Rico CP Set Up, Adopts Action Program," *Daily Worker* (New York), March 24, 1946.

81. As Pujals points out, the PPD's 1952 slogan, *Pan, Tierra, y Libertad* (Bread, land, and liberty), was "a carbon copy of a local communist party slogan in the late 1930s." "Soviet Caribbean," 265.

82. James S. Allen, "Santos, Puerto Rico C.P. Leader, Tells 'Daily' of Independence Aim," *Daily Worker* (New York), October 8, 1943, 2.

83. Santos Rivera, *Puerto Rico ayer*, 10–11.

84. Santos Rivera, *Puerto Rico ayer*, 33.

85. See, for example, the six-part series on Puerto Rico in the *Daily Worker* (New York), February 16–September 14, 1947.

86. "Foster Tells of Dire Poverty in Puerto Rico," *Daily Worker* (New York), March 16, 1948, 5; Foster, *Crime of El Fanguito* (emphasis in original).

87. "El jefe nacionalista dijo que ha llegado la hora de la decisión," *El Mundo* (San Juan, Puerto Rico), December 15, 1947, 1.

88. "Puerto Rican Communists Expel Juan Corretjer," *Daily Worker* (New York), March 22, 1948. The party also expelled Lee Tapia, presumably for the same reason.

89. Guadalupe de Jesús, *Sindicalismo y lucha política*, 71.

90. Díaz, "El gobierno," chap. 5, 28.

PART II

Latin American Communism in the Cold-War Frame (1945–1989)

Latin America and the Communist World in the Early 1950s

The Networks of Soviet Pacifism and Latin American Anti-Imperialism

ADRIANA PETRA

In the first half of the 1950s, a substantial number of Latin American intellectuals formed a political-cultural activist network in line with the pacifist and noninterventionist politics that the Soviet Union promoted through the world peace movement. In the context of the peak years of the first Cold War and "Late Stalinism," writers, artists, and scientists from across the continent embraced a reborn anti-imperialism. They participated in a transnational circuit of trips, publications, and gatherings that linked Latin American capitals with Moscow, Prague, and Beijing. They combined their long-standing hemispheric anti-imperialist goals and values with those of like-minded peoples in Asia—particularly in China, but also in Soviet Central Asia and the Caucasus. Communism had achieved popular support among prominent cultural figures, ranging from progressive liberals to nationalists and from famous individuals to lesser-known ones. Together, they contributed to the legitimization and advancement of intellectual alternatives that the communist world offered, even with the ups and downs the heteronomous nature of the parties inevitably engendered.[1] The Brazilian Jorge Amado, Chilean Pablo Neruda, Colombian Jorge Zalamea, Cubans Nicolás Guillén and Juan Marinello, Guatemalan Miguel Ángel Asturias, Mexicans Vicente Lombardo Toledano and Diego Rivera, Uruguayan Jesualdo Sosa, and Argentines Alfredo Valera and María Rosa Oliver were all central nodes in a transnational network that constitutes a virtually unexplored chapter in the history of Latin American communism. On those rare occasions this network is recognized, it is seldom associated with the anti-imperialist and Third World internationalist currents of the "new left" or the revolutionary left movements of the second half of the twentieth century. Indeed, it is often portrayed as being opposed to them.

This chapter analyzes this "anti-imperialist *moment*." By "moment," I refer to the contingent and temporary nature of this network as well as the sense of opportunity it presented. I take as a starting point the figure of María Rosa Oliver (1898–1977), an Argentine writer who was one of the pillars of this network that spread across all five continents and who was most active from 1950 to 1955. Although the world peace movement included world-renowned Latin Americans, such as the poet Neruda and the painter Rivera, Oliver was not a familiar figure to many. Yet although she was not a central figure in either the literary or the scientific world, she possessed certain social and cultural qualities that enabled her to mediate and organize exceptionally well. These skills explain why she played an essential role in building and maintaining the network. They also highlight the feminization of organizational work that occurred in left and revolutionary groups, an important topic that lies beyond the scope of this chapter.[2]

Oliver was closely tied to Victoria Ocampo (1890–1979), with whom she played a central role in the periodical *Sur*, which Ocampo founded in 1931 with the participation of U.S. writer Waldo Frank. Ocampo was an Argentine writer, essayist, translator, and cultural promoter. She founded and directed *Sur* until her death, financing a cultural enterprise of enormous scope and continental, even transatlantic, importance almost entirely with her personal resources. She was an active feminist and antifascist activist. In the 1950s, in the context of the Cold War, she participated in and supported the activities of the Congress for Cultural Freedom, a self-styled anti-totalitarianism organization that opposed Soviet pacifism.

Sur was one of the most ambitious and long-lasting cultural projects in Latin America. As scholar John King has pointed out, members of *Sur* built bridges with other cultures, primarily European, through travel, personal contacts, and a fantastic ability to translate.[3] The team that worked on the periodical dominated Argentine culture for more than thirty years. They formed a cultural elite with strong international ties. Contemporary critics, from both the political left and the nationalist right, attributed their outlook and their modernizing cosmopolitan critiques to their "aristocratic" origins, including those of Oliver herself. For this reason, her ability to mediate and maneuver in Latin American political and cultural networks is inseparable from the social position she established for her Popular Front politics and the causes of antifascism, women, and communism, three themes that readily intersected at this time. Rebelling against her class but without renouncing its cultural preferences and relations, María Rosa Oliver thus invites us to consider both the heterogeneity of the intellectual commitment to communism and to explore, from her particular perspective, a "moment" of Latin American intellectual communism that in the early 1950s combined support for a communism that was expanding through the countries of Eastern Europe and China with the goals of anti-imperialism and national liberation. The latter, while in line with the processes of decolonization and the nationalist struggles underway at the time, also conjured up the anti-imperialist imaginary and struggles of the 1920s and 1930s.

This was an ephemeral, loosely systematized, and contingent "moment." It was itself a product of movements that, although promoted by the communist states, were not state controlled. Instead, they were organized through preexisting political and cultural networks and connections. Because of this, Oliver's archive, especially her correspondence with certain Latin American intellectuals and politicians, as well as her memoirs and personal papers, provide an opportunity to observe this period "from below," that is, from the point of view of one of its unique protagonists. This stage in the history of communism has only recently garnered attention. Combined with renewed interest in the 1950s and the first Cold War, this attention has given rise to research on Soviet cultural diplomacy in the post-Stalin period, relations between Latin America and East Europe, and, above all, the role of the People's Republic of China in the expansion of anti-imperialist sentiments, emancipatory geographies, and the "experiences of the world" that an important segment of Latin American literary elites enjoyed.[4] As such, its reconstruction contributes to research that examines the role of communism in the construction of an anti-imperialist imagination, forged in the years prior to the formation of the Popular Front in 1935. These experiences left an internationalist memory and practice that we can trace through the anticolonial and national liberation struggles that developed after World War II.[5] More generally, such an approach to this moment and this network of transnational militancy can also contribute to uncovering earlier traces of internationalism in the Global South before the "Third World-ism" of the 1960s.

An Aristocratic Communist

Oliver played an indispensable role in the creation of a network of Latin American activists tied to the Union of Soviet Socialist Republics (USSR). A member of the Argentine aristocracy, when she was ten years old she suffered from polio and could not walk without help.[6] This physical limitation was not an obstacle to her cultural activism, which combined her own social dispositions stemming from her class origins with an early political commitment. Although she had already been involved in editorial work through bohemian and vanguardist circles in Buenos Aires, it was her role in the creation of *Sur*, alongside Frank and Ocampo, that placed her at the nerve center of Latin American cultural networks. Her friendship with Frank, an "idealist and mystical communist," was her entry into the world of progressive artists and intellectuals in the United States (which also was manifested through her work translating U.S. social-realist writers). Her "Americanist" consciousness was developed in discussions with Alfonso Reyes from Mexico and Pedro Henríquez Ureña from the Dominican Republic, two "itinerant intellectuals" who were central figures in the establishment of Latin American studies as an academic discipline in the first half of the twentieth century.[7] Reyes, in his diplomatic capacity, lived for extended periods in Buenos Aires, and Henríquez Ureña arrived in the city in 1924 and stayed until his death in 1946. Both had a close relationship with Oliver, which facilitated the formation of *Sur*'s editorial committee. This connection, along with their ties to Frank, was fundamental in the development and consolidation of their intellectual exchanges throughout the Americas during President Franklin D. Roosevelt's Good Neighbor policy and the U.S.'s subsequent entry into World War II.

In the 1930s Oliver moved closer to communism by way of antifascism, following a generational shift that went beyond Argentina. Although some writers argue that she joined the Partido Comunista de Argentina (PCA, Communist Party of Argentina), her role was always that of a "fellow-traveler." Party members highly valued her participation because it offered social prestige, which advanced Popular Front initiatives and a defense of the Soviet Union.[8] In this sense, her ideological profile can be characterized more as that of a leftist humanist than that of a typical Stalinist communist. Throughout the decade, she helped create the Argentine Women's Union, the Committee for Victory, and the Argentine Commission for Aid to Spanish Intellectuals. She also took part in the Asociación de Intelectuales, Artistas, Periodistas y Escritores (AIAPE, Association of Intellectuals, Artists, Journalists, and Writers) and the Committee against Racism and Anti-Semitism.[9] Communists were the principal force in all of these efforts, in contrast to their marginal role during the preceding period. They brought their organizing expertise, perseverance, discipline, and transnational structures through which they promoted a strong concept of internationalist community and fraternity. Even though the PCA was forced underground for forty years after the coup of 1930, its antifascist work allowed it to play a role in Argentine politics.[10] At least until the 1960s, this work was identified with the liberal-democratic antinationalist tradition and, after 1945, with Peronism. After Juan Domingo Perón gained the loyalty of the working class, the PCA became a party whose main base was among the urban middle class. The PCA developed and maintained this support through a cultural apparatus that included various publishers, magazines, and groups.

In 1942, thanks to her credentials as a proven antifascist, especially in the U.S. diplomatic corps in Buenos Aires (some of whom were family friends), Oliver was invited to work in the Department of Cultural Affairs of the Coordinating Office of Interamerican Affairs that Nelson Rockefeller led. This office formed part of the orbit of U.S. Vice President Henry Wallace, who, in turn, became a personal friend, a personality in the pacifist movement, and a prestigious figure among Latin American communists.[11] As part of her work in the department, Oliver advised those who were organizing cultural propaganda. Her main role was to avoid common stereotypes about the countries in the region. She spent

Figure 2. María Rosa Oliver discusses contemporary Latin American literature during a luncheon conference in the Green Room at Warner Bros. studio in Burbank, California, ca. 1940. María Rosa Oliver Papers, C0829, Manuscripts Division, Department of Special Collections, Princeton University Library, Serie 5.

two years in the United States, during which time she functioned as a cultural ambassador under Rockefeller, which increased her Latin American connections, especially among leftists and communists from Mexico, Brazil, Colombia, and Bolivia who, within the context of the alliance between the United States and the Soviet Union, occupied positions and gained public visibility that had previously been inaccessible to them. Oliver observed this paradox somewhat skeptically. As she wrote in her memoirs: "For the first time I met daily with people from all over Latin America, creating the absurdity that I had to come to Washington to meet my people."[12] She also met African American activists, such as W. E. B. Du Bois and Paul Robeson, who strengthened her understanding of the role of racism in the United States.

Oliver traveled to Washington with the conviction that above all other political and ideological considerations, it was necessary to defeat Nazism. This conveniently aligned with the policy of U.S. Communist Party leader Earl Browder.[13] Like many other progressives, left liberals, and not a few communists, she had confidence that the government of Roosevelt, despite the limitations of his Good Neighbor policies, would guarantee that U.S. corporations and trusts would not impose their will upon Latin America and that his administration would reach an agreement with the Soviet Union (figure 2). After Oliver's return to Buenos Aires in 1944, however, she became steadily more committed to the Soviet Union in the wake of Roosevelt's death, the anticommunist persecution of her friends and relatives, and U.S. President Harry S. Truman's anticommunist foreign policy. The Soviet Union, in the immediate postwar period, enjoyed tremendous moral prestige as a result of its leading role in the defeat of Nazi Germany and the near certainty that after the human and economic tragedy caused by World War II, the Soviet state wanted to prevent another world conflict.

Oliver's experience as a leading member of a well-oiled diplomatic machine and her cultural connections added to the political and cultural network centered around *Sur*, her feminist activism, and her Popular Front antifascism. Together these factors shaped the nature of her contacts and connections for her later role intermediating transnational communism during the Cold War. In 1952, during the depths of the Cold War, when Oliver had already become pro-Soviet, she wrote extensively to her friend and ex-mentor Rockefeller, explaining her decision. She revealed, once again, her ability to navigate between worlds. Recalling that she had gone to the United States ten years earlier to work under the Roosevelt administration, she noted that she "fondly remembered the hospitality that was offered me in Washington, D.C." But, she added, "What I am most grateful for is the opportunity [I had] to join in the struggle against fascism and help, with limited means and immense desire, to close ranks against those who threatened, in writing, to dominate the world and turn the countries of the southern part of America into Nazi colonies. They called us 'land of monkeys' with the same racist hate with which they sent the German Jews to concentration camps." She continued,

> I went to Washington with the belief that after the war ended and Hitler was defeated, the victorious countries, unified in peace as they had been in war, would give humanity a better world. This—and not any defense of any economic or political regime—compelled me to lend my modest assistance to the United States government.
>
> Nelson, I am giving you this explanation for two reasons: first . . . because I completely disagree with the international policy of the State Department and if something has changed, it is not my morality or conduct but the morality and conduct of U.S. foreign policy.[14]

Her positions had both political and personal consequences. They distanced Oliver from intellectual circles, especially those of her dear friend, Ocampo, who had become a central figure in the Argentine section of the anticommunist Congress for Cultural Freedom (an organization that the U.S. government

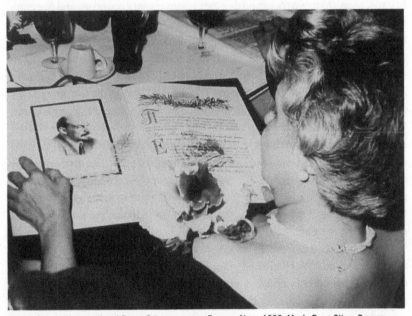

Figure 3. Lenin International Peace Prize ceremony, Buenos Aires, 1958. María Rosa Oliver Papers, C0829, Manuscripts Division, Department of Special Collections, Princeton University Library, Serie 5.

promoted, and the CIA secretly funded). When Oliver received the Lenin Prize in 1958 "for building peace among peoples," the hostile comments that *Sur* published provoked a bitter polemic between the two writers, and Oliver resigned from the editorial board of the journal she had helped found (figure 3).[15] As scholar Alvaro Fernández Bravo noted, "Oliver is a prism, through which we can observe how the networks she participated in (and often led) helped in the formation of groups and collective representations, including a Latin American collective identity that emerged after the Second World War."[16]

The World Peace Movement and Cold War Culture Battles

In the post–World War II context, the Soviet Union promoted a movement of intellectuals, scientists, and public figures who spoke out against the dangers of a Third World war. They called for the peaceful resolution of conflicts between countries and opposed the use of nuclear arms. French and Polish communists launched the initiative at a meeting in Wroclaw, Poland, in 1948. Five hundred delegates from more than forty countries attended the meeting and agreed to create an international committee headquartered in Paris. The following year the inaugural meeting of the first World Congress of Partisans for Peace was held in Paris. More than two thousand delegates from seventy countries and five continents participated in the congress, which changed its name to the World Peace Council (WPC) the following year.[17] French physicist Frédéric Joliot-Curie was the organization's first president. Neruda and Amado, who were both living in exile in France, represented Latin America, as did Cuban intellectual Marinello and Mexican trade unionist Lombardo Toledano.[18] Initially, the movement was mainly concerned with European themes, first and foremost the situation in Germany. With the outbreak of war in Korea in 1950, the organization shifted its attention to Asia and later to Africa. The major conflicts between the two superpowers unfolded in these two regions in tandem with the disintegration of European colonial empires. Given this new geopolitical reality, the battle for peace was closely tied to issues such as people's right to self-determination, the principle of nonintervention, and support for independence and national liberation movements.

The global peace movement was the cultural front's most important initiative in the post–World War II era and played a key role in the cultural and ideological battles that occurred during the Cold War. As soon as it began, anticommunists and liberals labeled it as nothing more than a façade that the Soviets erected to manipulate well-meaning Western intellectuals. These forces created their own organization, the Congress for Cultural Freedom, in Berlin in

1950 with the mission of fighting totalitarianism.[19] Recent investigations have questioned the rather simplistic characterization of the World Peace Council as nothing more than a passive instrument of Soviet foreign policy. Instead, some scholars have pointed out that the WPC's strategies were more recipro-cal than unidirectional and that they corresponded to the different members' own interests, priorities, and perspectives in addition to their support for the Soviet Union. In other words, although the Soviet state and communist parties around the world promoted the pacifist movement, these forces did not control its operations. To understand this movement, it is necessary to examine the role of the participants, the connections they maintained, and the various mean-ings that could be given, across the extensive world occupied by international communism, to topics such as the defense of peace, national sovereignty, and anti-imperialism.[20] This is particularly important when we observe that the international appeal communist pacifism engendered not only garnered the attention of well-known cultural figures but also influenced world public opin-ion. This happened at the same time as the Soviet Union went through one of its greatest periods of cultural darkness that was characterized, at least until Joseph Stalin's death in 1953, by the isolation, chauvinism, and the struggle against "cosmopolitanism" that went so far as to prohibit marriage with foreigners and included anti-Semitic persecution.[21] All the communist parties that embraced this discourse of cultural nationalism replicated this dogmatic approach while trying to adapt it to their own national culture and local idiosyncrasies, as was the case in Argentina.

This is why it is difficult to explain how the call for cultural nationalism and the emphasis on localism coalesced with the demands of internationalism unless we understand how figures such as Oliver simultaneously and skillfully found ways to interpret Moscow's mandates in their own fashion and, at the same time, avoided alienating themselves from communist leaders in their own countries. The idea of manipulation or bewitchment, which had been widely reproduced in Western studies of communist intellectuals but is now largely discredited, stems from this top-down vision and, as a result, does not help to unravel the complexities of individual trajectories.

Although important Latin American artists, writers, and noted personalities supported it, pacifist activism encountered many obstacles in developing and gaining public support. The Latin American democratic spring that blossomed following World War II died quickly in the inclement climate of the Cold War. Military coups occurred in Colombia and Venezuela while other governments in the region launched anticommunist crusades, banned a number of communist parties, increased repression against public activities, and imprisoned or exiled leftist leaders and important cadres. The United States, for its part, backed broadly defined anticommunist repression that even extended to nationalist and developmentalist governments it had previously backed, as the overthrow of Jacobo Árbenz in Guatemala in 1954 dramatically demonstrated. Adding to the difficulties Latin American communists faced, the World Peace Council's top authorities paid no attention and gave little support to Latin America during these years. As a result, economic and logistical aid was scarce and, at times, nonexistent. Correspondence from this period reveals this reality. For example, the Cuban writer Marinello complained about the disconnected and isolated nature of the work of the peace organization throughout Latin America and added that it was plagued by "indecision and vagueness."[22] Jorge Regueros Peralta, a journalist and one of the founders of the Communist Party of Colombia, insistently attempted to convince the World Peace Council that the subcontinent was strategically important as "the rearguard of the enemy and a source of raw materials." For those reasons, Regueros believed it was urgent that the WPC create a Latin American secretariat that would efficiently coordinate the work of the national committees, which often acted in a chaotic manner.[23]

The Latin American peace movement's first activity was the American Continental Congress for Peace, which took place from September 5 to 11, 1949, in Mexico City. Fifteen hundred delegates from nineteen countries participated. At the urging of trade unionist Lombardo Toledano, former Mexican president Lázaro Cárdenas attended along with other political figures, such as the former Chilean leader Carlos Ibáñez del Campo, Cuban Fulgencio Batista, and former vice president Wallace. The congress declared that Wallace was "one of the period's foremost fighters for peace."[24] This event marked a return to the nationalist and anti-imperialist themes that dominated much of the global communist discourse in the postwar period. However, in the case of Latin America, these goals connected to a cultural tradition that had existed since the end of the previous century and had focused much of its criticism on the United States, its values, and its imperialist practices. Thus, without hiding its evocation of the Arielist argument, Argentine communist Ernesto Giudici criticized the utilitarianism, commercialism, and lack of "soul" that characterized U.S. culture.[25]

Giudici, like many of his comrades, retained their anti-imperialist and internationalist memories from the 1920s and early 1930s. During those years Latin American communist militants belonged to a network that brought together anticolonial, Pan African, and antiracist currents from around the world. As scholars Sabine Dullin and Brigitte Studer have pointed out, following the decoupling of communism and the anti-imperialist and anticolonial struggles that the Comintern's antifascist strategy engendered, the decolonization scenario reactivated an interwar internationalism, which had a demonstrably strong attraction for nationalist elites all over the world, from the Pan Africanism of George Padmore and Jomo Kenyatta to Jawaharlal Nehru and Latin American Marxists.[26] Indeed, China, which for the Comintern had been a vantage point for interpreting the peripheral regions, was now a central player and an example of a successful revolution that offered the communists extended domination over vast regions of the world.

Oliver was part of the group that pushed for the creation of an Argentine-based headquarters of the World Peace Council a few weeks before the American Continental Congress for Peace opened in Mexico.[27] She was not part of the delegation that traveled to Paris for the first peace congress, but in 1950 she was named as a delegate to represent a women's group (Friends of Peace Association) at the second world meeting that took place in Warsaw in December. Oliver wrote an extensive chronicle of that congress that was published in French in the magazine *Europe*, founded by the pacifist Romain Rolland in 1923, in which she praised the liberation of the downtrodden Polish people as well as her fraternal encounters with old friends, such as Neruda, Marinello, Lombardo Toledano, German writer and feminist Ana Seghers, U.S. writer and activist Joseph Starobin, and French writer Joseph Kessell (who was born in Argentina).[28]

A range of previously existing political and personal relationships underlay the Soviet peace network. Oliver greeted this new stage of political activism with the same cosmopolitan spirit she had displayed in all her previous engagements. What emerges from these encounters is the image of a family reunion whose members, dispersed throughout the world, share both the same language and a common memory. The correspondence between and among these individuals constantly evokes the sense that their relationships constituted a convergence of equals based on the web of camaraderie forged across a trajectory of Americanism (in the hemispheric sense), antifascism, and an ecumenical commitment to humanistic causes and values. They were all dedicated to boosting membership in a global peace movement, a job that demanded, in the first place, a loosening of its close relations with the communist parties. Thus, for example, when Oliver wrote to her close friend, Chilean poet and diplomat Gabriela Mistral, she remarked upon the presence of representatives from a number of different political tendencies, even "the spectrum of religious faiths," in the meeting in Poland. She noted,

> When we finally decided to create the World Peace Council we sent you a telegram that Pablo Neruda, Juan Marinello, Jorge Amado, and I had signed asking if you wanted to become a member. Did you receive this request? I assume that

your position as a diplomat prevented you from joining. I also thought that the political sympathies of the signers could lead you to believe that it was a [Communist] party congress. That would be a mistake. People with a range of political beliefs attended, as I have already told you. [People from] Asia were well represented and formed a compact bloc. For example, half the Indian delegation (of more or less seventy members) supported Nehru while the other half opposed the government. The delegates from Korea, China, Vietnam, and Indonesia, however, spoke with one voice; there were no differences among them.[29]

Oliver's insistence convinced Mistral to head the list of political and cultural personalities who convened the Continental Conference for Peace, the realization of which depended, to a large degree, on Oliver's organizational expertise and her skill at leveraging her social capital and cultural connections. In her position as secretary of the conference, Oliver managed to bring together figures from various Latin American countries, the United States, and Canada and overcome a number of bureaucratic, political, and police barriers.[30] Concretely, the meeting was supposed to take place in Rio de Janeiro, but the Getúlio Vargas government first authorized it, then prohibited it. Attempts to have it move to Santiago were fruitless. Finally, Oliver was able to secure a place for the conference in Montevideo, Uruguay, after President Andrés Martínez Trueba, of the Colorado Party, authorized it.[31] When the government withdrew its authorization at the last minute, the conference took place clandestinely. Nevertheless, close to five hundred delegates arrived from Argentina, Bolivia, Brazil, Chile, Colombia, Guatemala, Paraguay, Puerto Rico, the United States, and Venezuela. They met in basements and cultural centers. Many had to return to their countries or were not even able to leave them in the first place, because the Uruguayan government denied them visas. This happened to the Canadian, Mexican, and Cuban delegates. Following three days of deliberations, the delegates approved a public statement and an eight-point resolution that called for progressive disarmament, the prohibition of nuclear weapons, the regulation of atomic energy, a campaign against sending troops to Korea, and condemnation of the "militaristic policy" of the U.S. ruling class.[32]

Despite the adverse conditions, Oliver managed both to bring together writers and artists from across the continent and to take the first steps toward the construction of a structure in which activist intellectuals could operate. The project advanced so much it was able to hold a Continental Congress of Culture the following year in Chile.[33] Despite the challenges it had faced, the Montevideo meeting had agreed to organize a gathering that would address cultural issues, artistic creation, and the chronic dispersion and lack of communication that affected Latin American intellectuals. The country chosen to hold the conference was Chile, then under the presidency of Ibáñez del Campo. Predictably, Neruda, who had just returned to his country after four years in exile, hosted it. In addition, Mistral, Baldomero Sanín Cano, and Joaquín García Monge issued the call inviting people to the congress.[34] The event was an unqualified success, as even the anticommunist press recognized. The two hundred delegates included representatives from Argentina, Bolivia, Brazil, Chile, Colombia, Costa Rica, Cuba, Guatemala, Haiti, Mexico, Paraguay, Uruguay, the United States, and Venezuela. A number of famous intellectuals, including Amado, René Depestre, Jorge Icaza, Reyes, Rivera, Siqueiros, Guillén, Betty Sanders, and Gabriel Bracho attended.[35]

The congress issued a statement on the problems of cultural creation in Latin America and called for a meeting of intellectuals from the United States, Great Britain, the Soviet Union, China, and France (the "five great powers") to be held in a Latin American country at which they could freely express their agreements and disagreements regarding "world peace." Several national organizations emerged from the Chilean meeting that backed their proposals. The following year the Argentine Congress for Culture and the Argentine House of Culture formed. Both institutions affirmed that the defense of national identity was inseparable from any form of political or cultural submission and emphasized their solid support for the anti-imperialist principles of Argentine intellectual life.[36] A network of publications on both a regional and transatlantic scale based on the slogans of pacifism and anti-imperialism developed following the congress. A number of publications emerged as well, including *Revista Para Todos* in Brazil, *Paz y Democracia* in Colombia, the monthly *Paz* in Mexico, *Mass and Mainstream* in New York, *Por la Paz*, which María Rosa Oliver led, and, as a key node in the network, *Défense de la Paix* (subsequently *Horizons*), which was edited in thirteen languages and distributed in twenty countries.

China, the Pacific, and Latin American Anti-Imperialism

Latin American communist discourse in the 1950s had a new geography of transnational activism. This reflected changes in postwar geopolitics with the addition of Eastern Europe to the Communist world, the Cold War framework for understanding decolonization, and, above all, the Chinese Revolution. From its origins this revolution differed from the Soviet model while reenergizing the dormant revolutionary instincts of many communists. Praise of these Eastern European and Chinese people's democracies abound in contemporary memoirs and correspondence but not to the extent of what Argentine communist writer Héctor Agosti described as the "outburst of Chinese enthusiasm" among communists, sympathizers, and fellow travelers. Referring to Montevideo as her "traveling congress," Oliver emphasized, along with Mistral, the need for her involvement in the peace movement. She drew parallels between Asians and Latin Americans:

> The Cold War is making life more difficult for Latin Americans each day: the cost of living rises steeply, the few freedoms that we have left are being curtailed, and the pressure grows to send soldiers to fight in distant wars. . . . How can a Coya or a Guaraní hate a Korean? They share the same physique and living conditions. There were many *inditos* [little Indians] among the delegates and they look toward Asia, not toward Europe or the United States.[37]

This connection of Asia to Latin America had a point of reference in the Peace Conference of Asia and the Pacific Region, held in Beijing between October 2 and 12, 1952, just seven months after the Montevideo event. It was the first international meeting organized by the New China and the first in which Latin American and Caribbean intellectuals met their Asian counterparts. It was one of the so-called other Bandungs that gave shape to networks and languages of solidarity, internationalism, and Afro-Asian unity that the more famous April 1955 conference in Indonesia later crystallized.[38]

The period after the Chinese Revolution's triumph in 1949 underlined the Pacific region's role as a strategic area in international politics, marked by the start of the Korean War—which highlighted the division between the Soviet Union and the United States as well as the debut of China as a regional power. The United States' presence in South Korea and Taiwan threatened China's continental security, as did Japan's rearmament. These threats were the basis for the 1952 conference. Local affiliates of the WPC issued a statement that asserted the need to make the Pacific an ocean of unity instead of war, the need to "oppose the rearming of Japan by the United States in order to safeguard the security of Asia and of the Pacific regions[,] . . . oppose the intervention of any nation in the internal affairs of another nation in order to safeguard the independence and sovereignty of nations as well as to ensure the peaceful co-existence of nations with different systems." It further "insist[ed] upon the peaceful settlement of the existing conflicts in order to restore and develop the normal trade relations and interflow of culture among nations."[39]

Opposition to U.S. intervention in the region and the danger of a new war dominated the conference's agenda. At the same time, the meeting also discussed the promotion of cultural exchanges, national independence, and women's roles in the region's struggles for liberation. Four hundred and seventy-eight delegates and observers met in Beijing, representing more than fifty countries, including those in Asia and Oceania and several Pacific Rim countries in North, Central, and South America. A painting by Rivera was exhibited during the sessions alongside Pablo Picasso's famous *Dove of Peace*. In the opening session, the vice president of the People's Republic of China, Song Qingling, recalled the meeting in Montevideo and referred to the protests that swept through Latin America against the sending of troops to Korea. Song emphasized the core beliefs of communist pacifism during the Cold War, which highlighted the essential relationship between the struggle for peace, national independence, and the principle of nonintervention.[40]

Neruda, head of the Chilean delegation, discussed the impact the Chinese Revolution had on the other side of the ocean. He emphasized that it raised the possibility of turning the huge expanse of water between the two regions into a bridge between the newly powerful China and the impoverished and subject countries of Latin America.[41]

The Asia-Pacific Peace Conference opened a path for pilgrimages to the "New China" that took the form of dozens of books and hundreds of articles and accounts by artists, intellectuals, and professionals from all over the world. Oliver visited China in early 1953, after spending Christmas in the Soviet Union, which she had been officially invited to visit after participating in the Congress of the Peoples for Peace in Vienna in December (figures 4 and 5). She was part

Figure 4. María Rosa Oliver visits China, 1953. María Rosa Oliver Papers, C0829, Manuscripts Division, Department of Special Collections, Princeton University Library, Serie 5.

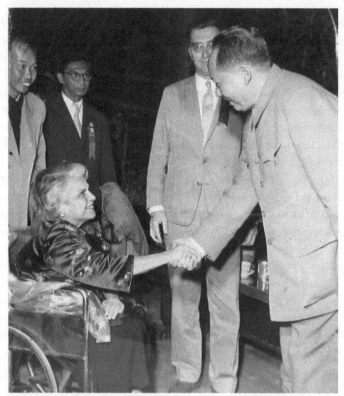

Figure 5. María Rosa Oliver meets Mao Zedong in China, 1953. María Rosa Oliver Papers, C0829, Manuscripts Division, Department of Special Collections, Princeton University Library, Serie 5.

of a delegation with ten other Argentines, including Norberto A. Frontini, with whom she wrote an account of this trip, *Lo que sabemos, hablamos: testimonio sobre la China de hoy* (What we know, we say: Testimony on the China of today).[42] The visit to China, unlike that to the Soviet Union, made a huge impression on her, both for its revolutionary vitality and the many similarities between Asian and Latin American countries. The book draws analogies, from the physical appearance and style of the handicrafts to the predominantly rural character of the countries and the oppressive weight of economic dependence and colonialism.

Zalamea from Colombia attended the Beijing conference, and his experience mirrors the impact the gathering had on Oliver and other members of the peace movement. He was a poet, dramatist, novelist, and Liberal Party diplomat, who went into exile in Buenos Aires after the assassination of Colombia's Liberal Party presidential candidate Jorge Eliécer Gaitán in 1948 and the popular uprising known as the "Bogotazo." His friendship with Oliver dated from his time as the Colombian ambassador in Mexico during World War II. Through this friendship he joined *Sur* and attended the Continental Conference in Montevideo. There he became reacquainted with communist lawyer Diego Montaña Cuellar, with whom he had been active in the campaigns for justice for the murder of Gaitán. Montaña Cuellar convinced him to join the Colombian delegation to the Beijing meeting and from there traveled to the Soviet Union. Zalamea was particularly interested in Soviet Central Asia.[43] Montaña Cuellar recalled that this trip had a strong impact on Zalamea, despite his being "closed off, resentful, and drunk" because of his exile.[44] Experiences such as this one demonstrate how effective Chinese cultural diplomacy was in making the Beijing peace conference into a highly emotional "theatrical symbol." As scholar Rachel Leow has noted, this was crucial for the mobilization of more popular forms of Afro-Asian internationalism, as well as demonstrating the space that Latin Americans now occupied in this new geography.[45] In just a few months, Zalamea was named a member of the inaugural Latin American secretariat of the World Peace Council and settled in Vienna until returning to Colombia at the end of the 1950s. From there he engaged in broad outreach in cultural diplomacy and insisted on promoting an anti-imperialist discourse that emphasized the common interests between Latin America and those African and Asian countries that had thrown off the yoke of colonialism.[46] Zalamea's case shows how the retreat from democracy in Latin America in the early Cold War, the Chinese Revolution, and decolonization successfully converged with the political-intellectual networks in the WPC that extended across all five continents. This political confluence helped shape an anti-imperialist discourse and an early Third World-ism among a segment of Latin American intellectuals.

The Crisis of Communist Pacifism

In November 1956 Oliver took part in a meeting of the leadership bureau of the World Peace Council that marked the beginning of the decline of communist pacifism. It was organized initially to discuss the British-French-Israeli invasion of Egypt in response to the latter's nationalization of the Suez Canal. The crisis in Eastern Europe, the tragic corollary of which was the Soviet invasion of Hungary, forced two successive postponements and the moving of the meeting from Stockholm to Helsinki after the Swedish government prohibited the gathering. Still reeling from the impact of Nikita Khrushchev's statements at the Twentieth Congress of the Communist Party of the Soviet Union (CPSU), where he denounced the crimes of Stalinism and the cult of personality before an engrossed audience, several of the delegates who arrived in the Finnish capital had abandoned the usual camaraderie for open hostility and distrust.

The Hungarian Revolution provoked an enormous crisis in the communist world and opened the door to a large number of desertions and resignations in the months and years following the Twentieth Congress, most especially in intellectual circles. Along with the imperialist intervention in Egypt, which ended with Arab nationalist leader Gamal Abdel Nasser's victory and France's and Great Britain's humiliating withdrawals, which socialist and social democratic forces had supported, Hungary was the spark that generated, in different ways and degrees, the birth of the New Left.

Oliver spoke briefly at the Helsinki meeting, the atmosphere of which she defined as tragic. She recognized that the Hungarian events raised a fundamental question: the entrance of Soviet tanks in Hungary directly contradicted the principle of nonintervention, one of the movement's fundamental pillars. This, moreover, was particularly serious for the peoples of Latin America, since they were so exposed to the threat that their protests would be smothered by "U.S. bombardments" that their own governments opportunely requested. Oliver commented,

> In reality, there was a struggle in the conscience of all those present at the Helsinki meeting between defending the principle of noninterference from a moral point of view versus having to admit the political justification we were given for its violation. That is why . . . our meeting was tragic. Anyone who does not recognize the tremendous moral tragedy that was Hungary, does not deserve to be a member of our movement, nor of any responsible political party.[47]

The World Peace Council issued a statement that admitted that the internal differences expressed at the conference prevented its members from formulating a shared assessment of what had happened in Hungary. Their unanimous mourning of the spilling of blood allowed the council to maintain an image, albeit limited, of independence and autonomy that, in any case, was not enough to forestall a large list of former allies, comrades, and sympathizers from abandoning their commitments to communist pacifism. The crisis in the communist world was palpable by the end of 1956. The beginnings of China's separation from the Soviet bloc, which became a reality a few years later, aggravated the crisis. One direct consequence of this rupture was that several Latin American parties in countries with a broad peasant base declared themselves Maoist.

Oliver left the world peace movement in 1962, after fourteen years of intense activism, including her membership in the organization's executive committee. In the years that followed, Oliver did not abandon her political commitment and continued to support both Cuba and China, although she devoted a significant part of her time to writing the three volumes of her memoirs. In the last decade of her life, she became interested in liberation theology and embraced a kind of Christian socialism. She died in Buenos Aires in 1977 at the age of 78. During the 1950s, as I have noted, the network in which she was a key actor brought together thousands of intellectuals, political personalities, and workers in a circuit that united Latin American capitals with Moscow, Paris, Beijing, and Eastern Europe. It developed a series of understandings and interpretations regarding the place of Latin America on the political map of the Cold War. It reinvigorated the language of anti-imperialism to defend peace and national independence and built links and relations with the Afro-Asian world, what we now call the Global South, prior to the dissemination of Third World–ist ideas. As part of a growing interest in the 1950s, which had been eclipsed by the political and cultural power of the 1960s, a detailed study of this "moment" of communism constitutes a historical contribution to the anti-imperialist imagination and tradition of Latin America, along with its global connections. At the same time, it completes a chapter in the political history of intellectuals and cultural elites and allows us to think about the way in which webs of solidarity among Latin America, Africa, and Asia were articulated in a series of events that occurred across the twentieth century.

Notes

1. On the partisans for peace movement in Latin America, see Iber, *Neither Peace nor Freedom*. I have dealt with the Argentine case in Petra, *Intellectuals and Communist Culture*. For an analysis that emphasizes the alternative intellectual system of legitimization that the USSR promoted during the Cold War, see Ridenti, "Jorge Amado."

2. Oliver wrote works of fiction, film scripts and plays, articles, and translations, although she only published *Geografía argentina*; *América vista por una mujer argentina*; with Norberto A. Frontini, *Lo que sabemos*; and the three volumes of her memoirs: *Mundo, mi casa*; *La vida cotidiana*; and *Mi fe es el hombre*.

3. King, *Sur*.

4. Rupprecht, *Soviet Internationalism after Stalin*; Zourek, *Praga y los intelectuales latino-americanos*; Locane, "Del orientalismo a la provincialización."

5. From the 1920s until at least 1935, when the strategic shift toward the politics of anti-fascist popular fronts took place, anti-imperialism effectively brought together hundreds of communist organizations, militants, and sympathizers from all corners of the globe and gave rise to a gigantic network of transnational activism, starting from the creation of the league against Imperialism and Colonial Oppression in 1927, within the framework of the Anti-Imperialist Congress in Brussels. Although it was led by the communists, the league drew from a broad social and political-ideological spectrum,

including nationalists, syndicalists, socialists, and pacifists as well as peasants, workers, the middle classes, and intellectuals. Dullin and Studer have drawn attention to the "forgotten connections" that can be established between this transnational moment of communism and the anti-imperialist, third-world, and national liberation movements of the 1950s and 1960s. See Petersson, "La Ligue anti-impérialiste"; Dullin and Studer, "Communisme + transnational"; Kersffeld, *Contra el imperio*; and the many writings of Melgar Bao, among them "Cominternismo intelectual."

6. Oliver's physical infirmities are worthy of more study. Some writings have dealt specifically with this topic when discussing her memories of her youth. See Lojo, "Memoria, género y enfermedad."

7. On the links between Oliver, Reyes, and Henríquez Ureña from the point of view of their role in the formation of a Latin American network during World War II, see Fernández Bravo, "Redes latinoamericanas."

8. Clementi, *María Rosa Oliver*; Fernández Bravo, introducción.

9. Deutsch, "Mujeres."

10. Halperín Dongui, *La Argentina*.

11. On Wallace's relationship with Latin America, see Pavilack, "Henry A. Wallace."

12. Oliver, *Mi fe es el hombre*, 151.

13. On Browderism in Latin America, see Caballero, *Latin America and the Comintern*, 134–48, and Margaret M. Power's chapter in the current volume.

14. María Rosa Oliver to Nelson Rockefeller, April 9, 1952, Buenos Aires, box 5, folder 57, María Rosa Oliver Papers (hereafter referred to as Oliver Papers), Manuscripts Division, Department of Special Collections, Princeton University Library, Princeton, New Jersey. Unpublished texts written in Buenos Aires.

15. "Premios literarios argentinos," 104.

16. Fernández Bravo, "María Rosa Oliver," 133.

17. Some of the delegates and guests were forced to meet in Prague because the French government denied them visas to enter the country.

18. Neruda, Marinello, Lombardo Toledano, the former Mexican president Lázaro Cárdenas, Uruguayan Julia Arévalo, and Argentinians Julio Luis Peluffo and Gerardo Scolamieri formed part of the organization's first leadership body. See "El congreso de París," *Orientación* (Buenos Aires), May 4, 1949.

19. Iber, *Neither Peace nor Freedom*, 83–115.

20. See Bayerlein, Braskén, and Weiss, "Transnational and Global."

21. The *Diccionario soviético de filosofía* defined "cosmopolitism" as a theory that had its origins in the bourgeoisie and drew on a universalist and humanist rhetoric to express an imperialist will to rule while calling on people to deepen their patriotic feelings about their national culture and traditions. Latin American communist writers, artists, and intellectuals used this term frequently during the period covered in this chapter. See Rosental and Iudin, *Diccionario soviético de filosofía*, 89.

22. Juan Marinello to María Rosa Oliver, October 22, 1952, Havana, box 4, folder 58, Oliver Papers.

23. Jorge Regueros Peralta to María Rosa Oliver, May 3, 1952, Bogotá, box 5, folder 53, Oliver Papers.

24. Wallace was unable to attend so a number of Latin American artists and intellectuals, including Juan Marinello, Pablo Neruda, David Alfaro Siqueiros, Nicolás Guillén, and Miguel Otero Silva, sent him a letter of support. D. A. Siqueiros to Henry A. Wallace, September 8, 1949, Henry A. Wallace Collection, Iowa Digital Library. Also see Iber, *Neither Peace nor Freedom*, 72.

25. Ernesto Giudici, "Realidades americanas en el Congreso de México," *Orientación* (Buenos Aires), November 2, 1949. *Ariel*, an essay by Uruguayan José Enrique Rodó, was published in 1909 and became one of the fundamental texts of Latin American thought. Directing his arguments primarily at young people in the Americas, Rodó defines Latin America as spiritualist and idealist in opposition to the United States, which is materialist and centered on utilitarianism.

26. Dullin and Studer, "Communisme + transnational," 30.

27. Oliver did this publicly in the Argentine city of La Plata in August 1949. The meeting was banned, and the police dispersed the gathering. See "Declaración y llamamiento del Congreso Argentino de Partidarios de la Paz," *Orientación* (Buenos Aires), August 24, 1949.

28. Oliver's text was published as "Les fleurs de Varsovie," *Europa*, February 1951. The names were listed in II Congreso Mundial de Partidarios de la Paz de Varsovia, box 1, folder 51, Oliver Papers.

29. María Rosa Oliver to Gabriela Mistral, February 2, 1951, Buenos Aires, Colección Digital Fondo Gabriela Mistral, Biblioteca Nacional Digital de Chile, Santiago.

30. In addition to Gabriela Mistral, the appeal was supported by Benjamín Cevallos Arízaga, president of the Supreme Court of Justice of Ecuador; the then–vice president of the Chilean Senate, Salvador Allende; president of the National Congress of Guatemala, Roberto Alvarado Fuentes; writer and former president of Peru José Gálvez Barrenechea; the Brazilians Candido Portinari, Oscar Niemeyer; and the magistrate João Pereira de Sampaio; African American singer and activist Paul Robeson; the U.S. Christian-ethics professor Joseph Fletcher; Ecuadorian writer and diplomat Manuel Benjamín Carrión; Mexican writers Alfonso Caso and Enrique González Martínez; Cubans José Elías Entralgo and Carlos García Vélez; Paraguayan musician José Asunción Flores; Guatemalan Luis Cardozo y Aragón; Canadian religious leader James Endicott; Colombian philosopher Baldomero Sanín Cano; Argentine writer Leónidas Barletta; the Uruguayan Jesualdo Sosa; and the Costa Rican writer Joaquín García Monge, among others.

31. Announcement from the American Continental Conference for Peace, signed by María Rosa Oliver, Branca Fialho, and Juan Lamatta, February 9, 1952, Río de Janeiro, Colección Digital Fondo Gabriela Mistral, Biblioteca Nacional Digital de Chile, Santiago. The Colorado Party is, along with the White or National Party, one of the traditional political parties in Uruguay.

32. "Pese a todas las trabas la Conferencia Continental por la Paz se realizó con éxito," *Nuestra Palabra* (Buenos Aires), March 25, 1952, 5; "Resoluciones de la Conferencia Continental por la Paz," *Nuestra Palabra*, April 2, 1952, 5.

33. Alburquerque, *La trinchera letrada*.

34. Gabriela Mistral's real support for the congress was confusing since she later denied to the international press that she backed it. See Alburquerque, *La trinchera letrada*.

35. The agenda of the congress was organized as follows: proclamation to the intellectuals of the peoples of America; cultural exchange: declaration of the intellectuals to the peoples of America; and exhortation to governments, cultural and professional entities and intellectuals of America. Archivo Juan Antonio Salceda, private archive, Tandil, Argentina. The resolutions of the Congress were published in the cultural magazine of the PCA, *Cuadernos de Cultura* 12, July 1953, 1–22.

36. "La Casa de la Cultura Argentina," Buenos Aires, ca. 1952, 2, and "Casa de la Cultura Argentina: Declaración de Principios," Buenos Aires, ca. 1953, both Archivo Juan Antonio Salceda, private archive, Tandil, Argentina.

37. María Rosa Oliver to Gabriela Mistral, September 5, 1952, Buenos Aires, Colección Digital Fondo Gabriela Mistral, Biblioteca Nacional Digital de Chile, Santiago.

38. Lewis and Stolte, "Other Bandungs."

39. Peace Conference of the Asian and Pacific Regions (Beijing, 1952), "A Call for the Convention of a Peace Conference for Asia and the Pacific Regions," ca. September 1952, W. E. B. Du Bois Papers (MS 312), Special Collections and University Archives, University of Massachusetts Amherst Libraries.

40. Quoted in Ibarra Arana and Hao, "Peace Conference," 792. I thank Mónica Ni for help in translating the material from Chinese.

41. Ibarra Arana, Ignacio, and Hao, "Peace Conference," 793–94.

42. Hubert, "Intellectual Cartographies."

43. Jorge Regueros Peralta to María Rosa Oliver, April 27, 1952, Bogota, box 5, folder 53, Oliver Papers.

44. López Bermúdez, *Jorge Zalamea*, 346.

45. Leow, "Missing Peace," 28.

46. See Jorge Zalamea to María Rosa Oliver, February 18, 1957, box 7, folder 13, Oliver Papers.

47. World Peace Council, memoirs, Notas manuscritas sobre la reunión del Bureau del Consejo Mundial de la Paz reunido en Helsinki en 1956, box 1, folder 2, Oliver Papers.

Breaking the Silence

Communist Women, Transnationalism, and the Alianza Femenina Guatemalteca, 1947–1954

PATRICIA HARMS

Women associated with Guatemala's Communist Party played a critical role in shaping both the social and the political reforms undertaken during the country's revolutionary decade (1944–1954). Given that the communist party was illegal for the majority of that time, communist women operated primarily through the women's organization, the Alianza Femenina Guatemalteca (AFG, Guatemalan Women's Alliance), where they developed critical connections with the Women's International League for Peace and Freedom (WILPF) and the Women's International Democratic Federation (WIDF), transnational organizations that became vital to AFG's ideological formation. Fusing gender and ethnic analysis with a class-based theoretical foundation, these transnational relationships helped them identify the inequitable schisms within Guatemala and the impacts of historic imperialism, becoming the lifeblood for their theoretical development. Finding commonalities between their condition and that of women worldwide, Guatemalan communist women integrated the theoretical tools developed by their international partners on issues of inequality, illiteracy, lack of access to land, and poverty into their deeply patriarchal society.

Across Latin America, the experiences of communist women prior to 1954 have largely been erased from public memory and historical records, within a multilayered context of entrenched patriarchy and the global Cold War, creating a distorted and incomplete understanding of their contributions.[1] Historian Sandra McGee Deutsch argues that histories of women in communist parties have been ignored due to the emphasis on political campaigns for suffrage and maternal-based social-reform movements, stories that have tended to homogenize women and erase their political experience and multiple identities.[2] This silence has been broken by several recent works that have begun to restore the role of communist women. *Queridas camaradas* (Dear comrades), *Feminism for the Americas* and "Las comunistas de la decada" chart the work of socialist- and communist-affiliated women's organizations between the 1940s and 1960s shifting the existing paradigms of women's activism.[3] In Guatemala the media have contributed to the obfuscation of communist women's activism by failing to recognize their individual agency. As Antonio Obando Sánchez, the founder of the Guatemalan Communist Party, recalled, "communist women, the official [Guatemalan] press repeated tirelessly, were lovers, both of the cheerful life (dancing and drinking), and of their communist comrades and chiefs, who shared them among all."[4] This media-driven perspective became embedded within Guatemalan scholarship, which as scholar Ana Cofiño Kepler argues, stereotyped communist women as devoid of sociopolitical agency and tangentially as victims of repressive dictatorships but never as independent actors.[5] Through the hypermasculinized Cold War lens, the U.S. State Department further solidified this stereotype referring to women in the Alianza as the "wives and lovers" of communist men and simultaneously concluding that communist men were hard working and incorruptible.[6]

To compound their invisibility further, the dual machinations of a national patriarchal structure and a Cold War context had such a powerful effect on these women that they essentially silenced themselves. María Vilanova de Árbenz, the wife of president Jacobo Árbenz (1951–1954), avoided any discussion of her critical leadership within the Alianza and an important social-welfare institution, Asociación de Comedores y Guarderías Infantiles (Association of Nutrition and Daycare Centers), limiting herself to a few dismissive sentences. "During the period I lived in Guatemala, a social group began that wanted to get women involved in politics," she states in her autobiography. "This movement was determined to make an advance in [women's] political participation."[7] Her vague description of the Alianza's political activities exemplifies the phenomenon of silencing identified by historian Patrick Iber, who argues that individuals literally reworked their personal stories to align with acceptable Cold War narratives.[8] This includes even less-prominent women, such as Alianza executive secretary Ester de Urrutia, who literally erased her extensive activism by burning her personal papers during the terrifying days following the resignation of Jacobo Árbenz, when she and her family were targeted by anticommunist vigilantes.[9]

In light of this reality, the lack of archival sources poses significant challenges to the recovery of communist women's activities. I have found a parallel methodological research strategy employed to unearth Indigenous histories a useful guide for excavating the stories of communist women. In those cases where no records were available (written or oral), I have used actions to reliably decode meaning.[10] Adopting this approach, I have made connections between women's presence at specific events and the reported outcomes of their activism, which establishes the incontrovertible contributions of Guatemalan communist women made despite gaps within the archival sources.

The Partido Guatemalteco del Trabajo

The Guatemalan Communist Party first formed during the 1920s and emerged from activist labor union and mutual-aid-association circles dating back to the 1890s, of which at least twenty-two were women's organizations.[11] Founder Antonio Obando Sánchez led the first manifestation of the party until the 1930s when it was violently repressed by the Jorge Ubico dictatorship (1930–1944). In 1934 Ubico's fear of communism erupted into paranoia and dozens of Guatemalan communist and labor leaders were jailed, tortured, and executed (Obando Sánchez escaped execution but not prison). On September 17, 1934, a firing squad killed a dozen men, and one week later another five men were executed.[12] Although Ubico's reconfiguration of Guatemala's gender norms explicitly denied women political agency, scholars Arturo Taracena Arriola and Omar Lucas Monteflores identified the arrest and torture of dozens of women identified with the Communist Party during this same period.[13]

The 1944 revolution shifted Guatemala's sociopolitical context substantially, initiating what was referred to as the "ten years of spring." Two democratically elected presidents, Juan José Arévalo (1945–1950) and Árbenz (1951–1954) introduced sweeping sociopolitical reforms. Embracing a self-described spiritual socialism, Arévalo initiated moderate reforms reminiscent of U.S. President Franklin D. Roosevelt's New Deal, introducing labor codes and social security, while Árbenz brought in more structural socioeconomic reforms. The 1952 agrarian reform became the most consequential of these structural transformations drawing opposition from the U.S.-based United Fruit Company (UFC), whose fallow landholdings were purchased by the Guatemalan government and redistributed to more than a hundred thousand landless families. In June 1954, the UFC, the U.S. State Department, and internal, political opposition to Árbenz colluded to overthrow his administration in a military coup, essentially ending a decade of socioeconomic and political progress.

The Guatemalan revolution was part of a broader democratic resurgence across Latin America in the immediate aftermath of World War II. However, that brief opening rapidly ended amid a mounting Cold War emphasis on military security. Latin American political exiles sought refuge throughout Guatemala's democratic decade, bringing with them a diversity of political ideas to a country that had historically been intellectually isolated. Guatemala City played host to an eclectic community of Latin American political exiles including Apristas from Peru, Nicaraguan communists, Argentine anti-Peronists, Venezuelan social democrats, and Cuban *antibatistianos*.[14] The influence of these intellectual and political exiles was particularly critical during the formative years of the Arévalo administration. Chilean Virginia Bravo Letelier served as an adviser and member of the council for Arévalo's educational reforms. Salvadoran political refugees Graciela Amaya de García and Matilde Elena López joined with Guatemalan labor activist Hortensia Hernández Rojas to organize several labor unions that were rapidly developing during the embryonic revolutionary months. They also participated in the formation of the Alianza Femenina Guatemalteca and later to the revival of the Guatemalan Communist Party.

The Partido Guatemalteco del Trabajo (PGT, Guatemalan Worker's Party), as the Communist Party called itself, remained a small and unofficial party for most of the revolutionary decade. José Manuel Fortuny, Alfredo Guerra Borges, and Víctor Manuel Gutiérrez formed a clandestine forerunner of the PGT in 1949, the Vanguardia Democrática (Democratic Vanguard), with forty-three members.[15] Unlike the experience of communist women whose participation in the Alianza and transnational organizations supported and developed their theoretical platform, the PGT developed in relative isolation.[16] As Fortuny, Carlos Manuel Pellecer Durán and Guerra Borges recounted to historian Piero Gleijeses, Guatemala was perceived to be too backward a country and its communists too few to attract the attention of a Latin American communist movement.[17] "'We were a provincial party; we didn't look beyond our village; we didn't even have an international committee,' stated Fortuny. 'The party's leaders were very busy: We were overwhelmed with work.'"[18] Members of the PGT only had sporadic contacts with Western European and Soviet-bloc communist parties during the Árbenz era but maintained regular contacts with communist parties in Mexico and Cuba.[19] Guerra Borges and Fortuny reported to Gleijeses that only the Cuban communists were really interested in helping the Guatemalans. "The PSP [Partido Socialista Popular (PSP, Cuban Communist Party)] was the only Communist party that had the vision to see that a strong Communist party could be created in Guatemala," Guerra Borges said.[20]

The PGT's identity as an urban ladino organization was critical to their ideological development and recruitment of rural and Indigenous members. While the term "*ladino*" had been replaced by "*mestizo*" in the rest of Central America, it remained an identifiable ethnic category in Guatemala, following the rise of Liberalism and its construction of a coffee economy.[21] The state solidified the binary identity between ladino and Indigenous due to its need for Indigenous labor, which was forcibly elicited through labor drafts.[22] As René Reeves notes, Indigenous and non-Indigenous identity was cultural rather than biological. "Acculturated Maya could be brought into the body politic by 'becoming' ladinos. This required them to detach themselves from their community of origin and to forfeit their corporate land rights."[23] Despite the fact that the term itself is highly unstable, during the revolutionary decade, this racialized structure continued to serve as an important signifier of opportunity and social status in a country deeply divided by race and class.[24]

Legalized during the Árbenz administration in 1952, the PGT adopted its labor-oriented name precisely to attract rural, working-class, and Indigenous Guatemalans who held deep suspicions about an urban ladino organization. PGT member Bernardo Alvarado Monzón describes PGT's divergence from the classic Leninist party structure and adaptation to the Guatemalan context:

> Our workers, our peasants, and our middle class are very backward because of the semi-feudal conditions in our country and because of the tyrants who oppressed us for so long. But these are our people, in whose midst we must forge our party. . . . This is why we are critical of those comrades who look down on our new members and welcome only those who are already "well prepared." They forget that communists are molded within the party. . . . The belief that the party should be small, that it should be primarily a school of Marxist theory, and that its prospective members should arrive well-qualified . . . has isolated us from the masses and restricted the party's growth.[25]

Although the vast majority of its members were not steeped in orthodox Marxist-Leninist ideology, the PGT's identification of Guatemala's deep socioeconomic inequalities and its support of the Decree 900 Agrarian Land Reform in May 1952 drew many rural and working-class members.[26] The efficacy of their adapted approach became evident as their membership swelled to five thousand by the end of the revolution in 1954.[27] These efforts represented a marked departure from the approach of President Arévalo, whose suspicion of rural organizing "limited the revolution's early actions."[28] While they only ever held four of the fifty-eight congressional seats, following the election of

Árbenz in 1950, the PGT leadership formed the president's trusted inner circle before their formal political recognition in 1952.[29]

The Alianza Femenina Guatemalteca

Communist women found an autonomous political space in which to advocate for their social and political ideals in the Alianza Femenina Guatemalteca.[30] While women were increasingly recognized as a significant political force, they confronted an entrenched patriarchal political system, a highly gendered and stratified system that remained unaltered throughout the revolutionary decade. In order to contain the women's growing influence, male politicians employed a strategy of creating female affiliates, a tactic that at once mobilized women on behalf of specific political parties and simultaneously marginalized the women from leadership and policy-making power.[31] The Alianza became a sanctuary for women from a variety of prorevolutionary parties and was a vital women's association willing to engage with gender analysis within a political milieu that had marginalized women from mainstream parties and defined gender as secondary to other dimensions of analysis.

Women embraced a particular strategy for their political engagement in the face of their small numbers and the opposition they experienced from the majority of their male peers.[32] Unwilling to build ideological barriers by differentiating themselves from other politically active women, communist women developed a multiparty strategy that included membership in a variety of noncommunist political parties, avoiding the label of socialist or communist.[33] De Urrutia exemplifies this approach, belonging to several prorevolutionary parties, including the Renovación Nacional (National Renovation), the Partido Acción Revolucionaria (Revolutionary Action Party), and then the Partido de la Revolución Guatemalteca (Guatemalan Revolutionary Party), before joining the PGT once it was formed in 1951. A representative of the labor union the Trabajadoras de Beneficios de Café (Coffee-Processing Workers), Hernández Rojás was also the leader of the female affiliate of the Comité Político Nacional de los Trabajadores (National Workers Political Committee) and member of the executive committee of the Confederación de Trabajadores de Guatemala (CTG, Confederation of Guatemalan Workers); both she and López were executive members of the Partido Revolucionario Obrero de Guatemala (PROG, Workers Revolutionary Party of Guatemala). Carmen Vargas de Amezquita became the leader of the female affiliate of the Partido de la Revolución Guatemalteca (PRG, Guatemalan Revolutionary Party), a party that united all noncommunist parties in support of the Árbenz presidency. During the early 1950s the leadership of the PRG and that of the Alianza were virtually indistinguishable at times.[34]

Drawn together by a shared feminist and class consciousness, the Alianza served as an incubator in which women identified and integrated gender analysis into their existing class critiques.[35] The Alianza's significance for communist women was confirmed by the leader of the PGT women's affiliate, Irma de Alvarado, in a 1952 report to the PGT's second congress. "It is critical for the party to make more of a commitment to work with the Alianza Femenina Guatemalteca, a powerful mass organization that raises and addresses the issues of better working conditions for women and children."[36] In turn, communist women played key leadership roles within the Alianza, which achieved some of the most important social reforms for women during the early 1950s. The most prominent communist women in the Alianza were Hernández Rojas, Haydeé Godoy, Chávez de Alvarado, de Urrutia, López, and Dora Franco y Franco, although many women were likely involved in the activism but did not maintain formal memberships in the PGT or any political party. These leaders brought Lenin's conviction to the Alianza that the success or failure of the revolution was directly dependent upon the participation of women.[37] Adopting this political ideology as the barometer for their activism, the communist women were pivotal in integrating gender equality into the foundation of the Alianza's sociopolitical platform.

The Alianza's theoretical development undergirding its sociopolitical agenda was facilitated by its relationships with transnational women's organizations. The organization was itself born in the aftermath of the First Inter-American Congress of Women, held in Guatemala City in August 1947, a hemispheric conference that the U.S. section of the WILPF initiated. WILPF was created in 1915 in The Hague, the Netherlands, by a group of women dedicated to peaceful solutions in the midst of World War I. Within an ambitious agenda, its organizers were advocates of a wide range of women's rights, including suffrage. Through WILPF and other organizations represented at the congress, the nascent Alianza members were exposed to hemispheric organizations and ideas, a transformative experience for a community long isolated by dictatorial regimes. The topics presented throughout the congress were highly democratic, anti-imperialistic, egalitarian, and transnational in scope.[38] Its delegates advocated for principles that transcended nationalistic concerns, including the call for an improvement in the quality of life for those without access to basic human rights, including education, adequate nutrition, and healthcare, drawing direct inspiration from the 1945 Chapultepec Conference.[39] Held in March, the Chapultepec Conference was convened to strengthen wartime cooperation against possible military threats. Its resolutions emphasized that all activities be consistent with the principles of the emerging United Nations. The Guatemalan delegation at Chapultepec recommended the condemnation of intervention by a state in the internal or external affairs of another state. Guatemala also recommended that all American republics abstain from recognizing and maintaining relations with antidemocratic regimes, especially those that had come to power through a coup against a democratically elected government. The subsequent resolutions approved during the 1947 congress advocated for the extension of democracy by raising the standard of living for all peoples and fostering civil rights for women.[40] The congress also addressed global warfare and the role of U.S. foreign policy and militarization. In short, the congressional resolutions reflected a clarity regarding the needs of women living in Latin America.

The women who formed the Alianza immediately following the congress were electrified by its sociopolitical critiques. Without the theoretical background to name Guatemala's enormous socioeconomic challenges, they had been identifying their historic inequalities in what scholar Devaleena Das refers to as as "the epistemological tool of experience."[41] For at least some of the future Alianza members, their interactions with participants at the Congress gave them the ideological tools they had been lacking. First lady Árbenz recalled they were introduced to Marxist ideas that finally gave them the language and intellectual ideas surrounding the complex interplay among class, gender, and economics that resonated with the Guatemalan context.[42] Precisely when women formed the Alianza Femenina Guatemalteca following the 1947 congress is unclear, as no records remain of its founding. The first public reference to the Alianza appears in October 1947, less than two months after the congress, in a public newspaper, and several sources list members of the Alianza during its early years.[43] Some of those early leaders include María Isabel Foronda de Vargas Romero, who was identified as the secretary general; Hortensia Hernández Rojás as secretary; Romelia A. de Folgar as responsible for legal matters; Franco y Franco as treasurer; and Matilde Elena López in charge of propaganda. What is clear from these sparse records is that women who became members of the PGT during the 1950s had been critical to the creation of the Alianza in 1947.

The Inter-American Federation of Women was formed at the end of the congress, and the Alianza joined it immediately.[44] Designed as an umbrella organization to facilitate hemispheric communication and alliances, the federation created an essential network of transnational solidarity for Guatemalan women through which they could exchange sociopolitical ideals.[45] Its organizers envisioned the Federación de Mujeres de las Américas to be merely the first step in the creation of a larger women's confederation, the Confederación Interamericana de Mujeres (Inter-American Confederation of Women). The federation hoped to spread its message of unity and democracy through the educational systems, workers' networks, literature and literacy campaigns, and the construction of schools.[46] During the Alianza's formative years, the federation played a key role in helping its members to develop hemispheric relationships. The Alianza listed its federation affiliation within Alianza brochures and political pamphlets, its membership critical to their sense of place within the Americas. As federation affiliates, they sent letters to the U.S. Secretary of State in response to labor disputes between the United Fruit Company and Guatemalan workers. Within months the Alianza had hosted delegates traveling to other such conferences, maintained contact with the WILPF organizers, and hosted a delegation from the United Nations.[47] The Alianza's affiliations with the federation and WILPF along with high-ranking members of the Arévalo government gave Alianza members unusual access for such a young organization to international associations.

The Alianza's ideological platform fused the economic and political critiques articulated during the 1947 congress with the existing maternal Guatemalan feminism, creating a feminist ideology with a high degree of class and gender consciousness.[48] During the Arévalo administration, parallel gender structures had been celebrated, demarcating the realm of social reforms; describing the care of children, orphans, and the disabled as essentially women's work; and affirming and solidifying the gendered binary of masculine and feminine spheres.[49] While this approach had effectively elevated maternalism as an influential voice within the social reform movement, it also essentially depoliticized women. The Alianza, by contrast, insisted that women must participate within the revolutionary political sphere: "Women cannot abandon the problems of agrarian reform, industrialization, the peace movement and national sovereignty to the realm of men[,] and society cannot be separated into two spheres."[50] For the Alianza, addressing gender inequalities was just as pivotal to revolutionary reforms as was class, and Alianza members emerged as tireless advocates for a wide variety of working-class and rural women. The Alianza approach developed new questions regarding healthcare, education, and the nutritional status of children, identifying the devastating realities of Guatemala's historic class, racial, and gender inequities. The necessary language and tools Alianza members developed during the Arévalo era enabled them to enact structural reforms during the Árbenz era.

During the first months of the Árbenz presidency, the Second Inter-American Congress held in Mexico City in 1951 affirmed the Alianza's focus on the well-being of women and children.[51] Alianza members were involved in the congressional preparations and ultimately sent ten representatives, including de Urrutia, Godoy, and Hernández Rojas from the PGT.[52] The congressional conclusion that activists must "intensify the campaign to aid children in whom the future of nations lies" led directly to one of the Alianza's most important initiatives.[53] Upon their return, the women launched the Conference on the Defense of Children held in Guatemala City, December 14–21, 1951. In her capacity as director of the child associations, first lady and Alianza member Árbenz initiated the conference, and PGT female affiliate leader Chávez de Alvarado organized the entire event. Although the conference was the idea and work of PGT women and the Alianza, the public president and vice presidents were all male, reflecting the patriarch barriers political activists faced. It is also possible having the director of public education and other powerful male figures involved in the conference meant that its resolutions had a better chance of implementation. PGT members Foronda de Vargas Romero, Haydée Godoy, López, and Hernández Rojás represented the Alianza at the conference. Its conclusions included a call for a national minimum wage for rural and urban workers, access to education, and laws to protect children and provide for maternity leave, representing a fundamental and systematic restructuring of Guatemala's socioeconomic infrastructure.[54]

The 1951 Congress also appears to have influenced the Alianza's work to reform Guatemalan gender norms. One of its resolutions called for a broad-based program to educate men and women on the need to create, in their words, "the good man." The congress urged countries throughout the Americas to establish education in the home, school, and society to help all people understand and practice the ideas of equality for the effect of joint responsibility and collaboration in all domestic and social tasks.[55] Integrating this affirmation of new gender roles into their expanding sociopolitical agenda, the Alianza, at their only national conference in 1953, provided an analysis of the impact of Guatemala's patriarchal system within every public and private sector of society (President Árbenz was overthrown seven months later). Amidst their far-ranging conclusions, the Alianza members identified the plight of domestic workers, among the most invisible of Guatemala's workforce, whom the 1947 Labor Code had overtly excluded from any sort of labor protection or law.[56] Alianza members publicly denounced sexual abuse of those women who historically have been seen as sexually available to male members of Guatemalan households. They reported instances when if a domestic worker became pregnant, she was dismissed or forced to abandon her child because such pregnancies carried the obvious signs of patriarchal misbehavior.[57] The Alianza's public acknowledgment of this type of sexual abuse represented an unprecedented gendered indictment of Guatemala's patriarchal system, and the organizers launched plans for a domestic workers' union.[58]

During the last year of its existence, the Alianza fused gender analysis with Guatemala's agrarian reform, facilitating a new direction in their activism. Its relationship with the WIDF accelerated this expanding political agenda, helping the Alianza contextualize the issue of land reforms. Founded on November 29, 1945, at the International Congress of Women in Paris, the WIDF rapidly became the largest women's organization in the world, drawing its membership from a wide variety of women's organizations. Despite its involvement with the United Nations, the U.S. State Department saw the WIDF's large membership from countries within the Soviet sphere and global south as placing it firmly on the wrong side of the Cold War. The WIDF initiated the 1975 UN International Women's Year, a turning point for large-scale activities directed at improving women's status worldwide.

The WIDF's interrelated conceptual emphasis on antifascism, global peace, women's rights, and better living conditions for children resonated deeply with the Alianza's ideals for its sociopolitical context.[59] Just when the Alianza joined the WIDF is not clear. The WIDF had sent teams into Latin America to make contacts with local women's organizations during the late 1940s, but it is likely that Alianza's relationship with the Federation of Women and WILPF facilitated a contact.[60] However the Alianza connected with the WIDF, the WIDF's use of maternalist language to legitimate women's sense of neutrality in their observations of conflict and politics fit well with the Alianza's feminisms.[61] Several members of the Alianza, including de Urrutia and Franco y Franco, attended the WIDF conference in Copenhagen in June 1953. Here they found a common sense of purpose and a renewed direction with its Declaration on the Rights of Women, which included all women irrespective of their "race, nationality and position in society."[62] Included within the list of rights, the "rights of peasant women to own land and to the fruits of the land," the granting of the same rights to agricultural as to industrial women workers in regards to wages, measures of security at work, and the protection of mother and child, and the "right to vote and to be elected to all state bodies, without restrictions and discrimination" were pivotal to the work of the Alianza.[63] Just days after the delegates returned from the 1953 congress, they issued the following statement that echoed every element of the WIDF's resolutions: "The working woman and the peasant woman should find a place in the Alianza Femenina Guatemalteca from which to fight for improved salaries and living conditions of children and women, and to work with other social sectors for progress and independence, as well as the peace and happiness of the Guatemalan home."[64] As María Jérez de Fortuny would later claim, Alianza's relationship with the WIDF allowed them to establish contacts with organizations in other countries that amplified their understanding of what were called women's problems.[65]

The Alianza sent Franco y Franco, de Urrutia, and Daisy Alfaro, who were also members of the PGT, into the rural areas to meet with rural and Indigenous women. The three women visited farm communities on a weekly basis (every Sunday, the only day rural women had time off from work) to understand their challenges and develop an awareness regarding their rights as women and workers during the Árbenz era of land reform.[66] The Alianza's records suggest that their message resonated primarily in rural agricultural areas that the United Fruit Company dominated.

The Alianza's commitment to working-class women brought them into direct confrontation with Guatemala's patriarchal attitudes toward the economic contributions of women following the 1952 agrarian-reform law Decree 900. Women's work, particularly, rural and Indigenous women's work, had been historically ignored despite their incontrovertible contributions within such fields as the agricultural sector. Although women dominated the coffee-picking workforce, the job of coffee picker did not appear on the national census as late as 1921. While the redistribution of land had an immediate positive economic impact on rural families, the government directed its policy at male heads of household, excluding countless single mothers from this essential economic reform. In response, rural women began to petition the Alianza directly with regard to the inequitable distribution of land, and the Alianza presented these stories to the National Agrarian Reform Commission. One such situation described by Alianza executive secretary de Urrutia, revealed that a single mother was denied her request for land as head of her household based solely on her identity as a woman. In her letter of support, de Urrutia highlighted the intersection of gender and class: "In countries that have maintained backward feudalism, they have also preserved habits and mentality including a false morality that authorizes men to reduce women to objects without property, supreme servitude, and obedience."[67] One particular confrontation with male bureaucrats made its way onto the front pages of several national newspapers. Using the man's name directly, the Alianza challenged one local agrarian-reform committee member in the coffee-growing area of Alotenango.[68] His response was simply, "I refuse to give land to women." In the face of this intransigence, the Alianza resolved to integrate women into the national agrarian-reform program through equal access to credit, fair prices for their crops, and improved agricultural technology.

The Alianza's policy shift to address Guatemala's historic, structural gendered inequity had immediate results. By late 1953 their advocacy on behalf of rural and Indigenous women had increased their membership by 600 percent from the preceding year, extending the organization into twelve departments.[69] The *Alianza* encouraged rural women to form committees in order to identify their specific social and economic needs. Once the group reached ten people, the Alianza incorporated them as an official affiliate. The ideological structure undermining these committees was a grass-roots approach based upon the belief that women were capable of identifying their own needs, which, no doubt, was attractive to many rural women whose concerns had been historically ignored. Rural women rapidly outnumbered the original urban members, in a similar pattern to the PGT party itself. By the time the Alianza held its first and only national congress in 1953, at least 1,377 separate committees were represented, including 450 groups from the capital city, 677 from Escuintla, and 250 from Santa Rosa. Although the exact number of members remains unclear, calculating these numbers suggests that at least 13,770 women were associated with the Alianza. Although it existed as a national organization, led by politically powerful women, such as first lady Árbenz, the Alianza comprised primarily small, localized committees, most of whose members were rural and working class.[70]

Despite the groundswell of rural and working-class membership, one of the unanswered questions is the Alianza's perspective on Guatemala's majority Indigenous population, particularly in light of its prevalence at the 1951 Inter-American Congress in Mexico City. One of Mexico's delegates led the discussion over the nature of education within Indigenous communities and their economic participation within the nation-state, acknowledging that "the Indian population of the Americas" had not been given the same opportunities as other citizens.[71] The delegates identified the need for educational materials to be produced in Indigenous languages in order to preserve their cultures and to enrich the literature and histories of the entire community.[72] Furthermore, the delegates called for competent teachers (presumably those who could speak the community language) to be engaged in the process of education. The congressional delegates also called for broad-based economic reforms so that Indigenous peoples could be taught how to improve their economic standard of living without "attempting to change their customs."[73]

These resolutions regarding Indigenous communities represented a radical departure from conclusions reached by the Guatemalan section of the inter-American agency, the Instituto Indigenista Interamericano (III), which defined its attempts to integrate Indigenous communities into the dominant national culture as a breakdown of the traditional structure in order to create a new civilization, in other words, to integrate Indigenous peoples into the modern nation-state. Antonio Goubard Cabrera, III director, defined "*indigenismo*" as "an awareness of social problems involving the adjustment of the Indian to occidental civilization. He goes on to say,

> I cannot ignore the many social values found in the different cultures of ethnic groups throughout the world . . . but it would seem that in breaking up of present civilization, an active attitude, a positive attempt to unify values, appears to be the one that will build a new civilization. This attempt is a process of simplification which arises from an understanding of diverse values, and is a concomitant in the development of civilization. In other words, and in regard to Guatemala, this attempt means a homogeneous nation.[74]

There are few documents to indicate how the Alianza responded to the III's work in Guatemala or the 1951 congressional call to reform the state's relationship with Indigenous peoples. In a singular 1953 example, a manifesto that the Alianza issued on International Women's Day included an acknowledgment of the reality that Guatemala's Indigenous people (who made up 70 percent of the country's rural population) had an incredibly low economic income.[75] The Alianza's actions support this example and demonstrate a consistent understanding of the ways in which women and particularly Indigenous women were doubly discriminated against within Guatemala's institutional structures. The Alianza's policies and solidarity with rural and Indigenous women, agricultural and factory workers, and domestic and market women filled a gendered gap where unions and land reformers could only imagine men as recipients of reform. During its last year, Alianza included in its agenda a call for constitutional reforms to the definition of citizen, which at the time explicitly denied illiterate women the right to vote and which, according to national figures from 1950, represented roughly 95 percent of Indigenous women and 55 percent of Spanish-speaking women.[76] Its focus on structural labor and land reforms as well as on the political rights of illiterate women indicates the development of an understanding of Guatemala's structural racism within the Alianza.[77]

The experiences of communist women within the Alianza with their transnational partners played a significant role, particularly, for women from a less-powerful country. Guatemalan women had been isolated by decades of dictatorial regimes, unable to travel and exchange ideas with other women's organizations. Connections with the WILPF and WIDF filled this historic vacuum, creating a network with other Latin American women and across the global south. For women from Guatemala's small Communist Party, their transnational contacts created a sense of global solidarity, encouraging them to take their rightful place nationally on sociopolitical problems. They used these transnational affiliations to claim authority within Guatemala, consistently identifying themselves as the members of the Inter-American Federation of Women in every public declaration and activism.

These transnational events also demonstrated the multidimensional possibilities and benefits for women in less-powerful countries. The Guatemalan child social reforms represented by the *comedores infantíles* (nutrition centers), and *guarderías infantíles* (childcare centers) were on full display during the 1947 congress, and delegates toured the facilities in and around Guatemala City.[78] The centers gained international attention, receiving accolades from the Universidad Femenina de México in 1949 and Eva Perón, the spouse of Argentine president Juan Domingo Perón.[79] Alianza members brought their hard-earned experiences to the discussions on the status of children at the 1951 Second Inter-American Congress in Mexico City, where they highlighted child-welfare reforms developed by a cross-class alliance between Elisa Martínez de Arévalo, wife of President Arévalo, and the working-class and market women in Guatemala City in 1945 into the comprehensive socioeconomic solutions to childhood poverty. The Alianza's contribution to the child-reform movement in the Americas displayed empowering elements of transnationalism, shifting the dominant currents of knowledge within transnational women's associations that had historically flowed from north to south.[80]

Alianza's transnational connections became increasingly important as its members reached out to both the WILPF and the WIDF as the rumors and fear of an invasion grew during the first months of 1954. For its part, the WILPF actively advocated on Guatemala's behalf, declaring the threatened invasion to be imperialistic and illegal according to international law and sending letters to the U.S. Secretary of State in response to labor disputes between the United Fruit Company and Guatemalan workers. Heloise Brainerd, the head of the U.S. section of WILPF, petitioned the U.S. State Department directly to advocate on Guatemala's behalf. In the following months, she and others continued to inform their global partners of the threat to the Árbenz government.[81] WIDF members petitioned the U.S. government to halt its support and intervention in Guatemala, and in the months following the 1954 political overthrow of Jacobo Árbenz, the new WILPF chair, Carolyn B. Threlkeld, sent out notices to the membership regarding this injustice. U.S. members of both WILPF and WIDF continued to publicly denounce their own government for its participation in the 1954 military coup d'état against Árbenz. These transnational connections were severed for members of the Alianza, however, as their leadership, including many of its communist members, went into exile, and their national cross-class feminist organizing was permanently ruptured amid the political terror of the following decades.

Conclusion

Transnational connections were pivotal to the Alianza's theoretical and political development. As a dynamic and evolving organization, these connections facilitated a consciousness of Guatemala's gendered and class stratification and simultaneously enabled women within the Alianza to share experiences with women across the globe. Through the Alianza, communist women were responsible for some of the most important socioeconomic reforms of the democratic decade. They embraced democratic principles and suffrage for all women, including all illiterate women, explicitly calling for the inclusion of Indigenous women. They demanded women's right to land ownership during the 1952 pivotal Agrarian Reform Program, along with increased social safety nets for children. They insisted that class, gender and ethnic analyses be integrated into all state-sponsored social reforms. While they remained rooted within their national context, their activism was informed and expanded by their relationships with the WIDF and the WILPF. Their connection to a transnational community offered women from a small Communist Party within a patriarchal society common ground with the global female condition, bound together by sociopolitical inequality and imperialist domination.

Notes

1. A historiographic analysis is beyond the purview of this essay.

2. Deutsch, "New School Lecture," 99.

3. See Valobra and Yusta Rodrigo, *Queridas camaradas*; Cofino, "Las comunistas de la decada"; Marino, *Feminism for the Americas*, 166.

4. Ruano Najarro and Obando Sánchez, *Comunismo y movimiento obrero*, 32.

5. Cofiño, "Huellas de las comunistas," 2.

6. Gleijeses, *Shattered Hope*, 78–79. This trend has been identified by historians Jadwiga Pieper-Mooney and Francisca de Haan. See Mooney and Lanza, *De-centering Cold War History*; Haan, "Continuing Cold War Paradigms." The most notable of this interpretation is found in the works of Schneider, *Communism in Guatemala*; Poppino, *International Communism in Latin America*; and James, *Red Design for the Americas*. The role of the Alianza has not been examined since.

7. Vilanova de Árbenz, *Mi esposo*, 38.

8. See Iber, *Neither Peace nor Freedom*.

9. Julia Urrutia, in-person interview with author, July 2004. Guatemala City.

10. McDonnell, *Masters of Empire*, 14.

11. For further information, see Wagner, *History of Coffee*. In fact, these unionist circles were responsible for the proposal of universal suffrage in 1920, which missed approval by one vote.

12. Randolph, "Diplomatic History," 68, 75.

13. See Cofiño, "Las primeras comunistas," 177. Cofiño's source was Taracena Arriola and Lucas Monteflores, *Diccionario biográfico*. The women arrested include María Ákvarezm, María Paniagua, Juana M. Corea G., María C. Cruz, Marcelina Dávila, Manuela Cleopatra Dávila, Sotera Flores Morales, Lucrecia Galeano, Reyes Girón de Masay, Francisca González, Petrona González, Felisa Juárez, Natalia viuda de Saquilmer, Petrona Saquilmer, Dolores Masaya, Teresa Masaya de Juárez, Ángela Mota, Filomena Mungía Sibaja V. de Guardían, Victorinana Soto Gómez, Violeta Téllez, and Rosa Valenzuela. The Archivo General de Centro América, Guatemala City, also contains references to the arrest and imprisonment of women by Ubico's forces but does not provide any further evidence.

14. Anderson, *Che Guevara*, 126.

15. Gleijeses, *Shattered Hope*, 186. Guatemala established diplomatic relations with the USSR in April 1945.

16. Gleijeses, *Shattered Hope*, 184.

17. Gleijeses, *Shattered Hope*, 186. One of the most important leaders, José Fortuny only traveled to the Soviet Union in 1957.

18. Gleijeses, *Shattered Hope*, 189.

19. Historian Greg Grandin agrees with this conclusion and demonstrates their increased international contacts during the post-1954 era. Grandin, *Last Colonial Massacre*, 89.

20. Gleijeses, *Shattered Hope*, 185. It also appears that Víctor Manuel Gutiérrez traveled to Moscow in 1951 following the World Federation of Trade Unions meeting in Berlin.

21. Smith, introduction, 3.

22. Taracena Arriola, *Etnicidad*, 1:416.

23. Reeves, *Ladinos with Ladinos*, 10.

24. For further analysis see Herrera, *Natives, Europeans, and Africans*; Hale, *Más que un Indio*; Casaús Arzú, *Guatemala*; Konefal, *For Every Indio Who Falls*.

25. "Informe presentado por el camarado Bernardo Alvarado M. a nombre de la comisión del comité central en la conferencia nacional de organización del Partido Guatemalteco del Trabajo-8 y 9 de Agosto de 1953," *Organización* 7, September 1953, 7–8, Guatemalan Documents Collection (hereafter referred to as GDC), Library of Congress, Washington, DC.

26. See Grandin, *Last Colonial Massacre*; Gleijeses, *Shattered Hope*.

27. Gleijses, *Shattered Hope*, 195. The PGT was an urban-based Ladino Party led by middle-class intellectuals. It grew to include a significant number of agricultural workers, including Indigenous men.

28. Carey, "Rethinking Representation," 156.

29. Gleijses, *Shattered Hope*, 147.

30. A total of thirty-five PGT women were members of the Alianza.

31. Miller, *Latin American Women*, 112.

32. Ríos Tobar, "Feminism Is Socialism," 132.

33. The Guatemalan Communist Party records confiscated by the U.S. State Department and now held in the GDC contain only four women's names, including Dora Franco y Franco.

34. Container 9; container 15, October 31, 1946; container 9, June 1951; Matilde Elena López, "Publicaciones del Comité Central del Partido Revolucionario Obrero de Guatemala, (PROG), Bosquejo Histórico Universal, Guatemala," June 1951, report, container 9, n.d., all GDC.

35. Hojas Sueltas, 1950, Archivo General de Centro América, Guatemala City, Guatemala.

36. Irma del Alvarado, "Intervención especial sobre el trabajo en el Frente femenina a cargo del Irma del Alvarado en el Segundo Congreso de Partido Guatemalteco del Trabajo," December 1952," file, 5, GDC.

37. Alvarado, "Intervención especial sobre el trabajo," 2; Cofiño, "Huellas de las comunistas," 6.

38. Wamsley, "Hemisphere of Women," 244; Marino, *Feminism for the Americas*, 226.

39. Longley, *In the Eagle's Shadow*, 187; Immerman, *CIA in Guatemala*, 94.

40. "Proyecto de reglamente del congreso interamericano de mujeres," file, 3, Archivo General de Centro América, Guatemala City, Guatemala.

41. Devaleena Das, Transnational Feminism Workshop, McMaster University, Ontario, May 12, 2018.

42. Gleijeses, *Shattered Hope*, 141.

43. Carrillo Samayoa and Torres Urizar, *Nosotras*, 154. The newspapers *Nuestro Diario* (Guatemala City), May 7, 1948, and *Diario de Centro América* (Guatemala City), September 1, 1949, provide the first full listing of the Alianza executive.

44. For further information on the 1947 Inter-American Congress of Women, see Harms, *Ladina Social Activism*, chap. 5.

45. *Federación de Mujeres de las Américas*, March 1951; *El Imparcial* (Guatemala City), August 29, 1947; Heloise Brainerd, November 1, 1947; and Carolyn B. Threlkeld, Chairman of the Latin American Committee on the Issue of the 1954 overthrow of Árbenz, November, 1954, all in Women's International League for Peace and Freedom (hereafter referred to as WILPF), U.S. section, reel 130.30, DG43, Swarthmore College Peace Collection (hereafter referred to as SCPC), Swarthmore College.

46. To date, no other primary documents relating to this organization have been discovered. The few remaining references to it remain within the WILPF papers, and it is never referred to within Guatemalan newspapers. The U.S. section of the WILPF joined the federation during its annual board meeting in Boston, October 24–26, 1947.

47. Over the next several years, the newspaper *Nuestro Diario* (Guatemala City) ran a series on high-profile visits between women of the Unión de Mujeres Democráticas and former delegates of the 1947 congress. The first occurred on November 13, 1947. In 1948 *Nuestro Diario* noted visits with international delegates on February 26, March 18, and March 22, 1948.

48. Maternal feminism is the belief that women as caregivers have an important role to play in society and politics.

49. *Diario de Centro América* (Guatemala City), October 8, 1948.

50. "Congreso de la mujer guatemalteca," editorial, *Diario del Pueblo* (Guatemala City), publication of Partido de la Revolución Guatemalteca (PRG), November 25, 1953, GDC.

51. There are very few records of this second congress. A two-page document titled "Federación de Mujeres de las América" and a small pamphlet on the program contents were found among the Guatemalan Documents Collection in the Library of Congress and the Women's International League for Peace and Freedom Papers at Swarthmore College. See Heloise Brainerd, February 17, 1951, WILPF, U.S. section, reel 130.30, DG43, SCPC.

52. *Resolutions of the Second Inter-American Congress of Women*, Mexico City, October 12–19, 1951, WILPF, reel 130.30, DG43, 1–6, SCPC. Guatemalan C. Otilia de Balcárcel led the fourth commission, which called for adequate laws in public health and the spread of disease.

53. Federación de Mujeres de las Américas, "Segundo congreso interamericano de mujeres que se efectuara en la ciudad de México, capital de la república Mexicána, del 12 al 19 de octubre de 1951," 1, GDC.

54. There is little direct evidence of how these resolutions were implemented. However, the 1952 agrarian reform law addressed many of these economic inequities.

55. *Resolutions of the Second Inter-American Congress of Women*, Mexico City, October 12–19, 1951, WILPF, reel 130.30, DG43, 3, SCPC.

56. Forster, *Time of Freedom*, 102.

57. "Informe de la comisión de AFG, situación de las mujeres que trabajan," container 6, 3, GDC.

58. The Alianza disbanded in July 1954 following the overthrow of Árbenz, and it is likely the union was not established.

59. Haan, "Continuing Cold War Paradigms," 550.

60. Armstrong, "Before Bandung." Within the surviving documents, the Alianza makes a reference to the WIDF by the late 1940s.

61. Donert, "From Communist Internationalism," 333.

62. Women's International Democratic Federation (WIDF), *World Congress of Women*, 254.

63. WIDF, *World Congress of Women*, 255.

64. File, container 9, July 1, 1953, 7, GDC; WIDF, *World Congress of Women*, 254.

65. Stoltz Chinchilla, *Nuestras utopías*, 151.

66. "Informe de la comisión de AFG, situación de las mujeres que trabajan," container 6, GDC.

67. Editorial, *Diario del Pueblo* (Guatemala City), November 25, 1953.

68. *Diario de Centro América* (Guatemala City), February 8, 1954.

69. "Informe de la secretaria general de A.F.G.," November 1953, 4, container 6, GDC.

70. Harms, *Ladina Social Activism*, 165. According to the 1950 census, rural Ladina and Indigenous women had literacy rates of 29 percent and 4 percent, respectively.

71. *Resolutions of the Second Inter-American Congress of Women*, Mexico City, October 12–19, 1951, WILPF, reel 130.30, DG43, 2, SCPC.

72. From the scant existing sources, this concern was raised by a Mexican delegation, but it is unclear as to why their approach differed so dramatically from the contemporary dominant approaches.

73. Resolutions of the Second Inter-American Congress of Women.

74. Antonio Goubard Cabrera, Instituto Indigenista Interamericano, *América Indígena* (Mexico) 5, no. 4 (1945): 377.

75. *Nuestro Diario* (Guatemala City, Guatemala), March 9, 1953.

76. Dirección General de Estadística, *Censos*.

77. The PGT's thinking about the role of ethnic identity evolved during the 1960s and 1970s as its members worked with Indigenous communities during the thirty-six-year civil war.

78. For further information on these centers, see chap. 3, Harms, *Ladina Social Activism*.

79. Container 3, March 11, 1952, GDC. In a note from María Árbenz to the Guatemalan ambassador, Árbenz thanks Eva Perón for her financial contributions to the nutrition centers. Other evidence suggests a professional relationship as first ladies between Eva Perón and Elisa de Areválo.

80. For further analysis on the flows of knowledge within traditional transnational movements, see Briggs, McCormick, and Way, "Transnationalism," 627.

81. Carolyn B. Threlkeld, chairman of the Latin American Committee on the Issue of the 1954 overthrow of Árbenz, November 1954, WILPF, U.S. section, reel 130.30, DG43, SCPC.

Transnational Youth and Student Groups in the 1950s

MARC BECKER

In 1951 two communist youth leaders, one of whom had been to Moscow, returned from Europe to their homes in Colombia. Their international experiences had energized and inspired them, and they immediately set to work to rejuvenate youth organizations in their country. Fortuitously, a student delegation from neighboring Ecuador soon arrived. Together, the activists planned a visit to Venezuela to propose the creation of a Gran Colombian student federation, with a founding congress to be held in Bogotá on October 12, 1951. The goal was to build a strong and powerful youth movement, not only in their individual countries but across the region.[1]

The students ultimately were not successful in creating the planned federation, but their attempt highlights the interest, desire, and value that young activists found in cultivating transnational connections. This encounter across multiple borders is only one of many examples of how international travel, both within the Americas as well as globally, during the early post–World War II period both revitalized domestic organizing efforts in Latin America and contributed to the construction of powerful left-wing transnational networks. Before the military coup backed by the U.S. Central Intelligence Agency (CIA) overthrew the progressive government of Jacobo Árbenz in 1954, Guatemalan communists were also particularly active in encouraging transnational connections in order to build both domestic and international support for the reforms they sought to implement. Similarly, Chilean communists benefited from travel even though they faced a less-favorable environment at home and sometimes encountered serious sanctions upon their return. That repression, however, did not stop their activity, and, in fact, that sense of international solidarity inspired them to continue their struggles.[2]

The connections that students and other young people developed between different Latin American countries and with their counterparts around the world challenged the Cold War that was looming on the horizon. Their meetings laid important organizational groundwork for the Latin American left, and they transnationally linked together parties, movements, and organizations that otherwise would not have been in contact. In turn, these international encounters shifted the thinking, internal cultures, and horizons that helped foster the emergence of a strong Latin American left.

While these interactions have been largely forgotten or ignored, in retrospect their size, frequency, intensity, and ramifications are impressive. Evron Kirkpatrick, a propagandist, Cold War warrior, and husband to U.S. President Ronald Wilson Reagan's hawkish ambassador to the United Nations Jeane Kirkpatrick, noted that from 1953 through 1956, "Several thousand Latin Americans have visited behind the Iron and Bamboo curtains under Communist auspices or attended international front meetings outside the Western Hemisphere."[3] United States officials and their allies among the Latin American ruling class feared this movement. For a time those transnational connections challenged their ability to subjugate popular demands for a more peaceful, equal, and just world. More broadly, these networks in the 1950s laid the basis for much more militant actions that would soon emerge in what has come to be known as the "global 1960s."

Much of this travel in the 1950s occurred under the auspices of newly formed mass organizations—what opponents derogatorily referred to as communist front groups. The largest and best known of these mass organizations was the World Peace Council (WPC), which organized a series of international congresses and peace petitions.[4] Similarly, the second most-significant mass organization, the World Federation of Trade Unions (WFTU) along with its regional affiliates, including the Confederación de Trabajadores de América Latina (CTAL, Confederation of Latin American Workers), gained a global presence among workers. While these peace and labor groups had the largest participation and, hence, attracted the most attention, other mass organizations also fostered transnational connections among communist militants and others with similar progressive interests and concerns. These included the Women's International Democratic Federation (WIDF), the International Association of Democratic Lawyers (IADL), the World Federation of Scientific Workers

(WFSW), and the World Federation of Teachers' Union (FISE, from the French Federation Internationale Syndicale de L'Enseignement). All of these were founded between 1945 and 1946, most commonly in either London or Paris, and were headquartered in Europe. During the 1950s these mass organizations sponsored an ever-increasing number of delegations with more participants and a wider geographical spread that reached across the American hemisphere and linked the Americas with communist countries in Europe and Asia.[5]

Significantly, travel was not only in one direction. In 1955, for example, while almost two hundred delegations journeyed from Latin America to communist countries, the continent received twenty-nine return visits from communist countries. After the Chinese revolution in 1949, these exchanges were increasingly with Asia. At the same time, contacts also flourished within the Americas. While logically the most-active Latin American countries were those with the strongest communist parties (particularly Brazil, Mexico, Chile, Argentina, Uruguay, and Cuba), the travel extended to almost every country in the region. The largest number of delegations from Latin America involved cultural exchanges, youth and student groups, peace and friendship initiatives, and labor unions, though travel for scientific conferences, women's issues, trade fairs, and sports events was also significant. Visitors from communist countries to Latin America mostly arrived as part of cultural exchanges or for trade fairs, with most delegations arriving either to Argentina or Mexico because of their larger economies.[6] Those participating on these international trips often enjoyed a good deal of prestige upon their return to their home countries, both among their communist comrades as well as with the general public. They brought with them material for distribution at home, wrote articles or books, delivered lectures, and granted press interviews that reflected positively on the communist countries they had visited. Their experiences influenced public attitudes and general perceptions that extended well beyond the confines of their communist parties.[7] Those activities and contacts reflected the appeal that communist promises for peace and prosperity held for marginalized peoples in Latin America.

Rather than dedicating attention to communist party or labor leaders, this chapter examines the activities of young people and students whose international travels were just as important and compelling as those of labor confederations and peace campaigns. The number of youth and student groups and the frequency of their meetings ranked third, right behind their peace and labor counterparts. Many of the youth and student international meetings were organized under the umbrella of the World Federation of Democratic Youth (WFDY) and the International Union of Students (IUS, or UIE—Unión Internacional de Estudiantes—in Spanish). Both organizations emerged in the aftermath of World War II with the goal of uniting young people behind an antifascist platform that was broadly propeace, anti–nuclear war, and anti-imperialist and emphasized friendship between the youth in capitalist and socialist countries. One estimate from 1955 gave the membership of the WFDY as eighty-five million from ninety-seven countries, and the IUS as six million from seventy-two countries.[8] These were not insignificant organizations. For a brief period in the late 1940s, the WFDY was the most important mechanism for transnational networking among communist parties. Initially, both organizations were strongly European-oriented, but in the 1950s their influence spread out to Asia, Africa, and Latin America, thereby bringing those regions into a transnational orbit. In the process, they helped foster the organizational and political capacity of communist movements in what later came to be known as the global south.

While the number of travelers fluctuated year to year, depending on what opportunities presented themselves and what meetings took place, over the course of the 1950s the total only tended to increase. Fewer than one hundred Latin Americans traveled to Europe for peace and youth conferences in 1950, but by 1953 as the presence and strength of the mass organizations increased, one thousand did. That number dropped in 1954 with fewer transnational meetings but then doubled to a record of more than one thousand in 1955 with labor groups responsible this time for a large share of those expeditions.[9] Some traveled individually to study at a university, while others joined small groups or even large delegations. Scholarships, all-expense-paid tours, opportunities for scientific exchange at international congresses, and business opportunities all contributed to interest in such ventures.[10]

Unfortunately, young people and students left behind few surviving traces of their travels. Documentary evidence from the organizations they represented is scant, and their own writings are scattered among small periodicals that were often ephemeral in nature and, thus, difficult to locate in the standard repositories. In contrast, U.S. government officials kept copious records on these travels. Both the CIA and the State Department, including its Office of Intelligence Research (OIR), as well as other government agencies, generated voluminous amounts of data on communist activities that provide an excellent basis on which to reconstruct transnational activities. Although the data they generated are not exhaustive, they do thoroughly document how deeply these transnational connections reached into Latin America. The surveillance highlights not only government fears of losing geopolitical space to the Soviet Union and the socialist bloc internationally but also the nature of their ideological battle in Latin America against communist promises of a more equal and just world. Those factors explain why officials tracked international travel and sought to counter it.

World Federation of Democratic Youth (WFDY)

The WFDY was an initiative that emerged out of a World Youth Conference in November 1943 that encouraged youth to fight against fascism. Two years later and with the war recently concluded, five hundred delegates from sixty-five countries representing fifty million young people gathered in London to found the federation. The WFDY adopted a pledge for peace and international solidarity; organized campaigns for peace, democracy, human rights, and youth rights; and stood against war and oppression. By 1948 the WFDY claimed forty-eight million members in fifty-seven countries.

Although thirty-eight delegates and official observers from eight Latin American countries participated in the founding conference of the WFDY, those representatives played a relatively minor role, and at first the federation garnered little attention in the region. WFDY leaders, however, made strenuous efforts to extend the federation's reach. In order to understand better the lives and struggles of young people and to strengthen their ties with a global democratic youth movement, the WFDY sent its representatives around the world, including to Europe, Asia, Africa, the Middle East, and Latin America.[11] It supported the end of colonialism, including in Puerto Rico and Panama.[12] In the space of a couple years the WFDY quickly acquired a significant presence among young people in the Americas. In part this reflected the leftist tendencies of Latin American student organizations, but it was also a result of the appealing nature of its goals. Local affiliates became particularly active in Mexico, Cuba, and Venezuela.[13] Members embraced the federation as a global force for positive social change.

To foster these developments, WFDY headquarters in Paris published bulletins in Spanish that included information on youth struggles in Latin America as well as translations of material on the federation's international efforts. An issue from March 1949 included calls for an upcoming youth festival and for youth participation in a Paris peace congress as well as news from Europe, the United States, and Africa. Notes from Latin America denounced military repression in Venezuela, celebrated youth protests against the economic penetration of the United Fruit Company in Guatemala, condemned United States Marines who had defaced a José Martí monument in Cuba, and published a manifesto from the Brazilian student union in support of world peace.[14] The WFDY also translated and distributed articles from federation members around the world. In one issue treasurer Frances Damon outlined the federation's goals, and executive-committee member Ignacio Gallego discussed the struggle in Spain against fascism.[15] Another periodic bulletin transmitted information in Spanish for a Latin American audience on an upcoming Коммунистический Союз Молодёжи (Komsomol, All-Union Leninist Young Communist League) congress in Moscow.[16] These publications highlight the importance that the WFDY headquarters gave to Latin America, as well as the role it played in connecting young people with each other and with a global struggle.

State Department analysts complained that the "extreme left" dominated the local affiliates of the WFDY. As further evidence of that affiliation, the sole Latin American member of the executive council and six of the ten council members from Latin America selected at the London conference were "known or suspected Communists." Rather than a legitimate mass organization designed to advance common goals of a better and more just world, they painted the WFDY as nothing more than a communist front group with harmful and subversive intent. The analysts concluded, "The real goal of the WFDY in Latin America is to organize effective support, particularly among the youth, for Soviet policy at home and abroad."[17] CIA analysts similarly complained that "the WFDY has become an increasingly effective arm of Communist propaganda." This included an accelerated campaign to bolster "Latin American support for the Soviet drive in 'defense of peace.'"[18] U.S. officials could not conceive of a progressive movement outside of the confines of their Cold War blinders, and their reaction reflects both their knee-jerk anticommunism as well as the strength of these mass organizations.

As the federation became more closely aligned with communist goals and more loudly denounced Yankee imperialism, it also earned a significant degree of hostility from conservative Latin American governments. Those ruling-class representatives created barriers to holding youth conferences in the hemisphere, and at the same time they sought to foster an oppositional anticommunist youth organization. That objective was less than successful because their nascent federation was "strikingly similar to that of the WFDY, minus the pro-Communist and pro-Soviet slant of the latter."[19] As an astroturf organization without the organic basis and political drive of the WFDY, it did not realize significant success.

International Union of Students (IUS)

The International Union of Students has its roots in a gathering held in Prague, Czechoslovakia, in November 1945. Many of the participants at that meeting came from London, where they had just formed the WFDY. A hotly debated issue was whether a need existed for separate youth and student groups, particularly since most students were also young people. Some wanted to make the IUS subordinate to the larger WFDY. Another disagreement was whether the IUS should limit itself to a narrow subset of student issues, such as tuition payments and curricular concerns, or whether it should engage larger political issues that emerged out of the recently concluded world war including peace, social reform, and opposition to the resurgence of fascism. In the end the resulting organization attempted to reach a middle ground of defending the rights and interests of students, promoting improvements in their welfare and standards of education, and preparing them for their tasks as democratic citizens.[20] Delegates discussed how centrally organized the new organization should be and whether the secretariat would have power to act on its own or whether it should be limited to implementing resolutions passed at its congresses. Underlying all of these debates was how closely the organization should be associated with communist ideologies. These disputes soon led to a split in the organization, with a dissident anticommunist wing leaving to found the International Student Conference (ISC) that collapsed after revelations emerged in 1967 that it was a front group dependent on CIA funding.[21]

Activists formally founded the IUS as an association of university-student organizations at a World Student Congress in August 1946. The IUS had six main departments: travel and exchange; intellectual cooperation; relief and reconstruction; economic, social, and health; sports; and press and information. A president, four vice presidents, a secretary-general, and a secretariat composed of student representatives from various countries ran the organization. Those representatives worked full-time at the headquarters in a modern, recently constructed building near the center of Prague, where they received on-the-job training and guided the activities that the secretariat would undertake in their home regions.[22] The primary decision-making organ was a seventeen-member executive committee that met once a year. The IUS initially claimed to represent two and a half million students in forty-three countries, a number that subsequently grew to six million students from seventy-eight countries as the organization expanded its reach out of its base in Eastern Europe.

Like the WFDY, the IUS initially had a minimal presence in Latin America, but it soon achieved a global reach. As part of its efforts to solidify connections in the Americas, in 1947 the executive committee mandated Angel Vásquez, a representative of the Federación Estudiantil Universitaria (FEU, Federation of University Students) in Cuba, to implement a work program upon his return to his home country. Vásquez and a "Fernández-Gámiz" in representation of

Mexico and El Salvador attended the next executive committee meeting in the Rumanian capital, Bucharest, in May 1948, which discussed the accomplishments of the IUS in Latin America and the need for more cooperation between the IUS and the WFDY.[23]

Despite the resources the IUS put forward to build the student movement in Latin America, Vásquez failed to follow through with his commitments. The executive committee then decided to send the Spanish activist Arturo Acebez on a tour of the region. He planned to attend a congress of the Democratic Youth of Latin America in Mexico in April 1948, but his failure to secure a visa in time prevented him from being able to do so. Despite visa problems and other obstacles that prevented him from achieving all of his goals, Acebez expressed optimism that what he accomplished would provide a solid base for future work of the IUS in addressing the most-important problems that students in Latin America faced.[24]

Acebez returned with a lengthy, detailed, and critical report that provides insightful glimpses into the strengths and challenges of the student movement in Latin America. On one hand, over the previous years students had played a key role in bringing about the downfall of detested dictators, such as Gerardo Machado in Cuba, Juan Vicente Gómez in Venezuela, Jorge Ubico in Guatemala, and Gualberto Villarroel in Bolivia, as well as in mobilizing opposition to granting the United States access to military bases in Panama and against petroleum concessions in Brazil and sugar in Cuba. On the other hand, the semi-feudal character of Latin American countries created a great weakness for the student movement. "It must be remembered," Acebez stated, "that the vast majority of the students, more so than in Europe, come from the well-to-do classes and even from the families of landowners." Those material interests limited their democratic aspirations and frustrated the ability of the IUS to extend its reach into Latin America.[25] That would change over the course of the twentieth century as rising literacy rates and educational opportunities brought more children of workers into universities.

After Vásquez's disappearance from the IUS, an Ecuadorian was the only official delegate from Latin America who received credentials for an annual council meeting in Paris in September 1948. Two accredited observers from Venezuela attended, but those who had been invited from other Latin American countries (including Brazil, Chile, Colombia, Cuba, Guatemala, Mexico, Panama, and Puerto Rico) did not. This was the case even though the IUS secretariat had sent invitations that stressed the importance of participation and included logistical information and information on the steps necessary to secure visas for travel to France.[26]

Over time both the IUS and WFDY council meetings, which were always held in Europe, expanded to include more representatives from Latin America. One of the first and most reliable delegates was Ecuadorian student Rafael Echeverría, who lived in Prague. He had married a Czechoslovakian woman named Ana Bartonova and was probably the Ecuadorian at the September 1948 meeting in Paris.[27] Initially, Echeverría was the only representative from Latin America at executive committee meetings. Together with others from European, Asian, and Pacific countries, they met in Sofia, Bulgaria; London, England; Moscow, USSR; and Berlin, Germany.[28] Probably because he already lived in Prague, Echeverría was elected as one of four vice presidents for the IUS (together with others from China, France, and the Soviet Union).[29] Echeverría went on to play a significant role in the Ecuadorian left. These international experiences provided training grounds that molded young activists for their future endeavors.

In preparation for the September 1948 meeting, the IUS executive council assembled a massive packet of material almost five hundred pages in length. Among the documents was one that discussed the work of the IUS secretariat in Latin America. It expressed a "special interest to get in touch with the great mass of democratic and progressive students" in the hemisphere and to become acquainted with their problems, activities, and needs, even as the secretariat struggled to maintain its contacts in the region. Until recently these were "very slight or almost non existent [sic]" due in large part to "the apathy and lack of responsibility" that Vásquez had shown in his work. At a meeting in Prague in January 1949, the executive committee decided to dedicate the resources necessary to strengthen those connections. This included sending representatives and more bulletins and other publications to the continent. This time the IUS succeeded in establishing permanent relations with student groups in Cuba, Brazil, Ecuador, Panama, and Mexico. Those efforts paid dividends, with the IUS reporting that during the past eight months they had more communication than during the previous two years. Furthermore, with the encouragement of the IUS, student groups had been relaunched in Puerto Rico and Guatemala, and they were in the process of establishing connections with groups in Argentina and Venezuela. The secretariat pledged to continue to provide moral and political aid to the Latin American student movement to achieve the best solutions to their problems.[30]

By 1950 the IUS claimed six hundred thousand members in Latin America. The extent of penetration varied. Chilean student groups, for example, had not formally affiliated with the IUS despite a strong communist presence. Meanwhile, some anticommunist student groups in Cuba had voted to withdraw from the IUS. Nevertheless, State Department analysts reported, "Communist activity carried on through student-youth fronts is now significant in all Latin American countries of any importance except Argentina, Colombia, and Peru."[31] With the assistance of people like Echeverría, the IUS had gained a large presence, both in Latin America and in the minds of U.S. government officials. It was primarily through the WFDY and the IUS that many of those youth and student groups maintained their transnational ties, and through participation in world festivals those connections flourished.

Youth and Student Festivals

A series of world youth festivals and congresses that the WFDY and the IUS sponsored throughout the 1950s highlights the growing importance of transnational connections that drew young people into a global environment. In turn, the meetings strengthened the Latin American left as more and more people from the Americas participated. The biannual festivals brought youth and students from around the world together in massive celebrations for peace and friendship that included social, cultural, and sporting events. The festivals provided multiple opportunities for Latin American activists to travel and exchange experiences with their counterparts around the world and to bring their experiences back home. As these transnational ties strengthened, attempts by U.S. government officials and their allies in the domestic ruling classes to derail their activities intensified. If success can be judged in terms of the opposition a mobilization engenders, the student mobilizations were hitting their mark.

The WFDY held its first World Youth Festival in Prague in August 1947, and it lasted almost four weeks, the longest in the history of the festivals. Seventeen thousand people from seventy-five countries participated.[32] Among those from Latin America who planned to attend were Alberto Almeida Hidalgo and Jorge Espinosa Flor, two student activists from the Federación de Estudiantes Universitarios del Ecuador (FEUE, Federation of Ecuadorian University Students), although apparently only Almeida Hidalgo managed to travel. That he would do so was not unusual. Since 1939 he had visited Panama, Colombia, Czechoslovakia, France, and the United States. His older brothers, Rafael and Jorge, had also been student activists who traveled internationally. As was common for delegates who participated in international meetings, Almeida Hidalgo stayed in Europe for several months after the congress and planned to visit Moscow.[33] At the end of the year, he was still in Paris. According to the CIA, he had requested "a transit for the American Zone of Germany in order to proceed to Bulgaria for a period of two months." The WFDY was "sponsoring a 'peace train' with 800 youths who will work on 'youth railways' in Slovakia and Moravia and (or) will join youth brigades in Bulgaria, Poland, and Rumania."[34] Almeida Hidalgo's involvement with student activism in Europe is representative of the deepening of political activism that resulted from these transnational ties.

As a regional counterpart to the youth festival in Prague, the WFDY in collaboration with the IUS attempted to organize a Latin American youth congress in January 1948. Initially, plans were to hold the event in either Chile or Cuba. The goals of the congress included a consolidation of peace, support for the United Nations, a fight for democracy and against fascism, promotion of economic development and agricultural reform, advocacy for independence for Puerto Rico, abolishment of racial discrimination against Blacks and Indigenous peoples, improved living conditions for youth, and the unity of youth. A hope was that much like the youth festival in Prague, the congress would contribute to intensified activism in Latin America.[35]

The proposed congress ran into difficulties when host governments refused permission to hold the assembly in their countries and denied visas to delegates. Finally, after repeated delays, the congress convened in Mexico City on April 30, 1948, thanks in large part to pressure the labor leader and CTAL president Vicente Lombardo Toledano placed on the government. Twenty-six delegates from nine Latin American countries attended, plus representatives from Puerto Rico and the United States and observers from the WFDY and the IUS. The congress passed resolutions calling for greater democracy and national independence (including for Puerto Rico) and denounced Yankee imperialism and its support for dictatorships in Latin America. It pledged support for universal disarmament, including abolition of nuclear weapons. Other resolutions called for a right to work, social security, education, sports, and recreation. The congress culminated with a call for peace and democracy and a denunciation of imperialism.[36] Holding the meeting despite extraordinary repression represented a significant advance, and organizers expressed hope for the future of student and youth movements in Latin America.[37]

Despite continual difficulties and hurdles, the Mexican meeting fostered the growth and strengthening of transnational connections within the Americas. In January 1949, for example, the Mexican youth leader and president of the Confederación de Jovenes Mexicanos (Confederation of Mexican Youth) Manuel Popoca Estrada arrived in Quito as an emissary of the WFDY. At a youth congress of the Ecuadorian socialist party, he presented the WFDY as the legitimate heir of the youth who fought the fascists and Nazis in the last war. Their struggle had not ended with the defeat of Adolf Hitler, Michinomiya Hirohito, and Benito Mussolini, and "victory would not be complete as long as there existed oppressed peoples." The fight continued in Spain, Greece, China, and Puerto

Rico. In response to his appeal, the youth congress voted to affiliate with the WFDY. While in Quito, Popoca Estrada also addressed a special meeting of the leftist provincial Federación de Trabajadores de Pichincha (FTP, Pichincha Workers Federation). FTP president César Humberto Navarro responded positively to his description of the work of the WFDY and declared that the labor movement should adopt a similar agenda. Opponents typically presented the WFDY and IUS as merely communist fronts, but notably absent in U.S. embassy reports, whether due to failures in their surveillance operations or an intentional decision on the part of the organizers, was any mention of Popoca Estrada meeting with explicitly communist organizations.[38] The transnational student movement was having broad, regional repercussions across Latin America, and that frightened government officials.

Building on previous successes, the WFDY and IUS held their second World Festival of Youth and Students in Budapest in August 1949. Organizers proclaimed that festival would "be one of the greatest events in the history of the international student movement." They encouraged students to send those who were most active in defending student interests, but they also urged engagement with progressive writers, artists, and scientists in order to assure "the participation of outstanding men [sic] of art and culture." Even those who were unable to attend should be informed of and kept involved in the work of the student movement. An explicit intent was to use the meeting to mobilize activists well beyond those who were able to travel to Budapest. Particularly important was that the festival "be truly representative of our student members all over the world." Since "student organizations in colonial countries may encounter considerable financial and other difficulties in sending a proper representation to the Festival," organizers asked "student organizations in other countries to adopt a number of representatives of colonial and fighting youth and to collect money in order to support them." Through their participation, "the democratic students of the world will once again demonstrate their friendship and solidarity with the students and youth of Republican Spain, democratic China, fighting Greece, Vietnam and Indonesia, and with all the oppressed youth of colonial and dependent countries." Since Latin America was included in what was considered the colonial world, this call involved an explicit intent to incorporate that region fully into its organizational process.[39] Their efforts paid dividends. For two weeks, twenty thousand young people from eighty-two countries, including delegates from Argentina, Brazil, Bolivia, Chile, Puerto Rico, and Venezuela, engaged in cultural, sporting, and political activities at the festival. Reflecting these transnational initiatives, festival participants pledged their solidarity with the "anti-colonialist struggle" of the peoples of Indonesia, Malaysia, and French

Indochina as well as their support for the "anti-fascist struggle" of the Spanish and Greek peoples.[40] These international meetings actively and intentionally build transnational networks that pressed for political changes in a postcolonial world.

Immediately following the youth festival in Budapest, the WFDY held its Second World Youth Congress. In a call to the youth of the world to attend the congress, the WFDY proclaimed that it represented "over 50 million young men and women of 63 countries." The federation called on its members to organize meetings and distribute material in preparation for the meeting. "Let every young worker, every young peasant or farmer, every student know about the work of the WFDY," organizers declared, as they joined together in a struggle for a better future.[41] Seven hundred delegates from sixty countries, including representatives from thirteen Latin American countries, attended that congress. A large portion of the Latin American delegation—maybe as many as half—were students already residing in Europe. A persistent problem was that a lack of funds and visas prevented more students from traveling from the Americas. Apparently, only the Ecuadorians were able to secure proper documentation. Nevertheless, many of those who did manage to travel took maximum advantage of the opportunity. Following the congress, some Latin American delegates continued to Moscow, and some of those proceeded to Beijing.[42] Those who arrived in Beijing toured China for a month and participated in a variety of communist celebrations.[43] Even with all of the difficulties and limitations, these international gatherings provided remarkable opportunities to share experiences with their counterparts around the world. Reflecting the growing incorporation of the Americas into these transnational networks, Flavio Bravo from Cuba and Meir Benaim from Brazil were elected to the WFDY executive council.[44]

Over the next several years, international youth and students' meetings as well as other regional peace and labor conferences led to a significant increase in activism in Latin America. Guy de Boysson, a French leader of the WFDY, expected that thirty-two hundred young people "of all political, religious and pacifist tendencies" from Latin America would attend the Third World Youth Festival for Peace in Berlin in August 1951.[45] Although ultimately reality did not match Boysson's lofty goals in terms of mobilizing participants, organizers still managed a sizable achievement. The assembly marked "the largest Latin American attendance at any non-hemispheric Communist-sponsored conference to that date."[46] Youth and student groups in a dozen Latin American countries mobilized to send delegations. Local groups held congresses and passed resolutions in favor of peace and against imperialism. Particularly, in Guatemala and Ecuador, delegations gained governmental support. In part this was due to cabinet-level changes that brought in leftist ministers of education who were willing to back such initiatives.[47] Nine Ecuadorians sailed from the port of Guayaquil on July 6, 1951, for the Berlin festival, the largest group from Latin America up to that point to travel to an international meeting. At the head of the delegation was the communist leader Enrique Gil Gilbert, nephew of the vice president Abel Gilbert, who was currently acting president while the regular office holder Galo Plaza Lasso was visiting the United States. Vice president Gilbert's daughter Areceli joined the group in Berlin. With such high-profile participation, the festivals were gaining a good deal of legitimacy.[48]

In Ecuador the recently appointed socialist minister of education Carlos Cueva Tamariz (and the father of Patricio, one of the delegates) had applied for official passports for the delegates. The foreign office refused that request under intense pressure from the United States ambassador but did issue ordinary passports when socialists threatened to withdraw their support from the government.[49] For their part CIA officials blamed this support on "a naiveté" among local officials "regarding the Communist nature of the festival."[50] An additional and perhaps larger problem for U.S. government officials was funding for travel that they contended came from foreign sources. In their eyes, that challenged the legitimacy of the meetings, and their goal was to convince the general public to share that perception. One report claimed, "Money for travel and other expenses came from national peace committees, the World Peace Council and other Communist sources." One tactic was for mass organizations to hold contests in literature, art, and music with the winners receiving free trips to the festival. U.S. officials claimed that while "peace and other front groups sponsored money raising campaigns," those efforts were designed "to conceal the fact they were receiving funds from abroad."[51] "Although some money was evidently raised locally," CIA analysts wrote, "there is little doubt that the larger part of the delegates' expenses is being financed from abroad." Thoughtful observers noted, "The cost of international meetings, large-scale publications, and the other activities in which they engage, are beyond the financial resources of university students."[52] In fact, almost all student organizations relied on external revenue streams, not just communist-oriented groups, so in that sense the WFDY and IUS were by no means unique.[53] The hypocrisy of the CIA's criticism of external funding became even more readily apparent when revelations emerged in 1967 that the agency provided most of the financial support for anticommunist student organizations.[54]

The Berlin festival took place against the backdrop of the Korean War and amidst growing tensions between the Soviet Union and capitalist powers. The theme of the festival appropriately was "Youth, United in the Struggle for Peace against the Danger of a New War." Local youth groups hosted the event with the support of an international festival committee and the government of the German Democratic Republic. The growing size and support for a progressive youth movement that stood firmly against United States imperial interests logically engendered stiff opposition. U.S. officials expressed their concern that "the extent and intensity of the preparations added up to a major propaganda effort and one of the most ambitious single undertakings of the 'peace' offensive."[55] State Department analysts complained, "Communists used the Berlin Youth Festival as the occasion for an unprecedented movement of Latin Americans to Communist European headquarters." Of the 26,000 people from 104 countries who attended, around 300 delegates and observers came from 17 Latin American countries. In total, about 250 of these participants traveled directly from Latin America by plane or ship while the rest were Latin Americans who were already living or traveling in Europe. According to the OIR, the delegations comprised primarily "Communists, fellow-travellers, or champion athletes going along for the ride."[56]

As before, many of the delegates to the festival took advantage of their presence on the continent to travel to Eastern Europe and the Soviet Union. State Department analysts worried, "The large deployment of Latin American youth elements to Soviet-held areas may have served as a shield for a program of indoctrinating younger Communist elements that are more and more important to the movement in Latin America." The Cuban delegation was of particular concern "because of reported WFTU plans to train young Cuban workers in Europe, and the unexplained travel of Cuban workers to Moscow and other parts of Europe in the previous quarter."[57] Those international experiences would build a stronger Latin American left, and for that reason U.S. government officials worked hard to stop them.

The presence of the general secretary of the Brazilian student congress along with a group of other Latin American students in Berlin before the festival and in Bucharest afterward reflected the growing interest that the IUS had in Latin America. As the transnational connections strengthened, more and more Latin American students continued to travel to Europe for IUS council meetings. Delegates at an IUS meeting in Warsaw elected a Cuban and an Ecuadoran to its executive committee and reserved a place on the board for representatives of Brazil's National Student Union.[58] Another meeting in Bucharest in September 1952 included about half a dozen representatives from Bolivia, Chile, Cuba, Ecuador, Panama, and Venezuela, even though the Ecuadorian delegate was the only one that "represented an IUS affiliate of national importance." That affiliate, FEUE, had elected six delegates to attend the council meeting. The U.S.

ambassador in Quito commented that this delegation "of self-styled Socialists will probably depart with ordinary passports," though doing so could result in repressive measures against the socialist and communist parties from the new incoming administration of the conservative populist José María Velasco Ibarra.[59] The Cuban Lionel Soto also became a member of the executive committee. Council members at the meeting "mapped out a program of support for the International Conference in Defense of the Rights of Youth which is scheduled to convene in Vienna during February 1953."[60] Latin American participation in these events only grew even as conservative opposition intensified.

From July to September 1953 the WFDY and the IUS staged a series of three very successful international meetings. The centerpiece event was the Fourth World Festival of Youth and Students for Peace and Friendship held in Bucharest in August. The WFDY's Third World Youth Congress preceded it in Bucharest, and the IUS's Third World Student Congress followed in Warsaw. More than thirty thousand young people from 111 countries attended the youth festival. Of this number, six hundred came from Latin America—double the number that had participated in the last festival in Berlin in 1951. The delegates represented seventy-six student unions from twenty countries and included a range of individuals from different political persuasions and with different motivations. Financing international travel presented a perennial problem, with everyone searched for different sources of funding. Some delegations received some financial support from official sources in their own countries. In Brazil, organizers held contests in writing, musical composition, motion pictures, and the fine arts, with the prize being a free trip to the festival. In Ecuador the FEUE advertised a raffle for a free passage to the festival that featured symphony concerts, operas, ballets, musicals, dances, and sports events.[61] The appeal extended well beyond narrow political interests.

About 130 delegates planned to attend from Chile, including 18 federal deputies who represented a variety of political parties.[62] They were responsible for their own passage, but the Communist Party had invested a significant amount of effort into building interest for the congress. "Party funds" would cover "all other expenses connected with the trip." Student and youth groups had also engaged in a wide variety of fund-raising activities to cover their expenses. These included the showing of a film on U.S. bacteriological warfare in Korea that a Chinese delegate to a recent continental cultural congress in Santiago had brought to Chile.[63]

With the support of the progressive Árbenz government, another sizable delegation of at least thirty planned to travel from Guatemala for the congress. The group included political exiles from several countries including the Dominican

Republic, Nicaragua, and El Salvador, as well as deputies from the Guatemalan congress. As in Chile, the delegates were organizing fund-raising events to cover their expenses, with the government paying the rest.[64] A group of Colombians also planned to attend.[65]

The Federation of Students of Panama planned to send a delegation that would include "dancers of the tamborito, punto, bamboreras and zapateo; performers of folk music and sportsmen, especially swimmers." The press and information department of the IUS included this information in its promotional material for the festival together with a photograph of the dance troop. The IUS invited the youth ballet from Brazil to participate in the cultural programs at both the festival and subsequent student congress. Director S. W. Ribeiro "promised to do everything possible to bring the company to Europe for these events." From Ecuador the FEUE wrote that Antonio Canadas, president of the university sports league, had formed a local committee to promote attendance at the festival. Committee members "promised to work hard to make the Festival in Bucharest a success, 'where young people from the whole world will come together for peace.'"[66] The attraction of and participation in the festivals continued to expand well beyond narrowly drawn communist circles.

The goals of the youth festival included protesting the Korean War and supporting the anticolonial movements in the French colonies of Algeria and Vietnam. Even so, U.S. officials noted "a relative absence of direct, vituperative attacks on the Western democracies and on their policies by WFDY-IUS officials from the Soviet Bloc." Rather, "this was left to participants from non-Communist areas, especially from colonial countries." In addition, "a number of Latin American delegates took the opportunity to attack their own governments for their 'repressive' actions against youth."[67] The implication was that participants were stooges of an international communist conspiracy who had been put up to such nefarious activities, but that ignores that they had their own motivations. The gatherings strengthened domestic organizing efforts even as they also advanced the political agendas of the international organizations; transnational connections assured that the two would be ever more tightly bound together.

A commission for the activity of youth in the colonial and underdeveloped areas proposed resolutions at the Bucharest festival for regional meetings that the entire body had willingly adopted. The IUS congress at Warsaw similarly adopted a resolution of solidarity with students from colonial, dependent, and underdeveloped countries that urged the organization of national and regional student meetings in Latin America, Asia, and Africa. The festival established a Latin America bureau to pursue those objectives. Inspired by those initiatives and following the success of the Bucharest festival, the WFDY and the IUS pursued plans for two regional youth congresses in the Americas: a Festival of Students and Youth of South America in Santiago, Chile, and a Festival of Friendship of the Youth of Central America and the Caribbean in Guatemala. Both festivals were initially planned for October 1954. It was an appropriate time to launch such an initiative because both groups had experienced significant growth in membership and had achieved a geographic reach across the region. The WFDY had increased from seven affiliates in six countries in Latin America in 1948 to twelve affiliates in eleven countries in 1950. In 1948 the IUS claimed thirteen affiliates in nine Latin American countries. By August 1951, it had assembled nineteen affiliates in fifteen countries of Latin America with a total membership of 680,000.[68]

In response, students formed a South American preparatory committee that consisted of twenty-five members from eight countries (Argentina, Bolivia, Brazil, Chile, Ecuador, Paraguay, Peru, and Uruguay) to send out invitations and make international arrangements for the Santiago festival. Among its goals were an interchange of folklore and the arts, organization of sports competitions, contributions toward international understanding, broadening horizons for youth, assurance of employment at a decent wage, adequate education, security, and the realization for youth of "a present more worthy of them, a future of peace and happiness." A Chilean preparatory committee with representatives of labor, youth, student, and political groups began meeting in December 1953 to make local arrangements in Santiago. Preparatory sessions were successful, with a variety of student, youth, cultural, labor, and municipal groups pledging their support. Organizers expected more than seventeen hundred delegates to attend from across the continent.[69]

Activists established a parallel organizing committee for the festival of friendship of the youth of Central America and the Caribbean planned for Guatemala. The festival was to be "a great sports and cultural event, in which all young people of good will can participate, whatever their political or cultural bent." In preparation for the October festival, organizers held a three-day national youth festival in Chimaltenango, Guatemala, in February 1954 with thirteen hundred people in attendance. The plans for the festival collapsed, however, in the face of a CIA-backed coup in June 1954 that replaced the progressive Árbenz administration with the repressive right-wing military dictatorship of Carlos Castillo Armas. Guatemala had previously provided a very conducive environment for such initiatives, but that was to be no more. With the coup, United States officials effectively eliminated one of the principal centers of progressive agitation in the region.

South American activists similarly struggled to bring the planned youth festival in Chile to fruition. Although delegates from Argentina, Bolivia, Brazil, Chile, Ecuador, Paraguay, Peru, and Uruguay planned to attend, organizers pushed the date back from October 1954 to January 1955.[70] The State Department instructed its embassy to put pressure on local governments to deny visas for travel to the meeting. In response, the conservative government of Carlos Ibáñez del Campo opposed holding the meeting in Chile. The government denounced the "preparations which are being made with respect to the Congress of Youth People scheduled for next year and secretly sponsored by international communism," and "agreed to prevent its taking place as it is designed to serve the subversive and anarchistic purposes of this totalitarian sect."[71] Organizational success exacerbated conservative opposition, which significantly increased the level of difficulty of holding such meetings.

Finally, the Chilean government banned the youth festival outright. In response, activists shifted their plans for the festival to São Paulo, Brazil, in February 1955. Once again, the U.S. embassy went on the offensive and mobilized its diplomatic missions to urge local governments to deny travel documents for the meeting.[72] In Ecuador, U.S. ambassador Sheldon Mills faithfully passed this information on to the minister of foreign affairs Luis Antonio Peñaherrera. Considering that previously the Ecuadorian government had taken "such pertinent measures as the Constitution of Ecuador permits to discourage the attendance of Ecuadoran Nationals at Communist activities of this nature," the ambassador said, "this information is transmitted to the Ministry for such measures as it may wish to take."[73] Ecuador's foreign minister informed the embassy that it had passed this information on to the conservative minister of government Camilo Ponce Enríquez, the left's chief nemesis, so that he could take the necessary measures to comply with the request within the limits of constitutional guarantees.[74] Similar to how the interests of a transnational left coalesced, the political agenda of the U.S. government and the conservative domestic ruling class also reinforced each other.

The U.S. Information Service (USIS) was particularly determined to denounce the festival as a communist event. The agency noted that several of its posts in Latin America had already "supplied material exposing communist nature of so-called South American youth festival" and asked its officials to "watch for and supply for use press service other media any material which will help expose this communist festival."[75] In response to this pressure, just as the event was to start, the governor of São Paulo and the Brazilian president, João Fernandes Campos Café Filho, banned the event. Government repression, both internal and external, prevented the festival from taking place. Even so, those who were already present held a meeting though much-reduced in size.[76] Organizers were determined not to allow the repression to stop their efforts. U.S. officials and their allies in the local ruling class were equally determined to keep up the pressure against such initiatives. The U.S. Information Agency (USIA) asked its representatives to be on watch for other similar gatherings and pledged to mobilize its forces against other planned meetings, including the upcoming Fifth World Festival of Youth and Students to be held in Warsaw in 1955.[77]

Opposition to their efforts did not immobilize the WFDY and the IUS. The WFDY mailed material to encourage attendance at the Warsaw festival, and their efforts paid off: it was the largest of the festivals to date. Over thirty thousand people from 114 countries attended, although (as is usually the case with these types of international meetings) many of those came from Poland or neighboring countries. Among the delegates and observers were over five hundred from nineteen Latin American countries. Luigi Einaudi, who oversaw Latin American affairs in the U.S. National Student Association for the CIA, speculated that many of the students who traveled "from Mexico, Brazil, Ecuador, and Chile who attended the Soviet-backed World Youth Festival in Warsaw in 1955 did so out of curiosity."[78] Others, of course, were much more ideologically and politically motivated. As always, Latin Americans participated in planning meetings before and after the festival, although by this time constant right-wing pressure meant that only the FEUE from Ecuador formally belonged to IUS. Leaders stayed to participate in WFDY and IUS council meetings following the festival, while other participants (including delegations from at least ten Latin American countries) as always took advantage of their travel opportunities to visit neighboring countries as well as the USSR and China. Among new members admitted to the WFDY at its council meeting were youth groups from Argentina and Uruguay.[79]

Latin Americans took advantage of international festivals to assume leadership positions in organizational headquarters or to pursue university studies in Europe. Five students from Ecuador were among the 650 students from 38 countries who attended a World Student Congress in Prague in 1956, with another student joining the group who planned to study in Rumania on an engineering scholarship.[80] Included in the group was Jorge Rivadeneira, the vice president of the Juventud Comunista del Ecuador (JCE, Young Communists of Ecuador) and of the FEUE, who "quietly left for Prague by plane on July 1." He was scheduled to replace Jorge Arellano Gallegos as vice president for Latin America for the IUS.[81] Eventually, these two would go in dramatically different directions, with Rivadeneira joining their predecessor Rafael Echeverría in leading a Maoist-inspired guerrilla insurgency in Ecuador while Arellano Gallegos assumed a dogmatically anticommunist position.[82] The outcome of involvement in these transnational assemblies was not always the same, nor was it necessarily predictable.

The Sixth World Festival of Youth and Students held in Moscow in 1957 attracted thirty-four thousand people from 130 countries, including many from Latin America.[83] It was the first youth festival to be held in the Soviet Union, and it also led U.S. government officials and their allies among the Latin American ruling class to double down on their opposition to it. Despite the success of the festival, those conservative opponents continued their drive to fracture student federations in Latin America and to break them away from the WFDY and IUS. The Moscow festival was a highpoint, and even though the festivals continued to meet on a regular basis, they began to decline in size and importance. In part this was a result of the organized anticommunist opposition, but it also reflected the fallout at the twentieth congress of the Communist Party of the Soviet Union (CPSU) in February 1956 from Nikita Khrushchev's denunciation of Joseph Stalin's crimes, followed in October 1956 by an uprising in Hungary that a large Soviet military force crushed. Those and other events sent shock waves that affected communist parties as well as mass organizations around the world.

In 1959 the Seventh World Youth Festival was held in Vienna. Similar to previous gatherings, it included discussions, seminars, special attractions, galas, and sports programs, though in the face of intense right-wing Cold War–opposition, it was smaller and included fewer Latin American participants.[84] Furthermore, among many leftists, political support was shifting away from the Soviets and mass organizations associated with them that were now seen as too accommodating with the capitalist world and, instead, toward the Chinese and Cubans, whose revolutions appeared to present more radical alternatives. As the world moved into the turbulent 1960s, political strategies mutated, and together with that, the nature and purpose of the festivals changed as well. For a time in the 1950s, however, youth and student festivals had played a key role in encouraging the development of strong transnational organizing strategies.

Rather than decreasing in importance, during the early Cold War communists paid more attention to international youth and student mass organizations, including the WFDY and the IUS. Although largely ignored in the literature, at the time those mass organizations dedicated significant attention to Latin America and brought the youth of that region into their transnational orbits. Their strength and importance concerned U.S. officials, with the ironic result that their surveillance effectively documented a struggle for a more just and peaceful world that might otherwise be forgotten or lost to history. Students and young people, as with others who sought to travel to participate in these international meetings, faced constant hurdles owing primarily to the difficulties of securing visas and funding for their travels. In Latin America, antagonistic governments repeatedly sought to shut down meetings that they opposed. Even with all these barriers, many people managed to attend and establish transnational connections. These meetings laid an important organizational groundwork for the Latin America left, and those transnational linkages fostered its strength. Those encounters shifted thinking and strategies, which contributed to heightened levels of militancy in what have come to be known as the "global 1960s."

Notes

1. "Communism in the Other American Republics: Quarterly Survey, April–June 1951," July 19, 1951, Office of Intelligence Research (OIR), in U.S. Department of State, *Latin America*. This source does not name the two young people or provide more information on their specific activities in Europe. From 1950 to 1953, these quarterly OIR reports tracked transnational movements, leaving scholars with a useful documentary record of activities.

2. "Communism in the Other American Republics: Quarterly Survey, January–March 1953," April 23, 1953, OIR, in U.S. Department of State, *Latin America*.

3. Kirkpatrick, *Year of Crisis*, 260. Kirkpatrick acknowledges that he drew on government research for the information in his anticommunist books, but what he does not admit is that this publication was propaganda that the U.S. Information Agency (USIA) had sponsored. Nevertheless, the data he presents appears to be largely accurate even though its intent was to make people fear a looming communist menace.

4. Becker, "Latin American Peace Movement."

5. Kirkpatrick, *Year of Crisis*, 394–95.

6. Kirkpatrick, *Target*, 108–9.

7. Kirkpatrick, *Target*, 330.

8. Kirkpatrick, *Target*, 35.

9. OIR, U.S. Department of State, "Communism in Latin America," 87.

10. Kirkpatrick, *Year of Crisis*, 260–61.

11. "Call of the Executive Committee of the World Federation of Democratic Youth for the Second World Youth Congress," attached to Jacobs to State, April 27, 1949, entry #2396, box 51, Record Group 84 (hereafter referred to as RG84), National Archives and Records Administration, College Park, Maryland (hereafter referred to as NARA). The WFDY included in its category of "colonial and dependent countries" those of Africa, Asia, and Latin America. See "WFDY Activity in Asia and Latin America," November 1, 1955, CIA Electronic Reading Room, *Central Intelligence Agency*, https://www.cia.gov/readingroom/ (hereafter referred to as CIA Electronic Reading Room).

12. Quito to State, March 10, 1949, entry #2396, box 51, RG84, NARA.

13. "The World Federation of Democratic Youth: Part Two," June 1, 1948, OIR, in U.S. Department of State, *Latin America*.

14. *Servicio de Información* 43 (March 25, 1949), in "Propaganda Material," August 9, 1949, CIA Electronic Reading Room.

15. *Servicio de Artículos* 9 (March 1949), in "Propaganda Material," August 9, 1949, CIA Electronic Reading Room.

16. *Bulletin de Estudio y Documentación* 2 (March 1949), in "Propaganda Material," August 9, 1949, CIA Electronic Reading Room.

17. "World Federation . . . Part Two."

18. "Weekly Summary Number 34," January 14, 1949, CIA Electronic Reading Room.

19. "World Federation . . . Part Two."

20. "The IUS Constitution," in Maanen, *International Student Movement*, 289–300.

21. Altbach, "International Student Movement," 161.

22. "The Operational Pattern of International Communism in Latin America," March 5, 1956, CIA Electronic Reading Room.

23. "International Communist Movements 1 May 48–1 September 48," September 1, 1948, CIA Electronic Reading Room.

24. Arturo Acebez, "The Situation and the Problems of Students in Latin America," included in "International Union of Students/World Federation of Democratic Youth," January 28, 1949, CIA Electronic Reading Room.

25. Acebez, "Situation and the Problems."

26. "International Union of Students/World Federation of Democratic Youth," January 28, 1949, CIA Electronic Reading Room. The available documentation does not indicate whether the other delegates failed to attend for financial, logistical, or political reasons or if they simply had not made the effort to do so.

27. "International Communist Movements," May 1, 1949, CIA Electronic Reading Room.

28. "International Communist Movements," June 8, 1950, and September 1, 1950, CIA Electronic Reading Room.

29. Jacobs to State, April 27, 1949, entry #2396, box 51, RG84, NARA.

30. The documents from the IUS council meeting made their way in the CIA library and were subsequently released as part of the CIA's online database. See "The Work of the Secretariat of the UIE among the Student Organizations of Latin America," in "International Union of Students/World Federation of Democratic Youth," January 28, 1949, CIA Electronic Reading Room.

31. "Communism in the Other American Republics: Quarterly Survey, January–March 1951," April 17, 1951, OIR, in U.S. Department of State, *Latin America*.

32. Quito to State, March 10, 1949, entry #2396, box 51, RG84, NARA. On the festivals, see Cornell, *Youth and Communism*, 137–52.

33. CAS (controlled American source), "Information on Ecuadorian participation in World Federation of Democratic Youth," December 5, 1947, entry #2396, box 43,

RG84, NARA. "Controlled American source" (CAS) was used as a euphemism for a CIA officer or station, which given the covert nature of the agency's work was not technically supposed to exist.

34. Caffery to State, July 27, 1948, 822.00B/7-2748, Record Group 59, NARA.

35. OIR, "World Federation . . . Part Two."

36. OIR, "World Federation . . . Part Two."

37. Acebez, "Situation and the Problems."

38. Quito to State, March 10, 1949, entry #2396, box 51, RG84, NARA.

39. "The IUS Appeals to the Students of the World," attached to Jacobs to State, April 27, 1949.

40. "International Communist Movements," September 1, 1949; "International Communist Movements 1 September 1949–1 January 1950," January 1, 1950, CIA Electronic Reading Room.

41. "Call of the Executive Committee of the World Federation of Democratic Youth for the Second World Youth Congress," attached to Jacobs to State, April 27, 1949, entry #2396, box 51, RG84, NARA.

42. "Communism in the Other American Republics: Quarterly Survey, July–September 1950," October 13, 1950, OIR, in U.S. Department of State, *Latin America*.

43. "Communism . . . October–December 1950," January 12, 1951, in *OSS/State Department Intelligence and Research Reports*.

44. "International Communist Movements," September 1, 1949, and "International Communist Movements 1 September 1949–1 January 1950," January 1, 1950, CIA Electronic Reading Room.

45. "Current Intelligence Bulletin—1951/07/12," July 12, 1951, CIA Electronic Reading Room.

46. "Latin American Attendance at 1951 and 1953 Communist Youth Festivals," in Streibert, USIA Circular, April 19, 1955, entry #2396, box 61, RG84, NARA.

47. "Communism . . . April–June 1951."

48. Daniels to State: July 9, 1951, 722.001/7-951; July 20, 1951, 722.001/7-2051; and March 5, 1952, 722.001/3-552; and Wight to State, February 11, 1952, 722.001/2-1152, all in Record Group 59, NARA; and Mayers to Eden, "Ecuador: Annual Review for 1951," Quito, January 23, 1952, AE 1011/1, in Dunkerley, *British Documents on Foreign Affairs*, series D, part 5, doc. 34, 2:291.

49. Daniels to State, July 9, 1951, RG59, 722.001/7-951, NARA; Daniels to State, July 20, 1951, RG59, 722.001/7-2051, NARA; Daniels to State, March 5, 1952, RG59, 722.001/3-552, NARA; Wight to State, February 11, 1952, RG59, 722.001/2-1152, NARA; Mayers to Eden, "Ecuador: Annual review for 1951," Quito, January 23, 1952, AE 1011/1, in Dunkerley, *British Documents on Foreign Affairs*, series D, part 6, vol. 2, doc. 34, 291.

50. "Office of Current Intelligence Daily Digest," July 13, 1951, CIA Electronic Reading Room.

51. "Latin American Attendance."

52. "Office of Current Intelligence Daily Digest," July 13, 1951.

53. Altbach, "International Student Movement," 167.

54. Stern, "Short Account."

55. "Latin American Attendance."

56. "Communism . . . July–September 1951," October 24, 1951.

57. OIR, "Communism in the Other American Republics: Quarterly Survey, July–September 1951." Also see "Cuban Delegates to WFDY Meeting," July 9, 1951, CIA Electronic Reading Room.

58. "Communism . . ., July–September 1951."

59. Daniels to State, August 1, 1952, 722.00(W)/8-152, Record Group 59, NARA.

60. "Communism . . . June–September 1952," October 20, 1952.

61. "Communism . . . April–June 1953," August 11, 1953.

62. "Latin American Attendance at 1951."

63. "Chilean Delegation to Third World Youth Congress of the WFDY in Bucharest," July 24, 1953, CIA Electronic Reading Room.

64. "Guatemalan Delegation to Fourth World Festival of Youth," August 4, 1953, CIA Electronic Reading Room.

65. "Colombian Delegates to Bucharest Youth Congress," August 20, 1953, CIA Electronic Reading Room.

66. International Union of Students, "Press and Information Department International Union of Students," (Prague), no. 11, June 1953, in CIA Electronic Reading Room.

67. "Latin American Attendance at 1951."

68. Maleady, "Memorandum," April 14, 1955, entry #2396, box 61, RG84, NARA.

69. Dulles, "Preparatory Meeting for the South American Youth Festival," May 6, 1954, entry #2396, box 61, RG84, NARA.

70. "Schedule of Communist-Sponsored Propaganda Activities," October 26, 1954, OIR, entry #2396, box 65, RG84, NARA.

71. Smith, "Communist Sponsored Youth Festival Scheduled for Santiago in January 1955," September 20, 1954, entry #2396, box 65, RG84, NARA; Mills to State, September 29, 1954, entry #2396, box 61, RG84, NARA.

72. Murphy, "Communist Sponsored South American Festival of Youth," January 14, 1955, entry #2396, box 61, RG84, NARA.

73. Mills, "Memorandum," January 24, 1955, entry #2396, box 61, RG84, NARA.

74. Peñaherrera to Embassy, February 3, 1955, RG84, Entry #2396, Box 61, NARA.

75. Washburn, USIS, Washington, circular telegram, January 21, 1955, RG84, Entry #2396, Box 61, NARA.

76. Kirkpatrick, *Target*, 139.

77. Streibert, USIA Circular, cover sheet, April 19, 1955, entry #2396, box 61, RG84, NARA.

78. Paget, *Patriotic Betrayal*, 165.

79. Kirkpatrick, *Target*, 126, 140–41, 330.

80. Maanen, International Student Movement, 128.

81. Bragonier to King and Sanders, "Communism in Ecuador," August 28, 1956, entry #2396, box 73, RG84, NARA.

82. Villamizar Herrera, *Ecuador*; Arellano Gallegos, *La subversión*.

83. Kotek, *Students and the Cold War*, 63–64; Peacock, "Perils of Building Cold War Consensus."

84. "An Operational Estimate of the Seventh World Youth Festival Vienna 26 July–4 August 1959," April 1, 1959, and "Recent Information Concerning the Seventh World Youth Festival, Vienna, 25 July–4 August 1959," August 1, 1959, both in CIA Electronic Reading Room.

Our Vietnamese *Compañeros*

How Salvadoran Guerrillas Adapted
the "People's War" Strategy

KEVIN A. YOUNG

Comparisons of El Salvador to Vietnam were widespread in the 1980s. "El Salvador is Spanish for Vietnam," warned U.S. peace activists.[1] By supporting the brutal Salvadoran oligarchy and military, they argued, the U.S. government was waging an immoral and catastrophic war. Revolutionaries in El Salvador celebrated the Vietnamese struggle. For them, the victory of the "heroic and legendary *hermanos*" (brothers and sisters) of Vietnam proved "that when a people are willing to liberate themselves, there is no force capable of crushing them." A popular guerrilla song from the early 1980s proclaimed, "In El Salvador, just like in Vietnam."[2] U.S. and Salvadoran officials drew different lessons from the war in Vietnam, adapting the strategy of state terrorism for use against Salvadoran civilians.[3]

The international dimensions of the Salvadoran civil war (1980–1992) have received much attention. It is well established that Washington provided at least $6 billion to the Salvadoran government, which was responsible for 85 percent of the violence and most of the seventy-two thousand deaths.[4] The leftist guerrilla coalition, the Frente Farabundo Martí para la Liberación Nacional (FMLN, Farabundo Martí National Liberation Front), also had international connections. It took inspiration from victorious revolutions in Vietnam, Cuba, and Nicaragua and also received military training and weapons from those countries (though the aid was wildly exaggerated by the U.S. and Salvadoran governments).[5] The FMLN also won the sympathy of unarmed activists around the world. El Salvador was the focus of an extensive global solidarity movement in the 1980s.[6]

Although the history of these transnational alliances is well known, the transnational *influences* on the FMLN remain more obscure. Vietnam was especially important. It was not just Vietnamese heroism but also their strategy that inspired Salvadorans. Vietnamese communists' specific approach to guerrilla revolution, rooted in the notion of "people's war," distinguished their struggle from most other Third World revolutions. This idea was particularly influential in the Fuerzas Populares de Liberación Farabundo Martí (FPL, Farabundo Martí Popular Liberation Forces), one of the five organizations that united to form the FMLN in 1980. The FPL's strategy of "prolonged popular war" was an adaptation of the Vietnamese concept and earlier Chinese ideas.[7] It called for combining diverse forms of struggle over many years to prepare the ground for a final revolutionary offensive and transition to socialism. Its emphasis on political organizing work and mass participation, not just military action, differentiated it from other approaches to guerrilla war. This strategic orientation helps explain why the FPL became the largest of the five FMLN factions in the early 1980s and why it had a major presence in six of El Salvador's fourteen departments during the war.

Influence did not require direct contact. Although FPL leaders eventually cultivated ties with the Vietnamese—as they did with revolutionaries in Cuba, Guatemala, and Nicaragua—for most of the 1970s they learned the relevant lessons primarily by reading the Spanish translations of key Chinese and Vietnamese texts. Mao Zedong's *On the Protracted War* and Vo Nguyen Giap's *People's War, People's Army* both appeared in Spanish in the 1960s and circulated widely across Latin America and the Caribbean.[8] Gerson Martínez, the FPL chief of press and propaganda in the early 1970s, recalls that his organization began to reflect "Vietnamese influence without anyone having gone to Vietnam."[9] This learning process was facilitated by the FPL's relative ideological openness compared to some Marxist organizations. "We had quite diverse education," one FPL commander later recalled. "I don't remember any text being prohibited," said another.[10]

FPL leaders also learned from their experiences in El Salvador. Over the course of the 1970s they adjusted in response to pressures from the constituencies they sought to organize. The need for popular support led to a significant degree of flexibility in their revolutionary praxis. Moreover, as peasants, women, and other groups joined the FPL, they also helped modify its politics from within. The organization creatively adapted global ideas and applied them in the context of dynamic, two-way encounters with Salvadoran popular sectors.

The first section of this chapter introduces the strategy of prolonged popular war and why it appealed to FPL leadership. The following two sections analyze why the FPL leaders found the Vietnamese version most persuasive and how they adapted it for use in El Salvador. The final section addresses the guerrilla war that began in full force in 1981, showing that the FPL continued to prioritize popular organizing—partly from necessity, partly for ideological reasons—even in the midst of all-out war.

Prolonged Popular War in Global Context

Most of the movements that FPL leaders studied were Marxist-Leninist, which meant that their leaders deemed themselves a vanguard and sought to build parties based on democratic-centralist principles.[11] FPL leaders believed in that model. However, Marxist-Leninist movements since 1917 had varied widely in their strategic interpretation of it. Since the mid-1930s most of the Soviet-aligned communist parties in Latin America had eschewed class confrontation and armed struggle, instead seeking progressive reforms through interclass alliances and existing institutions. This orientation was guided by the Soviet Union's Popular Front policy, the essence of which continued after World War II. As such, the Partido Comunista de El Salvador (PCS, Communist Party of El Salvador) sent its members to work in the labor movement but with strict respect for the law. The party leaders promised that a future socialist society could be won "through gradual democratic victories."[12]

The 1959 triumph of the Cuban guerrillas punctured the hegemony of that strategy within the Latin American left, inspiring a wave of similar guerrilla campaigns across the region. The Cuban revolution influenced numerous Salvadoran revolutionaries, including the FPL's founders. For Martínez and other young radicals, Che Guevara offered an "ethical paradigm," an example of moral valor.[13] Cuba also showed that an armed revolution could be successful. This lesson had a major impact on the baker and Communist leader Salvador Cayetano Carpio, who had spent years as a successful union organizer and PCS leader before growing disenchanted with the party's legalism. Carpio resigned from the party and formed the FPL with six comrades in 1970. Cuba had shown Carpio "that it was necessary to apply Marxism in a non-dogmatic way, according to the conditions of the country."[14] The founding premise of the FPL was that El Salvador's political channels were closed to challengers and that armed struggle was the only viable option for transforming the country. The FPL's early propaganda identified "legalism, reformism, and economism" as key obstacles on the left.[15]

The FPL did not embrace the specifics of the Cuban strategy, though. The defeat of all the Cuban-inspired Latin American guerrilla movements of the 1960s, including in El Salvador itself in the early 1960s, made Carpio and others doubt whether Fidel Castro and Guevara's success in the Sierra Maestra could ever be replicated. They thus rejected the Cuban *foco* strategy, which was based on the idea that a small group of rural guerrillas could ignite a successful revolution. Carpio would later criticize "the conception of guerrillas as a few heroes isolated from the people," a small "elite that acts upon the people." He scorned the notion that the people "would receive them as their saviors, mesmerized by their great exploits."[16]

Similarly, the FPL criticized the "insurrectionist" tendency found in many revolutionary movements at the time. This perspective assumed that the ground was ripe for a seizure of state power. It prioritized military preparations among the guerrillas and efforts to win over the regime's own military officers. This strategy was influential within the Ejército Revolucionario del Pueblo (ERP, People's Revolutionary Army), which formed in El Salvador in 1972.[17] Carpio and others thought this approach was destined to fail because it neglected mass political work. In Russia in 1917 the Bolsheviks had seized power quickly, aided by a context of mass strikes and protests against wartime misery. El Salvador in 1970 was a very different scene. The capitalist agricultural economy, which revolved around coffee, cotton, and sugar, was dominated by a narrow oligarchy that ruled in close alliance with the military. There was little sign of militancy among the rural poor. Though the cities were more industrialized than elsewhere in Central America, the revolutionary groups lacked a large base among urban workers. There was no indication that rank-and-file soldiers were about to revolt, as they had in Russia. Consequently, the political terrain in El Salvador demanded a more long-term, "integrated" approach, in order to build a mass movement that could confront the regime through both armed and unarmed means.[18]

When the FPL first adopted the prolonged-popular-war strategy, its main reference point was China. Mao had written about the strategy in the 1930s during the Chinese war of resistance against Japan. He affirmed the possibility of victory but warned against the illusion of "quick victory." The war would progress in three stages, he said: a first stage in which the resistance was on the defensive, a second stage of "strategic stalemate" in which the invaders were forced onto the defensive, and a final stage of "strategic counter-offensive." Mao emphasized the importance of political organizing and agitation alongside military operations: "The contest of strength is not only a contest of military and economic power, but also of human power and morale," including among the civilian population. He thus advocated "making the political mobilization for the war a part of our daily work."[19] The Vietnamese resistance against the French and the United States employed a similar strategy, but the Chinese experience had more influence on the FPL in its early years, probably due to the earlier triumph of the Chinese revolution and Chinese efforts to spread Maoist thought in Latin America.[20]

The prolonged popular war seemed to FPL leaders a more realistic model in a poor country that was dominated by reactionary elites allied with a foreign empire. It took account of the movement's initial weakness and offered a strategic vision for how to achieve, over time, a shift in power relations in preparation for a seizure of the state. Mao's three stages were apparent in early FPL theoretical writings, which envisioned moving "from a situation of great disadvantage in the correlation of forces with the enemy, to a situation of equilibrium of forces, and finally, to the creation of a correlation of forces favorable to the revolutionaries," which would "make viable the triumph of the revolution." The combination of military and political tactics was especially attractive given the shortage of "revolutionary consciousness" and "revolutionary organization of the working-class and peasant masses and other sectors." While "the objective conditions for carrying out a popular revolution are present in abundance," the "subjective" conditions of consciousness and organization "lag behind."[21] This context demanded the prioritization of political work—that is, mass education efforts and aggressive campaigns for better wages, land, public services, and political freedoms—in addition to military preparation and small-scale armed actions.

The prolonged popular war was still open to much interpretation, however. Mao's version actually became a target of FPL criticisms by the start of the civil war. In her 1982 study of the Vietnamese revolution, FPL second-in-command Mélida Anaya Montes ("Ana María") repeatedly criticized Mao's neglect of nonpeasant sectors, contrasting his peasant-based strategy with the worker-peasant alliance of the Vietnamese. She blamed the devastating losses of the Long March of 1934–1935, in which nine-tenths of Mao's army perished, on the movement's failure to cultivate an organized support network in the cities that could have aided the rebels as they were being hunted by Chiang Kai-shek's forces.[22]

Several other Latin American guerrilla organizations adopted the prolonged-popular-war strategy, but they often interpreted it quite differently from the Salvadorans. In Argentina the approach of the Partido Revolucionario de los Trabajadores-Ejército Revolucionario del Pueblo (PRT-ERP, Revolutionary Workers' Party–People's Revolutionary Army) was weighted much more heavily toward military tactics.[23] Conversely, the group within Nicaragua's Sandinista National Liberation Front that advocated prolonged popular war was focused largely on propaganda and deemphasized the role of armed action, at least in the early 1970s. Like Mao's movement, its area of operations was mainly rural.[24] FPL leaders likely had some knowledge of these groups but were not in close contact with them and did not mention their texts as having been influential.[25]

As these examples suggest, the prolonged popular war was a general strategic orientation, not a detailed blueprint for revolution. Different revolutionaries interpreted the strategy differently, with widely varying degrees of success. The FPL's gravitation toward the Vietnamese model, and its success in adapting it for El Salvador, therefore merits closer attention.

Vietnam and the Worker-Peasant Alliance

FPL interviews and writings from the late 1970s and early 1980s mention Vietnam more frequently than China, Cuba, or neighboring Nicaragua and Guatemala.[26] In 1982 Anaya Montes published a whole book on the lessons of Vietnam. The organization also reprinted large quantities of books by Vo Nguyen Giap and another Vietnamese theoretician, Truong Chinh.[27] It was the Vietnamese conception of prolonged popular war that FPL leaders found most compelling. The Vietnamese communists, like the Chinese, had argued that "an insurrection could not be victorious without a deep and wide political movement waged by the revolutionary masses."[28] Building that movement required education and organizing work so that civilians would be prepared, both to support the guerrillas and to confront landlords, employers, and the state directly. One significant difference from the Chinese, however, was the importance that the Vietnamese placed on a worker-peasant alliance. They envisioned a coalition of wage workers (both urban and rural) and rural smallholders "under the leadership of the working class."[29]

The worker-peasant alliance was likewise a constant theme in FPL propaganda. According to Carpio, "the great lesson of Vietnam" was that a Marxist-Leninist party had succeeded by building itself "upon the basis of a firm worker-peasant alliance."[30] The FPL argued that fully proletarianized workers should exercise more influence than peasant smallholders, since the former had "absolutely nothing to lose"; they were also in a more strategic position to disrupt the capitalist economy, both in the cities and on the plantations.[31]

For the FPL the worker-peasant alliance was an alternative to the vertical interclass alliances promoted by some of its competitors on the left, including the ERP and the Resistencia Nacional (RN, National Resistance). It firmly opposed any coalition that might subordinate the interests of workers and peasants to those of more privileged classes. While it did not rule out temporary "tactical" alliances with "progressive" and "democratic" segments of the middle class and petty bourgeoisie, it prioritized the development of a "strategic" alliance among those groups that shared "the same fundamental objectives." That strategic alliance could then neutralize the power of more privileged classes in any future tactical alliance.[32] A related argument of the FPL was that the Salvadoran military regime was not fascist but rather *fascistoide*, meaning with fascistic tendencies. The mischaracterization of the regime as fascist led some of its rivals on the left to ally out of "desperation" with any and all "democratic" sectors, regardless of who was steering those alliances or what impact they had on "the development of the revolutionary struggle."[33]

Starting in 1972 the FPL elaborated its internal position on mass organizing. Despite the FPL's theoretical emphasis on the proletariat and the relatively large size of the country's industrial sector, the urban working class was only a secondary focus for its organizing. FPL leaders viewed the urban labor movement as dominated by "reformism," bureaucracy, and workers' fear of layoffs. They saw teachers, students, and rural workers and peasants as the groups most likely to join a revolutionary coalition. Teachers were the "most combative" sector of working people in the early 1970s and were often supported by their students. Though the rural poor had not shown widespread militancy in recent decades, they were facing increased impoverishment and also represented the majority of El Salvador's population.[34]

The FPL hoped that with the help of the teachers' union it "could extend the movement" among students and the rural poor, "and that's what happened."[35] It initiated a series of publications, both general and sector-specific, including one called *Campo Rebelde* ("Rebel countryside") that ran for at least fourteen issues in the late 1970s. In 1974 it channeled "the large majority of cadres" into mass organizing work. Most went to rural areas, where they focused on "the training of reliable peasant cadres" who could represent the FPL in the countryside.[36] The following year FPL leaders helped form the Bloque Popular Revolucionario (BPR, Popular Revolutionary Bloc), a civilian coalition that included peasant smallholders and rural wage workers, high school students, teachers, university students, and urban workers and slum dwellers, in roughly descending numbers. These groups occupied factories and rural land, demanded better wages, and denounced state violence. Each supported the others in their campaigns. This commitment to solidarity stands out in oral histories with survivors. Peasant activist Rosa Rivera, for instance, recalls how everyone in her area of Chalatenango "mobilized in solidarity with the students" after the regime murdered dozens of student marchers in San Salvador on July 30, 1975. Many rural activists, including Rivera, were captured and tortured for participating in protests against the massacre.[37] The explosive growth of the BPR between 1975 and 1980, registered in both its numbers and militancy, proved that a worker-peasant alliance (or a worker-peasant-student alliance) was possible.

The FPL's organizing was greatly facilitated by the work that other groups had carried out since the late 1960s. The national teachers' union, founded in 1965, had waged two nationwide strikes in 1968 and 1971, and its progressive political demands had placed it at the forefront of resistance to the military regimes. Its head was Anaya Montes, who was recruited to join the FPL in the early 1970s by fellow trade unionist Carpio. Anaya Montes also served as general secretary of the BPR in the mid-1970s before going underground in preparation for the war.[38]

In the countryside, most of the prior organizing work had grown out of the Catholic Church. By the early 1970s, thousands of peasant catechists and lay leaders had been trained to read, write, and facilitate Bible study. Discussions of the Bible led to increased political organizing by peasants, an outcome often unintended by Church officials. This path is exemplified by the life of Apolinario Serrano. Initially educated by the Church as a lay worker, in 1974 he was elected as organizing secretary of the Federación Cristiana de Campesinos Salvadoreños (FECCAS, Christian Federation of Salvadoran Peasants). He soon became the most important peasant leader in the country and by the late 1970s was a high-level militant in the FPL.[39]

While the FPL's coalition-building work benefited from some favorable circumstances, its analysis, strategy, and dedication were also important. Its suspicion of alliances with dissident elites and its rejection of electoral politics may have cost it some support in the early 1970s, but by 1975 that analysis resonated widely among its target constituencies due to the military regime's fraud in the 1972 election and the increased state repression against nonviolent activists.[40] Its commitment to building the worker-peasant alliance, largely inspired by the Vietnamese, was unequaled elsewhere on the Salvadoran left. Even so, forging an urban-rural coalition was no easy feat. The FPL's success depended partly on its particular approach to organizing, which helped it win the sympathies of diverse groups. The Vietnamese, too, influenced that approach.

Active, Direct, Conscious Participation

The FPL considered itself a vanguard, but this self-perception was tempered by a strong emphasis on *el pueblo* (the people) as the protagonist of revolution. This idea was evident in the title of Giap's book *People's War, People's Army*. Like Mao before him, Giap argued that "the people are to the army what water is to fish" and that the army must obey a strict code of honor in dealing with the people. Beyond simply respecting and defending the people, though, the revolutionaries must also foster mass participation. In Giap's words, the revolution must involve "a deep and wide political movement waged by the revolutionary masses."[41] This broad participation was essential to people's war. Giap proclaimed, "Every resident a soldier, every village a fortress, every party cell and every communal administrative committee, a military command."[42]

Some of the FPL's propaganda slogans echoed Giap's call. "Let us make every *barrio* (neighborhood) and canton a fortress for the revolution," read a spray-painted slogan in a guerrilla stronghold outside San Salvador in 1981.[43] Like Giap, FPL leaders emphasized not just respect for the people but "the growing incorporation of the people into the tasks of the war." In the early 1970s they determined that this "would be the yardstick for measuring the advances of the war."[44] A 1976 BPR manifesto, which clearly bears the mark of FPL thought, condensed key lessons from revolutionary movements around the world. One of the most important was "that without the ACTIVE, DIRECT, AND CONSCIOUS participation of the popular masses no revolutionary process can develop." The document cited Mao Zedong on the need for the party to learn from the masses, and Giap on the worker-peasant alliance.[45]

A tight connection with the masses was also a key theme in FPL writings on the role of the vanguard party. "The revolutionary vanguard must emerge from the people themselves," said another document from the mid-1970s. It must guide, not replace, the people.[46] In Carpio's words, the FPL had "a superior quality" that enabled it to guide the revolution, but ultimately "it is the people who make their Revolution," and "a true Marxist Party does not substitute for the people." Furthermore, the party "needs to be fused [*fundido*] with the people" and constantly "taking the temperature of the people." Proclaiming a party line was meaningless "if the people do not take it in their hands and make it a living reality." If they refused, it meant the vanguard had failed to take a position "aligned with the needs and realities of the people." Elaborating the line should be an iterative process, with continuous revisions based on the infusion of "knowledge about how it's being applied and how 'it has stuck' among the people and why."[47]

The fight for reforms was to be an indispensable educational process that would prepare the masses to play a revolutionary role. Struggles for better wages, working conditions, and other "immediate interests" would produce "direct confrontation with the class enemy," which would, in turn, help people to understand the deeper "roots of exploitation." With the party's guidance, the people would come to "understand the need to wage a revolutionary struggle to put an end to the regime of exploitation and oppression."[48]

Though this conception of mass participation drew from Mao's and Giap's emphasis on the need for a mass-based political movement, the FPL arguably went further than the Chinese and Vietnamese in its insistence on "active, direct, and conscious" popular participation. According to the BPR's 1976 manifesto, the masses "are not simply a source of support for the revolutionary struggle, as many in Latin America have wrongly argued in years prior, but rather the *actors* in those struggles, their MOTOR FORCES. They must participate with the highest level of consciousness and conviction."[49] The FPL did not seek direct control over labor unions and other mass organizations and privately criticized other FMLN factions for doing so. For Carpio, popular organizations "should have their own character before the masses, so as to be able to win over all of the most exploited sectors." Another commander likewise said, "We view the mass organizations as the broad channels and in that sense we cannot destroy those open structures. Nor do we have the right to deprive the masses of their right to build their trade organizations."[50] Even the BPR was no mere front organization: though FPL members played a key role in the coalition's formation in 1975, its member groups "had their own life, their own dynamics," in the words of former BPR general secretary and FPL leader Facundo Guardado.[51]

Had the FPL tried to convert its mass constituencies into automatons, it would have been unsuccessful. María Elmma Landaverde, a former rural organizer from the Aguilares region north of San Salvador, recalls the dynamic between peasants and organizers who arrived from outside their communities. Once "some of them arrived with hammocks, which for us was a petty-bourgeois attitude," since "we had to sleep on the floor." A small act like sleeping in a hammock could poison the relationship if it was seen as an indication of pretension or selfishness. "If you are a revolutionary you have to change your perceptions and your behavior, because you can't be a social fighter if you want to dominate the peasant [*si te quieres llevar en medio de tus pies al campesino*]."[52] Adherence to this ethos of respect was essential to the FPL's successes. Its organizers were usually able to minimize tensions by adapting to their surroundings.

Peasants also influenced the FPL's political thought and praxis, both directly and indirectly. The very need to recruit peasants brought changes in the organization. One major example was its 1975 overture to Catholics. In an open letter to the "progressive priests" who were then working in many parts of the countryside, the initially atheistic FPL now argued that "religious work and revolutionary activity can be fruitfully combined in the interest of the *pueblo*."

Religion and Marxism could be "two tributaries of the same river," as FPL leader Lorena Peña later characterized the message. The letter affirmed the importance of interpreting Marxism with a "creative spirit," of maintaining "revolutionary humility," and of recognizing that no group had "a monopoly over the truth."[53] This changed stance on religion was partly influenced by global shifts within the left. The rise of liberation theology in the 1960s and early 1970s had led many secular revolutionaries in Latin America to rethink their suspicions toward Christianity. FPL leaders cited Guevara's statement that "when Christians join the revolution it will be invincible." They likely also knew of the Vietnamese communists' long-standing view that revolution and religion were compatible. The biggest reason for the FPL leaders' shift on religion, however, was the local impetus: openness to religious believers was "a strategic necessity" in El Salvador because the "peasant and worker masses" were "fundamentally Catholic."[54]

Organizing the mass base necessary for a prolonged popular war required the FPL to accommodate its target constituencies. This lesson was originally based on the writings of Chinese and Vietnamese revolutionaries. But it was the organization's on-the-ground work in the 1970s that gave it concrete form. FPL strategy by the late 1970s reflected a successful adaptation of the prolonged popular war to the Salvadoran context—so successful that its enemies responded with their own strategy of mass extermination to crush the threat.

Popular War in the 1980s

The start of the Salvadoran civil war is usually associated with the formation of the FMLN in October 1980 and the major guerrilla offensive of January 1981. Up to that point the armed activities of the guerrillas had consisted only of small-scale acts like sabotage, robbery, and targeted assassination of abusive local elites. The state and large landowners, however, had practiced systematic terrorism against the civilian population for most of the prior decade. In 1980 alone the military and right-wing death squads killed around ten thousand civilians.[55] The survivors from unarmed movements joined the guerrillas, fled the country, or went inactive in the hope of avoiding repression.

The new context inspired changes in the FPL's strategy, beyond just the obvious shift toward military operations. The decision to join the FMLN coalition was itself a significant concession for Carpio, whose distrust of rival revolutionary leaders is legendary.[56] Carpio's own resistance notwithstanding, most FPL leaders began to look more favorably on political alliances, both with the other guerrilla groups and with nonradical forces. This reevaluation was largely due

to the July 1979 triumph of the Nicaraguan Sandinistas, who had not significantly influenced the FPL's thinking until then. According to Gerson Martínez,
the success of an interclass coalition in the fight against the Anastasio Somoza
dictatorship awakened FPL leaders to the importance of alliances with a broad
range of "antidictatorial forces." Martínez recalls being "impressed by the matu-
rity and political flexibility with which the Sandinista Front had fostered the
convergence of all these actors." The Nicaraguan victory also illustrated the
importance of "insurrectionary" tactics, which the Sandinistas had increasingly adopted in the late 1970s. Their success made the FPL leadership rethink
its dedication to a gradual accumulation of revolutionary momentum. "From
then on, we became more convinced of the role of insurrection as part of the
strategy of popular war. This was summarized in the slogan 'Long live armed
insurrection with prolonged popular war!'"[57]

The shift to all-out war also led the FPL and the broader FMLN to place
greater priority on cultivating international support. They engaged in concerted outreach to potential supporters in the United States, Europe, Mexico,
Nicaragua, and elsewhere, and with great success. The U.S.-based Committee
in Solidarity with the People of El Salvador (CISPES), which had strong sympathies for the FPL, eventually included more than one hundred local chapters
across the United States.[58]

The FMLN also forged closer military ties with foreign allies. Nicaragua
became the headquarters for the top command, and many lower-level militants
also did political work there. Cuba provided artillery training for FMLN officers,
medical and educational services for wounded guerrillas, advice about military
strategy, and various other support.[59] Vietnam helped train the FPL's newly
created special forces, which performed "sapper" actions, including infiltrat-
ing behind enemy lines during offensives. The Vietnamese were renowned on
the global guerrilla left for their expertise in that realm. Some trainees traveled directly to Vietnam, while others received Vietnamese-inspired training
in Cuba. Anaya Montes led a 1981 delegation to Vietnam, where she gathered
material for her 1982 book on military and political strategy. Vietnam also provided M-16 rifles, most of which came indirectly from the United States, which
had sent them to South Vietnam during its occupation.[60]

In other ways, however, the FPL's strategy remained consistent during the
war years. While military operations and discipline necessarily assumed more
importance, political organizing and popular participation—the essence of
"popular war"—were still a priority. Again, the Vietnamese were a significant
influence. The combination of political and military operations was a key focus
of Anaya Montes's book on Vietnam. She quoted a famed woman general, "the

compañera Nguyen Thi Dinh," on the need for continued political work amid military struggle: "We need arms, arms, and more arms. That doesn't mean abandoning the political struggle."[61]

The political struggle in FPL-controlled territories took innovative forms. The eastern part of Chalatenango department featured new experiments in popular democracy, known as local-popular-power councils. The councils oversaw food production and the provision of healthcare, education, security, and other needs in the war zones. They functioned with a large degree of autonomy from the FPL command and became key sites of popular empowerment, including for the emergence of feminist consciousness among peasant women.[62] Autonomy was partly necessitated by the desperate context, but it also reflected a conscious ideological decision. Felipe Peña Mendoza, one of the most dogma-averse leaders of the FPL, had advocated participatory councils prior to his death in 1975.[63] Even Carpio, who is often remembered as a more vain and dogmatic figure, wrote of the need to let the masses "come to insurrection through their own modalities." The popular-power councils, he hoped, would become the "thresholds into a new society."[64] Other participants described the councils as a new application of the prolonged-popular-war strategy, in that they embodied the FPL's emphasis on the "active and growing participation of the people."[65] Thus the intensification of the military war did not bring an end to political organizing. In some ways it gave that work a more revolutionary character.

The strength of popular organizing helped the FPL survive the crisis of April 1983, when it lost its top two commanders, Carpio and Anaya Montes, in a shocking murder-suicide. Over the previous two years Carpio had grown more distant from other FPL leaders, particularly over the question of negotiating with the regime. He accused the advocates of negotiations of "petty bourgeois" tendencies and singled out Anaya Montes as the main culprit. Though there is still some debate about whether Carpio directly ordered her murder, he killed himself after he was accused of the crime. The scandal caused a schism within the FPL.[66] An organizational trauma of this magnitude could only be overcome because the FPL had other able leaders, both at the top and at the grassroots, who could fill the vacuum. The group's survival is a testament to the "popular" nature of its war. That the guerrillas ultimately failed to overthrow the regime should not obscure that fact.[67]

Conclusion

Salvadoran revolutionaries of the 1970s and 1980s learned from a broad array of global experiences. Although this chapter has focused on just one faction of the FMLN, the fact that the FPL was the biggest of the five factions owed in large part to its innovative application of global ideas.

Chinese and Vietnamese conceptions of "popular" or "people's" war were especially important in shaping the FPL's thought and praxis. China and Vietnam informed the FPL's emphasis on mass-based political work and on the worker-peasant alliance as the central axis of a revolutionary movement. For most of the 1970s this transnational learning process occurred indirectly, through reading and secondhand interactions, rather than through personal contact with Chinese or Vietnamese revolutionaries. By the early 1980s the FPL leadership developed direct relationships with Vietnam's government, which provided it with military training, arms, and advice.

The importance of these transnational influences can easily be overstated, however, as the Salvadoran and U.S. regimes did when they painted the insurgents as puppets of foreign powers. Rather than copying the Chinese or Vietnamese models, the FPL adapted their lessons selectively and creatively. The FPL's growth depended on its ability to apply global ideologies and strategies in dialogue with El Salvador's peasants, workers, and students. Its success in doing so belies common characterizations of the Salvadoran insurgents as rigid and sectarian.[68] Those negative tendencies were indeed present, but they coexisted with more dynamic qualities, including the emphasis on fostering a self-critical "creative spirit" and learning from others.[69] The future of El Salvador's left depends in large part on whether it can recapture that creative spirit.

Notes

Thanks to my interviewees for sharing their memories and analysis and also to María Socorro Álvarez, Joaquín Chávez, Van Gosse, Verónica Guerrero, Carlos Henríquez Consalvi, Diana Sierra Becerra, and the four volume editors.

1. The slogan appeared on a bumper sticker circulated by the San Francisco–based Planetary Peace Alliance. See Midwest Chicano/Latino Activism Collection, Special Collections Division, Michigan State University Libraries, https://d.lib.msu.edu /michilac/190.

2. Comandante Ana María, *Experiencias vietnamitas*, dedication; Salvador Cayetano Carpio ("Marcial") in Carpio and Montes, *La guerra popular*, 21; Torogoces de Morazán, "Toda Centroamérica," undated, https://www.youtube.com/watch?v=Lkzht3QqHDA.

3. Grandin, *Empire's Workshop*, 100.

4. Schwarz, *American Counterinsurgency Doctrine*, 2; Hoover Green and Ball, "Civilian Killings and Disappearances"; Commission on the Truth for El Salvador, *From Madness to Hope*, 43.

5. For relatively sober takes by counterinsurgent intellectuals, see Spencer, *From Vietnam to El Salvador*; Rosello, "Vietnam's Support."

6. See, for instance, Gosse, "North American Front."

7. In Spanish the term was *guerra prolongada popular* or sometimes *guerra prolongada del pueblo*, which were used interchangeably. I use "people's war" and "popular war" interchangeably here.

8. A Spanish translation of Mao's was issued by the Chinese government in 1960: *Sobre la guerra prolongada*. A translation of Giap's was apparently first published by the Cuban government in 1964, as *Guerra del pueblo, ejército del pueblo*; publishers in Argentina and Mexico issued their own editions in 1965 and 1971, respectively.

9. Gerson Martínez, interview by Carlos Henríquez Consalvi, San Salvador, January 15, 2020. Transcripts of all unpublished interviews are available at the Museo de la Palabra y la Imagen in San Salvador.

10. Atilio Montalvo ("Salvador") and Gerson Martínez ("Valentín") in Harnecker, *Con la mirada en alto*, 93–94. Another FPL commander interviewed in 1981 said that "other peoples' liberation struggles" were a focus of political education efforts in the guerrilla camps. Comandante Jesús in Carpio and Montes, *La guerra popular*, 103.

11. Democratic centralism can be more or less democratic in practice. In basic terms it involves free internal debate prior to arriving at a decision and disciplined respect for the decision by all members thereafter.

12. Facundo Guardado, qtd. in Harnecker, *Con la mirada en alto*, 31. See the FPL critiques of the PCS in Harnecker, *Con la mirada en alto*, 31–32, 54–59.

13. Gerson Martínez interview.

14. Carpio in Harnecker, *Pueblos en armas*, 157.

15. "Guerra revolucionaria prolongada del pueblo," *El Rebelde* 10, 1973, 5. All FPL periodicals cited in this chapter were consulted at the Centro de Información, Documentación y Apoyo a la Investigación, Universidad Centroamericana José Simeón Cañas, San Salvador, El Salvador. Issues of *Estrella Roja* are also available online through the Servicio Informativo Ecuménico y Popular, https://ecumenico.org.

16. Carpio, "Cuaderno no. 4: Introducción y algo más sobre la necesidad de que las FPL se transformen en el verdadero partido Marxista-Leninista del proletariado salvadoreño," October 1982, in Carpio, *Nuestras montañas*, 176.

17. There was a current within the ERP that favored a strategy more similar to the FPL's conception of prolonged popular war. The Resistencia Nacional faction split from the ERP in 1975, partly over the ERP's lack of emphasis on political organizing. See Martín Álvarez and Cortina Orero, "Genesis and Internal Dynamics."

18. Carpio, "Testamento político," April 1, 1983, in Carpio, *Nuestras montañas*, 220–21; Carpio in Harnecker, *Con la mirada en alto*, 103.

19. Mao, *On the Protracted War*, 3, 41, 43, 53, 74.

20. Gerson Martínez in Harnecker, *Con la mirada en alto*, 110. On Vietnamese strategy, see Giap, *People's War*, esp. 111–27. On Chinese efforts, see Rothwell, *Transpacific Revolutionaries*, esp. 18–25.

21. "Las condiciones objetivas y subjetivas para la lucha revolucionaria," *Estrella Roja* 1, 1973, 13, 15.

22. Comandante Ana María, *Experiencias vietnamitas*, 109, 134–35, 192. China's esteem among Latin American revolutionaries declined in the 1970s for various other reasons, including Mao's support for the Pinochet regime in Chile. Rothwell, *Transpacific Revolutionaries*, 25.

23. Carnovale, "La guerra revolucionaria."

24. Zimmerman, *Sandinista*, 168–70, 180, 189–90. The strategy of the Ejército Guerrillero de los Pobres (EGP, Guerrilla Army of the Poor) in Guatemala was closer to that of the FPL.

25. Harnecker, *Con la mirada en alto*, 93–94, 203.

26. Though the FPL expressed solidarity with those other countries, its ties to them were initially quite limited. It did not have "very close or systematic relations" with the Sandinistas prior to 1979. It had a closer relationship with Guatemalan revolutionaries, from whom it received some military support. The lack of more international outreach was due in part to FPL leaders' belief that "the internal class struggle is the motor force in every true revolutionary process," and that any successful revolution initially "supported itself through its own efforts." Mao made this point in his 1937 text *On Contradiction*, which was widely read among FPL militants in the 1970s. See Gerson Martínez in Harnecker, *Con la mirada en alto*, 93, 98, 203–7 (first quote, 203); Facundo Guardado, interview by author, San Salvador, May 22, 2015; Carpio, "Testamento político," in Carpio, *Nuestras montañas*, 223 (second quote); Comandante Ana María, *Experiencias vietnamitas*, 156 (third quote, in reference to Vietnam).

27. Comandante Ana María, *Experiencias vietnamitas*; Carpio and Montes, *La guerra popular*, 21, 93, 151, 255; Carpio, "Cuaderno no. 4," 188; Harnecker, *Con la mirada en alto*, 95; Pearce, *Promised Land*, 206–8.

28. Giap, *People's War*, 88. Cf. Mao, *On the Protracted War*, 72–74.

29. Giap, *People's War*, 35–36.

30. Carpio, "Cuaderno no. 4," 188. FPL leaders also studied urban-based guerrilla movements, including the Montoneros in Argentina and the Tupamaros in Uruguay. Atilio Montalvo in Harnecker, *Con la mirada en alto*, 94.

31. FECCAS-UTC, "La estrategia de los trabajadores," n.d., folder 6, Federación de Trabajadores del Campo collection, in Centro de Información, Documentación y Apoyo a la Investigación, Universidad Centroamericana José Simeón Cañas, San Salvador, El Salvador, 3, 6. Although the FPL distinguished landless rural workers from smallholders, its organizers informally used the term *campesino* in reference to both groups. In practice most of the rural poor combined wage labor and subsistence cultivation. Unless otherwise specified, I use *peasant* here in this more inclusive sense.

32. FECCAS-UTC, "La estrategia," 11; Pearce, *Promised Land*, 133–34.

33. BPR, "La alternativa del pueblo: El Bloque Popular Revolucionario," July 11, 1976, folder 8, BPR collection, in Centro de Información, Documentación y Apoyo a la Investigación, Universidad Centroamericana José Simeón Cañas, San Salvador, El Salvador, 4.

34. Harnecker, *Con la mirada en alto*, 91, 108–09, 115, 123–28, 146–52 (quotes from Facundo Guardado, 146, 125); Guardado interview.

35. Facundo Guardado in Harnecker, *Con la mirada en alto*, 125.

36. Gerson Martínez in Harnecker, *Con la mirada en alto*, 119, 151.

37. Rosa Rivera Rivera, interview by author and Diana Sierra Becerra, April 10, 2015, Arcatao; Miguel Franco, interview by author, May 21, 2015, Arcatao.

38. Anaya Montes, *La segunda gran batalla*; Carpio and Montes, *La guerra popular*, 85–89.

39. This summary draws from Cabarrús, *Génesis de una revolución*; Cardenal, *Historia de una esperanza*, 433–603; Pearce, *Promised Land*, 97–190; Palencia, *Para que no olvidemos*, 96–140; Chávez, *Poets and Prophets*, 72–105; and author interviews with María Delia de Cornejo, April 25, 2015, San Salvador; Rosa Rivera Rivera and María Helia Rivera, April 10, 2015, Arcatao; Celestino Rivera, April 11, 2015, Arcatao; and Facundo Guardado.

40. The FPL's rejection of vertical class alliances was apparently a factor in the 1975 decisions of FECCAS and the teachers union to join the FPL-aligned BPR, which meant abandoning the rival mass organization, the Frente de Acción Popular Unificada (FAPU, United Popular Action Front); Pearce, *Promised Land*, 136. The BPR then became the largest mass organization in the country.

41. Giap, *People's War*, 65, 88, 141.

42. Qtd. in Carpio and Montes, *La guerra popular*, 244. For similar phrasing, see Comandante Ana María, *Experiencias vietnamitas*, 125.

43. Qtd. in Carpio and Montes, *La guerra popular*, 245.

44. Gerson Martínez in Harnecker, *Con la mirada en alto*, 79.

45. BPR, "La alternativa del pueblo," 4–5; capitalization in original.

46. FECCAS-UTC, "La estrategia," 6.

47. Carpio, "Cuaderno no. 5: El partido debe estar íntimamente ligado al pueblo, a las masas," October 1982, in Carpio, *Nuestras montañas*, 191–94. See also "Breve exposición de la línea de la organización," *Estrella Roja* 2, 1975, 5.

48. BPR, "La alternativa del pueblo," 6; FECCAS-UTC, "La estrategia," 5.

49. BPR, "La alternativa del pueblo," 5; emphasis and capitalization in original.

50. Carpio, "Cuaderno no. 5," 197; Comandante Ricardo in Carpio and Montes, *La guerra popular*, 147.

51. Guardado interview. This statement is especially notable since Guardado has long since broken with the left.

52. María Elmma Landaverde, interview with author, May 1, 2015, Santa Tecla.

53. "Presentación," 2; "Nuestra actitud ante la religion," 25; "Las FPL son una organización Marxista-Leninista," 7; "En cuánto a nuestros órganos de comunicación con las masas populares," 16; all in *Estrella Roja* 2, 1975; Lorena Peña ("Rebeca") in Harnecker, *Con la mirada en alto*, 65.

54. "Nuestra actitud ante la religion," 25. More recently Fidel Castro had praised revolutionary Christians during his 1971 visit to Chile. "Discurso pronunciado por

el Comandante Fidel Castro Ruz," December 2, 1971, http://www.cuba.cu/gobierno/discursos/1971/esp/f021271e.html.

55. McClintock, *American Connection*, 266.

56. Other FPL leaders attributed that distrust to Carpio's dogmatic arrogance, the way he "came to see himself as infallible." Atilio Montalvo in Harnecker, *Con la mirada en alto*, 331. The five factions retained separate command structures but collaborated on major decisions.

57. Gerson Martínez in Harnecker, *Con la mirada en alto*, 206. These shifts were not uncontested, even after Carpio's death in 1983. For one internal critique of "the new revisionism," see "La entronización del revisionismo de nuevo tipo en nuestra línea estratégica," doc. 620, folder 3, Archivo Comandante Chana, Museo de la Palabra y la Imagen, San Salvador. The unsigned document warns that the Sandinistas have "exerted influence obliging us to adopt similar positions."

58. On CISPES, see Gosse, "North American Front."

59. Kruijt, *Cuba and Revolutionary Latin America*, 161–64. Despite Fidel Castro's critique of the prolonged-popular-war strategy, during the 1980s the FPL received more Cuban aid than other FMLN factions because of its comparative size and strength. Kruijt, *Cuba and Revolutionary Latin America*, 162.

60. U.S. propaganda always overhyped the importance of foreign sources: Many FMLN arms were captured or bought from the Salvadoran military, and material aid from the Soviet Union was not significant. But the existence of those other foreign connections is not in doubt. My summary is based on Comandante Ana María, *Experiencias vietnamitas*; Spencer, *From Vietnam to El Salvador*; Rosello, "Vietnam's Support"; and author interviews with former FPL and ERP militants.

61. Comandante Ana María, *Experiencias vietnamitas*, 17.

62. Pearce, *Promised Land*, 241–87; Sierra Becerra, "For Our Total Emancipation."

63. Gerson Martínez in Harnecker, *Con la mirada en alto*, 107, 131.

64. Carpio, "Cuaderno no. 4," 178.

65. "Raúl" in Carpio and Montez, *La guerra popular*, 193.

66. For other FPL leaders' accounts, see Harnecker, *Con la mirada en alto*, 325–43 (quote from Atilio Montalvo, 333). For a perspective more sympathetic to Carpio, see José Antonio Morales Carbonell, "El suicidio de Marcial," in Carpio, *Nuestras montañas*, 53–112.

67. On the origins and content of the 1992 peace accords, see Wood, *Forging Democracy from Below*, 52–107; Chávez, "How Did the Civil War in El Salvador End?"

68. See, for instance, Grenier, *Emergence of Insurgency*. For FPL leaders' self-criticisms, see Harnecker, *Con la mirada en alto*, 344–51.

69. "Las FPL son una organización Marxista-Leninista," 7.

Afterword

Remapping the Past

TANYA HARMER

More than a hundred years after the Bolshevik Revolution, historians are still grappling with its global reach and impact. New archival access and the revolution's centenary added impetus to the need to capture its transnational resonance and ramifications. As the preceding chapters so ably demonstrate, one result of such an endeavor has been to make visible those previously rendered invisible. Another has been to remap the way we conceptualize the past: to challenge the silos historians have tended to draw around geographical spaces and the people who live within them. This is an exciting and necessary venture, joining some of the most innovative new histories of global communism, Latin America's Left(s), and anti-imperialism in recent years. Yet, as Victor Figueroa Clark noted in a recent survey of Latin American communism, it is also challenging "in part because much of the historiography is anti-communist in its perspective, which has had the effect of entrenching multiple misconceptions about communists and communist parties, and in part because of a dearth of material due to repression and the clandestine nature of some communist activities."[1]

In questioning national scales of analysis and showcasing the different constituent groups advocating for revolutionary change, this volume addresses many of misconceptions head on. It takes communist movements and militants seriously and examines them on their own terms, in their own contexts. It also reveals the benefits transnational methods can offer as a means of dealing with a scarcity of sources. This afterword points to some of the most significant ways our knowledge of communism in the Americas is advanced by the contents of this book and how a new understanding of transnational approaches can affect the way we rethink histories of the twentieth century, revolutionary movements, and the Cold War.

Despite new access scholars have had to archival sources—either through declassification of state records, personal papers, oral histories, memoirs, and digitization initiatives—documenting the history of communism in the Americas and beyond remains a problem. As Marc Becker notes in his chapter, young communists and students left behind "few surviving traces" of their beliefs, travels, and interactions. Their publications were "ephemeral," and the records they kept of their world were incomplete. Self-censure either through destruction of records or an unwillingness to share them was also routine among communist activists in the past and to some degree remains so. Strategic or, more commonly, defensive reasons impelled communists to limit what was known of their undertakings and beliefs. To survive Cold War violence meant staying quiet or diminishing roles and relevance. Historians' choices about whom to study and the sources they have had to work with have compounded absences from the historical record. The silencing of women within accounts of politics and revolution has long since been a particularly persistent problem. As Patricia Harms reminds us in her chapter on the Alianza Femenina Guatemalteca, this is both due to patriarchal power structures *and* the repressive Cold War forces who systematically sought to wipe out voices of difference and dissent.

Crucially, however, transnational networks were often used by local actors as a means of asserting a voice, resisting repression, or overcoming internal constraints and challenges. As the contributors to this volume demonstrate, these networks can, in turn, provide historians with a lens through which to track the stories of those within them. Papers pertaining to the Women's International League for Peace and Freedom, for example, help piece together the transnational activism of those who connected through it, including the Guatemalan women at the heart of Harms's study. The papers also show the ways in which local actors were able to use transnational organizations to transcend constraints they faced at home. Harms describes, "Roots within transnational community offered women from a small communist party within a patriarchal society common ground with the global female condition." We learn that a transnational encounter in Guatemala in 1947 also directly inspired local actors, giving birth to the Alianza and providing women an autonomous political space. In her chapter, Adriana Petra similarly recovers the power that women had to convoke and to lead regional transnational meetings as well as benefit from them. Moreover, her study of Argentine writer and intellectual María Rosa Oliver reveals the impact these transnational encounters had on global politics. Becker similarly uses records about and pertaining to postwar mass organizations like the World Democratic Federation of Youth and the International Union of Students to trace Latin American youth activism on a world stage in the 1950s. In short, reading transnational institutional histories for what they reveal about the identity, beliefs, and actions of those who participated within them can help us to recover the significance and standing of protagonists otherwise silenced locally as a result of national censorship, circumstances, and scant surviving archival records.

As well as providing a means to capture lost voices of the past, the transnational histories of communism in this volume showcase a multitude of mobilities and interactions across borders. At the heart of these stories is migration. To be sure, we already know that migration underpins the story of the Americas and that migrants very often carried with them ideas and influences that shaped politics, society, culture, and economics in both their countries of origin as well as those they traveled through and to. However, the centrality of migration (either by force or voluntarily) to histories of communism in the Americas is worth underlining. Whether in the case of the seventy thousand Puerto Ricans living in New York by 1940 or the hundreds of thousands of Afro-Caribbean migrants living in the United States and Central America in the late nineteenth and twentieth centuries, migratory networks shaped the evolution of intellectual and political projects. The communist movement, quite simply, would not have evolved in the Americas without immigrant communities' influence on local communist activism and strategies. Jacob A. Zumoff's chapter in this volume, for example, points to the centrality of Caribbean migrants living in the United States to the turn in the Communist Party of the United States (CPUSA) to emphasize Black oppression as constitutive to capitalist evolution in the country. Black Caribbean immigrants, Zumoff argues, offered the CPUSA a "bridge to the broader Black population" in the United States through recruitment and a reframing of the urgency of anticolonialism, anti-imperialism, and socialist transformation. Focusing in on Cuba, Frances Peace Sullivan similarly explores the role that migration of Antillanos had on workers' movements and communist organizing on the island in the 1930s. However, she also reveals the power Afro-Cuban communists like Sandalio Junco had to mobilize support for antiracist and anti-imperial campaigns against U.S. companies in the greater Caribbean region through speeches and attendance at major transnational communist conferences in Uruguay and Argentina at the end of the 1920s. Travel throughout the region provided a means for individuals, many of them Comintern representatives, to campaign for working-class solidarity and Black liberation in the Americas.

Refuge and exile in the context of repression and conflict also shaped the ways communism evolved (or did not). Actors fleeing persecution or in search of support did not necessarily receive the solidarity and reception they sought. Margaret M. Power reveals how Puerto Rican Nationalists, forced into exile in the context of debilitating setbacks and repression in the 1930s, established close relations and collaborated in various ways with their communist counter-parts and allies in the CPUSA. The Puerto Rican Nationalists struggled, how-ever, to persuade them that independence had to be prioritized at all costs in the context of the shifts and turns associated with the Comintern in the 1930s and 1940s. Meanwhile, as Lazar Jeifets and Víctor Jeifets argue, Nicaraguan resistance leader Augusto César Sandino arrived in Mexico as a political and military figure with ambitions to speak to the Mexican government but was ostracized, dismissed, and treated as a political refugee. The Communist Party of Mexico did not help, demanding international tours and a visit to Moscow in return for support but failing to provide the means by which Sandino could travel. Even so, exile abroad tended to alter political trajectories, projects, and opportunities. Sandino's problematic encounters in Mexico confirmed to him that he needed to return to Nicaragua as soon as possible. Jacob Blanc's study of Luís Carlos Prestes's years of exile in Bolivia, Argentina, Uruguay, and the USSR provides insight into the radicalizing effect of transnational encounters. It was in Bolivia and Argentina that Prestes first read Marx and Lenin in earnest. In Buenos Aires and Uruguay, he was also in close contact with communist mili-tants who helped orient and inspire him. Indeed, it was the "web of relation-ships" that Prestes developed in exile, Blanc contends, that explains Prestes's subsequent role as secretary general of the Partido Comunista Brasileira (PCB, Brazilian Communist Party) thereafter.

Other protagonists of communism in the Americas traveled for work and training. Zumoff and Sullivan recount West Indian migrants' experience of work in Central America, the Caribbean, and the United States, revealing the multiple ways work, in turn, shaped identities and politics. Elsewhere, Puerto Rican Alberto Sánchez joined the Communist Party of the United States while working in factories in the United States. Power's chapter recounts the way this then launched him on a return journey to Puerto Rico to found the island's own Communist Party. Although beyond the scope of this volume, Burak Sayim's recent work on Comintern organizing and activism in Istanbul in the 1920s and 1930s reminds us to look closely at sailors as political agents and transna-tional actors who facilitated the growth of global networks.[2] Latin Americans, meanwhile, worked in administrative, political, journalistic, and organizational roles directly for the Comintern in Moscow, for its Caribbean and South American Bureaus, or for the World Peace Council in Vienna, as was the case with Jorge Zalamea of Colombia. From these positions, as Petra and Blanc note, these Latin Americans were able to insert Latin American interests and peoples into global anti-imperialist communities.

Tony Wood shows in his chapter on Latin Americans who spent time in the USSR during the 1920s and 1930s that people also moved in search of learning and insight, which they received as university students and travelers. Mass organizations like the World Democratic Federation of Youth similarly convened congresses that brought tens of thousands of people from around the globe together. The rapid rise in numbers attending such meetings in the 1950s that Becker details in his chapter are striking, growing from seven hundred delegates at the start of the decade to five times that number from almost double the number of countries by 1957. But as Becker notes, youth festivals and congresses themselves were only part of a much-larger story of transnational travel and linkages. For Latin American youth delegates, at least, mass events became a springboard for travel itineraries that took them across the Iron Curtain and back, criss-crossing from south to north and back again. International organizing and institution building were thus rooted in mobility and helped spur connections across borders. In this context, mass movement of rank-and-file militants provided insight, intelligence, and know-how to mass organizations who sponsored encounters *and* facilitated the spread of ideas, experiences, and influences back to the home countries of delegates who traveled. It is worth underlining Becker's final point here that without the mass mobilization and new transnational linkages of the 1950s, it is difficult to make sense of the global 1960s that followed. It was not just people who moved extensively during these decades. As Kevin Young comments, "influence did not require direct contact." Chinese and Vietnamese influences in El Salvador initially relied on translation of key works of revolutionary strategy. Vietnamese training in Cuba or Vietnam followed, but it arose from the dissemination of ideas and goods initially.

A third major contribution of this volume is what it reveals about the way global contexts resonated locally. Events across the world were not simply a backdrop. Very often, they provided a frame, a reference, and a guide for the way transnational figures acted in the way they did, and we are thus reminded of the need to pay more attention to them. To some extent, these shifts were mediated through what Power calls the "political twists and turns" of the Comintern's directives. The chapters in this volume recount the mental and strategic gymnastics that followed as militants and party leaderships struggled to respond to instructions and political shifts. However, these twists also responded to changing broader international dynamics. The global antifascist struggle that dominated world politics in the 1930s and 1940s, for example, had a tremendous impact on Latin Americans, serving as an entry point into politics and transnational activism, as Adriana Petra relates in her study of María Rosa Oliver. The developing Cold War in the late 1940s and 1950s further served to render regional conflicts globally significant as the ideological superpower battle expanded into "new geographies." For those like Oliver involved in Soviet-sponsored activism around the world, this stretched horizons in the 1950s and shifted focus toward Asia and Africa and to the Korean War, decolonization, the right to self-determination, and support for movements of national liberation. Detailing Latin American encounters with Asia and zooming in on the Conference for Peace in Asia and the Pacific Region, which took place in Beijing in 1952, Petra joins others who have recently pushed us to think about "other Bandungs" shaping transnational networks that followed.[3] Rather than being born in 1955 with the meeting of Afro-Asian solidarity as is commonly suggested, the language of solidarity, internationalism, and integration that came to define third-world groupings in the late 1950s and 1960s arose within a variety of different networks and encounters.

Which brings me to a fourth significant contribution that transnational histories of communism in the Americas, both in this volume and those awaiting to be written, collectively offer by way of considering alternative geographies and maps of the past. The Comintern's organizing bodies for the Americas brought communities together to work directly under its different offices. The Caribbean Bureau and the South American Bureau divided Latin America, bringing the Hispanic and Anglophone Caribbean populations into direct dialogue and collaboration with their U.S. counterparts. As Sullivan writes, the Caribbean Bureau became a new transnational "nexus" in New York, bringing together "Marxist intellectuals, party members, and union organizers from across the Caribbean."

Yet, as long as colonial orders have sought to subdivide the world as a means of controlling it, people have refused to be categorized and contained in neat groupings. And the same is also true of the Comintern's awkward administrative denomination of Latin America as part of the "colonial and semicolonial" world, which outlived the organization and found echoes in the way the World Democratic Federation of Youth conceived of the world. What is clear from new transnational histories is that despite these efforts to map the world by delineating separate spheres, there was an extraordinary mixing and meeting of peoples *across* divides. This was true within the Comintern's subregional constructs in the Americas and between its inhabitants and the rest of the world throughout the twentieth century. The resulting encounters established not one alternative to the predominant international order but *many*, particularly when it came to simplistic ideas of a world divided between East and West during the Cold War.

As well as encouraging us to think about the linkages, itineraries, and exchange across the Iron Curtain, transnational histories can also challenge highly problematic terms like the "Global South." As Pablo Palomino has recently argued, such terminology serves to hide and distort heterogeneous experiences within the supposed "South" as well as to blind us to the connections between it and the "Global North." He comments, "'Global south' . . . suggests a view from above—not from the political perspective of actors on the ground." If, as he underlines, it is ahistorical to subdivide the world when charting the history of anarchism or capitalism or to suggest liberation theology arose exclusively in the "South," the same is obviously true of the history of communism, which necessitates a transnational and global frame.[4] In this context, we must acknowledge the decisive significance of the Soviet Union in sponsoring and facilitating interactions through institution building, travel, culture, and networks around the world—just as the United States strove to do the same to promote its own worldview and priorities. Rather than putting up borders, in fact, Cold War strategies were invested in mobility and exchange as they simultaneously strove (unsuccessfully) to contain the reach and movement of others.

There is, however, a caveat to this remapping and transnationalism. As I've written elsewhere, it is important that we do not automatically equate interaction with cooperation and solidarity.[5] To the contrary, as the authors in this volume reveal, cross-border interactions and mobility could very often cause or reveal rifts and ruptures. There were "disparate responses," Wood tells us, to Latin Americans' experience in the Soviet Union in the 1920s and 1930s, "from deepening loyalty to stark estrangement." Petra reminds us of the "enormous crisis" the Soviet Union's invasion of Hungary caused on the global left and the seeds it offered for growth of a New Left thereafter. And Zumoff's comparative study of Afro-Caribbean involvement in communist militancy in Costa Rica and Panama (in contrast to the United States) illustrates the impediment to working-class unity that religion, language, and race could have on effective solidarity.

Tracing such disjuncture—as well as conjuncture—is important. It offers the opportunity to probe the coherence of left-wing projects and revolutionary movements, to understand their trajectories, and to draw lessons for the future. To be sure, studying transnational encounters can teach about the way strategies evolved from shared experiences and discussions. Kevin A. Young, for example, underlines the significance of mediated adaptation in the "general strategic orientation" rather than "detailed blueprint" Vietnam's experience offered Salvadorans. In a fascinating study of Vietnam's pivotal influence and significance for El Salvador, he persuasively forces us to think globally when examining revolutionary movements in the twentieth century. Yet, very often what we learn from encounters are the limitations that communist parties faced either as a result of structural conditions or those conditions they placed on themselves that exacerbated both internal cleavages and those between themselves and others.

Lazar Jeifets and Víctor Jeifets's study of the Comintern's failings in its dealings with Sandino in Nicaragua is exemplary in this regard. It reveals the significance personal differences, ignorance, and logistical constraints had in exacerbating bad strategy. Zumoff reminds us of competing transnational projects by contrasting Afro-Caribbean political allegiances in the United States, Costa Rica, and Panama either to communist parties or Marcus Garvey's competing Universal Negro Improvement Association, whose origins and influence were also the product of migration and mobility. Power's study of the Puerto Rican Communist Party and National Party, meanwhile, shows the way that transnational encounters could contribute to and exacerbate divisions within anticolonial movements. Rather than strengthening Puerto Ricans' challenge to U.S. imperialism, the PCP's alliance with the Communist Party of the USA ironically echoed "Washington's colonial connection to Puerto Rico." In sum, as historians we need to be alert not only to the collective power that transnational connections offered local actors but, in many cases, also the asymmetries and inherent colonial logics that infused them, as well. Tracing transnational encounters and mobility is just the first step. Accounting for the ways and extent to which this affected change (or not) and why is equally important if we are to learn from the past.

What is abundantly clear from the chapters in this volume and the renewed interest in global and transnational histories of communism is that historians paying closer attention to Latin Americans' interaction with each other and the wider world is not the whim of historiographical turns. Rather, it reflects a belated acknowledgment by historians of the Americas of the intricate linkages that have long since existed across borders, oceans, and metaphorical curtains. To paraphrase Fernando Lacerda's critique of the Comintern's belated focus on the Americas, which Wood quotes in the opening of his chapter, it is not that

Latin America has suddenly started engaging with the world in recent decades but that historians for the first time are taking a serious scholarly interest in the region's long established global reach and resonance.

Notes

1. Figueroa Clark, "Latin American Communism," 388.
2. Sayim, "Occupied Istanbul."
3. Lewis and Stolte, "Other Bandungs."
4. Palomino, "On the Disadvantages," 29, 32–33.
5. Harmer and Martín Álvarez, *Toward a Global History*, 15.

Bibliography

"VIe Congrès Mondial de l'International communiste. Trente-sixième séance, 18 août (matin)." *La Correspondance Internationale* 130, October 30, 1928, 1419.

Acosta-Belén, Edna. *Puerto Ricans in the United States: A Brief Chronology.* New York: Center for Puerto Rican Studies, 2015.

Acuña Ortega, Víctor H. *La huelga bananera de 1934.* San José, Costa Rica: CENAP, 1984.

Adi, Hakim. *Pan-Africanism and Communism: The Communist International, Africa, and the Diaspora, 1919–1939.* Trenton, NJ: Africa World, 2013.

Aguilar Camín, Héctor. "El camarada Vadillo." *Nexos* 147, March 1990.

——. "En busca de Vadillo." *Nexos* 149, May 1990.

Alarcón, Agustín. "¿Nación Negra? ¡No!" *Adelante* 2, no. 18, November 1, 1936, 12.

Alburquerque Fuschini, Germán. *La trinchera letrada: intelectuales latinoamericanos y Guerra Fría.* Santiago, Chile: Ariadna ediciones, 2011.

Alexander, Robert J. *Rómulo Betancourt and the Transformation of Venezuela.* New Brunswick, NJ: Transaction, 1982.

Alfaro, Olmedo. *El peligro antillano en la America Central.* Panama City: Imprenta nacional, 1924.

Altbach, Philip G. "The International Student Movement." *Journal of Contemporary History* 5, no. 1 (1970): 156–74.

Anaya Montes, Mélida. *La segunda gran batalla de ANDES.* San Salvador: Editorial Universitaria, 1972.

Anderson, Jon Lee. *Che Guevara: A Revolutionary Life.* New York: Grove, 1997.

Anderson, Moji. "Imperial Ideology: 'Subjects,' 'Objectivity,' and the Use of 'Empire' in the 1918–19 Banana Workers' Strike in Costa Rica and Panama." Working paper.

Mona, Jamaica: Institute of Social and Economic Research University of the West Indies, 1998.

Andreu Iglesias, César. *Independencia y socialismo*. San Juan, Puerto Rico: Librería Estrella Roja, 1951.

Arango Durling, Virginia. *La inmigración prohibida en Panamá y sus prejuicios raciales*. Panama City: Publipan, 1999.

Aránguiz Pinto, Santiago. "El 'viaje revolucionario': el relato testimonial como 'utopía realizada': Rusia soviética y la prensa comunista chilena (1922–1927)." In *Los comunismos en América Latina: Recepciones y miliancias (1917–1955)*, edited by Santiago Aránguiz Pinto and Patricio Herrera González, 1:75–100. Chile: Historia Chilena, 2018.

Arellano Gallegos, Jorge. *La subversión en Ecuador*. Quito: Editor Luz de América, 2003.

Arias Gómez, Jorge. *Farabundo Martí: Esbozo biográfico*. San Jose, Costa Rica: Editorial Universitaria Centroamericana, 1972.

Armstrong, Elisabeth. "Before Bandung: The Anti-Imperialist Women's Movement in Asia and the Women's International Democratic Federation." *Signs* 41, no. 2 (2016): 305–31.

Arredondo, Alberto. *El negro en Cuba: ensayo*. Havana, Cuba: Editorial Alfa, 1939.

——. "El negro y la nacionalidad." *Adelante* 1, 10, March 1, 1935, 6.

Ayala, César J., and Rafael Bernabe. *Puerto Rico in the American Century: A History since 1898*. Chapel Hill: University of North Carolina Press, 2007.

Barima, Kofi Boukman. "Caribbean Migrants in Panama and Cuba, 1851–1927: The Struggle, Opposition, and Resistance of Jamaicans of African Origin." *Journal of Pan African Studies* 5, no. 9 (2013): 43–62.

Basbaum, Leôncio. *Uma vida em seis tempos: memórias*. São Paulo: Editora Alfa Omega, 1976.

Bastos, Abguar. *Prestes e a revolução social: fatos políticos, condições sociais e causas econômicas de uma fase revolucionária do Brasil*. São Paulo: Editora HUCITEC, 1986.

Bayerlein, Bernhard, Kasper Braskén, and Holger Weiss. "Transnational and Global Perspectives on International Communist Solidarity Organisations: An Introduction." In *International Communism and Transnational Solidarity: Radical Networks, Mass Movements, and Global Politics, 1919–1939*, edited by Holger Weiss, 1–27. Leiden: Brill, 2017.

Becker, Marc. "A Latin American Peace Movement on the Margins of the Cold War." *Peace & Change* 45, no. 4 (2020): 513–42.

——. "Mariátegui, the Comintern, and the Indigenous Question in Latin America." *Science & Society* 70, no. 4 (2006): 450–79.

Beluche, Olmedo. "El problema nacional: Hispanoamérica, Colombia, y Panamá." *Revista Colombiana de Sociología* 10 (2003): 9–30.

Berger, Susan A. *Guatemaltecas: The Women's Movement, 1986–2003*. Austin: University of Texas Press, 2006.

Bergin, Catherine. "The Russian Revolution and Black Radicalism in the United States." *Soundings* 68 (2018): 65–77.

———. "'Unrest among the Negroes': The African Blood Brotherhood and the Politics of Resistance." *Race & Class* 57, no. 3 (2016): 45–58.

Botey, Ana María. *Costa Rica entre guerras, 1914–1940*. San José: Editorial de la Universidad de Costa Rica, 2005.

Botey, Ana María, and Rodolfo Cisneros. *La crisis de 1929 y la fundación del Partido Comunista de Costa Rica*. San José: Editorial Costa Rica, 1984.

Bourgois, Philippe I. *Ethnicity at Work: Divided Labor on a Central American Banana Plantation*. Baltimore, MD: Johns Hopkins University Press, 1989.

Boyce Davies, Carole. *Left of Karl Marx: The Political Life of Black Communist Claudia Jones*. Durham, NC: Duke University Press, 2007.

Briggs, Laura, Gladys McCormick, and J. T. Way. "Transnationalism: A Category of Analysis." *American Quarterly* 60, no. 3 (2008): 625–48.

Broué, Pierre. *Histoire de l'Internationale communiste: 1919–1943*. Paris: Fayard, 1997.

Browder, Earl. *Democracy or Fascism: Earl Browder's Report to the Ninth Convention of the Communist Party*. New York: Workers Library, 1936.

Buchenau, Jürgen. "Calles y el Movimiento Liberal en Nicaragua." *Boletín del Fideicomiso Archivos Plutarco Elías Calles y Fernando Torreblanca* 9 (1992): 3–32.

Caballero, Manuel. *La Internacional Comunista y la revolución latinoamericana, 1919–1943*. Caracas, Venezuela: Editorial Nueva Sociedad, 1987.

———. *Latin America and the Comintern, 1919–1943*. Cambridge: Cambridge University Press, 1986.

Cabarrús, Carlos Rafael. *Génesis de una revolución: análisis del surgimiento y desarrollo de la organización campesina en El Salvador*. Mexico City: Centro de Investigaciones y Estudios Superiores en Antropología Social, 1983.

Campbell, Susan. "'Black Bolsheviks' and Recognition of African-America's Right to Self-Determination by the Communist Party USA." *Science & Society* 58, no. 4 (1994): 440.

Campos Domínguez, Teresa de Jesús. "La Revista *Mundo Obrero* (1930–1933) y el Buro del Caribe de la IC." *Pacarina del Sur En Línea* 4, no. 16 (2013).

Campos Ponce, Xavier. *Los yanquis y Sandino*. Moscow: Progreso, 1965.

Cardenal, Rodolfo. *Historia de una esperanza: vida de Rutilio Grande*. San Salvador: UCA Editores, 2002.

Cardoso da Silva, Matheus. "Do antirracismo local ao antifascismo global: a transnacionalização do movimento negro nos EUA entre as duas guerras mundiais." *Revista Electrônica da ANPHLAC* 27 (August–December 2019): 144–84.

Carey, David, Jr. "Rethinking Representation and Periodization in Guatemala's Democratic Experiment." In *Out of the Shadow: Revisiting the Revolution from Post-Peace Guatemala*, edited by Julie Gibbings and Heather A. Vrana, 145–72. Austin: University of Texas Press, 2020.

Carnovale, Vera. "La guerra revolucionaria del PRT—ERP." *Sociohistórica* 27 (2010): 41–75.

Carpio, Salvador Cayetano. *Nuestras montañas son las masas: con una nota de Tulita Alvarenga*. 2nd ed. San Salvador: Carpio-Alvarenga Editores, 2011.

Carpio, Salvador Cayetano, and Mélida Anaya Montes. *La guerra popular en El Salvador*. Mexico City: Ediciones de la Paz, 1982.

Carr, Barry. "From Caribbean Backwater to Revolutionary Opportunity: Cuba's Evolving Relationship with the Comintern, 1925–1934." In *International Communism and the Communist International, 1919–43*, edited by Tim Rees and Andrew Thorpe, 234–53. Manchester, UK: Manchester University Press, 1998.

——. "Identity, Class, and Nation: Black Immigrant Workers, Cuban Communism, and the Sugar Industry, 1925–1943." *The Hispanic American Historical Review* 78, no. 1 (1998): 83–116.

——. *Marxism and Communism in Twentieth-Century Mexico*. Lincoln: University of Nebraska Press, 1992.

——. "Mill Occupations and Soviets: The Mobilisation of Sugar Workers in Cuba 1917–1933." *Journal of Latin American Studies* 28, no. 1 (1996): 129–58.

——. "Pioneering Transnational Solidarity in the Americas: The Movement in Support of Augusto C. Sandino 1927–1934." *Journal of Iberian and Latin American Research* 20, no. 2 (2014): 141–52.

Carr, Edward Hallett. *Foundations of a Planned Economy, 1926–1929*. New York: Macmillan, 1971.

——. *Twilight of the Comintern, 1930–1935*. New York: Pantheon, 1982.

Carrillo, Ana Lorena, and Norma Stoltz Chinchilla. "From Urban Elite to Peasant Organizing: Agendas, Accomplishments, and Challenges of Thirty-Plus Years of Guatemalan Feminism, 1975–2007." In *Women's Activism in Latin America and the Caribbean: Engendering Social Justice, Democratizing Citizenship*, edited by Elizabeth Maier and Nathalie Lebon, 140–56. New Brunswick, NJ: Rutgers University Press, 2010.

Carrillo Samayoa, Andrea, and Jacqueline Torres Urizar, eds. *Nosotras, las de la historia: mujeres en Guatemala (siglos XIX–XXI)*. Guatemala City: Ediciones La Cuerda, 2011.

Carter, Dan T. *Scottsboro: A Tragedy of the American South*. Baton Rouge: Louisiana State University Press, 1979.

Casaús Arzú, Marta. *Guatemala: linaje y racismo*. San José, Costa Rica: FLACSO, 1992.

Casey, Matthew. *Empire's Guestworkers: Haitian Migrants in Cuba during the Age of US Occupation*. Cambridge: Cambridge University Press, 2019.

Castro Fernández, Silvio. *La masacre de los Independientes de Color en 1912*. Havana, Cuba: Editorial de Ciencias Sociales, 2002.

Cerdas Cruz, Rodolfo. *The Communist International in Central America, 1920–36*. Basingstoke, UK: Macmillan, 1993.

——. *La hoz y el machete: la internacional comunista, America Latina y la revolucion en Centro America*. San Jose, Costa Rica: Editorial Universidad Estatal a Distancia, 1986.

Chacón Araya, Germán. "Recordando la Fundación del Partido Comunista de Costa Rica." *Reportorio Americano* 27 (January–December 2017): 125–28.

Charney, George. *A Long Journey*. Chicago: Quadrangle, 1968.

Chase, William J. *Enemies within the Gates? The Comintern and the Stalinist Repression, 1934–1939*. New Haven, CT: Yale University Press, 2001.

Chávez, Joaquín M. "How Did the Civil War in El Salvador End?" *American Historical Review* 120, no. 5 (2015): 1784–97.

———. *Poets and Prophets of the Resistance: Intellectuals and the Origins of El Salvador's Civil War*. New York: Oxford University Press, 2017.

Chinchilla, Norma Stoltz. *Nuestras utopías: mujeres guatemaltecas del siglo XX*. Guatemala City: Agrupación de Mujeres Tierra Viva, 1998.

Ching, Erik. "El Partido Comunista de Costa Rica, 1931–1935: Los documentos del archivo ruso del Comintern." *Revista de Historia* 37 (1998): 7–224.

Chomsky, Aviva. "Afro-Jamaican Traditions and Labor Organizing on United Fruit Company Plantations in Costa Rica, 1910." *Journal of Social History* 28, no. 4 (1995): 837–55.

———. "'Barbados or Canada?': Race, Immigration, and Nation in Early Twentieth-Century Cuba." *Hispanic American Historical Review* 8, no. 3 (2000): 415–62.

———. *West Indian Workers and the United Fruit Company in Costa Rica, 1870–1940*. Baton Rouge: Louisiana State University Press, 1996.

Claudín, Fernando. *The Communist Movement: From Comintern to Cominform*. 2 vols. New York: Monthly Review, 1975.

Clementi, Hebe. *María Rosa Oliver*. Buenos Aires: Planeta, 1992.

Cofiño, Ana María. "Huellas de las comunistas en el movimiento de mujeres: de la revolución al feminismo contemporáneo." Ponencia presentada en las Jornadas sobre el PGT, Guatemala City, October 2014.

———. "Las comunistas de la decada, y el organo de prensa Mujeres de la Alianza femenina guatemalteca." *Nuestra Historia* 3 (2017): 127–141.

———. "Las primeras comunistas en Guatemala. De las dictaduras a la Revolución (1923–1954)." In *Queridas camaradas: historias iberoamericanas de mujeres comunistas*, edited by Adriana María Valobra and Mercedes Yusta Rodrigo, 173–92. Buenos Aires: Miño y Dávila Editores, 2017.

Comandante Ana María [Mélida Anaya Montes]. *Experiencias vietnamitas en su guerra de liberación*. Mexico City: Ediciones Enero 32, 1982.

Commission on Cuban Affairs and Buell. *Problems of the New Cuba: Report of the Commission on Cuban Affairs*. New York: Foreign Policy Association, 1935.

Commission on the Truth for El Salvador. *From Madness to Hope: The 12-Year War in El Salvador: Report of the Commission on the Truth for El Salvador*. New York: United Nations, 1993.

Communist International. *VI Congreso de la Internacional Comunista*. 2 vol. Mexico: Siglo XXI, 1978.

Communist Political Association. *The Path to Peace, Progress and Prosperity: Proceedings of Constitutional Convention of the Communist Political Association*. New York: n.p., 1944.

"Comrade Bukharin's Opening Speech" [July 17, 1928]. *International Press Correspondence* 8, no. 39, July 25, 1928, 705–6.

"Comrade Bukharin's Speech in Reply to the Discussion on the International Situation" [July 30, 1928]. *International Press Correspondence* 8, no. 49, August 13, 1928, 863–74.

Confederación Nacional Obrera de Cuba (CNOC). "Resolución sobre el trabajo entre los trabajadores negros." January 1934. In *El movimiento obrero cubano: documentos y artículos*, by Instituto de Historia de Cuba, 2:265–73. 2 vols. Havana, Cuba: Editorial de Ciencias Sociales, 1975.

Confederación Sindical Latino Americana (CSLA). *Bajo la bandera de la C.S.L.A.: Resoluciones y documentos varios del Congreso Constituyente de la Confederación Sindical Latino Americana efectuado en Montevideo en mayo de 1929*. Montevideo: Impr. La Linotipo, 1930.

Conniff, Michael L. *Black Labor on a White Canal: Panama, 1904–1981*. Pittsburgh, PA: University of Pittsburgh Press, 1985.

"Continuation of the Discussion on the Questions of the Revolutionary Movement in the Colonies" [August 17 and 18, 1928]. *International Press Correspondence* 8, no. 76, October 30, 1928, 1387–1426.

Corinealdi, Kaysha L. "Envisioning Multiple Citizenships: West Indian Panamanians and Creating Community in the Canal Zone Neocolony." *Global South* 6, no. 2 (2012): 86–106.

Cornell, Richard. *Youth and Communism: An Historical Analysis of International Communist Youth Movements*. New York: Walker, 1965.

Craske, Nikki. *Women and Politics in Latin America*. New Brunswick, NJ: Rutgers University Press, 1999.

Cuevas, Alexander. *El movimiento inquilinario de 1925*. Panama City: Centro de Estudios Latinoamericanos Justo Arosemena, 1980.

David-Fox, Michael. *Showcasing the Great Experiment: Cultural Diplomacy and Western Visitors to the Soviet Union, 1921–1941*. Oxford: Oxford University Press, 2012.

Debs, Eugene V. "The Negro in the Class Struggle." In *Class Struggle and the Color Line: American Socialism and the Race Question, 1900–1930*, edited by Paul M. Heideman, 44–47. Chicago: Haymarket, 2018. Originally published in *International Socialist Review* (November 1903). Citations refer to the Haymarket edition.

Degras, Jane. *The Communist International: 1919–1943*. 3 vols. London: Cass, 1971.

de la Cruz, Vladimir. "El Primer Congreso del Partido Comunista de Costa Rica." *Estudios Sociales Centroamericanos* 27 (1981): 25–64.

de la Fuente, Alejandro. *A Nation for All: Race, Inequality, and Politics in Twentieth-Century Cuba*. Chapel Hill: University of North Carolina Press, 2001.

——. "Race and Inequality in Cuba, 1899–1981." *Journal of Contemporary History* 30, no. 1 (1995): 131–68.

——. "Two Dangers, One Solution: Immigration, Race, and Labor in Cuba, 1900–1930." *International Labor and Working Class History* 51 (1997): 30–49.

Del Moral, Solsiree. *Negotiating Empire: The Cultural Politics of Schools in Puerto Rico, 1898–1952*. Madison: University of Wisconsin Press, 2013.

Del Vasto, César. *Historia del Partido Comunista de Panamá (1930–1943)*. Panama City: Universal Books, 2002.

Deutsch, Sandra McGee. "Mujeres, antifascismo y democracia. La Junta de la Victoria, 1941–1947." *Anuario IEHS* 28 (2013): 157–75.

———. "The New School Lecture 'An Army of Women': Communist-Linked Solidarity Movements, Maternalism, and Political Consciousness in 1930s and 1940s Argentina." *The Americas* 75, no. 1 (2018): 95–125.

Díaz, Luis. "El gobierno de Luis Muñoz Marín: la persecución política hacia los líderes del Partido Comunista de Puerto Rico de 1953 a 1960." Master's thesis, Centro de Estudios Avanzados, San Juan, Puerto Rico, 2019.

Dimitrov, Georgi. *Selected Works*. Vol. 2. Sofia, Bulgaria: Sofia, 1972.

Dirección General de Estadística. *Censos de la República de Guatemala, 1950*. Guatemala City: Talleres Gutenberg, 1951.

"Discussion on the Report of Comrade Bukharin" [July 25, 1928]. *International Press Correspondence* 8, no. 46, August 8, 1928, 811–22.

"Discussion on the Report of Comrade Bukharin on the Draft Programme of the Comintern" [August 9, 1928]. *International Press Correspondence* 8, no. 66, September 25, 1928, 1175–80.

Donert, Celia. "From Communist Internationalism to Human Rights: Gender, Violence, and International Law in the Women's International Democratic Federation Mission to North Korea, 1951." *Contemporary European History* 25, no. 2 (2016): 313–33.

Donoghue, Michael E. *Borderland on the Isthmus: Race, Culture, and the Struggle for the Canal Zone*. Durham, NC: Duke University Press, 2014.

Drachewych, Oleksa. *The Communist International, Anti-imperialism and Racial Equality in British Dominions*. New York: Routledge, 2019.

———. "The Communist Transnational? Transnational Studies and the History of the Comintern." *History Compass* 17, no. 2 (2019): e12521.

Drachewych, Oleksa, and Ian McKay, eds. *Left Transnationalism: The Communist International and the National, Colonial, and Racial Questions*. Montreal: McGill-Queen's University Press, 2019.

Drake, Paul W. *The Money Doctor in the Andes: The Kemmerer Missions, 1923–1933*. Durham, NC: Duke University Press, 1989.

Draper, Theodore. *American Communism and Soviet Russia: The Formative Period*. New York: Viking, 1960.

Dulles, John W. F. *Anarchists and Communists in Brazil, 1900–1935*. Austin: University of Texas Press, 1973.

Dullin, Sabine, and Brigitte Studer. "Communisme + transnational. L'équation retrouvée de l'internationalisme au premier XXe siècle." *Monde(s)* 10, no. 2 (2016): 9–32.

Dunkerley, James, ed. *British Documents on Foreign Affairs: Reports and Papers from the Foreign Office Confidential Print*. Bethesda, MD: University Publications of America, 1991.

Echeverri-Gent, Elisavinda. "Forgotten Workers: British West Indians and the Early Days of the Banana Industry in Costa Rica and Honduras." *Journal of Latin American Studies* 24, no. 2 (1992): 275–308.

Eley, Geoff. *Forging Democracy: The History of the Left in Europe, 1850–2000*. Oxford: Oxford University Press, 2002.

Enkevort, Maria Gertrudis van. "The Life and Works of Otto Huiswoud: Professional Revolutionary and Internationalist, 1893–1961." PhD diss., University of the West Indies at Mona, 2001.

Ewing, Adam. "Caribbean Labour Politics in the Age of Garvey, 1918–1928." *Race & Class* 55, no. 1 (2013): 31–35.

Fernández Bravo, Alvaro. Introducción to *Mi fe es el hombre*, by María Rosa Oliver, 9–49. Buenos Aires: Ediciones Biblioteca Nacional, 2008.

———. "María Rosa Oliver en las redes comunistas del siglo." *Mora* 23 (2017): 133–48.

———. "Redes latinoamericanas en los años cuarenta: la revista *Sur* y el mundo tropical." In *Episodios en la formación de redes culturales en América Latina*, edited by Claudio Maíz and Alvaro Fernández Bravo, 113–35. Buenos Aires: Prometeo Libros, 2009.

Fernández Robaina, Tomás. *El negro en Cuba, 1902–1958: apuntes para la historia de la lucha contra la discriminación racial*. Havana, Cuba: Editorial de Ciencias Sociales, 1990.

Ferreira Lima, Heitor. *Caminhos percorridos*. São Paulo: Brasiliense: Arquivo de História Social Edgard Leuenroth, UNICAMP, 1982.

Ferrer, Ada. *Insurgent Cuba: Race, Nation, and Revolution, 1868–1898*. Chapel Hill: University of North Carolina Press, 1999.

Figueroa Clark, Victor. "Latin American Communism." In *The Cambridge History of Communism: Volume 2: The Socialist Camp and World Power 1941–1960s*, edited by Norman Naimark, Silvio Pons, and Sophie Quinn-Judge, 388–413. Cambridge: Cambridge University Press, 2017.

Flynn, Elizabeth Gurley. *Earl Browder: The Man from Kansas*. New York: Workers Library, 1941.

Forster, Cindy. *The Time of Freedom: Campesino Workers in Guatemala's October Revolution*. Pittsburgh, PA: University of Pittsburgh Press, 2001.

Foster, William Z. *The Crime of El Fanguito: An Open Letter to President Truman on Puerto Rico*. New York: New Century, 1948.

French, John D. *The Brazilian Workers' ABC: Class Conflict and Alliances in Modern São Paulo*. Chapel Hill: University of North Carolina Press, 1992.

Fromm, Georg H. *César Andreu Iglesias: aproximación a su vida y obra*. Río Piedras, Puerto Rico: Ediciones Huracán, 1977.

Gandásegui, Marco A., Alejandro Saavedra, Andrés Achong, and Iván Quintero. *Las luchas obreras en Panamá, 1850–1978*. 2nd ed. Panama City: Centro de Estudios Latinoamericanos Justo Arosemena, 1990.

García, Angel, and Piotr Mironchuk. *Los soviets obreros y campesinos en Cuba*. Havana, Cuba: Editorial de Ciencias Sociales, 1987.

García Domínguez, Sthel, and Violeta Rovira González. "Los 'Soviets' de Nazábal, Hormiguero y Parque Alto de la provincia de Las Villas." *Islas* 18 (October 1968): 221–53.

García Muñiz, Humberto. "U.S. Military Installations in Puerto Rico: Controlling the Caribbean." In *Colonial Dilemma: Critical Perspectives on Contemporary Puerto Rico*, edited by Edwin Meléndez and Edgardo Meléndez, 53–66. Boston: South End, 1993.

García Treviño, Rodrigo. "El regreso de Evelio Vadillo." *Nexos* 156, December 1990.

Gatto, Ezequiel. "Harlem Radical African Blood Brotherhood: política afroamericana en tiempos de la Revolución Rusa." *Huellas de Estados Unidos* 3 (September 2012): 89–107.

Giap, Vo Nguyen. *Guerra del pueblo, ejercito del pueblo*. Havana: Editora Política, 1964.

———. *People's War; People's Army*. 2nd ed. Hanoi: Foreign Languages, 1974.

Gibbings, Julie, and Heather A. Vrana, eds. *Out of the Shadow: Revisiting the Revolution from Post-Peace Guatemala*. Austin: University of Texas Press, 2020.

Giovannetti-Torres, Jorge L. *Black British Migrants in Cuba: Race, Labor, and Empire in the Twentieth Century Caribbean, 1898–1948*. Cambridge: Cambridge University Press, 2018.

Gleijeses, Piero. *Shattered Hope: The Guatemalan Revolution and the United States, 1944–1954*. Princeton, NJ: Princeton University Press, 1991.

Gómez, J. "Party Cadres in the CPs of South American and Caribbean America." *International Press Correspondence* 12, no. 35, 1932, 743–44.

Gosse, Van. "'The North American Front': Central American Solidarity in the Reagan Era." In *Reshaping the US Left: Popular Struggles in the 1980s*, edited by Mike Davis and Michael Sprinker, 11–50. New York: Verso, 1988.

———. "'To Organize in Every Neighborhood, in Every Home': The Gender Politics of American Communists between the Wars." *Radical History Review* 50 (1991): 109–41.

———. *Where the Boys Are: Cuba, Cold War America, and the Making of a New Left*. London: Verso, 1993.

Gould, Jeffrey L., and Aldo Lauria-Santiago. *To Rise in Darkness: Revolution, Repression, and Memory in El Salvador, 1920–1932*. Durham, NC: Duke University Press, 2008.

Grandin, Greg. *Empire's Workshop: Latin America, the United States, and the Rise of the New Imperialism*. New York: Metropolitan Books, 2006.

———. *The Last Colonial Massacre: Latin America in the Cold War*. Chicago: University of Chicago Press, 2004.

Grant, Colin. *Negro with a Hat: The Rise and Fall of Marcus Garvey*. Oxford: Oxford University Press, 2008.

Greene, Julie. *The Canal Builders: Making America's Empire at the Panama Canal*. New York: Penguin, 2009.

Gregory, James. "Communist Party USA History and Geography." "Mapping American Social Movements Project." *University of Washington*, 2015. https://depts.washington.edu/moves/CP_intro.shtml.

Grenier, Yvon. *The Emergence of Insurgency in El Salvador: Ideology and Political Will*. Pittsburgh, PA: University of Pittsburgh Press, 1999.

Grobart, Fabio. "Preguntas y respuestas sobre los años 30." In *Trabajos escogidos*, edited by Luis M. Traviesas Moreno, 89–112. Havana, Cuba: Editorial de Ciencias Sociales, 1985.

Guadalupe de Jesús, Raúl. *Sindicalismo y lucha política: apuntes históricos sobre el movimiento obrero puertorriqueño*. San Juan, Puerto Rico: Editorial Tiempo Nuevo, 2009.

Guerrón-Montero, Carla. "Racial Democracy and Nationalism in Panama." *Ethnology* 45, no. 3 (2006): 209–28.

Guridy, Frank Andre. *Forging Diaspora: Afro-Cubans and African Americans in a World of Empire and Jim Crow*. Chapel Hill: University of North Carolina Press, 2010.

Haan, Francisca de. "Continuing Cold War Paradigms in Western Historiography of Transnational Women's Organisations: The Case of the Women's International Democratic Federation (WIDF)." *Women's History Review* 19, no. 4 (2010): 547–73.

Hale, Charles R. *Más que un Indio = More Than an Indian: Racial Ambivalence and Neoliberal Multiculturalism in Guatemala*. Santa Fe, NM: School of American Research Press, 2006.

Halperín Donghi, Tulio. *La Argentina y la tormenta del mundo: ideas e ideologías entre 1930 y 1945*. Buenos Aires: Siglo Veintiuno Editores Argentina, 2003.

Hanglberger, Daniel. "Marcus Garvey and His Relation to (Black) Socialism and Communism." *American Communist History* 17, no. 2 (2018): 200–219.

Harmer, Tanya, and Alberto Martín Álvarez, eds. *Toward a Global History of Latin America's Revolutionary Left*. Gainesville: University of Florida Press, 2021.

Harms, Patricia. *Ladina Social Activism in Guatemala City, 1871–1954*. Albuquerque: University of New Mexico Press, 2020.

Harnecker, Marta. *Con la mirada en alto: Historia de las Fuerzas Populares de Liberación Farabundo Martí a través de entrevistas con sus dirigentes*. San Salvador: UCA Editores, 1993.

———. *Pueblos en armas*. Mexico City: Ediciones Era, 1984.

Harpelle, Ronald N. "Bananas and Business: West Indians and United Fruit in Costa Rica." *Race and Class* 42, no. 1 (2000): 57–72.

———. *The West Indians of Costa Rica: Race, Class, and the Integration of an Ethnic Minority*. Montreal: McGill-Queen's University Press, 2001.

Hays, Arthur Garfield. *Report of the Commission of Inquiry on Civil Rights in Puerto Rico*. Washington, DC: Library of Congress Photoduplication Service, 1977.

Haywood, Harry. *Black Bolshevik: Autobiography of an Afro-American Communist*. Chicago: Liberator, 1978.

———. *The Road to Negro Liberation: The Tasks of the Communist Party in Winning Working Class Leadership of the Negro Liberation Struggles, and the Fight against Reactionary Nationalist-Reformist Movements among the Negro People: Report to the Eighth Convention of the Communist Party of the U.S.A., Cleveland, April 2–8, 1934*. New York City: Workers Library, 1934.

Helg, Aline. *Our Rightful Share: The Afro-Cuban Struggle for Equality, 1886–1912*. Chapel Hill: University of North Carolina Press, 1995.

Herbst, Josephine. "A Passport from Realengo." *New Masses*, July 16, 1935, 10–11.

Herrera, Robinson A. *Natives, Europeans, and Africans in Sixteenth-Century Santiago de Guatemala*. Austin: University of Texas Press, 2003.

Herrera Zúniga, José Roberto. "Nueve preguntas sobre el comunismo 'a la tica.'" *Revista de Filosofía de la Universidad de Costa Rica* 52, no. 133 (2013): 29–44.

Ho Chi Minh. *Selected Works of Ho Chi Minh*. Moscow: Foreign Languages, 1960. Marxists International Archive, https://www.marxists.org/.

Hoover, Herbert. *Public Papers of the President of the United States*. Washington, DC: US Government Printing Office, 1976.

Hoover Green, Amelia, and Patrick Ball. "Civilian Killings and Disappearances during Civil War in El Salvador (1980 1992)." *Demographic Research* 41, no. 27 (2019): 781–814.

Hubert, Rosario. "Intellectual Cartographies of the Cold War: Argentinean Visitors to the People's Republic of China 1952–1958." In *The Routledge Handbook of Literature and Space*, edited by Robert T. Tally, 337–48. New York: Routledge, 2017.

Ibarra Arana, David Ignacio, and Zhang Hao. "Peace Conference of Asia and the Pacific Region (October 1952): An Approach between China and Central America." *Revista Estudios* 33 (December 2016–May 2017): 788–815.

Iber, Patrick. *Neither Peace nor Freedom: The Cultural Cold War in Latin America*. Cambridge, MA: Harvard University Press, 2015.

Immerman, Richard H. *The CIA in Guatemala: The Foreign Policy of Intervention*. Austin: University of Texas Press, 1982.

Instituto de Historia de Cuba. *Historia del movimiento obrero cubano, 1865–1958*. 2 vols. Havana, Cuba: Editora Política, 1985.

———. *El movimiento obrero cubano: documentos y artículos*. 2 vols. Havana, Cuba: Editorial de Ciencias Sociales, 1975.

Instituto Indigenista Interamericano. *América Indígena* (Mexico) 5, no. 4 (1945): 363–97.

Isserman, Maurice. *Which Side Were You On? The American Communist Party during the Second World War*. Urbana: University of Illinois Press, 1993.

Ivanovich, Vladimir. *¿Por qué los EE.UU. combaten contra Nicaragua?* Moscow: n.p., 1927.

James, C. L. R. *World Revolution, 1917–1936: The Rise and Fall of the Communist International*. Durham, NC: Duke University Press, 2017

James, Daniel. *Red Design for the Americas: Guatemalan Prelude*. New York: Day, 1954.

James, Leslie. *George Padmore and Decolonization from Below: Pan-Africanism, the Cold War, and the End of Empire*. Houndmills, UK: Palgrave Macmillan, 2015.

James, Winston. *Holding Aloft the Banner of Ethiopia: Caribbean Radicalism in Early Twentieth-Century America*. London: Verso, 1999.

———. "In the Nest of Extreme Radicalism: Radical Networks and the Bolshevization of Claude McKay in London." *Comparative American Studies* 15, no. 3–4 (2017): 174–203.

Jeifets, Lazar, Víctor Jeifets, and Peter Huber. *La Internacional Comunista y América latina, 1919–1943. Diccionário biográfico*. Moscow: Instituto de Latinoamérica de la Academia de las Ciencias, 2004.

Jeifets, Víctor, and Lazar Jeifets. *América Latina en la Internacional Comunista, 1919–1943. Diccionario Biográfico*. Santiago de Chile: Ariadna, 2015.

———. "Haya de la Torre, la Comintern y el Perú: Acercamientos y desencuentros." *Pacarina del Sur* 4, no. 16 (2013).

———. "La Comintern, el PCM y el 'caso Sandino': historia de una alianza fracasada, 1927–1930." *Anuario Colombiano de Historia Social y de la Cultura* 44, no. 2 (2017): 63–86.

———. "La Comintern y la formación de militantes comunistas latinoamericanos." *Revista Izquierdas* 31 (December 2016): 130–61.

———. "La inserción internacional de la izquierda comunista anti-gomecista en el exilio venezolano, primeros años." *Revista Izquierdas* 25 (October 2015): 1–28.

Jiménez, Cristina Pérez. "Puerto Rican Colonialism, Caribbean Radicalism, and *Pueblos Hispanos*'s Inter-Nationalist Alliance." *Small Axe: A Caribbean Journal of Criticism* 23, no. 3 (2019): 50–68.

Jiménez de Wagenheim, Olga. *Puerto Rico's Revolt for Independence: El Grito de Lares*. Boulder, CO: Westview, 1985.

Johnson, Robert David. "Anti-Imperialism and the Good Neighbour Policy: Ernest Gruening and Puerto Rican Affairs, 1934–1939." *Journal of Latin American Studies* 29, no. 1 (1997): 89–110.

Kalmykov, Nikolai P., ed. *Historia de America Latina, 1918–1945*. Moscow: Nauka, 1999.

Kelley, Robin D. G. *Freedom Dreams: The Black Radical Imagination*. Boston: Beacon, 2002.

———. *Hammer and Hoe: Alabama Communists during the Great Depression*. Chapel Hill: University of North Carolina Press, 1990.

Kelly, Brian. "Du Bois's Prolific 'Error' and the Break with 'Color-Blind' Orthodoxy." *Labor* 12, no. 4 (2015): 11–15.

Kersffeld, Daniel. *Contra el imperio. Historia de la Liga Antiimperialista de las Américas*. Mexico City: Siglo Veintiuno, 2011.

———. "El Comité Manos Fuera de Nicaragua, primera experiencia del sandinismo." *Pacarina del Sur* 13 (2012).

King, John. *Sur: A Study of the Argentine Literary Journal and Its Role in the Development of a Culture, 1931–1970*. Cambridge: Cambridge University Press, 1986.

Kirasirova, Masha. "The 'East' as a Category of Bolshevik Ideology and Comintern Administration: The Arab Section of the Communist University of the Toilers of the East." *Kritika* 18, no. 1 (2017): 7–34.

Kirkpatrick, Evron M. *Target: The World: Communist Propaganda Activities in 1955*. New York: Macmillan, 1956.

———. *Year of Crisis: Communist Propaganda Activities in 1956*. New York: Macmillan, 1957.

Kirschenbaum, Lisa A. *International Communism and the Spanish Civil War: Solidarity and Suspicion*. New York: Cambridge University Press, 2015.

Konefal, Betsy. *For Every Indio Who Falls: A History of Maya Activism in Guatemala, 1960–1990*. Albuquerque: University of New Mexico Press, 2010.

Kotek, Joël. *Students and the Cold War*. New York: St. Martin's, 1996.

Kruijt, Dirk. *Cuba and Revolutionary Latin America: An Oral History*. London: Zed, 2017.

Lamb, Ariel M. *No Barrier Can Contain It: Cuban Antifascism and the Spanish Civil War*. Chapel Hill: University of North Carolina Press, 2019.

Lasso de Paulis, Marixa. "Race and Ethnicity in the Formation of Panamanian National Identity: Panamanian Discrimination against Chinese and West Indians in the Thirties." *Revista Panameña de Política* 4 (July–December 2007): 61–92.

Leeds, Asia. "Toward the 'Higher Type of Womanhood': The Gendered Contours of Garveyism and the Making of Redemptive Geographies in Costa Rica, 1922–1941." *Palimpsest* 2, no. 1 (2013): 1–27.

Leow, Rachel. "A Missing Peace: The Asia-Pacific Peace Conference in Beijing, 1952 and the Emotional Making of Third World Internationalism." *Journal of World History* 30, no. 1–2 (2019): 21–53.

Lewis, Su Lin, and Carolien Stolte. "Other Bandungs: Afro-Asian Internationalisms in the Early Cold War." *Journal of World History* 30, no. 1 (2019): 1–19.

Locane, Jorge J. "Del orientalismo a la provincialización de Europa. A propósito del viaje a los albores de la República Popular China." *Transmodernity: Journal of Peripheral Cultural Production of the Luso-Hispanic World* 9, no. 3 (2020): 56–73.

Lojo, María Rosa. "Memoria, género y enfermadad en *Mundo, Mi Casa* de María Rosa Oliver." *Confluencia* 30, no. 3 (2015): 17–24.

Lombardo Toledano, Vicente. *Un viaje al mundo del porvenir (seis conferencias sobre la U.R.S.S.)*. Mexico City: Publicaciones de la Universidad Obrera de México, 1936.

Longley, Kyle. *In the Eagle's Shadow: The United States and Latin America*. Wheeling, IL: Davidson, 2002.

López Bermúdez, Andrés. *Jorge Zalamea, enlace de mundos: quehacer literario y cosmopolitismo (1905–1969)*. Bogota: Editorial Universidad del Rosario, 2015.

Maanen, Gert van. *The International Student Movement: History and Background*. The Hague: International Documentation and Information Centre, 1967.

MacKenzie, Kermit E. *La Comintern y revolución mundial. 1919–1943*. Moscow: Tsentrpoligraf, 2008.

Mahler, Anne Garland. "Global Solidarity before the Tricontinental Conference: Latin America and the League against Imperialism." In *The Tricontinental Revolution: Third World Radicalism and the Cold War*, edited by R. Joseph Parrott and Mark Atwood Lawrence, 43–68. Cambridge: Cambridge University Press, 2022.

———. "The Red and the Black in Latin America: Sandalio Junco and the 'Negro Question' from an Afro-Latin American Perspective." *American Communist History* 17, no. 1 (2018): 16–32.

———. "South-South Organizing in the Global Plantation Zone: Ramón Marrero Aristy, the novela de la caña, and the Caribbean Bureau." *Atlantic Studies* 16, no. 2 (2019): 236–60.

Makalani, Minkah. *In the Cause of Freedom: Radical Black Internationalism from Harlem to London, 1917–1939*. Chapel Hill: University of North Carolina Press, 2011.

Mao Zedong. *On the Protracted War*. Beijing: Foreign Languages Press, 1960.

Marino, Katherine M. *Feminism for the Americas: The Making of an International Human Rights Movement*. Chapel Hill: University of North Carolina Press, 2019.

———. "Pan-American Feminism and the Origins of International Women's Rights: The Confederación Continental de Mujeres por la Paz." Paper delivered at the American Historical Association Annual Conference, Atlanta, Georgia, January 2016.

Martín Álvarez, Alberto, and Eudald Cortina Orero. "The Genesis and Internal Dynamics of El Salvador's People's Revolutionary Army, 1970–1976." *Journal of Latin American Studies* 46, no. 4 (2014): 663–89.

Martínez Verdugo, Arnoldo, ed. *Historia del comunismo en México*. Mexico City: Grijalbo, 1985.

Martínez Villena, Rubén. *El útil anhelo: correspondencia de Rubén Martínez Villena*. 3 vols. Havana, Cuba: Ediciones La Memoria, 2015.

McClintock, Michael. *The American Connection, Volume 1: State Terror and Popular Resistance in El Salvador*. London: Zed Books, 1985.

McDonnell, Michael A. *Masters of Empire: Great Lakes Indians and the Making of America*. New York: Hill and Wang, 2015.

McDuffie, E. S. *Sojourning for Freedom: Black Women, American Communism, and the Making of Black Left Feminism*. Durham, NC: Duke University Press, 2011.

McGuire, Elizabeth. *Red at Heart: How Chinese Communists Fell in Love with the Russian Revolution*. New York: Oxford University Press, 2018.

McKay, Claude, and A. L. McLeod. *The Negroes in America*. Port Washington, NY: Kennikat, 1979.

McLeod, Marc. "Undesirable Aliens: Race, Ethnicity, and Nationalism in the Comparison of Haitian and British West Indian Immigrant Workers in Cuba, 1912–1939." *Journal of Social History* 31, no. 3 (1998): 599–623.

McPherson, Alan L. *The Invaded: How Latin Americans and Their Allies Fought and Ended U.S. Occupations*. Oxford: Oxford University Press, 2014.

Medina Ramírez, Ramón. *El movimiento libertador en la historia de Puerto Rico*. 3 vols. Santurce, Puerto Rico: Print and Pub., 1950.

Melgar Bao, Ricardo. "The Anti-Imperialist League of the Americas between the East and Latin America." *Latin American Perspectives* 35, no. 2 (2008): 9–24.

———. "Cominternismo intelectual: Representaciones, redes y prácticas político-culturales en América Central, 1921–1933." *Revista Complutense de Historia de América* 35 (January 2009): 135–59.

———. "Rearmando la memoria: El primer debate socialista acerca de nuestros afroamericanos." *Humania del Sur* 2, no. 2 (2007): 145–66.

Meyer, Gerald J. "Pedro Albizu Campos, Gilberto Concepción de Gracia, and Vito Marcantonio's Collaboration in the Cause of Puerto Rico's Independence." *Centro Journal* 23, no. 1 (2011): 87–123.

Michel, Concha. *Marxistas y "marxistas."* Mexico City, 1934.

Milazzo, Marzia. "White Supremacy, White Knowledge, and Anti—West Indian Discourse in Panama: Olmedo Alfaro's *El Peligro Antillano en la América Central.*" *Global South* 6, no. 2 (2012): 65–86.

Miller, Francesca. *Latin American Women and the Search for Social Justice.* Hanover, NH: University Press of New England, 1991.

Miller, James A., Susan D. Pennybacker, and Eve Rosenhaft. "Mother Ada Wright and the International Campaign to Free the Scottsboro Boys, 1931–1934." *American Historical Review* 106, no. 2 (2001): 387–430.

Molina Jiménez, Iván. "Afrocostarricense y Comunista: Harold Nichols y su Actividad Política en Costa Rica." *Latinoamérica* 46 (2008): 141–68.

Mooney, Jadwiga E. Pieper, and Fabio Lanza. *De-centering Cold War History: Local and Global Change.* London: Routledge, 2012.

Moraes, Dênis de, and Francisco Viana. *Prestes: lutas e autocríticas.* 2nd ed. Rio de Janeiro: Mauad, 1997.

Naison, Mark. *Communists in Harlem during the Depression.* Urbana: University of Illinois Press, 1983.

Navas, Luis. *El movimiento obrero en Panamá, 1880–1914.* Ciudad Universitaria Rodrigo Facio, Costa Rica: Editorial Universitaria Centroamericana, 1979.

Núñez Machín, Ana. *Rubén Martínez Villena.* 2nd ed. Havana, Cuba: Editorial de Ciencias Sociales, 1974.

Olcott, Jocelyn. "'A Plague of Salaried Marxists': Sexuality and Subsistence in the Revolutionary Imaginary of Concha Michel." *Journal of Contemporary History* 52, no. 4 (2017): 980–98.

Olien, Michael D. "The Negro in Costa Rica: The Ethnohistory of an Ethnic Minority in a Complex Society." PhD diss., University of Oregon, 1967.

Oliveira de Mattos, Pablo de. "The Silent Hero: George Padmore, Diáspora e Pan-Africanismo." PhD diss., Pontifícia Universidade Católica do Rio de Janeiro, 2018.

Oliver, María Rosa. *América vista por una mujer argentina.* Buenos Aires: Salzmann y Cia, 1945.

——. *Geografía argentina.* Buenos Aires: Editorial Sudamericana, 1939.

——. *La vida cotidiana.* Buenos Aires: Editorial Sudamericana, 1969.

——. *Mi fe es el hombre.* Buenos Aires: Ediciones C. Lohlé, 1981.

——. *Mundo, mi casa; recuerdos de infancia.* Buenos Aires: Falbo Librero Editor, 1965.

Oliver, María Rosa, and Norberto A. Frontini. *Lo que sabemos, hablamos: testimonio sobre la China de hoy.* Buenos Aires: Ediciones Botella al Mar, 1955.

O'Reggio, Trevor. *Between Alienation and Citizenship: The Evolution of Black West Indian Society in Panama 1914–1964.* Lanham, MD: University Press of America, 2006.

Padmore, George. *The Life and Struggles of Negro Toilers.* London: RILU/ITUCNW, 1931.

Paget, Karen M. *Patriotic Betrayal: The Inside Story of the CIA's Secret Campaign to Enroll American Students in the Crusade against Communism.* New Haven, CT: Yale University Press, 2015.

Palencia, Jorge, ed. *Para que no olvidemos: Una recopilación de testimonios sobre el surgimiento de organizaciones populares salvadoreñas y sus luchas durante los años 1970 y 1980*. Madrid: Castilla La Mancha, 2008.

Palomino, Pablo. "On the Disadvantages of 'Global South' for Latin American Studies." *Journal of World Philosophies* 4, no. 2 (2019): 22–39.

Pappademos, Melina. *Black Political Activism and the Cuban Republic*. Chapel Hill: University of North Carolina Press, 2011.

Paralitici, Ché. *La represión contra el independentismo puertorriqueño: 1960–2010*. Río Piedras, Puerto Rico: Publicaciones Gaviota, 2011.

———. *Sentencia impuesta: 100 años de encarcelamientos por la independencia de Puerto Rico*. San Juan, Puerto Rico: Ediciones Puerto, 2004.

Pateman, Joe. "V. I. Lenin on the 'Black Question.'" *Critique* 48, no. 1 (2020): 77–93.

Pavilack, Jody. "Henry A. Wallace y sus 'amigos' en América Latina (1940–1949)." In *Los comunismos en América Latina: Recepciones y miliancias (1917–1955)*, edited by Santiago Aránguiz Pinto and Patricio Herrera González, 215–32. Chile: Historia Chilena, 2018.

Peacock, Margaret. "The Perils of Building Cold War Consensus at the 1957 Moscow World Festival of Youth and Students." *Cold War History* 12, no. 3 (2012): 515–35.

Pearce, Jenny. *Promised Land: Peasant Rebellion in Chalatenango, El Salvador*. London: Latin America Bureau, 1986.

Pereira, Astrojildo. *Formação do PCB, 1922/1928; notas e documentos*. Rio de Janeiro: Vitória, 1962.

Pérez de la Riva, Juan. "Cuba y la migración antillana, 1900–1931." In *La repúbica neocolonial. Anuario de estudios cubanos*, edited by Juan Pérez de la Riva, 1–75. Havana, Cuba: Editorial de Ciencias Sociales, 1979.

Pérez Rosario, Vanessa. *Becoming Julia de Burgos: The Making of a Puerto Rican Icon*. Urbana: University of Illinois Press, 2014.

Petersson, Fredrik. "La Ligue anti-impérialiste: un espace transnational restreint, 1927–1937." *Monde(s)* 10, no. 2 (2016): 129–50.

Petra, Adriana. *Intelectuales y cultura comunista: itinerarios, problemas, y debates en la Argentina de posguerra*. Buenos Aires: Fondo de Cultura Económica, 2017.

———. *Intellectuals and Communist Culture: Itineraries, Problems, and Debates in Post-War Argentina*. Translated by Rebecca Wolpin. New York: Palgrave Macmillan, 2022.

Petrukhin, Alexandr A., and Evguenii M. Churilov. *Farabundo Martí*. Moscow: Editorial Progreso, 1985.

Piazza, Hans, ed. *Die Liga gegen Imperialismus und für nationale Unabhängigkeit: 1927–1937*. Leipzig: Karl-Marx-Universität, 1987.

Pichardo Viñals, Hortensia. *Documentos para la historia de Cuba*. Nuestra Historia. 4 vols. Havana, Cuba: Editorial de Ciencias Sociales, 1980.

Pizzurno Gelós, Patricia, and Celestino Andrés Araúz. *Estudios sobre el Panamá republicano: 1903–1989*. Panama City: Manfer, 1996.

Pons, Silvio, ed. *The Cambridge History of Communism*. New York: Cambridge University Press, 2017.

Pons, Silvio, and Allan Cameron, eds. *The Global Revolution: A History of International Communism, 1917–1991*. Oxford: Oxford University Press, 2014.

Poppino, Rollie E. *International Communism in Latin America: A History of the Movement, 1917–1963*. London: Free Press of Glencoe, 1964.

Porras, Ana Elena. "Configuraciones de identidad nacional: Panamá, 1991–2002." PhD diss., Pontificia Universidad Católica del Peru, 2002.

Portes Gil, Emilio. *Quince años de política mexicana*. Mexico City: Ediciones Botas, 1941.

Portuondo Moret, Octaviano. *El "Soviet" de Tacajó*. Santiago, Cuba: Editorial Oriente, 1979.

Power, Margaret. "Friends and Comrades: Political and Personal Relationships between Members of the Communist Party USA and the Puerto Rican Nationalist Party, 1930s–1940s." In *Making the Revolution: Histories of the Latin American Left*, edited by Kevin A. Young, 105–28. Cambridge: Cambridge University Press, 2019.

———. "Nationalism in a Colonized Nation: The Nationalist Party and Puerto Rico." *Memorias* 10, no. 20 (2013): 119–37.

———. "Rise of the Puerto Rican Nationalist Party, 1922–1954." In *50 Events That Shaped Latino History: An Encyclopedia of the American Mosaic*, edited by Lilia Fernández, 295–312. Santa Barbara, CA: Greenwood, 2018.

"Premios literarios argentinos, el Premio Lenin." *Sur* 250 (January–February 1958): 104.

Prestes, Anita Leocádia. *Luiz Carlos Prestes: um comunista brasileiro*. São Paulo: Boitempo Editorial, 2015.

Prestes, Luís Carlos. "Como cheguei ao comunismo." *Problema da Paz e do Socialismo* 1 (1973): 1–13.

Priestland, David. *The Red Flag: A History of Communism*. New York: Grove, 2009.

Pujals, Sandra. "'Con Saludos Comunistas': The Caribbean Bureau of the Comintern, Anti-Imperialist Radical Networks, and the Foundations for an Anti-Fascist Culture in the Caribbean Basin, 1927–1935." In *Anti-Fascism in a Global Perspective: Transnational Networks, Exile Communities, and Radical Internationalism*, edited by Kasper Braskén, Nigel Copsey, and David Featherstone, 58–76. London: Routledge, 2021.

———. "De un pájaro las tres alas: el Buró del Caribe de la Comintern. Cuba y el radicalismo comunista en Puerto Rico, 1931–1936." *Op. Cit. Revista del Centro de Investigaciones Históricas* 21 (2012): 254–83.

———. "¡Embarcados!: James Sager, la Sección Puertorriqueña de la Liga Anti-Imperialista de las Américas y el Partido Nacionalista de Puerto Rico, 1925–1927." *Op. Cit. Revista del Centro de Investigaciones Históricas* 22 (2013): 105–39.

———. "La presencia de la Internacional Comunista en el Caribe, 1920–1940." Radio interview. *La Voz del Centro*, November 11, 2018. http://www.vozdelcentro.org/tag/dra-sandra-pujals/.

———. "A 'Soviet Caribbean': The Comintern, New York's Immigrant Community, and the Forging of Caribbean Visions, 1931–1936." *Russian History* 41, no. 2 (2014): 255–68.

——. "¿Una perla en el Caribe soviético? Puerto Rico en los archivos de la Komintern en Moscú, 1921–1943." *Op. Cit. Revista del Centro de Investigaciones Históricas* 17 (2006): 117–57.

Putnam, Lara. *Radical Moves: Caribbean Migrants and the Politics of Race in the Jazz Age.* Chapel Hill: University of North Carolina Press, 2013.

Qayum, Seemin. "The German Blockade of the Caribbean in 1942 and Its Effects in Puerto Rico." In *Island at War: Puerto Rico in the Crucible of the Second World War,* edited by Jorge Rodríguez Beruff and José L. Bolívar, 139–68. Jackson: University Press of Mississippi, 2015.

"Questions of the Latin-American Countries: Co-Report of Comrade Humbert-Droz" [August 16]. *International Press Correspondence* 8, no. 72, October 17, 1928, 1299–1305.

Ramírez, Sergio, ed. *El pensamiento vivo de Sandino.* 2nd ed. 2 vols. Managua, Nicaragua: Editorial Nueva Nicaragua, 1984.

Randolph, David Eugene. "The Diplomatic History of Guatemala during the Administration of President Jorge Ubico: 1931–1944." Master's thesis, Arizona State University, 1980.

Rees, Tim, and Andrew Thorpe, eds. *International Communism and the Communist International, 1919–43.* Manchester, UK: Manchester University Press, 1998.

Reeves, René. *Ladinos with Ladinos, Indians with Indians: Land, Labor, and Regional Ethnic Conflict in the Making of Guatemala.* Stanford, CA: Stanford University Press, 2006.

Reiman, Richard A. *The New Deal & American Youth: Ideas & Ideals in a Depression Decade.* Athens: University of Georgia Press, 1992.

Reis Filho, Daniel Aarão. *Luís Carlos Prestes: um revolucionário entre dois mundos.* São Paulo: Companhia Das Letras, 2014.

Revueltas, José. *Las evocaciones requeridas: memorias, diarios, correspondencia.* 2 vols. Mexico City: Ediciones Era, 1987.

——. *Los errores.* Mexico City: Fondo de Cultura Económica, 1964.

Riddell, John, ed. *To the Masses: Proceedings of the Third Congress of the Communist International, 1921.* Leiden: Brill, 2015. Marxists International Archive, https://www.marxists.org/.

——. *Toward the United Front: Proceedings of the Fourth Congress of the Communist International, 1922.* Chicago: Haymarket, 2012.

Ridenti, Marcelo. "Jorge Amado e seus camaradas no círculo comunista internacional." *Sociologia & Antropologia* 1 (November 2011): 165–94.

Riga, Liliana. "The Ethnic Roots of Class Universalism: Rethinking the 'Russian' Revolutionary Elite." *American Journal of Sociology* 114, no. 3 (2008): 649–705.

Ríos Tobar, Marcela. "Feminism Is Socialism, Liberty, and Much More": Second-Wave Chilean Feminism and Its Contentious Relationship with Socialism." *Journal of Women's History* 15, no. 3 (2003): 129–34.

Rodríguez Beruff, Jorge. "Rediscovering Puerto Rico and the Caribbean: US Strategic Debate and War." In *Island at War: Puerto Rico in the Crucible of the Second World War,* edited by Jorge Rodríguez Beruff and José L. Bolívar, 3–28. Jackson: University Press of Mississippi, 2015.

Rodríguez-Fraticelli, Carlos. "Pedro Albizu Campos: Strategies of Struggle and Strategic Struggles." *Centro Journal* 4, no. 1 (1991–92): 25–33.

Rojas, Rafael. "Comunistas en democracia. El orden constitucional de 1940 en Cuba y la estrategia electoral del comunismo." *Conserveries mémorielles* 20, 2017.

Rojas Blaquier, Angelina. *El primer Partido Comunista de Cuba*. 3 vol. Santiago de Cuba: Editorial Oriente, 2005.

Rosa, Diógenes de la. *Diógenes de la Rosa: testigo y protagonista del siglo XX panameño: compilación de su obra*. Panama City: Academia Panameña de la Lengua, 1999.

Rosado, Marisa. *Pedro Albizu Campos, Las llamas de la aurora. Un acercamiento a su biografía*. 2nd ed. San Juan, Puerto Rico: n.p., 2003.

Rosas Sandoval, Francisco Javier. "La cultura de las clases trabajadoras urbanas de Costa Rica: El Caso de los Carpinteros y Ebanistas (1890–1943)." *Revista de Historia* 46 (2002): 111–48.

Rosello, Victor M. "Vietnam's Support to El Salvador's FMLN: Successful Tactics in Central America." *Military Review*, January 1990, 71–78.

Rosental, Mark, and Pavel Fedorovich Iudin. *Diccionario soviético de filosofía*. Montevideo: Pueblos Unidos, 1965.

Rothwell, Matthew D. *Transpacific Revolutionaries: The Chinese Revolution in Latin America*. New York: Routledge, 2012.

Ruano Najarro, Edgar, and Antonio Obando Sánchez. *Comunismo y movimiento obrero en la vida de Antonio Obando Sánchez, 1922–1932*. Guatemala City: Ediciones del Pensativo, 2007.

Rubenstein, Annette T. *I Vote My Conscience: Debates, Speeches, and Writings of Vito Marcantonio, 1935–1950*. New York: Calandra Institute, 2002.

Rupprecht, Tobias. *Soviet Internationalism after Stalin: Interaction and Exchange between the USSR and Latin America during the Cold War*. Cambridge: Cambridge University Press, 2015.

Santos Rivera, Juan. *Puerto Rico ayer, hoy y mañana: informe al comité central del Partido Comunista Puertorriqueño*. San Juan, Puerto Rico, 1944.

Sayim, Burak. "Occupied Istanbul as a Cominternian Hub: Sailors, Soldiers, and Post-Imperial Networks (1918–1923)." *Itinerario: European Journal of Overseas History* 46, no. 1 (2022): 128–49.

Schaffer, Alan. *Vito Marcantonio, Radical in Congress*. Syracuse, NY: Syracuse University Press, 1966.

Schneider, Ronald M. *Communism in Guatemala, 1944–1954*. New York: Praeger, 1958.

Schwarz, Benjamin C. *American Counterinsurgency Doctrine and El Salvador: The Frustrations of Reform and the Illusions of Nation Building*. Santa Monica, CA: Rand, 1991.

Secretariado Sudamericano de la Internacional Comunista. *El movimiento revolucionario latino americano: Versiones de la primera conferencia comunista latinoamericana, junio de 1929*. Buenos Aires: Revista La Correspondencia Sudamericana, 1929.

Selser, Gregorio. *Cronología de las intervenciones extranjeras en América Latina*. Mexico City: UNAM/UoM, 2001.

Senior, Olive. *Dying to Better Themselves: West Indians and the Building of the Panama Canal*. Kingston, Jamaica: University of the West Indies Press, 2014.

Serviat, Pedro. *El problema negro en Cuba y su solución definitiva*. Havana, Cuba: Editora Política, 1986.

Shipman, Charles. *It Had to Be Revolution: Memoirs of an American Radical*. Ithaca, NY: Cornell University Press, 1993.

Sierra Becerra, Diana Carolina. "'For Our Total Emancipation': The Making of Revolutionary Feminism in Insurgent El Salvador, 1977–1987." In *Making the Revolution: Histories of the Latin American Left*, edited by Kevin A. Young, 266–93. Cambridge: Cambridge University Press, 2019.

Siqueiros, David Alfaro. *Me llamaban el Coronelazo: memorias*. Mexico City: Grijalbo, 1977.

Smith, Carol A. "Introduction: Social Relations in Guatemala over Time and Space." In *Guatemalan Indians and the State: 1540 to 1988*, edited by Carol A. Smith, 1–30. Austin: University of Texas Press, 1990.

Soler, Ricaurte. *Panamá: historia de una crisis*. Mexico City: Siglo Veintiuno Editores, 1989.

Solomon, Mark I. *The Cry Was Unity: Communists and African Americans, 1917–36*. Jackson: University Press of Mississippi, 1998.

Soto, Lionel. *La revolución del 33*. Havana, Cuba: Editorial de Ciencias Sociales, 1977.

Soto-Quirós, Ronald. "Reflexiones sobre el mestizaje y la identidad nacional en Centroamérica: de la Colonia a las Repúblicas liberales." *Boletín de la AFEHC* 25 (2006): 1–39.

——. "Un otro significante en la identidad nacional costarricense: el caso del inmigrante afrocaribeño, 1872–1926." *Boletín de la AFEHC* 25 (2006): 1–32.

Spencer, David E. *From Vietnam to El Salvador: The Saga of the FMLN Sappers and Other Guerrilla Special Forces in Latin America*. Westport, CT: Praeger, 1996.

Spenser, Daniela. *The Impossible Triangle: Mexico, Soviet Russia, and the United States in the 1920s*. Durham, NC: Duke University Press, 1999.

Stein, Judith. *The World of Marcus Garvey: Race and Class in Modern Society*. Baton Rouge: Louisiana State University Press, 1986.

Stephens, Michelle Ann. *Black Empire: The Masculine Global Imaginary of Caribbean Intellectuals in the United States, 1914–1962*. Durham, NC: Duke University Press, 2005.

Stern, Sol. "A Short Account of International Student Politics with Particular Reference to the NSA, CIA, Etc." *Ramparts*, March 1967, 29–38.

Stevens, Margaret. "'Hands Off Haiti!' Self-Determination, Anti-Imperialism, and the Communist Movement in the United States, 1925–1929." *Black Scholar* 37, no. 4 (2008): 61–70.

——. *Red International and Black Caribbean: Communists in New York City, Mexico, and the West Indies, 1919–1939*. London: Pluto, 2017.

Studer, Brigitte. *The Transnational World of the Cominternians*. Houndmills, UK: Palgrave Macmillan, 2015.

Sullivan, Frances Peace. "'For the Liberty of the Nine Boys in Scottsboro and against Yankee Imperialist Domination in Latin America': Cuba's Scottsboro Defense Campaign." *Canadian Journal of Latin American and Caribbean Studies* 38, no. 2 (2013): 282–92.

Swagler, Matt. "The Russian Revolution and Pan-African Marxism." *Review of African Political Economy* 45, no. 158 (2018): 620–28.

Taracena Arriola, Arturo. *Etnicidad, estado y nación en Guatemala*. 2 vols. Antigua, Guatemala: Centro de Investigaciones Regionales de Mesoamérica, 2002–4.

Taracena Arriola, Arturo, and Omar Lucas Monteflores. *Diccionario biográfico del movimiento obrero urbano de Guatemala, 1877–1944*. Ciudad de Guatemala: Editorial de Ciencias Sociales, 2014.

Testa, Mary. "The Puerto Rican Nationalist Movement in New York City." In *Spanish Book*, reel 269, folder 9, January 11, 1939, WPA Federal Writers Project, New York City Municipal Archive.

Thompson, Robert. *The Path of a Renegade: Why Earl Browder Was Expelled from the Communist Party*. New York: New Century, 1946.

Tomek, Beverly. "The Communist International and the Dilemma of the American 'Negro Problem': Limitations of the Black Belt Self-Determination Thesis." *WorkingUSA* 15, no. 4 (2012): 549–76.

Torres Giraldo, Ignacio. *Cincuenta meses en Moscú*. Cali, Colombia: Universidad del Valle, 2005.

Ulianova, Olga. "El levantamiento campesino de Lonquimay y la Internacional Comunista." *Estudios Públicos* 89 (Summer 2003): 173–233.

U.S. Department of State. Office of Intelligence Research (OIR). "Communism in Latin America." In *Foreign Relations of the United States, 1955–1957. American Republics: Multilateral; Mexico; Caribbean, Volume 6*, edited by John P. Glennon, 83–89. Washington, DC: US Government Printing Office, 1987.

———. Office of Strategic Services (OSS). *Latin America, 1941–1961*. OSS/State Department Intelligence and Research Reports. Washington, DC: University Publications of America, 1979.

Vallejo, César. *Camino hacia una tierra socialista: escritos de viaje*. Buenos Aires: Fondo de Cultura Económica, 2014.

Valobra, Adriana María, and Mercedes Yusta Rodrigo. *Queridas camaradas: historias iberoamericanas de mujeres comunistas*. Buenos Aires: Miño y Dávila Editores, 2017.

Vega, Bernardo, and César Andreu Iglesias. *Memoirs of Bernardo Vega: A Contribution to the History of the Puerto Rican Community in New York*. New York: Monthly Review, 1984.

Vilanova de Árbenz, María. *Mi esposo, el presidente Árbenz*. Guatemala City: Editorial Universitaria, 2000.

Villamizar Herrera, Darío. *Ecuador: 1960–1990, Insurgencia, democracia y dictadura*. 2nd ed. Quito: Editorial El Conejo, 1994.

Waack, William. *Camaradas: nos arquivos de Moscou, a história secreta da revolução brasileira de 1935*. São Paulo: Companhia das Letras, 1993.

Wagner, Regina. *The History of Coffee in Guatemala*. Bogota: Villegas Editores, 2001.

Wamsley, Esther Sue. "A Hemisphere of Women: Latin American and U.S. Feminists in the IACW, 1915–1939." PhD diss., Ohio State University, 1998.

Weiss, Holger. *Framing a Radical African Atlantic: African American Agency, West African Intellectuals, and the International Trade Union Committee of Negro Workers*. Leiden: Brill, 2014.

Whitney, Robert. *State and Revolution in Cuba: Mass Mobilization and Political Change, 1920–1940*. Chapel Hill: University of North Carolina Press, 2001.

Women's International Democratic Federation (WIDF). *World Congress of Women, Copenhagen, June 5–10, 1953: Reports, Speeches (Extracts), Documents*. Berlin: Women's International Democratic Federation, 1953.

Wood, Elisabeth Jean. *Forging Democracy from Below: Insurgent Transitions in South Africa and El Salvador*. Cambridge: Cambridge University Press, 2000.

Wood, Tony. "The Problem of the Nation in Latin America's Second Age of Revolution: Radical Transnational Debates on Sovereignty, Race, and Class, 1923–1941." PhD diss., New York University, 2020.

Zenger, Robin Elizabeth. "West Indians in Panama: Diversity and Activism, 1910s–1940s." PhD diss., University of Arizona, 2015.

Zimmermann, Matilde. *Sandinista: Carlos Fonseca and the Nicaraguan Revolution*. Durham, NC: Duke University Press, 2001.

Zourek, Michal. *Praga y los intelectuales latinoamericanos (1947–1959)*. Rosario, Argentina: Prohistoria Ediciones, 2019.

Zumoff, Jacob A. "The 1925 Tenants' Strike in Panama: West Indians, the Left, and the Labor Movement." *The Americas* 74, no. 4 (October 2017): 513–46.

——. "Black Caribbean Labor Radicalism in Panama, 1914–1921." *Journal of Social History* 47, no. 2 (2013): 429–57.

——. *The Communist International and U.S. Communism, 1919–1939*. Historical Materialism Book Series. Chicago: Haymarket, 2014.

——. "Ojos Que No Ven: The Communist Party, Caribbean Migrants, and the Communist International in Costa Rica in the 1920s and 1930s." *Journal of Caribbean History* 45, no. 2 (2011): 212–47.

Contributors

MARC BECKER teaches Latin American history at Truman State University. He is the editor and translator of *Proceedings of the First Latin American Communist Conference, June 1929* (forthcoming) and author among other works of *Contemporary Latin American Revolutions* (2022); *The CIA in Ecuador* (2020); and *The FBI in Latin America: The Ecuador Files* (2017). He is currently working on a book on Philip Agee and the CIA in Ecuador in the early 1960s.

JACOB BLANC is a senior lecturer in Latin American history at the University of Edinburgh, where he teaches and studies about social movements, borderlands, and human rights. He is the author of *Before the Flood: The Itaipu Dam and the Visibility of Rural Brazil* (2019) as well as *The Prestes Column: An Interior History of Modern Brazil* (forthcoming).

TANYA HARMER is an associate professor of international history at the London School of Economics and Political Science. She is the author of *Allende's Chile and the Inter-American Cold War* (2011), *Beatriz Allende: A Revolutionary Life in Cold War Latin America* (2020) and, with Alberto Martín Alvarez, the editor of *Toward a Global History of Latin America's Revolutionary Left* (2021).

PATRICIA HARMS is an associate professor of history at Brandon University. She is the author of the award-winning *Ladina Social Activism in Guatemala City,*

1871–1954. She researches women and gender history in Central America, and her current project involves collecting testimonials from Spanish-speaking migrant women.

LAZAR JEIFETS is a professor of history at the Saint Petersburg State University. He is the author or coauthor of ten books, including *The Biographical Dictionary of the Comintern in Latin America*; *The Comintern in Latin America: People, Ideas, Structures*; and *Formation and Development of the Latin American CPs in the 1920s*.

VÍCTOR JEIFETS is a professor of history at the Saint Petersburg State University and the editor-in-chief of *Latinskaya Amerika* journal. He is the author, coauthor, or coeditor of eight books, including *The Biographical Dictionary of the Comintern in Latin America*; *The Comintern in Latin America: People, Ideas, Structures*; and *Rethinking Post-Cold War Russian-Latin American Relations*.

ADRIANA PETRA is a researcher at the National Council for Scientific and Technical Research of Argentina and professor at the School of Humanities of the National University of San Martín, where she also heads the Center for Latin American Studies. She is the author of the book *Intelectuales y cultura comunista: Itinerarios, problemas, y debates en la Argentina de posguerra* (2017, translated into English as *Intellectuals and Communist Culture: Itineraries, Problems and Debates in Postwar Argentina*, 2022), as well as numerous articles, chapters, and compilations. Her research interests are intellectual and cultural history and the history of the left, in particular, the Communist world.

MARGARET M. POWER is a professor of history at the Illinois Institute of Technology. She is the author, coauthor, or coeditor of six books, including *Right-Wing Women in Chile: Feminine Power and the Struggle against Allende, 1964–1973*. Her most recent book is *Solidarity across the Americas: The Puerto Rican Nationalist Party and Anti-imperialism*.

FRANCES PEACE SULLIVAN is an assistant professor of history at Simmons University, where she teaches Latin American, Caribbean, and global history. Her research addresses popular responses to imperialism and transnational social movements. Her forthcoming book, *Cuba's Cosmopolitan Enclaves: Foreign Capital and Popular Internationalism, 1919–1939*, explores internationalism among Cuban and immigrant sugar workers.

TONY WOOD teaches Latin American history at the University of Colorado Boulder. His work focuses on radical transnational debates on race, class, and the nationstate in Latin America in the 1920s and 1930s, retracing connections between Mexico, Cuba, and the USSR. Previously trained as a specialist on Russia and the former USSR, he is the author of *Chechnya: The Case for Independence* (2007) and *Russia without Putin: Money, Power, and the Myths of the New Cold War* (2018).

KEVIN A. YOUNG teaches Latin American history at the University of Massachusetts Amherst. He has published several books on social movements, revolutions, and political power in the Americas, including the edited volume *Making the Revolution: Histories of the Latin American Left* (2019).

JACOB A. ZUMOFF teaches history at New Jersey City University. He researches the labor movement, Communism, and race and ethnicity in the Americas. His most recent book is *The Red Thread: The Passaic Textile Strike* (2021).

Index

The University of Illinois Press
is a founding member of the
Association of University Presses.

University of Illinois Press
1325 South Oak Street
Champaign, IL 61820-6903
www.press.uillinois.edu